AI Governance Playbook

AI Governance Playbook

How to Secure, Control, and Optimize Artificial Intelligence Initiatives

Robert F. Smallwood

Chris Surdak, J.D.

BLOOMSBURY ACADEMIC
NEW YORK • LONDON • OXFORD • NEW DELHI • SYDNEY

Bloomsbury Publishing Inc, 1359 Broadway, 12th Floor, New York, NY 10018, USA
Bloomsbury Publishing Plc, 50 Bedford Square, London, WC1B 3DP, UK
Bloomsbury Publishing Ireland, 29 Earlsfort Terrace, Dublin 2, D02 AY28, Ireland

BLOOMSBURY, BLOOMSBURY ACADEMIC and the Diana logo are trademarks of Bloomsbury Publishing Plc

First published in the United States of America 2026

A catalog record for this book is available from the Library of Congress.

ISBN: HB: 979-8-8818-0083-3
PB: 979-8-8818-0084-0
ePDF: 979-8-7651-6018-3
eBook: 979-8-8818-0085-7

Typeset by Deanta Global Publishing Services, Chennai, India

For product safety related questions contact productsafety@bloomsbury.com.

To find out more about our authors and books visit www.bloomsbury.com and sign up for our newsletters.

Contents

Preface

Artificial Intelligence (AI) burst onto scene in late 2022 when OpenAI released ChatGPT. Suddenly, it seemed that AI was everywhere, being rolled out into consumer applications and providing eye-popping gains in functionality. And in 2024-25, agentic AI burst on the scene with the promise of fully automating business processes from end-to-end.

However, AI is not new; it has been part of the scientific, academic, and business consciousness for over eighty years and utilized in commercial software applications for over forty years. Since the cryptographers and mathematicians of the Second World War set their sights on using algorithms to understand human communication and thinking, we have been pursuing the realization of artificial humans and robots, envisioned a century before by fanciful dreamers.

Thesis

What is needed for organizations to capitalize on the capabilities of AI, yet manage the potential morass of issues and challenges, is a basic 'playbook' that spells out what key functions must accomplish at each phase of the AI development lifecycle. And that is what this book does, spelling out the required tasks methodically and simply.

Following the introductory seven chapters, which offer some basic definitions and information on standards and models, we have structured the book around the Information Governance Reference Model (IGRM), which has as its core facets data privacy, cybersecurity, IT, legal, risk management, records and information management (RIM), and business units. We have added a crucial chapter on the role of Audit in AI Governance, because without regular audits, there is no objective way to know how well the AI program rollout is hitting its metrics and addressing its stated business objectives.

The premise of this book is this: due to the present and future volume, variety, and velocity of data in organizations, governing it with Information Governance (IG) principles, tools, and Best practices is no longer optional. A focus on a major aspect of an AI initiative, such as data privacy or IT, will not yield a functioning system that a holistic approach will provide. To the contrary, deploying and employing effective IG mechanisms may be the single most important strategic initiative organizations must undertake in the coming decade. Get the balance of people, process, rules, and technology tools right, and your organization may flourish from gains in efficiency and effectiveness. Get this balance wrong, and your organization has a chance of fading away like Blockbuster or Kmart, or publicly imploding like Enron or FTX. Never before has the need for IG been greater than right now, regardless of when your 'right now' is occurring.

Fortunately, the tools, techniques, and tactics of IG are well-defined in the post-pandemic era, as scalability has been a driving goal of IG. Much like the rules, tools and frameworks of the world of finance are applicable regardless of an organization's size, so too do the tenets of IG scale both up and down, regardless of your organization's size. The key differentiator with effective use of IG is effectively deploying IT, and this is especially true when it comes to the deployment of a promising, yet potentially dangerous technology set called AI.

We once heard a saying that reflected the mindset that is required here: "Why do racing cars have brakes?" The answer? "So that they can go faster." Indeed, effective, strategic IG allows organizations to process information faster, produce results sooner, identify issues before they grow out of hand, and provide a degree of confidence required by executives in times of transformational change. This latest wave of information technology, punctuated by Generative Artificial Intelligence, Quantum Computing, Sustainable computing, and Zero Trust Security does not merely leverage effective IG, they depend upon it. Implementing any of these technologies without first having strategic IG is akin to subscribing to Netflix, Amazon.com, and Spotify without first having a connection to the Internet.

Purpose

In this book, which reflects the new realities of generative AI, we provide a structured approach, a construct based on IG models and Best Practices, which provides a framework for how to implement an effective, efficient program for the governance of AI. It is a balanced, holistic, cross-functional approach. We identify the key areas that must be considered, those aspects of each that determine the most effective solution for your organization, and the key factors for implementation and operational success throughout key phases of the AI development lifecycle. Again, effective IG is inherently scalable, so once you tailor it to your organizational needs, the framework should provide results that are specific to your organizational scenario.

And this approach has been proven in practice, as participants in the Certified Information Governance Officer in AI (CIGO/AI) training program from the CIGO Association (cigoa.org) have utilized this approach, with Leading organizations including many Fortune 1000 companies and major law firms have successfully governing their AI programs. In fact, the core content of this book comes from the CIGO/AI training and certification program.

Further, it is our goal not only to describe the "how" of IG for AI, but, more importantly, to explain the 'why' of IG for AI. For each of the techniques, tools, and tactics we outline, we provide the context behind their use. We believe that this understanding is critical in creating organizational as well as executive buy-in.

Goals

There are five main goals of this book; to present and explain:

1. What Information Governance is in context of AI program implementations.
2. Why Information Governance is a strategic imperative for AI in the coming decade.
3. Who should be involved in the strategic deployment of AI governance in your organization.
4. What each core function must accomplish at each phase of the AI development lifecycle.
5. How to implement an efficient and effective AI governance strategy in your organization.

We hope you will use this playbook we have constructed to implement AI in your organization ensuring it is secure, controlled, and best of all, optimized to meet your AI program objectives.

1 AI's Great Potential—and Governance Challenges

Most organizations today are using or considering artificial intelligence (AI) to streamline operations and improve business outcomes. In a recent survey, over 75 percent of companies globally have adopted AI technologies.[1] Furthermore, over 70 percent of organizations are using generative AI (GenAI) in at least one business function, and this continues to expand, demonstrating its rapid increase in adoption. And according to CFO.com, more than half (52%) of surveyed senior corporate leaders at companies that use generative AI, said they've also begun to leverage AI agents, and this is expected to continue to climb to 80% or more by 2027.

As the excitement surrounding AI applications escalates, dominating the headlines and spurring discussions, challenges remain for organizations to effectively implement responsible AI models in real-life scenarios. Surprisingly, only about half of AI initiatives progress from the initial pilot phase to full-scale production.[2] So there is much work to do.

What Is AI?

AI is a field of computer science that creates systems which can perform tasks that typically require human intelligence. These tasks include learning, reasoning, problem-solving, understanding natural language, perception, and even interacting with the environment. AI technologies, ranging from machine learning algorithms to advanced robotics, have demonstrated remarkable capabilities in various domains, transforming industries and enhancing efficiency.

The foundation of modern AI lies in the utilization of machine learning algorithms.[3] Within the realm of AI, there exist pivotal subfields, including, but not confined to:

- **Generative AI (GAI):** Referring to systems that employ data models to generate novel responses in the form of content, such as text, images, audio, software code, and other data modalities. These applications are typically trained on extensive real-world data and can approximate human-generated content from various prompts. Examples of GAI include OpenAI's ChatGPT, Microsoft's Copilot, Google's Gemini, Anthropic's Claude, and others.
- **Machine Learning (ML):** This type of AI software can continuously "learn" from outputs it generates, without human intervention. ML involves the creation of software components (models) that empower computers to discern and contextualize patterns in data without the need for explicit human programming of rules. Applications of ML can produce predictions, recommendations, or decisions based on statistical reasoning.
- **Natural Language Processing (NLP):** NLP involves the analysis and extraction of information from diverse human language sources, including text, images, videos, and audio data. It is commonly employed for language classification and interpretation. Many NLP applications not only process natural language but also generate content that emulates it.

To characterize generative AI, which has taken the world by storm since OpenAI released ChatGPT in November 2022, *generative AI creates entirely new content based on patterns and structures learned during its setup and training.*

Generative AI has found applications and use cases across industries, and its capabilities include content creation, text-to-speech synthesis, art/graphics generation, video creation, and more. Basically, you can ask a GAI system a question (a prompt), and it will give you an answer. However, the answers can at times be wildly incorrect (yet often convincing), referred to as "hallucinations." When this occurs, AI developers must reassess their approach to model setup and training and also examine the training data that was fed into the system for clues as to why the misfires are happening.

The capabilities of generative AI also raise ethical concerns, particularly in terms of generating realistic deepfake videos, text manipulation, or other content that could potentially be misused. As the field continues to advance, ongoing research and development aim to strike a balance between leveraging the creative potential of generative AI and addressing associated ethical challenges.

A **Large Language Model** (LLM) is a type of AI model that is trained on vast amounts of text and data to understand and generate human-like language. It has been posited that OpenAI and Google transcribed over a million hours of instructional YouTube videos to train their AI models, which raises ethical and legal copyright concerns.[4]

LLMs are characterized by their massive size, often containing billions or even trillions of parameters, enabling them to capture intricate patterns and nuances of language. LLMs are built on **neural network architectures** (the structural design of artificial neural networks, which includes the layout and connectivity of neurons (or nodes) within the network). These architectures dictate how data flows through the network and how the network processes information, typically using **transformer architectures**, and are capable of various language-related tasks such as natural language understanding, text completion, translation, and text generation. (Transformer architectures are a type of neural network architecture that has proven highly effective in various NLP tasks and other ML applications. They were introduced in the paper "Attention is All You Need" by Vaswani et al. in 2017. The transformer architecture has since become a foundational building block for many state-of-the-art AI models.)

Mathematics: The Universal Language

Transformers represent a breakthrough in modeling unstructured data such as language, pictures, or video. They work by transforming this unstructured data into mathematical equivalents that are easier for computers to understand. This transformation is based on matrix and vector mathematics, the bane of many engineering and science students in universities and colleges around the world.

From a governance perspective, this underpinning of LLMs represents a challenge, as relatively few professionals have mastery over such higher-order mathematics. While governance of GAI may not require a PhD in vector mathematics, it does require an understanding of the implications of vector mathematics.

Generative AI and LLMs are closely related, as many LLMs fall under the category of generative models. The primary function of these models is to generate coherent and contextually relevant text based on input prompts. They can create new content, complete sentences, or even generate entire paragraphs of text that are contextually consistent with the provided input.

The Appeal of GAI

It is notable that GAI, particularly in the form of LLMs, combines symbolic language and technology in an effort to replicate our humanness. It is not an accident that we find this technology compelling. When interacting with GAI, it is easy to be fooled into believing that we are interacting with another person.

This is both a feature and a bug of GAI. It is a feature because it resonates with neural pathways in our brains that have been created by both nature and nurture over thousands of generations. This makes GAI perhaps the most comforting of information technologies that humans have ever used. The technology seems to mold and yield to us, rather than the other way around. Anyone who has struggled to learn how to write software code knows of the historic difficulties of learning to communicate with earlier generations of information technology. Software has always had the nasty habit of doing exactly what we told it to do, rather than what we wished it would do.

Conversely, GAI is proving adept at understanding the nuance of what we ask of it, and then rendering these desires accurately in software code. If our organizational leaders find GAI compelling, it is because information technology might finally be on the cusp of allowing non-technical employees to produce technology-enhanced results without the need for highly trained intermediaries.

The downside of this combination is that, due to its familiarity and ease of use, GAI may fool us into a false sense of security and comfort. As we become ever more reliant on GAI systems, we will also become less and less able to confirm if it is telling us what we want to hear, rather than what we need to hear. Like a good friend trying to lessen the blow of some bad news or ill fortune, we must be cautious about believing everything that GAI tells us. This is where Information Governance (IG) professionals must step in and play the role of "adult in the room." The more we come to depend upon AI, the more we must remain vigilant of its use. Strict guardrails are needed, including AI Acceptable Use Policies, standards, frameworks, and models.

AI Wins in Daily Life

Award-winning science fiction writer William Gibson once said, "The future is already here but it's not evenly distributed." It is almost a certainty that you are already interacting with AI systems on a daily, if not hourly, basis. AI programs have been delivering significant business value for well over a decade. They are already deeply integrated into the lives of billions of people in developed nations. Some everyday examples of successful AI programs that have added significant value to businesses across different industries include:

1. **Amazon's Recommendation System**

   Amazon's AI-driven recommendation system analyzes customers' browsing and purchase history to suggest products they might be interested in. It also adjust pricing according to your past purchases and browsing history. This has substantially increased sales, customer engagement, and profitability.

2. **Netflix's Content Recommendation**

   Netflix employs AI algorithms to recommend TV shows and movies to its subscribers. These personalized recommendations play a crucial role in retaining and attracting customers and increasing their viewing time.

3. **Google's AdWords**

   Google's AdWords platform uses AI to match ads with relevant keywords and audiences, maximizing the effectiveness of online advertising campaigns. It is a major revenue driver for Google.

4. **IBM Watson in Healthcare**

   IBM Watson uses AI in healthcare settings by assisting clinicians with diagnosing diseases and suggesting treatment options. It can process vast amounts of medical data to help healthcare professionals make informed decisions.

5. **Tesla's Autopilot**

   Tesla's Autopilot system uses AI and machine learning for autonomous driving. It enhances safety and driving efficiency, and it is a key feature that attracts customers to Tesla vehicles.

These examples showcase the versatility and impact of AI across different sectors, from e-commerce and entertainment to healthcare and transportation. AI deployments have not only added value to these businesses but have also transformed the way they operate and interact with their customers.

Emerging Consumer-Facing AI Apps

Although AI has been around in basic forms for more than half-a-century, one of the biggest reasons for the recent frenzied buzz about AI is its move into consumer markets. As the examples above indicate, most implementations of AI thus far have been in highly controlled use cases, using carefully curated data, and maintained under strict control of the owner.

However, in 2022 OpenAI changed this paradigm forever when they released the LLM, Generative AI tool, ChatGPT, to the open market. With this one move, enterprise-scale AI tools went feral, allowing end users to interact with this technology whenever, however, and wherever they chose. Employees are using it to generate policy drafts, attorneys are using it to summarize documents and depositions,[5] and even soccer moms are using it to plan picnics and outings. This has fueled intense interest (and fear) in consumers for AI applications.

Some examples of newer consumer-oriented versions of AI include applications that can create an AI voice from scratch or even replicate your own voice; create professional videos from a written script where users can add realistic AI voices and matching footage and images from a licensed library of images, and add music in a few clicks; transform any input into slides, making it sort of the next-generation PowerPoint; transcribe spoken words with high precision; redesign photos by harnessing the power of AI to add color, enhance, and repair pictures, even having the capability to animate people in old photographs, giving them a fresh, lively appearance.

The Tremendous Potential of AI Programs to Build Business Value

Nearly all of the most valuable companies in the world earned their place at the top of the world's economy over the course of the last fifteen years. Simultaneously, all of them have adopted and implemented enterprise-scale data analytics and ML (also known as AI) into both their operations and their value-added products and services. While the relationship between the use of AI and value creation may not be causal, there is no doubt that it is highly correlated.

AI deployments add value to businesses and various sectors through several key mechanisms. First, AI excels in **automation**, handling repetitive and time-consuming tasks far beyond basic business process automation or **robotic process automation** (RPA). This not only increases efficiency but also frees human resources for more strategic and creative work, leading to cost savings and improved productivity.

Another significant contribution of AI is in **data analysis**. AI can rapidly process and analyze vast amounts of data, uncovering patterns, trends, and insights that would be challenging for humans to discover, especially in a short timeframe. This capability informs data-driven decision-making for knowledge workers.

AI also enhances **personalization**. Businesses can offer personalized experiences to customers, such as product recommendations, content, and marketing messages, thereby improving customer engagement and satisfaction and boosting revenues.

Predictive analytics is another area where AI proves invaluable, as it can forecast future trends, customer behaviors, and market shifts. This helps organizations make proactive decisions, optimize inventory, and reduce risks. It is also used in e-Discovery reviews during civil litigation.

In the realm of **customer service**, AI-powered chatbots and virtual assistants provide 24/7 support, answering common questions and handling routine tasks. This enhances customer service and reduces response times.

AI also contributes to **quality control** by operating in real - time to identify defects, errors, or anomalies during production, thereby reducing waste and production costs.

In **healthcare**, AI assists in improving the accuracy diagnosing diseases, analyzing medical images or X-rays, and predicting patient outcomes, which leads to better patient care and more efficient healthcare delivery.

The **financial services** sector benefits from AI through improved fraud detection, risk assessment, and trading strategies, resulting in more secure transactions and better investment decisions.

Supply chain optimization is another area where AI makes a significant impact by optimizing inventory levels, predicting demand, and improving logistics, which leads to cost savings and enhanced customer service.

In terms of **energy efficiency**, AI optimizes energy consumption in industries, equipment, and buildings, reducing costs and environmental impact.

The education sector also benefits from AI, as it provides **personalized learning experiences**, adapts content to individual students, and assesses their progress, thereby improving educational outcomes.

In **research and development**, AI accelerates scientific research by processing large datasets, simulating experiments, and identifying potential drug candidates, potentially leading to breakthroughs in various fields.

AI enhances **safety and security** by improving security systems, identifying threats, and detecting anomalies, which bolsters public safety and safeguards critical infrastructure.

Finally, in the development of **smart cities**, AI optimizes traffic management, energy consumption, waste management, and public services, making urban areas more efficient and sustainable.

In essence, AI's ability to rapidly process and understand data, automate tasks, and make predictions or recommendations empowers organizations to make informed decisions, enhance customer experiences, and achieve operational efficiencies. This ultimately adds substantial value across industries and applications. AI allows organizations to combine and optimize the very best characteristics of both humans and machines to produce optimal outcomes predictively in a lower-cost structure. The commercial and indeed ethical implications of this power are profound.

To Maximize Value and Reduce Risks, AI Programs Must Be Governed

In Steven Spielberg's movie "Jurassic Park," the two protagonists were arguing over the wisdom of bringing dinosaurs back to life in modern times. While the creator of the dinosaurs argued that his scientists had achieved things that had never been done before, Jeff Goldblum's character Dr. Ian Malcolm famously retorted, "Yeah, yeah, but your scientists were so preoccupied with whether or not they *could,* that they didn't stop to think if they *should.*" While prominent technologists may argue over the efficacy and safety of AI, the fact remains that this Pandora's Box was opened long ago. We cannot undo the use of this technology; the best we can achieve now is to properly govern and control it.

While technological advancements in AI software design and hardware processing capability hold immense promise, they at the same time give rise to a myriad of critical concerns, spanning safety, accountability, ethics, intellectual property rights, fairness, accuracy, bias, explainability, and privacy. As AI continues its evolution, seamlessly integrating into our daily lives and the physical world around us, the risks associated with its proliferation are destined to multiply.[6]

Issues in Training AI Models

Take the example of a company in Finland using prisoners to train their AI model.[7] While the lure of cheap labor may be attractive, the fact that the prisoners are paid a small hourly wage, rather than compensation based on quality, is inherently problematic. Prisoners naturally may have biases against the society that imprisoned them, and those biases most certainly could be expressed in their answers as they train the AI model. One must ask, "What could go wrong here?" Bias in AI models is a crucial issue that must be addressed so that we, as a society, develop AI models that are accurate, responsible, and ethical.

AI model training presents a range of challenges, both technical and organizational.[8] Here are some common issues faced by organizations today:

1. **Algorithm-Related Challenges**

   The algorithm forms the main structure of an AI model. Selecting the right algorithm is crucial, as different algorithms have varying strengths and weaknesses. **Overfitting** occurs when a model is too attuned to specific outcomes, missing other relevant results; that is, it cannot properly apply its training to real-world questions and scenarios. This can result from too few or overly homogeneous training data sets. Proper algorithm selection and training are essential to avoid these pitfalls.

2. **Data Set-Related Challenges**

   Training data sets are the foundation of AI models, dictating their accuracy. Common data issues include:

   Imbalanced Data: Biases in training data can skew results. For example, an AI model trained only on shoe data for a clothing retailer will not account for variables related to shirts or dresses.

   Insufficient Data: Small data volumes limit predictive accuracy. Adequate training data is necessary to refine outcomes and eliminate biases.

   Poor-Quality Data: Low-quality data leads to overall inaccuracies. Ensuring high-quality data sources is a crucial first step.

3. **Challenges in Hiring Skilled Talent**

   Developing AI models requires a team with specialized skills across technical disciplines. The high demand for AI talent makes hiring competitive. Organizations must move quickly to secure qualified professionals and may need to demonstrate their commitment to AI development, such as by establishing an AI center of excellence. A lack of experienced personnel can derail projects, leading to chronic inaccuracies or failure to complete initiatives.

4. **Project Management Challenges**

   Managing AI projects involves balancing technological, financial, and resource scheduling aspects. Effective communication is vital, as project managers must coordinate with various teams, including IT, legal, privacy, data science, security, risk, and end users. Misaligned expectations, often fueled by popular misconceptions about AI capabilities, need to be managed through clear communication about the project's goals and limitations.

5. **Data Management and Security Challenges**

   Data security is a significant concern at all stages of AI training. Issues include:

   Data Access and Ownership: Defining who has access to training data and results, and who manages the process, is essential. Sound data management strategies, like role-based access, are necessary to prevent logistical and security issues.

   Data Privacy and Security: Training data sets may contain sensitive information. Ensuring data privacy and security through encryption and data cleansing, as well as addressing standard cybersecurity concerns, is critical.

6. **Hardware and Software Challenges**

   AI model training requires substantial hardware and software resources. Limitations in computational power, storage capacity, software compatibility, and scalability can impede progress. IT departments need to ensure they have high-performance servers, ample storage, and compatible software tools and frameworks to handle large datasets and complex models, particularly for intensive projects.

Overcoming AI Model Training Challenges

Successfully navigating these challenges requires careful planning, efficient resource use, and consistent, inclusive communication. Technical solutions like data augmentation, regularization, and transfer learning (as described below) can address common issues. Organizational strategies such as establishing clear communication channels, fostering a culture of collaboration, diverse teams, and encouraging continuous learning are also crucial.

Organizational Solutions

- **Establish Clear Communication Channels:** Promote open communication about project goals and progress.
- **Create Diverse AI Governance Teams:** Including employees of various races, age groups, genders, and ethnicities will help foster a more inclusive approach and help to avoid bias and unfairness in setting up **hyperparameters** (those parameters and decisions made to set up the AI model initially, that do not change with new training data), selecting and processing training data, and AI query outcomes.
- **Foster a Culture of Collaboration:** Encourage constructive debate and respect among team members, and include multiple perspectives when arriving at decisions.
- **Encourage Continuous Learning:** Stay updated on AI advancements and integrate new strategies, skills, methods, and technologies into ongoing projects.

Technical Solutions

- **Data Augmentation:** Generating additional training datasets to enhance model training and to offset any tendencies toward bias or unfairness.
- **Regularization:** Techniques to mitigate **overfitting** (where the model performs well on training data queries but does not generalize well in live, real-world use) and improve model accuracy.
- **Transfer Learning:** Using existing algorithms as starting points for new projects, adapting successful models to new contexts.

By addressing both organizational and technical challenges, organizations can improve their AI model training processes and achieve more accurate and effective outcomes.

Introducing AI Governance

The rapid advancement of AI raises significant ethical, legal, and societal concerns, necessitating the implementation of **AI Governance**.

AI Governance is a multidimensional approach that involves the establishment of policies, processes, and frameworks to guide the ethical, legal, and societal aspects of developing, deploying, and using AI technologies. The need for AI Governance arises from several critical factors:

1. **Ethical Considerations:** AI systems can impact individuals, communities, and societies in profound ways. Ethical concerns may include issues related to bias and fairness, transparency, accountability, privacy, and the potential for discriminatory outcomes. AI Governance frameworks or "guardrails" are essential to ensure that AI technologies are developed and deployed ethically, taking into account the broader societal impact.
2. **Legal Compliance:** The use of AI often involves handling sensitive data and making decisions that have legal implications. AI Governance establishes legal frameworks to protect consumer rights, ensure fair and responsible use, and address potential risks. Compliance with existing laws and the creation of new regulations specific to AI are crucial elements of governance.
3. **Societal Impact:** AI technologies can have wide-ranging effects on employment, education, healthcare, and other societal aspects. AI Governance aims to mitigate negative impacts, promote positive contributions, and ensure that the benefits of AI are distributed equitably. It also addresses concerns related to job displacement, algorithmic decision-making, and the digital divide.
4. **Security and Safety:** As AI systems become more sophisticated, ensuring their security and safety is paramount. Governance frameworks help establish standards for cybersecurity, data protection, and system reliability. This is particularly important in critical applications such as autonomous vehicles, healthcare diagnostics, finance, and defense systems.
5. **Transparency and Accountability:** Building trust in AI systems requires transparency about their functioning and accountability for their actions. Governance mechanisms ensure that developers and organizations are transparent about their AI algorithms, disclose potential biases, and take responsibility for the consequences of their AI applications.

6. **International Collaboration:** AI technologies often operate across borders, requiring global cooperation to establish consistent standards and regulations. AI Governance facilitates collaboration between governments, businesses, researchers, and international organizations to harmonize policies and address global challenges associated with AI.

In summary, AI Governance is essential to harness the potential benefits of AI while providing guidelines to mitigate risks and ensure ethical, legal, and societal considerations are prioritized. By involving stakeholders from various domains and fostering international collaboration, AI Governance frameworks contribute to the responsible development, deployment, and use of AI technologies in a manner that aligns with human values and societal well-being.

The Role of Governments, Business, Researchers, Society, and Users

Governments play a crucial role in AI Governance by establishing regulatory frameworks to govern AI development and deployment. They enforce laws protecting consumer rights, ensuring fairness, and addressing potential risks.

Collaborating with international bodies to harmonize AI regulations across borders is also a key aspect. Examples include the **EU Artificial Intelligence Act,**[9] passed in 2024, which was the first comprehensive regulation on AI by a major regulator. The Act assigns applications of AI to three risk categories (Unacceptable, High-Risk, Others); the **General Data Protection Regulation (GDPR),** which went into effect in 2018 and sets standards for privacy and data protection impacting AI systems handling personal data; and the **Algorithmic Accountability Act of 2023** in the United States, which focuses on addressing bias and discrimination in AI algorithms. It requires companies to assess the impacts of the AI systems they use and sell, creates new transparency about when and how such systems are used, and empowers consumers to make informed choices when they interact with AI systems.

Businesses contribute to AI Governance by developing and adhering to ethical AI practices in their applications. They implement governance frameworks within their organizations to ensure responsible AI use and collaborate with industry peers and policymakers to contribute to the development of AI standards. Examples include **IBM's AI Ethics Principles**, emphasizing transparency, accountability, and fairness in AI technologies; and **Google's AI Principles**, outlining their commitment to ethical AI.

Researchers have a crucial role in AI Governance, conducting research to understand the ethical implications, risks, and societal impact of AI technologies. They develop best practices and guidelines for responsible AI development and engage in interdisciplinary collaboration to bring diverse perspectives to AI Governance. Examples include the **Fairness and Abstraction in AI (FAAI)** Research Group focusing on addressing biases in AI systems and the **Partnership on AI (PAI)**, a consortium of companies and organizations collaborating to address ethical challenges in AI.

Civil society advocates for transparency, accountability, and ethical considerations in AI systems. Monitoring and raising awareness about the societal impact of AI technologies, they engage in public discourse to ensure diverse voices are heard in AI Governance discussions. Examples include **Algorithm Watch**, a nonprofit organization analyzing and raising awareness about the impact of algorithms on society, and the **AI Now Institute**, an interdisciplinary research institute conducting research on the social implications of AI.

International organizations facilitate global collaboration on AI Governance standards and principles. They provide guidance and support for countries in developing AI policies and contribute to the development of ethical frameworks that transcend national borders. Examples include the **OECD AI Principles**, which provide principles for the responsible use of AI, and **UNESCO's Recommendation on the Ethics of Artificial Intelligence**, a global initiative to develop a standard-setting instrument on the ethics of AI. UNESCO's first-ever global standard on AI ethics—the "Recommendation on the Ethics of Artificial Intelligence"—was adopted by all 193 Member States in November 2021.

End users and community representatives play a role by providing input on the impact of AI technologies on local communities and individuals. They advocate for user rights, privacy, and fair treatment in AI systems, acting as watchdogs to ensure alignment with societal values. Examples include consumer advocacy groups representing consumer interests and community engagement initiatives allowing community members to voice concerns and contribute to AI Governance discussions.

The collaboration and active participation of these stakeholders ensure that AI Governance frameworks are well-rounded, reflecting a balance between innovation, ethics, and societal well-being, fostering a more inclusive and holistic understanding of the complex challenges associated with AI technologies.

Apply Proven Information Governance Models and Best Practices to AI Governance

Key to the successful deployment of AI applications is an effective **Information Governance** (IG) program. IG is a cross-functional discipline that aims to, "minimize information risks and costs, while maximizing value." IG can also be defined in short as "security, control, and optimization" of information. Think of IG as "AI readiness." Utilizing a cross-functional approach based on the **Information Governance Reference Model (IGRM)**, core groups include legal, risk management, data privacy, cybersecurity, information technology (IT), records and information management (RIM), and business units.

AI Governance is an offshoot of IG, and includes a comprehensive framework of principles, policies, regulations, and operational practices that steer the entire lifecycle of AI technologies, from problem definition to model evaluation and selection, to model training, to deployment, and finally to retirement. A multifaceted approach addresses a wide array of vital factors, such as ethics, accountability, transparency, fairness, privacy, and security.

The significance of AI Governance lies in its capacity to ensure the responsible and value-aligned evolution and application of AI technologies, serving the betterment of society as a whole. In the absence of robust governance, AI has the potential to amplify preexisting disparities, compromise individual rights, and introduce risks that may impact both individuals and society as a whole.

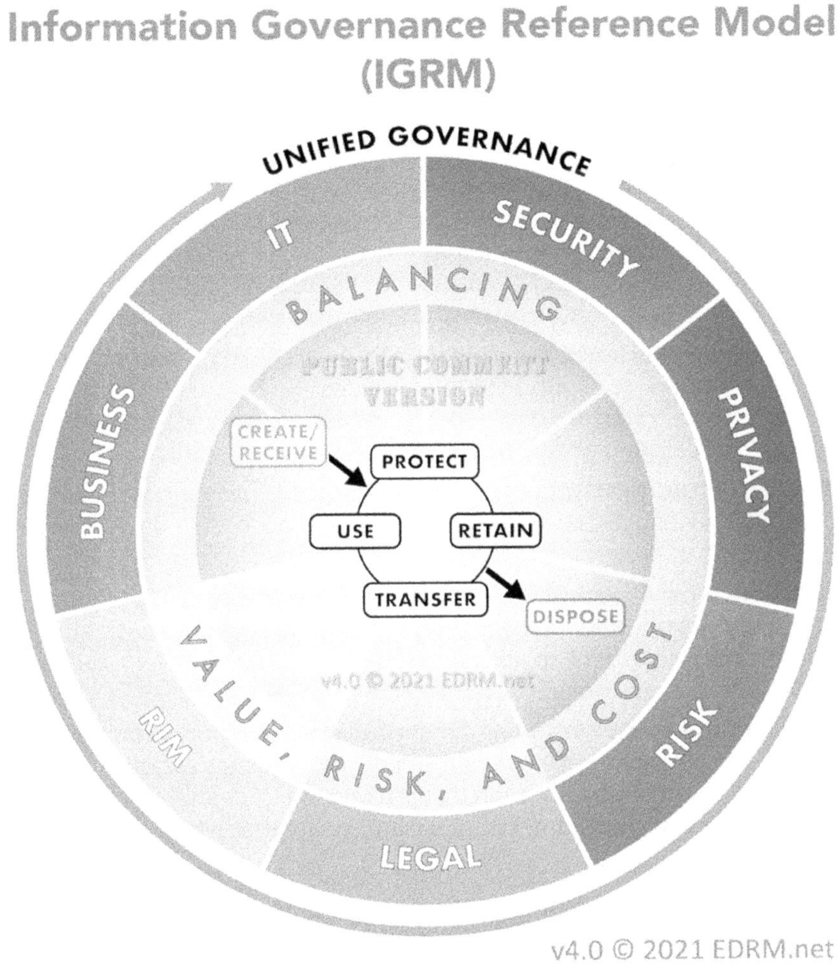

Figure 1.1 Information Governance Reference Model. Source: EDRM.net.

Without proper AI Governance controls and "guardrails" AI program deployments can suffer from:

1. **Bias and Discrimination:** Without proper governance, AI systems can perpetuate and even amplify biases present in training data, leading to discriminatory outcomes. This can have serious ethical and legal implications and harm marginalized communities. It can also severely impact a company's brand equity.
2. **Privacy Violations:** AI systems might inadvertently infringe on individuals' privacy by collecting, processing, or sharing personal data without proper or full consent.
3. **Security Risks:** Ungoverned AI deployments can become targets for cyberattacks. If AI systems are not adequately secured, they can be exploited, leading to data breaches, unauthorized access, or other security breaches. AI models can also be "poisoned" in that bad actors can insert volumes of erroneous training data to render the model useless, irrelevant or even damaging.
4. **Reputation Damage:** Poorly managed AI deployments can result in algorithmic errors or unintended consequences, which can tarnish a company's reputation and trustworthiness and reduce its brand value. Major companies in the AI marketplace have

had early missteps due to poorly trained models or overcompensating in attempts to create "politically correct" responses from the AI system or LLM.

5. **Regulatory Compliance Issues:** Failing to adhere to data protection and AI-related regulations can lead to legal issues, fines, sanctions, and penalties, which can be costly for businesses while burdening employees.
6. **Loss of Accountability:** Unclear responsibility for AI system outcomes can lead to a lack of accountability, making it challenging to rectify issues and assign responsibility when things go wrong. Clear lines of responsibility and tools like a responsibility assignment matrix (RAM), also known as a RACI matrix, can help clarify who on the AI team is Responsible, Accountable, Consulted, and Informed.
7. **Ineffective or Inefficient Operations:** Ungoverned AI might not operate optimally, leading to inefficiencies or errors in business processes. These errors can worsen over time, as the model "drifts" in a direction that amplifies biases and mistakes (commonly known as "hallucinations").
8. **Missed Opportunities:** Without proper governance, organizations might underutilize AI's potential, missing out on opportunities for automation, data-driven insights, and improved decision-making.
9. **Ethical Concerns:** AI deployment without ethical guidelines can raise moral questions about the technology's use in various applications, such as surveillance, autonomous weapons, or job displacement. Additionally, questions of data privacy must be kept at the forefront and continually monitored.
10. **Lack of Transparency:** Without governance, AI models might become "black boxes," making it difficult to understand their decisions and leading to a lack of transparency and trust. There are model-agnostic tools that can be used to "demystify" and explain complex models, such as LIME and SHAP values, which we will detail later.

To mitigate these dangers, it is crucial for organizations to establish robust AI Governance frameworks that include clear ethical guidelines, rigorous data handling and data protection procedures, security measures, and compliance with relevant laws and regulations. These measures must necessarily be far more rigorous, advanced, and comprehensive than prior attempts at IG, because AI is so much more powerful than earlier information technologies, and there are ongoing privacy and ethical concerns. Fostering a culture of responsibility and accountability within the organization is essential for safe and effective AI deployment.

Key Points

- Most organizations today are considering using generative artificial intelligence (AI) to streamline operations and improve business outcomes.
- There are everyday examples of successful AI programs that have added significant value to businesses across different industries from companies like Amazon, Netflix, IBM, and Tesla.
- One of the biggest reasons for the recent frenzied buzz about AI is its move into consumer markets.
- AI's ability to process and understand data, automate tasks, and make predictions or recommendations empowers organizations to make informed decisions, enhance customer experiences, and achieve operational efficiencies.
- While technological advancements in AI software design and hardware processing capability hold immense promise, they at the same time give rise to a myriad of critical concerns.
- AI model training presents a range of challenges, both technical and organizational.

- By addressing both organizational and technical challenges, organizations can improve their AI model training processes and achieve more accurate and effective outcomes.
- Governments play a crucial role in AI Governance by establishing regulatory frameworks to govern AI development and deployment.
- Businesses contribute to AI Governance by developing and adhering to ethical AI practices in their applications.
- International organizations facilitate global collaboration on AI Governance standards and principles.
- Key to the successful deployment of AI applications is an effective **Information Governance** (IG) program.
- IG is a cross-functional discipline that aims to, "minimize information risks and costs, while maximizing value."
- **AI Governance** is an offshoot of IG, and includes a comprehensive framework of principles, policies, regulations, and operational practices that steer the entire lifecycle of AI technologies.
- Without proper AI Governance controls and "guardrails" AI program deployments can suffer from bias, privacy concerns, security issues, compliance issues, and more, which can negatively impact the brand value and reputation of an organization.

Key Glossary Terms

AI Governance: A multidimensional approach that involves the establishment of policies, processes, and frameworks to guide the ethical, legal, and societal aspects of developing, deploying, and using AI technologies

Artificial Narrow Intelligence (ANI): A subtype of Narrow AI focusing on specific tasks. While excelling within predefined scopes such as voice recognition and image classification, ANI lacks versatility outside its narrow range.

Artificial Superintelligence (ASI): ASI surpasses human intelligence comprehensively, including problem-solving, creativity, and social skills. ASI, if realized, could potentially outperform humans in virtually every economically valuable work, raising concerns about control, safety, and societal impact. ASI remains a theoretical concept with significant technical, ethical, and philosophical challenges.

Computer Vision: Teaching machines to interpret and make decisions based on visual data, finds applications in image classification, object detection, facial recognition, gesture recognition, medical image analysis, visual search, OCR, augmented reality, visual inspection in manufacturing, surveillance and security, and satellite image analysis. These examples illustrate the diverse applications of AI-powered computer vision, showcasing its ability to extract valuable information from visual data in various domains.

Deep Learning: A specialized form of ML, involves neural networks with multiple layers (deep neural networks) capable of hierarchical abstraction. Effective in tasks like image and speech recognition, deep learning contributes to advancements in various domains.

General AI, or Artificial General Intelligence (AGI): Represents a theoretical concept embodying an AI system's ability to understand, learn, and apply knowledge across diverse tasks and domains, rivaling or exceeding human capabilities.

Generative AI: Referring to systems that employ data models to generate novel examples of content, such as text, images, audio, code, and other data modalities. These applications are typically trained on extensive real-world data and can approximate human-generated content from various prompts, even those that are limited or nonspecific.

Large Language Model (LLM): A type of AI model that is *trained on vast amounts of text data to understand and generate human-like language*. These models are characterized by their *massive size*, often containing billions or even trillions of parameters.

Machine Learning: This involves the creation of software components (models) that empower computers to discern and contextualize patterns in data without the need for explicit human programming of rules. Applications of machine learning can produce predictions, recommendations, or decisions based on statistical reasoning.

Natural Language Processing (NLP): NLP involves the analysis and extraction of information from diverse human language sources, including text, images, videos, and audio data. It is commonly employed for language classification and interpretation. Many NLP applications not only process natural language but also generate content that emulates it.

Reinforcement Learning: A type of ML, involves an agent learning to make decisions by interacting with its environment and receiving feedback in the form of rewards or penalties. Applied in autonomous vehicles, robotics, recommendation systems, finance, healthcare, education, natural language processing, and simulation environments, reinforcement learning showcases versatility in dynamic decision-making.

Strong AI: Includes Artificial General Intelligence (AGI), which also refers to highly autonomous systems or machines envisioned to outperform humans across a broad range of tasks.

Notes

1 "The State of AI: Global Survey," "AI in the Workplace: A Report for 2025," *McKinsey & Company*, accessed June 18, 2025, https://www.mckinsey.com/capabilities/quantumblack/our-insights/the-state-of-ai.

2 "Gartner Survey Reveals 80% of Executives Think Automation Can Be Applied to Any Business Decision," *Gartner*, accessed October 17, 2023, https://www.gartner.com/en/newsroom/press-releases/2022-08-22-gartner-survey-reveals-80-percent-of-executives-think-automation-can-be-applied-to-any-business-decision.

3 "Engaging with Artificial Intelligence," *Australian Signals Directorate*, last modified January 24, 2024, https://www.cyber.gov.au/resources-business-and-government/governance-and-user-education/governance/engaging-with-artificial-intelligence.

4 Cade Metz, Cecilia Kang, Sheera Frenkel, Stuart A. Thompson, and Nico Grant, "How Tech Giants Cut Corners to Harvest Data for AI," *New York Times*, April 6, 2024.

5 Liz Christman**,** "Obtain Fast Insights into Complex Legal Issues with Legal AI Summarization Tool," *Lexis Nexis*, April 24, 2024, https://www.lexisnexis.com/community/insights/legal/b/product-features/posts/obtain-fast-insights-into-complex-legal-issues-with-legal-ai-summarization-tool.

6 Dentons, Spatial Web Foundation, Verses, "The Future of Global AI Governance," July 2023, p. 5.

7 Morgan Meaker, "These Prisoners Are Training AI," *Wired Magazine*, September 11, 2023, https://www.wired.com/story/prisoners-training-ai-finland/.

8 Michael Chen, "6 Common AI Model Training Challenges," *OCI*, December 20, 2023, https://www.oracle.com/artificial-intelligence/ai-model-training-challenges/.

9 "What is the EU AI Act?" EU Artificial Intelligence Act, accessed July 16, 2024. https://artificialintelligenceact.eu/.

2 AI Governance Standards, Frameworks, and Models

Creating Guardrails

In this chapter, we will provide a wide discussion on the characteristics of an effective AI Governance framework. Any effective framework should be customized somewhat to the particular AI implementation.

Bear this in mind as you build an AI Governance framework; it will include not only a core framework but also the inclusion of relevant standards and models. It should be robust rather than rigid. It should anticipate change, not prevent it. It should clearly allow for updates, modifications, or additions, but not without meaningful contemplation. It should also reflect the fact that in governance, less is usually more. Say enough to get the job done, but after that use an economy of words, rules, and controls. In this way, you create governance that enables and enhances rather than constrains and confines.

AI Governance is crucial in ensuring the responsible and ethical development, deployment, and use of AI systems. The need for AI Governance standards, frameworks, and models arises from several key considerations, and their implementation brings various benefits. Here's a delineation of the need for and benefits of AI Governance in these three aspects:

Need for AI Governance Standards, Frameworks, and Models

The burgeoning field of AI brings forth many advancements and conveniences; yet, it also presents significant ethical, legal, and social challenges, necessitating the development and implementation of comprehensive AI Governance standards, frameworks, and models.

At the heart of these governance mechanisms lie ethical concerns, particularly regarding bias and fairness. AI systems, reflecting their training data, can inadvertently perpetuate or even amplify existing biases, leading to outcomes that lack fairness and equity. This issue underscores the importance of governance standards aimed at ensuring AI systems are developed and deployed in a manner that upholds fairness, transparency, and equity. Always keep in mind that efforts to identify, understand, and minimize bias in these systems are a never-ending effort against an ever-changing target. Even if it's not optimal, getting everyone on the same page is often a great first step. And there will be continual adjustments that will need to be made to accommodate changes in outputs, training data, and AI program goals.

Additionally, data privacy emerges as a major concern, given AI's capacity to process and analyze sensitive personal information, and the frequent use of personally identifiable information (PII) in AI models. Governance frameworks thus play a crucial role in establishing rigorous guidelines for the handling of personal data, aligning with privacy regulations and safeguarding individual rights. Many jurisdictions are considering, or have already adopted, strict privacy regulations pertaining to AI systems. Privacy must be at the forefront of any AI initiatives your organization may adopt.

Accountability and transparency form another critical axis of AI Governance. The complex nature of AI models, especially those based on deep neural networks, often results in systems that are difficult to interpret or explain. There are model-agnostic tools to assist in simplifying complex AI models to help explain them and their internal processes (which we will detail later in this book), and governance models can address this challenge by emphasizing the necessity for AI decisions to be understandable and explainable, thereby fostering trust and accountability. Furthermore, clear governance standards are instrumental in defining the responsibilities and accountability of stakeholders involved in the AI lifecycle, ensuring AI systems are used responsibly and ethically.

Security concerns are also significant, as AI systems are inherently reliant on vast datasets which may contain sensitive information. Governance frameworks are essential for establishing robust measures to protect data against unauthorized access and ensure its integrity. Moreover, the robustness of AI models is a focal point of governance standards, aiming to allow for planned interoperability while fortifying systems against adversarial attacks, thereby safeguarding their reliability and effectiveness.

Compliance with legal and regulatory frameworks is another vital aspect of AI Governance. The AI domain is governed by an evolving landscape of regulations and laws, making compliance a complex yet crucial requirement. Governance frameworks offer structured guidelines for navigating these legal complexities, helping organizations avoid potential legal entanglements and penalties.

Benefits of AI Governance Standards, Frameworks, and Models

AI Governance standards, frameworks, and models serve as cornerstone elements in the responsible development and deployment of AI technologies, offering a myriad of benefits that are essential for mitigating risks, building trust, fostering innovation, ensuring global alignment, and promoting long-term viability.

If an organization views governance as a necessary evil, or as something that will slow them down, they will likely prove themselves to be correct. We maintain that, "Brakes on racecars allow them to go faster," and that this maxim applies to AI initiatives. So, if an organization views governance as an enabling framework that will help to focus and accelerate their adoption of AI, they too will likely prove themselves to be correct. We urge you and your organization to choose wisely.

Risk mitigation is a chief benefit of implementing AI Governance mechanisms. AI Governance methods and best practices are instrumental in identifying and mitigating biases within AI models, thereby significantly reducing the risk of discriminatory outcomes that could arise from unchecked AI applications.

Additionally, adherence to established governance frameworks ensures compliance with legal requirements, minimizing the risk of encountering legal challenges and liabilities. This aspect is crucial as it helps organizations navigate the complex landscape of laws and regulations governing AI, ensuring their operations remain within legal boundaries.

The role of AI Governance in building trust and fostering adoption cannot be overstated. By adhering to **ethical AI principles**, organizations build trust among users, customers, and the wider public. This trust is foundational to fostering greater adoption of AI technologies, as it reassures stakeholders of the commitment to ethical considerations and the positive impact of AI on society. Companies that implement robust governance practices stand to significantly enhance their corporate reputation. Demonstrating a commitment to responsible AI practices distinguishes these organizations as leaders in ethical technology deployment, thus attracting more customers and partners.

Innovation thrives under the guidance of AI Governance frameworks. These frameworks offer a structured foundation for responsible and sustainable innovation, encouraging the development of AI advancements that are not only technologically advanced but also aligned with ethical principles. This approach to innovation ensures that AI technologies are developed with a keen awareness of their potential business and societal impact, driving progress in a manner that benefits the organization and quite possibly humanity as a whole.

Global alignment on AI ethics and regulations is facilitated through harmonized governance standards. Such standards promote international cooperation and ensure a consistent approach to AI Governance across borders. This global alignment is essential in today's interconnected world, where AI technologies and their implications transcend national boundaries. By fostering a unified stance on AI ethics and regulations, governance standards help create a level playing field and promote a shared understanding of responsible AI use worldwide.

Lastly, the sustainability and long-term viability of AI technologies are bolstered by ethical and responsible AI practices promoted by governance frameworks. These practices ensure that AI developments are conducted with an eye toward preventing negative externalities, thus contributing to the sustainable growth of AI technologies. By prioritizing ethical considerations and responsible deployment, AI Governance frameworks lay the groundwork for AI technologies to continue delivering value to society over the long term.

In summary, *the establishment of AI Governance standards, frameworks, and models is crucial for addressing a wide array of ethical concerns, ensuring accountability, enhancing security, achieving compliance with regulations, and involving a diverse set of stakeholders.* These governance mechanisms are fundamental to reaping the benefits of AI in a responsible and sustainable manner, paving the way for a future where AI technologies are developed and deployed in alignment with the highest ethical standards.

Beyond the Need for Technical Standards

Technical standards, often the unappreciated underpinning of technological societies, play a pivotal role in shaping the future landscape of AI regulation and governance. However, it is essential to recognize that relying solely on these standards may fall short of the comprehensive approach needed.

As the pace of technological change continues to accelerate, it grows ever more apparent that most of the challenges we face in adopting technology are personal and organizational. The gap between our technological prowess and our humanness grows greater with each technological advance. Hence, the challenges to our success with technologies like AI are necessarily rooted more in the psychological and social issues we face, rather than in technical or operational matters.

In May 2023, the G7 leaders issued a joint communiqué advocating for the development and global adoption of international technical standards governing AI's development and deployment.[1]

Similar calls for such standards have resonated from diverse private and public stakeholders. This is entirely justified, as historical precedents underscore how technical standards have been instrumental in shaping our modern world, delivering substantial benefits to governments, developers, manufacturers, and consumers. Andrew Russell and Lee Vinsel of *The New York Times* aptly noted, "Cars run on gas from any gas station, the plugs for electrical devices fit into any socket, and smartphones connect to anything equipped with Bluetooth. All of these conveniences depend on technical standards, the silent and often forgotten foundations of technological societies."[2]

Nonetheless, it is clear that, in this context, technical standards alone may not be sufficient. AI is poised to exert an unprecedented influence on both technology and society. The G7 communiqué astutely recognizes this tension by emphasizing the significance of "social implementation" of technical AI standards.[3] The US Department of Commerce's **National Institute of Standards and Technology** (NIST) has also *cautioned against an exclusive reliance on purely technical standards* when addressing AI, proposing a hybrid approach that integrates socio-technical standards. These socio-technical standards aim to bridge the gap between technology and society.

The development of socio-technical standards for AI Governance holds the promise of multiple advantages. Such standards can:

1. *Facilitate coordinated action* by governments and regulators to proactively ensure compatibility and compliance.
2. Provide a *flexible framework* allowing regulators across diverse regions to implement their unique AI regulations while maintaining global interoperability.
3. Critically, the standards would *take into account the potential trajectory of AI*, ranging from today's "narrow" AI designed for specific tasks within limited domains to the forthcoming "general" AI capable of learning, comprehending, and applying knowledge across diverse domains, and eventually to the future's "super-intelligent" AI surpassing human-level intelligence.

In essence, socio-technical standards may pave the way for AI Governance that keeps pace with the exponential evolution and growing autonomy of intelligent machines.

Relevant ISO Standards for AI Governance

Your organization may determine that adherence to all available standards is not necessary, depending on your business scenario and application requirements. Yet it is important to have as complete of a list as possible to consider:

ISO 24143:2022 – Information Governance: Emphasizes risk management and mitigation. It defines an IG program as a "strategic framework for governing information assets across an entire organization to enhance coordinated support for the achievement of business outcomes and obtain assurance that the risks to its information, and thereby the operational capabilities and integrity of the organization, are effectively identified and managed."

ISO/IEC 42001 – Artificial Intelligence: Specifies requirements for establishing, implementing, maintaining, and continually improving an Artificial Intelligence Management System (AIMS) within organizations. ISO/IEC 42001 is the world's first AI management system standard, providing valuable guidance for this rapidly changing field of technology. It addresses the unique challenges AI poses, such as ethical considerations, transparency, and continuous learning. For organizations, it sets out a structured way to manage risks and opportunities associated with AI, balancing innovation with governance.

ISO 31000 – Risk Management: The principles of ISO 31000 are based on value creation and protection. The principles are the foundation for *managing risk* and should be considered when establishing the organization's risk management framework and processes.

ISO/IEC 27001 – Information Security, Cybersecurity, Privacy Protection: The world's best-known standard for information security management systems (ISMS). It defines the requirements an ISMS must meet. It is an international standard to manage information security.

ISO 27701 – Privacy Information Management System (PIMS): Outlines a framework for Personally Identifiable Information (PII) Controllers and PII Processors to manage data privacy. It requires compliance with ISO 27001 as a prerequisite.

ISO 38500:2015 – Information Technology: Defines the governance of IT as a subset or domain of organizational governance, or in the case of a corporation, corporate governance.

ISO 15489-1: 2016 – Records Management: Defines the concepts and principles from which approaches to the creation, capture, and management of records are developed. It outlines the basics for records management practices.

Relevant IEEE Standards for AI Governance

IEEE (Institute of Electrical and Electronics Engineers): The world's largest technical professional organization, with over 400,000 members, dedicated to advancing technology for the benefit of humanity. IEEE and its organizational units engage in coordinated public policy activities at the national, regional, and international levels in order to advance the mission and vision of securing the benefits of technology for the advancement of society. IEEE has about forty technical societies, each focused on a certain knowledge area, which provide specialized publications, conferences, business networking, and other services. IEEE Societies include the IEEE Computational Intelligence Society, IEEE Computer Society, IEEE Robotics and Automation Society, and more. Below are some of the prominent standards relating to AI:

IEEE P7000 Series – Model Process for Addressing Ethical Concerns During System Design: The Institute of Electrical and Electronics Engineers (IEEE) has developed the P7000 series of standards focusing on various aspects of ethical considerations in AI, including transparency, accountability, and algorithmic bias. These standards aim to provide guidelines for incorporating ethical considerations throughout the design process.

IEEE P7001 – 2001 Transparency of Autonomous Systems: Measurable, testable levels of transparency, so that autonomous systems can be objectively assessed and levels of compliance determined, are described in this standard.

IEEE P7002 – Data Privacy Process: This standard specifies how to manage privacy issues for systems or software that collect personal data by defining requirements that cover corporate data collection policies and quality assurance.

IEEE P7003 – Algorithmic Bias Considerations: This standard focuses on providing guidelines for identifying and mitigating bias in algorithms, including those used in AI systems. It addresses the ethical implications of biased decision-making and aims to promote fairness.

IEEE P7004 – Standard for Child and Student Data Governance: This concerns the governance of data related to children and students. While not exclusively AI-focused, it is relevant to AI systems that involve the collection and processing of data from these populations.

IEEE P7005 – 2001 Standard for Transparent Employer Data Governance: Specific methodologies to help employers in accessing, collecting, storing, utilizing, sharing, and destroying employee data are described in this standard.

IEEE P7006 – (Working in Progress) Standard for Personal Data Artificial Intelligence (AI) Agent: This standard describes the technical elements required to create and grant access to a personalized AI that will comprise inputs, learning, ethics, rules, and values controlled by individuals.

IEEE P2874 – Standards: The IEEE P2874 standards are being developed to address the following needs as they relate to building a future global AI Governance framework:

1. Ensuring a shared understanding of meaning and context between humans and AI.
2. Ensuring explainability of AI systems, enabled by the explicit modeling of their decision-making processes.
3. Ensuring interoperability of data and models that enable universal interaction and collaboration across organizations, networks, and borders.
4. Ensuring compliance with diverse local, regional, national, and international regulatory demands, cultural norms, and ethics.
5. Ensuring authentication and credentialing, driving compliance and control over critical activities, with privacy, security, and explainability built in by design.

IEEE SA Ethics in Action: IEEE SA (Standards Association) has an "Ethics in Action" initiative, which includes efforts to develop standards and guidelines related to ethical considerations in various technologies, including AI. This initiative aims to ensure the responsible and ethical development and use of technology.

AI Standards from National Bodies

Various national standards bodies, such as NIST (National Institute of Standards and Technology) in the United States and BSI (British Standards Institution) in the UK, are also are developing standards or guidelines related to AI.

Emerging Agentic AI Standards

Major AI leaders are collaborating on emerging, vendor-neutral, open standards to ensure interoperability and safety in agentic AI development. Leading technical standards are the Model Context Protocol (MCP) from Anthropic, and the Agent-to-Agent (A2A) Protocol from Google.

Leading Agentic AI Standards and Protocols

Model Context Protocol (MCP): Originally developed by Anthropic and now an industry-wide open standard, MCP is a protocol that standardizes how AI systems connect with external data sources, memory stores, and tools. It provides a universal interface, enabling AI agents to access real-time information and execute functions securely across various platforms.

Agent-to-Agent (A2A) Protocol: Initiated by Google and stewarded by the Linux Foundation, A2A offers a universal standard for communication between AI agents, regardless of their underlying vendor or framework. This protocol facilitates seamless collaboration, coordination, and task hand-offs between different agents, enabling the creation of complex multi-agent systems.

Agent Communication Protocol (ACP): Launched by IBM under the Linux Foundation, ACP is an open, vendor-neutral standard for enterprise-scale communication and task management within agent networks.

Company-Specific Frameworks and Approaches

While contributing to open standards, leading companies also offer their own frameworks and best practices:

Google: Focuses on practical implementation through the "five core elements" of agentic solutions (reasoning, synthesizing, generating, taking actions, and memory) and the Agent Payments Protocol (AP2) for secure, verifiable transactions.

Anthropic: Emphasizes simplicity in design, the importance of measuring performance, and prioritizing transparency in planning steps. Anthropic also leads with a strong ethical approach known as Constitutional AI and was the first to achieve the ISO/IEC 42001:2023 certification for AI Governance.

OpenAI: Has developed the lightweight, client-side Swarm framework for building agentic workflows and has also integrated the Model Context Protocol (MCP) across its products. Their approach includes rigorous adversarial testing and a focus on robust safety guardrails.

NIST Risk Management Framework

The National Institute of Standards and Technology (NIST), part of the US Department of Commerce, in collaboration with the private and public sectors, issued the **AI Risk Management Framework** (AI RMF 1.0) in January 2023 to better manage risks to individuals, organizations, and society associated with AI. The RMF provides a comprehensive, flexible, repeatable, and measurable seven-step process that any organization can use to manage information security and privacy risk for organizations and systems, and links to a suite of NIST standards and guidelines to support the implementation of risk management associated with AI systems.[4]

The AI RMF refers to an AI system as an engineered or machine-based system that can, for a given set of objectives, generate outputs such as predictions, recommendations, or decisions influencing real or virtual environments. AI systems are designed to operate with varying levels of autonomy (adapted from: OECD Recommendation on AI: 2019; ISO/IEC 22989: 2022).

> *"The AI Risk Management Framework (AI RMF) is intended for voluntary use and to improve the ability to incorporate trustworthiness considerations into the design, development, use, and evaluation of AI products, services, and systems."*[5]

The primary objective of the AI Risk Management Framework (AI RMF) is to serve as a valuable resource for organizations engaged in the deployment and utilization of AI systems. Its purpose is to facilitate the effective management and reduction of risks associated with AI, ensuring the responsible development and use of this transformative technology.[6]

Aligned with the guidelines set forth by the **Organization for Economic Co-operation and Development** (OECD), the NIST AI Risk Management Framework addresses both organizations and individuals known as AI actors. These AI actors actively participate in various stages of the AI system lifecycle, encompassing deployment and operation.

The rapid evolution of AI has brought about significant advancements in multiple industries, unlocking novel opportunities. However, as AI gains prominence, it introduces distinctive risks and challenges. Potential threats include encroachments on civil liberties and individual rights. To address these concerns and emerging risks, the NIST AI Risk Management Framework has emerged. It not only tackles adverse effects but also strives to amplify the positive impacts of AI system implementation.

This comprehensive framework presents a methodical approach for identifying, assessing, and mitigating risks linked to AI systems. It equips organizations with the tools to navigate the complex landscape of AI technology, ensuring the ethical adoption of AI, safeguarding against potential harm, promoting accountability and transparency in AI implementation, and safeguarding the rights of individuals.

A companion NIST AI RMF Playbook has also been published by NIST along with an AI RMF Roadmap, AI RMF Crosswalk, and various Perspectives. In addition, NIST has made available a video explainer about the AI RMF.

On March 30, 2023, NIST launched the Trustworthy and Responsible AI Resource Center, which will facilitate the implementation of, and international alignment with, the AI RMF.

Presidential Executive Order and NIST

The US President's Executive Order (EO) on Safe, Secure, and Trustworthy Artificial Intelligence (14110), issued on October 30, 2023, charges multiple agencies—including NIST—with producing guidelines and taking other actions to advance the safe, secure, and trustworthy development and use of AI.[7]

The EO directs NIST to develop guidelines and best practices to promote consensus industry standards that help ensure the development and deployment of safe, secure, and trustworthy AI systems. Specifically, NIST is to:

- Develop a companion resource to the AI Risk Management Framework focused on generative AI.
- Develop a companion resource to the Secure Software Development Framework to incorporate secure development practices for generative AI and dual-use foundation models.
- Launch a new initiative to create guidance and benchmarks for evaluating and auditing AI capabilities, with a focus on capabilities that could cause harm.
- Establish guidelines and processes—except for AI used as a component of a national security system—to enable developers of generative AI, especially **dual-use foundation models** (those that can be used for "good" or "bad/evil" purposes), to conduct AI red-teaming tests for the deployment of safe, secure, and trustworthy systems. This includes:
  - Coordinating or developing guidelines related to assessing and managing the safety, security, and trustworthiness of dual-use foundation models and related to privacy-preserving machine learning.
- In coordination with the Secretary of Energy and the Director of the National Science Foundation (NSF), develop and help ensure the availability of testing environments, such as testbeds, to support the development of safe, secure, and trustworthy AI technologies, as well as support the design, development, and deployment of associated **privacy-enhancing technologies** (PETs).

- Develop a *report* to the Director of OMB and the Assistant to the President for National Security Affairs identifying existing standards, tools, methods, and practices, as well as the potential development of further science-backed standards and techniques, for:
  - Authenticating content and tracking its **provenance.**
  - Labeling synthetic content (e.g., **watermarking**).
  - Detecting **synthetic content.**
  - Preventing generative AI from producing Child Sexual Abuse Material or producing non-consensual intimate imagery of real individuals.
  - Testing software used for the above purposes.
  - Auditing and maintaining synthetic content.
- Create guidelines for agencies to evaluate the efficacy of differential privacy guarantee protections, including for AI.
- Develop guidelines, tools, and practices to support agencies' implementation of minimum risk management practices.
- Assist the Secretary of Commerce in coordinating with key international partners and standards development organizations to drive the development and implementation of AI-related consensus standards, cooperation, and information sharing. Then the Secretary of Commerce (coordinating with the Secretary of State and heads of other Federal agencies) will establish a plan for global engagement to promote and develop AI standards.
- These efforts are to be guided by principles set out in the NIST AI Risk Management Framework and the US Government National Standards Strategy for Critical and Emerging Technology, which is led by NIST.

In some assignments, NIST will be working on behalf of the Secretary of Commerce. NIST is to consult with other agencies in producing some of its guidance; in turn, several of those agencies are directed to consult NIST (directly or through the Secretary of Commerce) in accomplishing their actions under the EO. Most of the EO tasks assigned to NIST have a 270-day deadline.

In addition to working with government agencies, NIST intends to engage with the private sector, academia, and civil society as it produces guidance called for by the EO. NIST will build on and expand on current efforts in several of these areas. That includes the Generative AI Public Working Group established in June 2023.

Before the Trump inauguration in January 2025, federal regulatory action was guided by President Biden's Executive Order 14110: "Safe, Secure, and Trustworthy Development and Use of Artificial Intelligence." This was explicitly repealed on January 20, 2025. Trump's own EOs and AI Action Plan enable the Federal Government to withhold Federal funding from states that enforce state-level AI regulation; however, states can effectively regulate AI usage through existing, non-AI-specific state laws and regulations, for example privacy and consumer protection.[8]

An Overview: Frameworks, Guidelines, and Principles for AI Governance

1. **NIST AI Risk Management Framework:** Released on January 26, 2023, the Framework was developed through a consensus-driven, open, transparent, and collaborative process that included a Request for Information, several draft versions for public comments,

multiple *workshops*, and other opportunities to provide input. It is intended to build on, align with, and support AI risk management efforts by others *(see above for more detail).*

2. **OECD AI Principles:** The **Organization for Economic Co-operation and Development** (OECD) has developed principles for the responsible development and use of AI. These principles include fostering innovation, ensuring transparency, promoting accountability, and respecting human rights.
3. **EU Ethics Guidelines for Trustworthy AI:** The European Commission's High-Level Expert Group on AI has established guidelines for trustworthy AI. These guidelines emphasize human-centric AI, transparency, accountability, and the prevention of biases.
4. **AI Principles by IEEE:** The Institute of Electrical and Electronics Engineers (IEEE) has developed a set of principles to guide the development of ethical and accountable AI. These principles cover aspects such as transparency, accountability, privacy, and the consideration of societal impacts.
5. **IBM AI Ethics Principles:** IBM has outlined a set of AI ethics principles that focus on transparency, explainability, fairness, and accountability. These principles guide IBM's approach to developing and deploying AI technologies.
6. **Microsoft AI Principles:** Microsoft has established a set of AI principles that address fairness, transparency, inclusiveness, accountability, and reliability. These principles guide Microsoft's work in AI research and development.
7. **Google AI Principles:** Google has published a set of AI principles centered around being socially beneficial, avoiding biases, maintaining transparency, ensuring accountability, and incorporating privacy considerations into AI development.
8. **AI Ethics Guidelines by UNESCO:** The United Nations Educational, Scientific and Cultural Organization (UNESCO) has developed AI ethics guidelines to promote human rights, inclusivity, and the reduction of biases in AI systems.
9. **AI4People Ethical Framework:** AI4People, an initiative from the European AI community, has proposed an ethical framework for trustworthy AI. This framework covers principles such as fairness, transparency, accountability, and user empowerment.
10. **AITIC Ethics Guidelines:** The **AI Ethics Guidelines by the AI Trust and Implementability** Challenge (AITIC) aim to provide guidance on *ethical AI development*. The guidelines focus on accountability, transparency, and the consideration of societal impacts.

These frameworks contribute to the ongoing global conversation about AI Governance and ethics. Organizations are encouraged to adopt and adapt these principles to align with their specific contexts and values. It's essential to stay informed about updates and new developments in AI Governance frameworks, as the field continues to evolve.

AI and Information Governance Models

The **Information Governance Reference Model** (IGRM) serves as a comprehensive framework that provides guidance for managing information within organizations. When applied to AI Governance, the IGRM can be instrumental in highlighting various aspects of AI development and deployment, by functional role.

Here's an overview of how the IGRM's seven core facets—Legal, Privacy, Security, Risk Management, Records and Information Management, IT, and Business Units—contribute to guiding AI Governance:

1. **Legal**

   Regulatory Compliance: Ensure adherence to relevant AI regulations and legal frameworks.

   Contractual Agreements: Establish clear contractual agreements regarding AI development, deployment, and accountability.

   Intellectual Property: Define ownership and protection mechanisms for AI-generated intellectual property.

   Liability Framework: Develop guidelines for allocating liability in the case of AI-related incidents.

2. **Data Privacy**

   Data Protection: The Privacy facet focuses on safeguarding individuals' privacy, particularly concerning the use of personal data in AI systems. It guides organizations in implementing measures to protect sensitive information, ensuring compliance with privacy regulations.

   Privacy by Design: Integrate privacy considerations into the entire AI development lifecycle.

   Consent Management: Establish clear processes for obtaining and managing user consent for data usage.

   Anonymization and Pseudonymization: Implement techniques to protect individual identities in AI datasets.

   Data Subject Rights: Develop mechanisms for individuals to exercise their rights regarding AI-generated data.

3. **Records and Information Management**

   Data Governance: The RIM facet of the IGRM focuses on organizing and managing data throughout its lifecycle. In the context of AI, it guides organizations in establishing overarching policies for the collection, storage, and management of AI-related data, ensuring data quality, and maintaining documentation for transparency and accountability.

   Documentation: Maintain comprehensive records of AI development, training data, and model outcomes.

   Version Control: Implement versioning for AI models to track changes and updates.

   Audit Trails: Maintain audit trails for AI processes to ensure transparency and accountability.

4. **Cybersecurity**

   Data Security: The Security facet of IGRM addresses the *protection of data and AI models from unauthorized access*, ensuring the confidentiality, integrity, and availability of information. It guides the implementation of security measures to *prevent data breaches and attacks* on AI systems.

   Secure Development Practices: Integrate security measures into the AI development process.

   Access Controls: Implement robust access controls to protect AI models and data.

   Incident Response: Develop and test incident response plans specific to AI-related security breaches.

   Vulnerability Assessments: Regularly assess and address vulnerabilities in AI systems.

5. **IT**

   Technology Infrastructure Management: The IT facet addresses the technical aspects of AI implementation. It guides organizations in building and maintaining the IT infrastructure required for AI systems, including considerations for scalability, interoperability, and integration with existing systems.

   Integration with Existing Systems: Integrate AI systems seamlessly with existing IT architectures.

   Data Storage and Retrieval: Implement efficient mechanisms for storing and retrieving AI-related data.

   Interoperability: Ensure compatibility and interoperability with other IT systems and applications.

6. **Risk Management**

   Risk Assessment: The Risk Management facet of the IGRM helps organizations to focus on identifying and assessing risks associated with AI projects. It guides the development of risk management strategies to mitigate potential negative impacts, ensuring that AI initiatives align with organizational goals and values. Organizations must regularly assess the risks associated with AI applications and technologies.

   Risk Mitigation Strategies: Develop strategies to mitigate identified risks, including legal, ethical, and operational risks.

   Continuous Monitoring: Implement continuous monitoring mechanisms to identify emerging risks.

   Risk Reporting: Establish reporting mechanisms for timely communication of risks to relevant stakeholders.

7. **Business Units**

   Strategic Alignment: The Business Units facet ensures that AI initiatives align with organizational objectives and strategies. It guides the integration of AI into business processes, fostering collaboration between business units and AI development teams to maximize the value and impact of AI technologies.

   User Training and Awareness: Provide training to employees on AI systems, their capabilities, and ethical considerations.

   Cross-Functional Collaboration: Foster collaboration between business units, data scientists, and legal and compliance teams.

   Performance Measurement: Develop metrics to measure the performance and impact of AI applications on business outcomes.

This approach to AI Governance based on the **Information Governance Reference Model** emphasizes a holistic and integrated strategy that addresses legal, technical, and organizational aspects. Regular reviews and updates to the governance framework are crucial to adapt to evolving regulatory landscapes and emerging risks in the AI domain.

In summary, *the IGRM provides a guide for AI Governance by offering a structured approach to managing information across multiple functional groups, including legal, privacy, security, risk management, records & information management, IT, and business units.*

By incorporating these facets into AI Governance practices, organizations can develop and deploy AI systems in a manner that is ethical, responsible, and aligned with broader organizational goals.

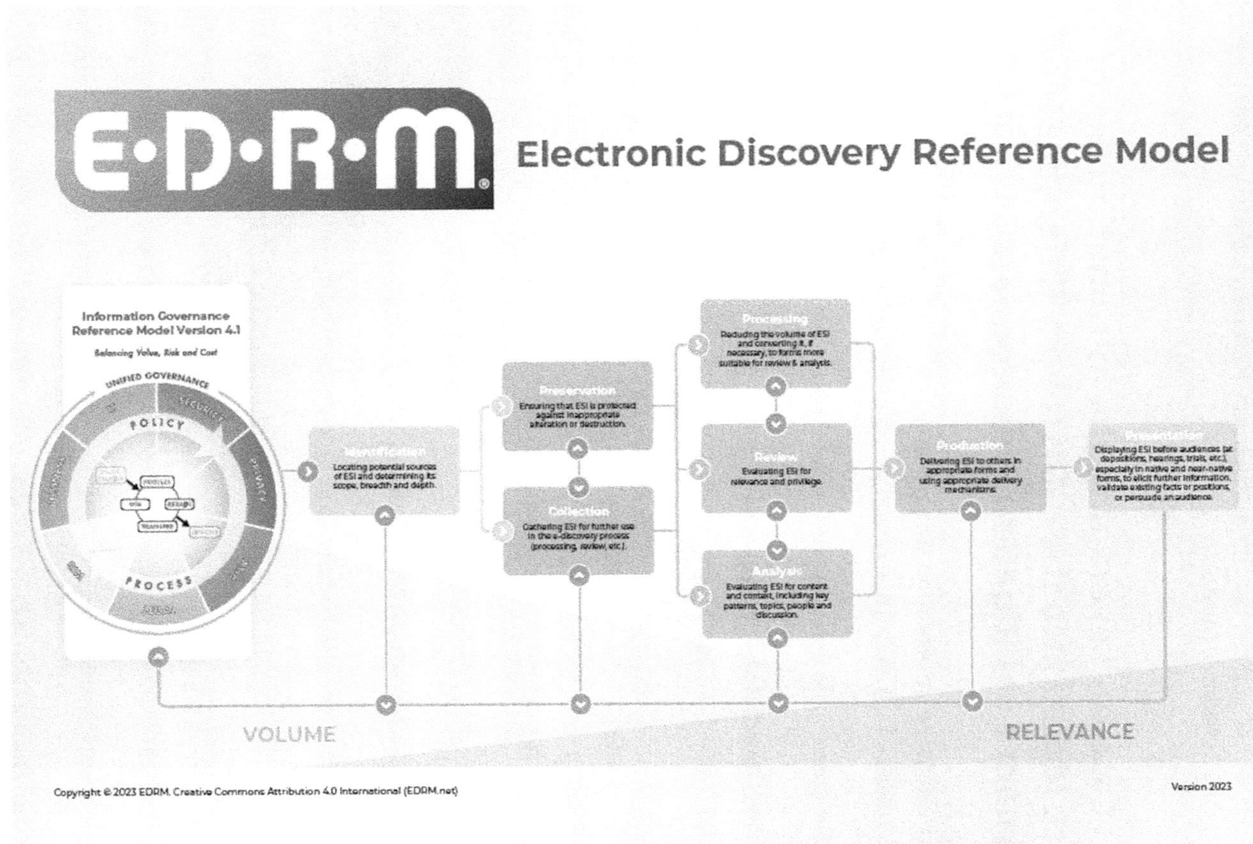

Figure 2.1 e-Discovery Governance Reference Model. Source: EDRM.net; https://edrm.net/edrm-model/current/.

Anticipating AI Litigation: Leveraging the IG Reference Model into the e-Discovery Reference Model

There is now, and undoubtedly will be much more, litigation associated with AI systems. To prepare for that, organizations should use the **e-Discovery Reference** Model (EDRM) as a high-level guide to align resources. Below you can see the **e-Discovery Reference Model (EDRM)**, which has, as the first step, the **IG Reference Model**:

Business Case for Leveraging the Information Governance Reference Model into the e-Discovery Reference Model for AI Governance in Litigation Preparedness

1. **Comprehensive Information Governance**

   By integrating the IG Reference Model into the e-Discovery process, businesses establish a *robust foundation for managing and governing information throughout its lifecycle.* This comprehensive approach ensures that data used in AI systems is well-managed, reducing the likelihood of legal challenges related to data quality, integrity, or compliance.

2. **Legal and Regulatory Compliance**

   Aligning AI Governance with the IG Reference Model ensures *adherence to legal and regulatory requirements.* This proactive approach helps businesses stay compliant with evolving laws, reducing the risk of legal challenges related to noncompliance and enhancing defensibility in litigation.

3. **Data Privacy**

   Embedding **dataprivacy** principles from the IG Reference Model into AI Governance ensures that sensitive information is appropriately handled. This approach helps in mitigating privacy-related litigation risks, demonstrating a commitment to protecting individual rights and data.

4. **Records and Information Management**

   The IG Reference Model emphasizes effective **Records and Information Management** (RIM), *enabling businesses to maintain records of training data and its provenance, a structured and organized repository of current data, and records of retired data sets or models.* This approach ensures that relevant information is readily available during e-Discovery, streamlining the process and minimizing the risk of spoliation claims.

5. **Cybersecurity Measures**

   The IG Reference Model includes **cybersecurity** considerations, which, when integrated into AI Governance, enhances the security posture of AI systems. Strengthened cybersecurity measures reduce the risk of data breaches and associated legal challenges, reinforcing trust in the AI technologies deployed.

6. **Risk Mitigation and Incident Response**

   The e-Discovery Reference Model, combined with the IG framework, *enables businesses to develop robust risk mitigation and incident response strategies.* This preparedness reduces the impact of potential legal actions arising from unforeseen issues with AI systems, showcasing a commitment to addressing challenges promptly and responsibly.

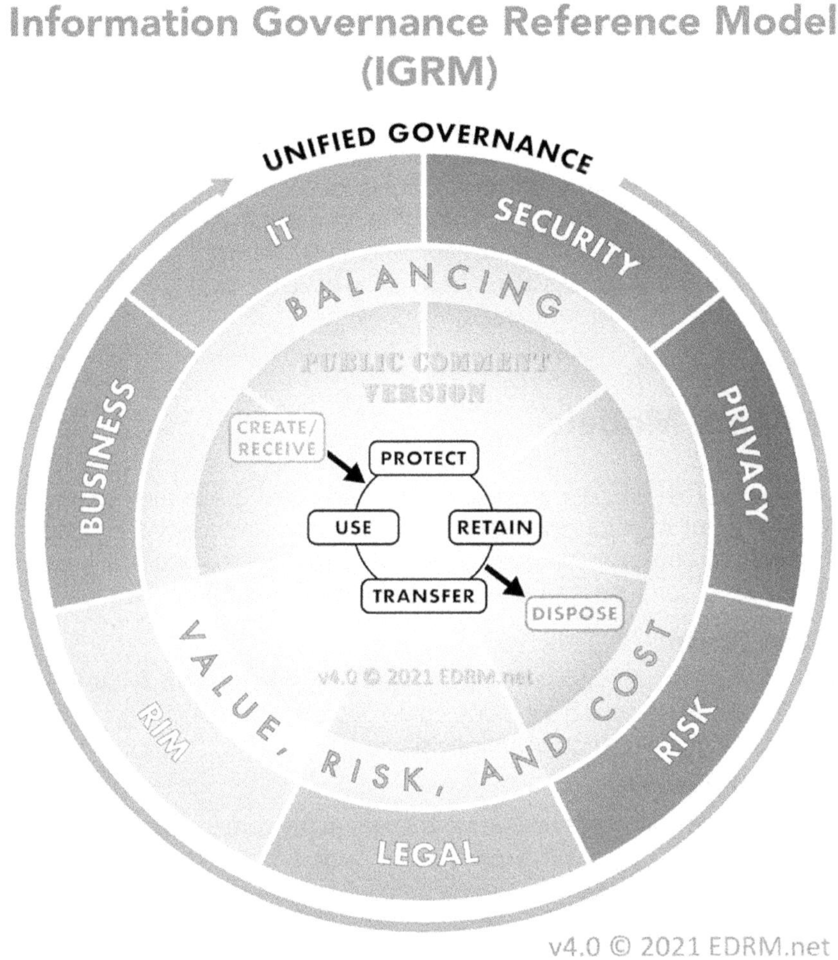

Figure 2.2 Information Governance Reference Model. Source: EDRM.net.

7. **Defensible Data Practices**

   Leveraging the IG Reference Model ensures that *data practices are defensible* in a legal context. This defensibility extends to AI-generated insights, fostering confidence in the reliability and validity of AI-derived evidence during litigation.

8. **Integration with e-Discovery**

   Processes By aligning AI Governance with the e-Discovery Reference Model, businesses seamlessly integrate AI-related data into the **e-Discovery** process. This streamlines the identification, preservation, and collection of relevant information, reducing the time and costs associated with e-Discovery.

9. **Cost-Efficiency and Resource Optimization**

   The unified approach provided by leveraging both models enhances operational efficiency. Businesses can *optimize resources by establishing standardized processes* for data management, governance, and e-Discovery, leading to potential cost savings in legal proceedings.

10. **Proactive Litigation Preparedness**

    The integrated approach helps to ensure that businesses *are proactively prepared for litigation* associated with AI systems. By implementing strong governance frameworks, they demonstrate a commitment to ethical and responsible AI practices, reducing the likelihood of legal challenges and fostering a positive legal standing.

In conclusion, *leveraging the Information Governance Reference Model into the e-Discovery Reference Model provides businesses with a holistic and proactive approach to AI Governance in the context of potential litigation.* This integrated strategy not only *mitigates legal risks but also establishes a foundation for ethical and responsible AI practices, aligning business operations with legal requirements and industry best practices.*

AI Governance Models

AI Governance models encompass a range of approaches to guide the ethical development, deployment, and use of AI. Additionally, the establishment of AI ethics committees, regulatory bodies, and standards-setting organizations plays a crucial role in shaping policies and guidelines. Here are descriptions of some existing AI models and related entities:

1. **Ethics by Design**

   This model emphasizes integrating ethical considerations into the entire lifecycle of AI systems, from design and development to deployment. It encourages proactive identification and mitigation of ethical risks.

2. **Human-Centered AI**

   Human-centered AI focuses on placing humans at the core of AI development, ensuring that AI technologies align with human values, preferences, and well-being. This model aims to create AI systems that augment human capabilities and enhance societal benefits.

3. **Explainable AI (XAI)**

   Explainable AI focuses on developing AI systems that provide clear and understandable explanations for their decisions. This model promotes transparency, accountability, and user trust by making AI decision-making processes interpretable.

4. **Responsible AI**

   Responsible AI encompasses a broad set of principles that guide ethical and accountable AI development. This includes considerations such as fairness, transparency, accountability, and the societal impact of AI technologies.

5. **AI for Social Good**

   This model emphasizes using AI technologies to address societal challenges and contribute to the greater good. It encourages the development of AI applications that have positive impacts on education, healthcare, environmental sustainability, and other areas.

6. **Privacy-Preserving AI**

   Privacy-preserving AI focuses on developing AI systems that prioritize the protection of user privacy. Techniques such as federated learning and homomorphic encryption are employed to ensure that sensitive data is kept confidential.

AI Establishments and Organizations

1. **AI Ethics Committees**

   Many organizations, both public and private, *establish AI ethics committees* to provide guidance on ethical AI development. These committees often consist of multidisciplinary experts who review and advise on AI projects, ensuring alignment with ethical principles.

2. **Regulatory Bodies**

   Regulatory bodies at national and international levels are being established to oversee AI development and deployment. These bodies work to create regulations, standards, and policies that address ethical considerations, safety, and fairness in AI systems.

3. **Standards-Setting Organizations**

   Organizations such as **ISO** (International Organization for Standardization) and **IEEE** (Institute of Electrical and Electronics Engineers) play a crucial role in developing standards for AI. These standards cover various aspects, including ethics, interoperability, and safety.

   ISO/IEC JTC 1/SC 42 - Artificial Intelligence: The International Organization for Standardization (ISO) and the International Electrotechnical Commission (IEC) established a joint technical committee, SC 42, to develop international standards for artificial intelligence.

4. **AI Regulatory Sandboxes**

   Some regulatory bodies and governments create AI regulatory sandboxes to foster innovation while ensuring ethical AI development. These sandboxes provide a controlled environment for testing and deploying AI technologies under regulatory supervision.

5. **Global Partnership on AI (GPAI)**

   GPAI is an international initiative that brings together leading experts and stakeholders to address challenges and opportunities in AI. It focuses on fostering collaboration on AI research, policy development, and best practices.

6. **AI Industry Alliances**

   Industry alliances, such as the **Partnership on AI** (PAI) and the **AI Infrastructure Alliance**, bring together companies to collaborate on the development of ethical guidelines, best practices, and standards for AI technologies.

7. **National AI Strategies**

   Many countries are developing national AI strategies that include governance frameworks, regulatory approaches, and investment plans. These strategies aim to position countries as leaders in AI while ensuring responsible development.

8. **AI Ethics Guidelines — UNESCO**

   The United Nations Educational, Scientific and Cultural Organization (UNESCO) has developed AI ethics guidelines to promote human rights, transparency, and the reduction of bias in AI systems.

These governance models, strategies, and entities collectively contribute to the establishment of ethical guidelines, regulatory frameworks, and standards for the responsible development and deployment of AI technologies. It's important to note that the AI Governance landscape is dynamic, and new models and organizations may emerge over time.

Key Points

- Ethical concerns for AI systems, particularly regarding bias and fairness reflected in their training data, can inadvertently perpetuate existing biases, leading to outcomes that lack fairness and equity.
- Governance frameworks play a crucial role in establishing rigorous guidelines for the handling of personal data.
- The complex nature of AI models often results in systems that are difficult to interpret or explain. Governance models address this challenge by emphasizing the necessity for AI decisions to be understandable and explainable.
- Robust cybersecurity is required to protect data against unauthorized access and ensure its integrity.
- Compliance with legal and regulatory frameworks is another vital aspect of AI Governance.
- AI Governance standards, frameworks, and models serve as cornerstone elements in the responsible development and deployment of AI and are essential for mitigating risks, building trust, fostering innovation, ensuring global alignment, and promoting long-term viability.
- Adherence to established governance frameworks ensures compliance with legal requirements, minimizing the risk of encountering legal challenges and liabilities.
- Global alignment on AI ethics and regulations is facilitated through harmonized governance standards. Such standards promote international cooperation and consistency.
- Technical standards, often the unappreciated underpinning of technological societies, play a pivotal role in shaping the future landscape of AI regulation and governance.
- In 2023, the G7 leaders issued a joint communiqué advocating for the development and global adoption of international technical standards governing AI.
- NIST has **cautioned against an exclusive reliance on purely technical standards** when addressing AI, proposing a hybrid approach that integrates **socio-technical** standards.
- Socio-technical standards aim to bridge the gap between technology and society.
- **ISO Standards** for AI Governance include: ISO 24143:2022 – Information Governance; ISO/IEC 42001 – Artificial Intelligence – the world's first AI management system standard; ISO 31000 – Risk Management; ISO/IEC 27001 – Information Security, Cybersecurity, Privacy Protection; ISO 27701 – Privacy Information Management System (PIMS) requires compliance with ISO 27001 as a prerequisite; ISO 38500:2015 – Information Technology; ISO 15489-1: 2016 – Records Management.
- **IEEE Standards** include the P7000 Series – Model Process for Addressing Ethical Concerns During System Design; IEEE P7001 Transparency of Autonomous Systems; IEEE P7002 Data Privacy Process; IEEE P7003 Algorithmic Bias Considerations; IEEE P7004 Standard for Child and Student Data Governance; IEEE P7005 Standard for Transparent Employer Data Governance; IEEE P7006 (Working in Progress) Standard for Personal Data Artificial Intelligence (AI) Agent; **IEEE P2874 Standards.**
- The NIST AI Risk Management Framework (AI RMF 1.0) was launched in January 2023. The RMF provides a 7-step process that any organization can use to manage information security and privacy risk in AI systems.

- **AI Frameworks** include the NIST AI Risk Management Framework, OECD AI Principles; EU Ethics Guidelines for Trustworthy AI, AI Principles by IEEE, as well as published AI principles from IBM, Microsoft, and Google.
- The **Information Governance Reference Model** (IGRM) serves as a comprehensive framework that provides guidance for managing information within organizations.
- When applied to AI Governance, the IGRM can be instrumental in highlighting various aspects of AI development and deployment, by functional role.
- By integrating the IG Reference Model into the e-Discovery process, along with the e-Discovery Reference Model (EDRM), businesses establish a foundation for governing information throughout its lifecycle and in preparing for litigation.
- Leveraging the IGRM into the EDRM provides businesses with a holistic and **proactive approach to AI Governance** in the context of potential litigation.
- AI Governance models like Human-Centered AI, Ethics by Design, Explainable AI (XAI), Responsible AI, and others encompass a range of approaches to guide the ethical development, deployment, and use of AI.

Key Glossary Term

Dual-use foundation models: Foundational AI models that have the potential for both beneficial and harmful purposes.

Notes

1 Kantaro Komiya and Supantha Mukherjee, "G7 Calls for Adoption of International Technical Standards for AI," *Reuters*, May 20, 2023. https://www.reuters.com/world/g7-calls-adoption-international-technical-standards-ai-2023-05-20/.

2 Andrew Russell and Lee Vinsel, "The Joy of Standards," *The New York Times*, February 16, 2019, https://www.nytimes.com/2019/02/16/opinion/sunday/standardization.html.

3 Dentons, Spatial Web Foundation, Verses, "The Future of Global AI Governance," July 2023, p. 6.

4 "AI Risk Management Framework," *National Institute of Standards and Technology*, accessed January 12, 2023, https://airc.nist.gov/AI_RMF_Knowledge_Base/AI_RMF.

5 Ibid.

6 "NIST AI Risk Management Framework (AI RMF 1.0) Explained," *Securiti*, accessed February 4, 2023, https://securiti.ai/nist-ai-risk-management-framework/.

7 "Executive Order on Safe, Secure, and Trustworthy Artificial Intelligence," *NIST*, accessed November 30, 2023, https://www.nist.gov/artificial-intelligence/executive-order-safe-secure-and-trustworthy-artificial-intelligence.

8 Email from Joe Shepley, Managing Director, Alvarez & Marsal, September 2, 2025

3 AI Governance in the Lifecycle of AI Development

In the 1980s, many organizations began adopting the Total Quality Management concepts first pioneered by W. Edwards Deming. Deming developed a range of principles and practices for improving production quality in Japan in the 1950s, which directly fed the economic growth of that country for the next quarter-century.

Key among Deming's principles was that "quality" was something that had to be built into products; it was impossible to effectively add quality to a product after the fact. As such, Deming sought to ensure products were manufactured correctly to begin with, rather than repaired after they were built incorrectly. When this philosophy was iterated many hundreds of times, products are produced to dramatically better standards than when they started, which creates economic benefits throughout an entire value chain.

This same philosophy applies to making governance a fundamental part of the AI lifecycle. Rather than applying governance as an afterthought and necessary cost of doing business, successful organizations will incorporate governance into all phases of AI adoption. In this way, AI can be deployed correctly from the start, and benefits can be accrued from this technology much more rapidly and cost-effectively.

Governance throughout the AI software development life cycle is crucial for reducing risks associated with the development and deployment of AI applications. Key parts of the AI software development life cycle that must be governed include the following:

1. Problem Definition and Project Initiation

Problem definition is the first step in the Project Initiation phase of the AI lifecycle where the specific problem that the AI system will address is identified and defined. This involves understanding the context of the problem, the stakeholders involved, and the desired outcomes. Additionally, the potential downsides or negative impacts of an AI system gone wrong, for various reasons (including unintentional bias in training data, model overfitting, or model drift), should be considered.

The Project Initiation phase is a crucial step in the AI software development life cycle, playing a pivotal role in shaping the trajectory of the project. In this phase, the scope, objectives, and expected outcomes of the AI project are defined to provide a clear direction.

The scope definition involves a comprehensive analysis of the problem domain, identification of key stakeholders, and the establishment of project boundaries in terms of data, technology, and business requirements. The deliverables include a **Project Scope Document** outlining these boundaries and objectives. Simultaneously, objectives and goals are established, and it is a best practice to align with the **SMART** criteria in breaking down tasks or milestones.

The "SMART" criteria are an acronym used to define the key characteristics of effective goals and objectives. Each letter in the acronym represents a different criterion, ensuring that goals are well-defined and achievable. The SMART criteria stand for:

1. **Specific**

   Goals should be clear, precise, and specific. They should address the who, what, where, when, and why of the objective, leaving no room for ambiguity.

2. **Measurable**

   Goals should include criteria that allow for measurement of progress and attainment. This involves defining concrete metrics or indicators to track the achievement of the objective.

3. **Achievable**

   Goals should be realistic and attainable. They should stretch individuals or teams to improve performance, but they should not be so challenging that they become unattainable.

4. **Relevant**

   Goals should be relevant and aligned with broader objectives and organizational strategies. They should contribute meaningfully to the overall mission and vision.

5. **Time-Bound**

   Goals should have a defined timeframe or deadline. This includes specifying when the goal needs to be achieved, providing a sense of urgency and promoting a time-conscious approach.

The SMART criteria are widely used in various contexts, including project management, performance management, and personal goal setting. Applying these criteria helps ensure that goals are well-articulated, focused, and conducive to successful planning and execution.

This analysis results in a document specifying the project's objectives and goals with defined success criteria. The expected outcomes of the project are then clearly stated, facilitating a common understanding of success through the development of **key performance indicators** (KPIs) and success metrics.

Establishing governance structures, roles, and responsibilities is equally critical during the Project Initiation phase. Governance structures are defined to ensure effective decision-making, risk management, and overall project control. This involves the establishment of a governance framework with roles and responsibilities, decision-making processes, and communication channels.

The deliverables include a **Governance Plan** outlining these aspects. Concurrently, roles and responsibilities are clearly defined for team members, stakeholders, and any external contributors. This ensures accountability and clarity throughout the project, with a **Roles and Responsibilities** matrix detailing the duties of each team member. It may be helpful to create a responsibility assignment matrix (RAM), also known as RACI, which defines specifically who is Responsible, Accountable, who is to be Consulted, and others who are to be Informed.

Risk management is addressed by identifying potential threats and opportunities, conducting risk assessments, developing mitigation strategies, and establishing processes for monitoring and responding to risks. The deliverable is a **Risk Register** outlining identified risks, their impact, and mitigation plans to offset or reduce those risks to acceptable levels.

Stakeholder engagement is another key facet of Project Initiation, involving the identification and engagement of stakeholders who have an interest in or are affected by the AI project. This requires understanding their interests, expectations, and concerns and developing a stakeholder engagement plan with effective communication strategies.

Additionally, ethical considerations are crucial, necessitating an ethical impact assessment, establishment of ethical guidelines, and alignment with industry best practices and standards. The deliverable is an **Ethical Considerations document** outlining guidelines and impact assessments.

Once the Project Initiation phase is complete, the AI development lifecycle progresses to subsequent phases, guided by the comprehensive foundation established in this critical initial stage. The governed aspects of the AI software development life cycle during Project Initiation ensure a strategic, ethical, and well-managed approach to AI project development and deployment.

2. Data Acquisition and Collection

All existing AI technologies have two core elements as their raw materials: algorithms and data. While varying the quality or appropriateness of the chosen algorithm can have material impacts on the resulting output, the choice of input training data has, by far, the greatest impact on AI outcomes. Organizations should plan for at least half of their total AI implementation budget to be associated with the acquisition, preparation, and confirmation of their input data.

This data may come from external sources, such as data brokers, or other third parties, which inherently carry more risk than collecting data from internal sources. So this risk must be considered. An example of an internal source can be files stored on shared drives, and these must be cleaned up, de-duplicated, and standardized from a metadata standpoint. Software tools can convert unstructured information such as MS Office files,. PDFs, and scanned documents into searchable structured data by converting to a standard format such as ASCII.

An example of this would be scanning in paper workers' compensation claims, then converting them to searchable ASCII text, and applying an AI engine to determine the causes behind the largest claims, and suggested ways to reduce those types of claims in the future. Harvesting data from unstructured documents is the Holy Grail of Information Governance.

Data acquisition and collection is a pivotal phase in the AI lifecycle, foundational for the successful development and deployment of AI models. This stage encompasses the processes of sourcing, cleansing, and structuring data, underpinned by the imperative to ensure its relevance, quality, and adherence to ethical standards. A thorough approach to the Data Acquisition and Collection phase involves not only the technical handling of data but also the rigorous implementation of **data governance** practices and consideration of ethical implications.

Implementing data governance practices is essential for ensuring both quality and compliance. *A comprehensive data governance framework outlines the policies, procedures, and responsibilities essential for effective data management throughout its lifecycle.* This includes defining data ownership to clarify roles and responsibilities for data custodianship, setting data quality standards to ensure accuracy, completeness, consistency, and timeliness, and ensuring compliance with relevant privacy and data protection regulations such as GDPR and HIPAA to address legal and ethical considerations. Furthermore, **data cataloging** and **metadata management** are crucial for maintaining the provenance or "data lineage" of datasets and providing detailed information about each dataset, including its origin, structure, and history, thereby ensuring transparency and facilitating effective use.

Assessing **data quality** is another critical step, involving the detection of anomalies, mitigation of data bias, and profiling to understand the nature of the data thoroughly. Alongside, robust **data privacy** and **cybersecurity** measures must be implemented, including data encryption, access controls, and techniques for anonymizing or pseudonymizing personal identifiers to protect sensitive information and comply with privacy regulations.

Ethical data collection and usage must also be established, starting with guidelines that address informed consent, data minimization, and user privacy. This ensures that data is collected and used in a manner that respects individuals' rights and minimizes risks.

Finally, establishing **data retention and deletion policies,** in collaboration with the **records and information management (RIM)** function, defines the duration data will be stored and outlines secure deletion methods to prevent unauthorized access once the data is no longer needed. Regular ethical audits, both internal and external, are instrumental in assessing compliance with these practices, ensuring that deviations are identified and rectified promptly.

In summary, the "Data Acquisition and Collection" phase is critical to the AI lifecycle, requiring not just technical diligence in handling data but also a commitment to ethical standards and governance practices. These efforts lay the groundwork for the development of AI systems that are not only effective but also responsible and aligned with societal values.

Here, we delve into the specific steps for the "Data Acquisition and Preparation" phase, emphasizing the implementation of data governance practices and ethical considerations:

1. **Implement Data Governance Practices for Quality and Compliance**

   a. Define Data Governance Framework

   Establish a comprehensive data governance framework that outlines policies, procedures, and responsibilities for managing data throughout its lifecycle. Key components include:

   Data Ownership: Clearly define ownership for each dataset, specifying roles and responsibilities for data custodianship.

   Data Quality Standards: Set standards for data accuracy, completeness, consistency, and timeliness to maintain high-quality datasets.

   Compliance Requirements: Ensure alignment with relevant regulations (e.g., GDPR, HIPAA) and industry standards, addressing legal and ethical considerations.

   b. Data Cataloging and Metadata Management:

   Create a centralized data catalog that provides metadata information for each dataset. Metadata should include:

   Data Origin: Document the source of each dataset, detailing its creation, format, and update frequency.

   Data Schema: Define the structure and relationships within the data, facilitating understanding and utilization.

   Data Lineage: Track the movement and transformations of data from its source to its utilization, ensuring transparency.

   c. Data Quality Assessment:

   Conduct thorough assessments to evaluate data quality. Implement tools and processes to:

   Identify Anomalies: Detect outliers, missing values, and inconsistencies that may affect model performance.

   Data Profiling: Analyze data distribution and statistical characteristics to understand its nature.

d. Data Privacy and Security Measures:

Implement robust measures to safeguard data privacy and security

Data Encryption: Apply encryption techniques to protect sensitive information during storage and transmission.

Access Controls: Define access levels and permissions to restrict data access based on roles and responsibilities.

Anonymization and Pseudonymization: Ensure personal identifiers are anonymized or pseudonymized to comply with privacy regulations.

2. Establish Processes for Ethical Data Collection and Usage

a. Ethical Data Collection Guidelines:

Define ethical guidelines for collecting data, addressing concerns related to:

Informed Consent: Clearly communicate the purpose of data collection and obtain explicit consent from individuals contributing data.

Data Minimization: Collect only the necessary data required for the intended purpose, minimizing the risk of unauthorized use.

User Privacy: Prioritize user privacy by anonymizing or aggregating sensitive information whenever possible.

b. Transparent Data Usage Policies:

Maintain transparency in how collected data will be used:

Data Usage Agreements: Clearly articulate how the data will be utilized, specifying model development, evaluation, and potential sharing with third parties.

Communication with Stakeholders: Keep stakeholders informed about data usage practices and any changes to the original agreements.

c. Data Retention and Deletion Policies:

Establish policies for the retention and deletion of data:

Data Retention Periods: Define the duration for which data will be stored, considering legal requirements and the data's relevance.

Secure Data Deletion: Ensure secure deletion methods are employed when data is no longer required, preventing overretention and unauthorized access.

d. Regular Ethical Audits:

Conduct regular ethical audits to assess compliance with ethical data usage practices.

Internal Audits: Periodically review data usage against established ethical guidelines, identifying and rectifying any deviations.

External Audits: Engage external auditors or ethics committees to provide independent assessments of ethical data practices.

By rigorously implementing data governance practices and prioritizing ethical considerations, organizations can enhance the reliability, quality, and ethicality of their datasets, ultimately contributing to the success of AI models developed in subsequent stages of the AI lifecycle.

3. Data Preparation: Exploration and Preprocessing

The Data Preparation phase includes data exploration and preprocessing. It is a crucial phase in the AI lifecycle for understanding the characteristics of the dataset and preparing it for model training and development. In this phase, practitioners aim to address biases in training data, ensuring fairness, and documenting preprocessing steps for transparency and reproducibility. Let's delve into the detailed steps involved.

To ensure data quality and compliance, organizations should first define a comprehensive data governance framework (see previous step for more detail).

This data governance framework outlines policies, procedures, and responsibilities for managing data throughout its lifecycle. It includes components such as clearly defined data ownership, specifying roles and responsibilities for data custodianship, and setting standards for data accuracy, completeness, consistency, and timeliness. Compliance requirements, aligning with regulations like GDPR and HIPAA, are crucial to addressing legal and ethical considerations.

Data cataloging and **metadata management** play a vital role in this phase. A centralized data catalog providing metadata information for each dataset is created. This metadata includes details on data origin, schema, and lineage, ensuring transparency in understanding and utilizing the data.

Bias detection and mitigation processes are necessary to prevent biased model outcomes, requiring regular audits and the application of fairness metrics. Transparency in data usage policies further reinforces ethical practices, specifying how data will be utilized and ensuring stakeholder communication.

The next step involves a thorough **data quality assessment**. Organizations should implement tools and processes to identify anomalies, address data bias, and conduct data profiling. This ensures that the dataset is free from outliers, missing values, and inconsistencies that may impact model performance. Additionally, data privacy and security measures must be implemented, including data encryption, access controls, and anonymization or pseudonymization of personal identifiers to comply with privacy regulations.

Ethical considerations are paramount. Regular ethical audits, both internal and external, should be conducted to assess compliance with ethical data usage practices, identifying and rectifying any deviations.

Furthermore, organizations need to establish policies, in consultation with the **records and information management (RIM)** departmental function, for data retention and deletion, defining retention periods and employing secure deletion methods.

By rigorously implementing data governance practices and prioritizing ethical considerations, organizations can enhance the reliability, quality, and ethicality of their datasets. This, in turn, contributes to the success of AI models developed in subsequent stages of the AI lifecycle. It ensures that the data used for model training is of high quality, ethically sourced, and aligned with regulatory and organizational standards.

4. Model Selection and Training

The **Model Selection and Training** phase is a pivotal stage in the AI lifecycle, where practitioners make critical decisions regarding the selection of algorithms and the development of models. This phase involves defining criteria for algorithm and model selection based on business requirements and implementing version control to track changes in algorithms and models.

By rigorously defining criteria for algorithm and model selection and implementing version control practices, practitioners ensure a systematic and transparent approach to the development of AI models. These steps contribute to the reliability, reproducibility, and maintainability of AI systems throughout their lifecycle. They can also be helpful in legal proceedings.

To define criteria for algorithm and model selection based on business requirements, practitioners start with a comprehensive understanding of the business context. This involves collaborating with stakeholders to gather requirements, identify business goals, objectives, and success criteria.

Key performance indicators (KPIs) are then defined, aligning with business objectives and encompassing relevant metrics such as accuracy, precision, and recall.

Algorithm selection criteria are established by:

1. Analyzing the nature of the problem;
2. Considering scalability requirements;
3. Evaluating interpretability versus complexity trade-offs; and,
4. Computational resource considerations.

Model selection criteria involve choosing performance metrics, evaluating model complexity, considering training time, and deciding between online and batch learning approaches.

Implementing **version control** to track changes in algorithms and models is crucial for maintaining transparency, reproducibility, and accountability in the development process. Practitioners choose a version control system, such as **Git** (a leading distributed version control system), to track changes in code, algorithms, and model files. Tagging releases and defining a branching strategy help manage different development stages and experimental features.

Git is a distributed **version control system** (VCS) widely used for tracking changes in source code during software development. Microsoft now owns GitHub, which is a popular code repository service built on Git. Microsoft acquired GitHub in 2018 for 7.5 billion US$. However, Git itself, the underlying version control system, remains free and open-source software and is not owned by Microsoft.

Git allows multiple developers to collaborate on a project, wherever they may be in the world, providing a mechanism to manage and coordinate changes to the project's files. Developed by Linus Torvalds (Linux inventor) in 2005, Git has become one of the most popular version control systems due to its efficiency, flexibility, and robust branching capabilities.

Key features of Git include:

1. **Distributed Version Control**

   Git is a distributed VCS, meaning that each developer has a complete local copy of the entire project history. This allows developers to work independently and efficiently without relying on a centralized server.

2. **Branching and Merging**

   Git excels in its branching and merging capabilities. Developers can create branches to work on specific features or fixes independently. Once the work is complete, branches can be merged back into the main codebase, allowing for parallel development without conflicts.

3. **Commit History**

   Git maintains a detailed and efficient commit history, tracking changes made to files over time. Each commit is uniquely identified, allowing developers to revert to a specific point in history or compare different versions of the code.

4. **Efficient Performance**

   Git is designed for speed and efficiency. Operations such as committing changes, creating branches, and switching between branches are performed quickly, enhancing the development workflow.

5. **Staging Area**

   Git introduces a staging area (index) where changes can be selectively added before committing. This allows developers to review and organize changes before finalizing them.

6. **Open Source and Cross-Platform**

   Git is an open-source project and is available for various operating systems, including Linux, macOS, and Windows. It is supported by a large community of developers and has a wealth of documentation and resources available.

7. **Support for Nonlinear Development**

   Git supports non-linear development workflows, enabling developers to work on multiple features or bug fixes simultaneously. This flexibility is crucial for complex projects with concurrent development efforts.

8. **Integration with Hosting Platforms**

   Git can be seamlessly integrated with hosting platforms like GitHub, GitLab, and Bitbucket. These platforms provide additional features such as issue tracking, pull requests, and collaboration tools.

9. **Security**

   Git ensures the integrity of the code by using cryptographic hashes to identify each commit. This makes it difficult to tamper with the commit history.

Overall, Git is a powerful and versatile version control system that has become an integral part of modern software development practices. Its ability to handle distributed development, efficient branching and merging, and support for diverse workflows makes it a preferred choice for teams of all sizes.

For code and algorithm versioning, practitioners use **tagging** to mark specific releases, major milestones, or experimental features. A branching strategy is defined to manage different development stages effectively.

Model versioning involves artifact storage, metadata logging, and the use of a model registry to manage and track different versions of models. Documentation practices, including changelogs and ReadMe files, ensure clear communication and understanding of changes made over time.

Collaboration and communication are facilitated through collaborative platforms, project management tools, and communication channels. Code reviews are implemented to ensure quality and consistency in changes, fostering a collaborative environment for knowledge sharing. **Continuous integration/continuous deployment** (CI/CD) practices are employed with automated testing and deployment automation to validate changes, ensure test coverage, and streamline the release of new algorithm versions or models.

By rigorously defining criteria for algorithm and model selection and implementing version control practices, practitioners ensure a systematic and transparent approach to the development of AI models. These steps contribute to the reliability, reproducibility, and maintainability of AI systems throughout their lifecycle.

Training and validation seek to implement predicted inputs into a model so that predictable outcomes result. It is essentially an enormous "if-then" exercise, where the algorithm is taught a series of conditional relationships based upon the data provided. The larger the number of these relationships, and the stronger or more obvious their correlation, the better the performance of the resulting AI.

What is often missing from this effort is the proactive training of exceptions, specifically **false positives** and **false negatives**. In the case of a false positive, a correlation appears to exist where it does not. In false negatives, a correlation exists but is missed. It has been said the, "false positives cost money, false negatives cost lives,' in the case of serious medical diagnoses. False positives and false negatives should be proactively defined, developed, and incorporated into the training regime of all AIs, and the performance of the AI against these signals should be verified.

Adding this mis-signaling to the training campaign is a critical success factor for AI systems, particularly those that contribute to mission-critical decision-making.

Key steps in the AI system training and validation phase include:

- Implement performance metrics and validation procedures.
- Monitor for overfitting and ensure model generalization.

The "Training and Validation" phase is a crucial step in the AI lifecycle where machine learning models are trained on data and validated to ensure their effectiveness and generalizability. This phase involves implementing performance metrics and validation procedures to assess model performance.

Overfitting is a common issue in machine learning where a model learns the training data too well, capturing noise and details that are specific to the training set but do not generalize well to new, unseen data. In other words, *an **overfit model** performs exceptionally well on the data it was trained on but fails to generalize its predictions to different or unseen datasets*. Overfitting can lead to poor performance when the model encounters new, real-world data, as it has essentially memorized the training data instead of learning the underlying patterns.

To ensure model generalizability, practitioners employ techniques to mitigate overfitting. These may include:

- **Regularization:** Applying techniques like L1 or L2 regularization (*L1 and L2 regularization are techniques used in machine learning to prevent overfitting and improve the generalization of models by adding a penalty term to the model's objective function. These regularization methods introduce a regularization term that penalizes the model for having overly complex or large parameter values. The goal is to discourage the model from fitting the noise in the training data and encourage it to learn the more essential underlying patterns*) to penalize overly complex models and prevent **overfitting**.
- **Dropout:** Introducing dropout layers in neural networks to randomly deactivate neurons (or nodes) during training, preventing the model from relying too heavily on specific neurons.

- **Data Augmentation:** Increasing the diversity of the training set to root out possible biases by applying techniques like rotation, flipping, or scaling to the input data.
- **Early Stopping:** Halting the training process when the model's performance on the validation set stops improving, preventing overfitting due to excessive training.

By checking for overfitting and implementing these techniques, practitioners ensure that the machine learning model generalizes well to new, unseen data, leading to more robust and reliable predictions in real-world scenarios.

Steps in the Training and Validation Phase

Firstly, performance metrics are defined by choosing relevant metrics based on the nature of the problem, such as accuracy, precision, and recall, often utilizing an F1 score *(The F1 score is calculated as the harmonic mean of precision and recall. A harmonic mean is a type of average calculated by summing the reciprocals of each value in a dataset and then dividing the number of values in the dataset by that sum. The value of the F1 score lies between 0 and 1, with 1 being a better, or mean squared error. These metrics are aligned with business objectives and stakeholder expectations. Evaluation criteria are established to assess model performance against set metrics, defining thresholds for acceptable performance).*

Validation procedures are then implemented, starting with a train-test split to create separate datasets for training and testing.

Cross-validation techniques, such as **k-fold cross-validation**, are employed for robust evaluation, particularly for smaller datasets.

K-fold cross-validation is a technique used to assess the performance and generalization ability of a machine learning model. It involves splitting the dataset into k (the number of folds) subsets, called **folds**, and performing the training and validation process k times. In each iteration, one of the folds is used as the validation set, while the remaining k-1 folds are used for training the model.

The choice of k (the number of folds) depends on the size of the dataset and computational resources. Common choices for k include five, ten, or even higher values. As a general guideline, larger values of k can provide a more accurate estimate of model performance but may be computationally expensive.

Overall, k-fold cross-validation is a valuable technique in AI system development for robustly evaluating model performance and improving the reliability of the results.

Hyperparameter tuning is conducted to optimize model parameters, and a validation set is introduced for iterative model improvement during training.

In the AI system development process, hyperparameter tuning refers to the optimization of hyperparameters to enhance the performance of a machine learning model. *Hyperparameters are external configuration settings that are not learned from the data during the training process but are set prior to training, and include all actions and decisions made in initially setting up the model.*

Examples of hyperparameters include the learning rate, regularization strength, the number of hidden layers in a neural network, or the depth of a decision tree.

The process of hyperparameter tuning involves searching for the best set of hyperparameter values that result in the optimal performance of the model. This is typically done through an iterative and automated approach, considering different combinations of hyperparameters and evaluating their impact on the model's performance.

Ensuring **model generalizability** is the next focus. Practitioners evaluate the model on previously unseen data, assessing its performance on a completely new test dataset to verify effective generalization. Techniques to detect and handle out-of-distribution data during deployment are implemented, ensuring the model's reliability on new inputs. Benchmarking against industry standards or benchmark models is conducted to validate competitive or superior performance.

The process concludes with the establishment of a feedback loop for continuous improvement based on real-world performance. Practitioners monitor the model's behavior in production, making updates as needed to maintain its effectiveness.

The "Training and Validation" phase is iterative, involving continuous experimentation and improvement. By implementing robust performance metrics, validation procedures, and monitoring for overfitting, practitioners ensure the development of machine learning models that not only perform well on training data but also generalize effectively to real-world scenarios.

5. Model Evaluation: Interpretability and Explainability in the AI Development Lifecycle

Key steps in the AI system Model Evaluation phase, which includes analyzing Interpretability and Explainability, include:

- Ensure that models are interpretable and decisions can be explained.
- Implement transparency measures for model outputs.

Interpretability and explainability evaluation in the AI development lifecycle is essential for ensuring that machine learning models are not black boxes and that their decisions can be understood and explained. This phase is crucial for building trust, meeting regulatory requirements, and addressing ethical concerns related to AI applications.

Key steps include:

The first step begins back in the **model selection** process, opting for models that inherently provide interpretability while carefully considering trade-offs between model complexity and interpretability. Feature importance analysis is then conducted to understand the impact of each input feature on the model's predictions, employing techniques like permutation importance or tree-based methods.

Explainable AI methods, such as LIME or SHAP, are leveraged to generate interpretable explanations for individual predictions, shedding light on the model's decision-making process. Essentially, these methods are ways to peer into a complex model and break it down to make it more simple and understandable.

1. **LIME (Local Interpretable Model-agnostic Explanations)**:

   LIME is a model-agnostic technique designed to explain the predictions of complex machine learning models by approximating their behavior locally. It focuses on creating interpretable and understandable explanations for individual instances or predictions.

   Here's how LIME works:

   - **Local Perturbation:** LIME perturbs the input features of a specific instance in the dataset, generating a set of perturbed instances.

- **Model Approximation:** For each perturbed instance, LIME obtains predictions from the black-box model, creating a local dataset.
- **Interpretable Model:** LIME then fits an interpretable and transparent model (e.g., linear regression) to the local dataset, approximating the behavior of the black-box model for that instance.
- **Explanation:** The coefficients of the interpretable model provide insights into the contribution of each feature for the specific prediction, offering a local and understandable explanation.
- **Local Perturbation:** LIME perturbs the input features of a specific instance in the dataset, generating a set of perturbed instances.
- **Model Approximation:** For each perturbed instance, LIME obtains predictions from the black-box model, creating a local dataset.
- **Interpretable Model:** LIME then fits an interpretable and transparent model (e.g., linear regression) to the local dataset, approximating the behavior of the black-box model for that instance.
- **Explanation:** The coefficients of the interpretable model provide insights into the contribution of each feature for the specific prediction, offering a local and understandable explanation.

2. **SHAP (SHapley Additive exPlanations)**:

   SHAP values are based on cooperative game theory and aim to fairly allocate contributions of each feature to the prediction across all possible feature combinations. SHAP values provide a global perspective on feature importance and can be used for individual instance explanations as well.

   Here's an overview of SHAP:

   - **Shapley Values:** SHAP values are based on Shapley values from cooperative game theory, which fairly distribute the value of each player in a coalition game.
   - **Feature Attribution:** SHAP values assign a contribution score to each feature for a specific prediction, considering all possible permutations of features.
   - **Additivity Property:** The contributions from each feature sum up to the difference between the model's prediction and the average prediction, ensuring additivity.
   - **Interpretability:** SHAP values can be used to explain both global model behavior by examining average contributions across the dataset and local predictions for individual instances.

Both LIME and SHAP are valuable tools for model-agnostic interpretability, allowing stakeholders to gain insights into how specific models arrive at their predictions. These methods contribute to transparency and trust in AI systems by providing understandable explanations, especially in cases where the underlying models are complex and lack inherent interpretability.

Additionally, **rule extraction** is employed to create human-readable rules from complex models, ensuring stakeholders can easily understand the underlying logic. To simplify complex models without sacrificing predictive performance, techniques like **model distillation** *(which refers to the process of transferring knowledge from a complex or large model [often referred to as the teacher model] to a smaller or simpler model [referred to as the student model]. The goal of model distillation is to retain or even improve the performance of the smaller model while reducing its computational complexity and memory footprint compared to the original larger model)*, or **regularization** *(model regularization refers to a set of techniques used during the training phase to prevent a machine learning model from overfitting to the training* data) are considered.

The implementation of transparency measures for model outputs is crucial. This includes providing clear output explanations and justifications, quantifying prediction confidence with confidence intervals or probability scores, and developing visualizations like decision plots or feature importance plots for better understanding. Comprehensive documentation detailing model architecture, hyperparameters, and the training process is essential, along with stakeholder education through training sessions to foster a shared understanding of the model's capabilities and limitations.

Addressing bias and fairness concerns is integral, involving the implementation of measures to identify and mitigate biases in model predictions and regularly assessing the model's fairness across different demographic groups.

Regulatory compliance is prioritized, ensuring that model explanations meet regulations, laws, and guidelines.

Continuous model monitoring is established to update explanations and transparency measures as the model evolves, and a feedback loop is implemented for users to provide feedback on model outputs, facilitating continuous improvement in explanations and addressing user concerns.

Interpretability and Explainability processes are ongoing and require collaboration between data scientists, domain experts, and end users. By ensuring models are interpretable, providing transparent explanations for outputs, and addressing bias and fairness considerations, organizations can enhance the trustworthiness and ethical use of AI systems.

Testing and Quality Assurance

Key steps in AI system testing and quality assurance include:

- Develop comprehensive testing protocols for AI applications.
- Establish quality assurance processes to identify and fix defects.

Testing and Quality Assurance processes are critical for ensuring the reliability, performance, and correctness of AI applications. These involve comprehensive testing protocols and quality assurance processes to identify and rectify defects.

Here are the detailed steps and considerations:

AI System Testing

The initial step includes **unit testing**, where individual components such as algorithms and data preprocessing modules are tested for functionality, covering edge cases, boundary conditions, and expected behaviors.

Integration testing follows, ensuring the seamless collaboration of system components and addressing potential integration issues.

Functional testing is then conducted to verify that the AI application meets specified functional requirements through various use cases and scenarios.

Performance testing evaluates the speed, responsiveness, and resource utilization of the AI system, while **robustness testing** assesses the system's resilience to variations in input data, including noisy or unexpected inputs.

Security testing is implemented to identify and address vulnerabilities, adhering to security best practices.

Usability testing focuses on assessing the user-friendliness of the AI interface, gathering feedback for improvements.

Regression testing is employed to detect unintended side effects of software code changes, automated for efficiency.

Ethical considerations testing evaluates the AI system for fairness, bias, and adherence to ethical guidelines, making adjustments to mitigate ethical concerns.

Edge case testing explores uncommon scenarios to identify potential issues. Quality assurance processes are then established to identify and fix defects. This involves defect tracking, root cause analysis to understand underlying issues, continuous quality monitoring, and the use of automated testing tools for consistency and reliability.

Documentation is crucial, maintaining records of testing protocols, identified defects, and resolution strategies for knowledge transfer and future consistency. It is recommended that the AI Governance team consult with the records and information management (RIM) staff to assist in maintaining documentation records throughout the process.

Feedback loops, including mechanisms for stakeholder feedback, **user acceptance testing** (UAT) with end users, and cross-functional collaboration between development, testing, and operations teams, contribute to continuous improvement.

Version control for models is implemented to track changes and ensure transparency and reproducibility in model development. Test environment management is carefully executed to replicate real-world conditions and maintain consistency between test and production environments.

The entire process is iterative, with lessons learned from defects incorporated into future development cycles. The dynamic and iterative nature of the "Testing and Quality Assurance" phase ensures that AI applications are robust, secure, and aligned with user expectations, contributing to their overall reliability and trustworthiness.

6. Model Deployment

Key steps in the AI system deployment phase include:

- User training and support
- Implement secure deployment practices, including access controls.
- Develop rollback plans in case of deployment issues.

User Training and Support

Key steps in AI system User Training and Support include:

- Provide training for end users and support personnel.
- Establish procedures for addressing user queries and issues

User Training and Support in the AI lifecycle is crucial for ensuring the effective adoption and ongoing operation of the deployed AI system. It has been stated over the years that, "The perfect new software application will fail without user acceptance." User training and support involve providing training for end users and support personnel, as well as establishing procedures for addressing user queries and issues.

To provide training for end users, organizations begin by understanding user roles, identifying the specific needs of different user groups, and tailoring training programs accordingly. *It is often a best practice to first survey users to determine what their greatest training needs are.*

Learning objectives are defined clearly, aligning with the tasks and responsibilities that end users will perform using the AI system. Interactive training materials, including videos, tutorials, and documentation, are developed, incorporating real-world examples and scenarios to make the training content practical. Scheduled training sessions, accommodating different time zones and learning preferences, are conducted, emphasizing hands-on practice with the AI system. A feedback mechanism is established to continuously improve training materials and sessions, and knowledge assessment tools, such as quizzes, are used to gauge user understanding. Certification programs may be implemented for advanced users.

Once users are trained, procedures for addressing user queries and issues are established. This includes setting up a dedicated helpdesk or support portal with multichannel support options. A comprehensive knowledge base is developed and maintained, featuring FAQs, troubleshooting guides, and step-by-step instructions. Users are empowered with self-help resources, and incident escalation paths are defined for complex issues. Timely responses are prioritized with **service-level agreements** (SLAs), and continuous improvement is fostered through feedback collection and root cause analysis. User community engagement is encouraged through forums and discussion groups, facilitating knowledge sharing among users.

User Training and Support are pivotal for the successful integration of the AI system into the operational environment. By providing effective training and establishing robust support procedures, organizations can enhance user competence, satisfaction, and overall system performance. Continuous improvement based on user feedback ensures that support mechanisms evolve alongside the changing needs of the user community.

In the "Deployment" phase of the AI lifecycle, the critical step of releasing the developed AI model or application into a production environment for end users requires careful planning and execution. The detailed steps and considerations for this phase involve implementing secure deployment practices and developing comprehensive rollback plans.

To ensure secure deployment, organizations focus on infrastructure security by adhering to best practices, implementing firewalls, encryption, and access controls based on roles. Network security protocols and encryption mechanisms are applied to protect data during transmission and at rest. Secure configuration practices are established, addressing default or unnecessary settings regularly.

Software source code and model security are prioritized through **code signing** to verify code integrity, protecting trained models from tampering, and securing application programming interfaces (APIs) with authentication and authorization mechanisms. Industry-standard encryption algorithms are utilized to safeguard data integrity and confidentiality.

In the context of AI system development, "code signing" is a security practice that involves digitally signing software code to verify its integrity and authenticity. This process helps ensure that the code has not been tampered with or altered since it was signed by its original author or source. Code signing is particularly crucial in the deployment phase of AI systems to enhance security and trust in the deployed application.

Here's an overview of how code signing works:

1. **Digital Signature:** When a developer or organization creates a piece of software, they use a cryptographic algorithm to generate a unique digital signature. This signature is based on the content of the code and the developer's private key.

2. **Embedding Signature:** The digital signature is then embedded or appended to the software code. This creates a signed version of the code that includes both the original code and the cryptographic signature.
3. **Verification:** Before deploying or executing the software, the system checks the digital signature using the developer's public key, which is available to anyone. If the signature is valid and matches the content of the code, it verifies that the code has not been altered since it was signed.
4. **Tamper Detection:** If the code has been tampered with, such as during unauthorized modifications or malicious activities, the digital signature verification will fail, indicating that the code's integrity has been compromised.

In the context of AI models and APIs, code signing is applied to the machine learning model files and code that expose and interact with the models. *By signing the code and model files, organizations can prevent unauthorized changes, tampering, or injection of malicious code* into the deployed AI system. Additionally, when securing APIs, code signing is often complemented by authentication and authorization mechanisms to control access to the APIs, ensuring that only authorized users or systems can interact with them.

Code signing is a fundamental security measure that helps maintain the integrity of AI systems during the deployment phase, contributing to the overall reliability and trustworthiness of the deployed application.

In case of deployment issues, organizations develop both automated and manual **rollback procedures** *(automated rollback scripts and procedures are created with checks and validations to revert to a stable state, and monitoring systems are implemented to detect anomalies in real-time, triggering automatic rollbacks based on predefined criteria).* **Manual rollback procedures** are documented, including step-by-step instructions for reverting to the previous version, and a communication plan is developed to notify stakeholders and define roles and responsibilities.

Rollback scenarios are tested through simulation of deployment issues, and backup and restore procedures are regularly performed and tested to ensure reliability. An **incident response team** is established to handle deployment issues promptly, and post-incident analyses are conducted to understand root causes and implement lessons learned for continuous improvement.

Key steps in AI system User Training and Support include:

- Provide training for end users and support personnel.
- Establish procedures for addressing user queries and issues.

User Training and Support in the AI lifecycle is crucial for ensuring the effective adoption and ongoing operation of the deployed AI system. It has been stated over the years that, "The perfect new software application will fail without user acceptance." User training and support involve providing training for end users and support personnel, as well as establishing procedures for addressing user queries and issues.

To provide training for end users, organizations begin by understanding user roles, identifying the specific needs of different user groups, and tailoring training programs accordingly.

Learning objectives are defined clearly, aligning with the tasks and responsibilities that end users will perform using the AI system. Interactive training materials, including videos, tutorials, and documentation, are developed, incorporating real-world examples and scenarios to make the training content practical. Scheduled training sessions, accommodating different time zones and learning preferences, are conducted, emphasizing hands-on practice with the AI system. A feedback mechanism is established to continuously improve training materials and sessions, and knowledge assessment tools, such as quizzes, are used to gauge user understanding. Certification programs may be implemented for advanced users.

Once users are trained, procedures for addressing user queries and issues are established. This includes setting up a dedicated helpdesk or support portal with multichannel support options. A comprehensive knowledge base is developed and maintained, featuring FAQs, troubleshooting guides, and step-by-step instructions. Users are empowered with self-help resources, and incident escalation paths are defined for complex issues. Timely responses are prioritized with service-level agreements (SLAs), and continuous improvement is fostered through feedback collection and root cause analysis. User community engagement is encouraged through forums and discussion groups, facilitating knowledge sharing among users.

User Training and Support are pivotal for the successful integration of the AI system into the operational environment. By providing effective training and establishing robust support procedures, organizations can enhance user competence, satisfaction, and overall system performance. Continuous improvement based on user feedback ensures that support mechanisms evolve alongside the changing needs of the user community.

Key steps in AI system User Training and Support include:

- Provide training for end users and support personnel.
- Establish procedures for addressing user queries and issues.

User Training and Support in the AI lifecycle is crucial for ensuring the effective adoption and ongoing operation of the deployed AI system. User training and support involve providing training for end users and support personnel, as well as establishing procedures for addressing user queries and issues.

To provide training for end users, organizations begin by understanding user roles, identifying the specific needs of different user groups, and tailoring training programs accordingly.

Learning objectives are defined clearly, aligning with the tasks and responsibilities that end users will perform using the AI system. Interactive training materials, including videos, tutorials, and documentation, are developed, incorporating real-world examples and scenarios to make the training content practical. Scheduled training sessions, accommodating different time zones and learning preferences, are conducted, emphasizing hands-on practice with the AI system. A feedback mechanism is established to continuously improve training materials and sessions, and knowledge assessment tools, such as quizzes, are used to gauge user understanding. Certification programs may be implemented for advanced users.

Once users are trained, procedures for addressing user queries and issues are established. This includes setting up a dedicated helpdesk or support portal with multichannel support options. A comprehensive knowledge base is developed and maintained, featuring FAQs, troubleshooting guides, and step-by-step instructions. Users are empowered with self-help resources, and incident escalation paths are defined for complex issues. Timely responses are prioritized with service-level agreements (SLAs), and continuous improvement is fostered through feedback collection and root cause analysis. User community engagement is encouraged through forums and discussion groups, facilitating knowledge sharing among users.

User Training and Support are pivotal for the successful integration of the AI system into the operational environment. By providing effective training and establishing robust support procedures, organizations can enhance user competence, satisfaction, and overall system performance. Continuous improvement based on user feedback ensures that support mechanisms evolve alongside the changing needs of the user community.

Key steps in AI system User Training and Support include:

- Provide training for end users and support personnel.
- Establish procedures for addressing user queries and issues.

AI Model Disgorgement

Understanding Model Disgorgement and Destruction

Model disgorgement, also known as algorithmic disgorgement or algorithmic destruction, refers to the deletion or destruction of models and algorithms. It can also mean clawing back the financial benefits that were gained through a model that was illegally trained, or where training data was stolen or used without authorization.

This process is typically undertaken to eliminate "bad" data from a model, where bad data encompasses information that was illegally obtained, used without consent, found to be invalid, or otherwise impacts the validity and legality of the model. While the terms destruction and disgorgement are sometimes used interchangeably, it is crucial to distinguish between them.[1]

Destruction involves rendering the entire model unusable, necessitating the creation of a new model from scratch. On the other hand, disgorgement entails removing the offending training data and its effects from the existing model, effectively erasing any trace of the data's use in the model's development.

The distinction between destruction and disgorgement becomes significant in the context of the complexity of model building. Model disgorgement can be a challenging or even impossible process, depending on how the model was constructed. In some cases, an order for disgorgement may effectively serve as a directive for model destruction, imposing a substantial burden due to the extensive resources required to train a new model. This becomes particularly pertinent in light of the rise of generative AI models that collect training data from diverse sources on the internet, emphasizing the need for an approach less drastic than total destruction.

Several model disgorgement techniques have emerged, and one prominent classification, proposed by Amazon Web Services AI researchers, categorizes these techniques based on two axes: the time during the model training process when the technique can be applied (reactive, proactive, or preemptive) and the "provability" of removing the effects of training data (deterministic or probabilistic).[2]

1. **Retraining (reactive, deterministic):** Involves complete model retraining after removing offending data, but it is becoming less viable due to the growing size of neural networks and resource constraints.
2. **Selective Forgetting/Unlearning (reactive, probabilistic):** Instead of retraining, this technique removes the effects of offending data on the model through a statistically provable process, reducing the impact to nearly zero.
3. **Compartmentalization (proactive, deterministic):** Utilizes subsets of the dataset to train smaller models, allowing the deletion and retraining of only the smaller models affected by offending data.

4. **Dataset Emulation (preemptive, deterministic):** Involves training on synthetic data rather than real datasets, with synthetic data generated in the style of a certain dataset but lacking identifiers to prevent privacy violations.
5. **Differential Privacy (preemptive, probabilistic):** Mathematically guarantees that the algorithm's output will remain virtually the same regardless of the addition or subtraction of other training data, protecting data subject privacy. This area is still under active research.

These emerging disgorgement techniques offer various approaches to address the challenges associated with model correction, catering to different stages of the model development lifecycle and providing options for both deterministic and probabilistic methods.

The iterative improvement process involves regularly reviewing and updating security measures and rollback procedures. User communication is emphasized, with clear and transparent notifications provided in case a rollback affects end users, along with instructions or support for those impacted.

In conclusion, the "Deployment" phase is a crucial step that requires meticulous planning and execution to ensure the smooth transition of the AI application from development to a production environment. By implementing secure deployment practices and having robust rollback plans in place, development teams can enhance the reliability, security, and resilience of AI systems in real-world scenarios.

Post-Deployment Monitoring and Evaluation

Key steps in the AI system Post-Deployment Monitoring and Evaluation phase include:

- Continuously monitor AI applications in real-world scenarios.
- Evaluating Long-Term Performance and Impact on Users and Stakeholders.

The "Post-Deployment Monitoring and Evaluation" phase is part of Deployment, and is critical for ensuring the ongoing success and optimization of AI applications in real-world scenarios. This phase involves continuous monitoring of AI applications and the evaluation of long-term performance and impact on users and stakeholders.

This phase in AI system development involves a comprehensive set of steps to ensure the continuous success, optimization, and ethical usage of AI applications in real-world scenarios.

1. **Continuously Monitor AI Applications in Real-World Scenarios:**
   a. **Establish Monitoring Infrastructure**: Define key performance indicators (KPIs) aligned with the application's objectives. Implement monitoring tools covering technical and user-centric aspects, including automated alerts, user feedback, and sentiment analysis.
   b. **Regular System Health Checks**: Conduct scheduled health checks, ensure data quality, perform security audits, and plan for infrastructure scaling to maintain optimal performance.

2. **Evaluate Long-Term Performance and Impact on Users and Stakeholders:**

   a. **User-Centric Performance Metrics**: Gather insights through user satisfaction surveys, analyze user engagement patterns, and identify trends indicating the acceptance of the AI application.

b. **Stakeholder Collaboration**: Engage with stakeholders to understand the perceived value of the AI application. Address concerns promptly and establish a feedback loop for continuous refinement.

c. **Long-Term Impact Assessment**: Assess the AI application's impact on business objectives, evaluate ethical and societal implications, and implement iterative model refinement based on real-world usage.

d. **Documentation and Reporting**: Maintain comprehensive documentation of long-term performance metrics, issues, and resolutions. Generate periodic reports to share insights with stakeholders and track the evolution of the AI application.

e. **Continuous Improvement**: Establish feedback loops between monitoring and development teams. Adapt to changing environments, staying aligned with organizational goals and addressing emerging challenges.

By systematically monitoring **key performance indicators** (KPI), conducting health checks, engaging stakeholders, and assessing long-term impact, organizations can foster continuous improvement, adapt to evolving conditions, and ensure the ongoing success and ethical usage of AI applications in real-world contexts. Regular documentation and reporting contribute to transparency, accountability, and the iterative refinement of AI systems over time.

Conclusion

The "Post-Deployment Monitoring and Evaluation" phase is a dynamic and continuous process that ensures the ongoing success, optimization, and ethical use of AI applications. By maintaining a robust monitoring infrastructure, engaging with stakeholders, and evaluating long-term impacts, organizations can refine and adapt their AI systems to meet evolving needs and challenges in the real-world environment.

7. Monitoring and Maintenance

In the generative AI lifecycle, the Monitoring and Maintenance phase is a continuous cycle of tracking, evaluating, and refining a model once it has been integrated into a production environment. Unlike traditional software, generative AI is dynamic; its performance naturally degrades as real-world data patterns shift—a phenomenon known as data or model drift.

Key Requirements for Post-Deployment

Infrastructure & Resource Management: Monitoring specialized computing resources (GPUs/TPUs) to track utilization, manage costs, and facilitate proactive scaling.

Observability Stack: Implementation of tools like Prometheus and Grafana for real-time visualization of system health and latency.

Security & Compliance: Ongoing screening for emerging security risks such as prompt injection and ensuring adherence to regulations like GDPR or the EU AI Act.

Feedback Loops: Mechanisms to collect direct user feedback (e.g., ratings) and human-in-the-loop assessments to ground model outputs in reality.

Steps in the Monitoring and Maintenance Process

1. **Establish Metrics & Baselines**: Define KPIs across two main buckets:
   - **Empirical Metrics**: Performance indicators like accuracy, response latency, and throughput.
   - **Generative-Specific Metrics**: Content quality scores for coherence, factuality (hallucination detection), and toxicity.
2. **Continuous Real-Time Monitoring**:
   - **Drift Detection**: Using statistical tests (like Population Stability Index) to identify when user inputs or model outputs diverge from the training distribution.
   - **Anomaly Alerting**: Setting up automated notifications to trigger when evaluation results or system errors hit critical thresholds.
3. **Active Content Auditing:**
   - **LLM-as-a-Judge**: Using a secondary, often larger, model to evaluate the output of the production model for quality and relevance.
   - **Adversarial Probing**: Regularly performing "red teaming" scans to identify new vulnerabilities to toxic or sensitive content generation.
4. **Strategic Maintenance & Optimization:**
   - **Regular Retraining**: Updating the model with new data or fine-tuning based on feedback to maintain relevance.
   - **Iterative Refinement**: Adjusting prompt templates, hyperparameters, or even swapping for newer base models as they become available.
5. **Governance & Documentation**: Maintaining detailed audit trails of model versions, input/output logs, and performance reports to ensure transparency and accountability.

8. Model Retirement

In the Model Retirement phase of the AI system lifecycle, several critical steps ensure a systematic and thorough approach to retiring AI models, maintaining operational efficiency, and preparing for future advancements.

Evaluation of Model Performance: This initial step involves rigorously assessing the AI model's performance against established metrics and criteria. The objective is to verify that the model has met desired standards and expectations in terms of accuracy, precision, recall, and other relevant measures. Activities include comparing the model's predictions with actual outcomes (ground truth data) across various scenarios. By conducting such evaluations, developers gain insights into the model's strengths and weaknesses, informing decisions on its continued deployment or retirement.

Assessment of Model Relevance: As technology evolves and business needs change, it becomes crucial to assess whether the AI model remains aligned with initial and current requirements. The objective here is to determine its ongoing relevance and effectiveness compared to newer models or techniques that may offer superior performance. Activities involve reviewing business goals, advancements in AI technologies, and market dynamics to gauge whether maintaining the current model aligns with organizational objectives or if a transition to newer solutions is advisable.

Impact Analysis: Retiring an AI model can have wide-ranging implications across stakeholders, operational processes, and downstream applications. The objective of impact analysis is to identify potential disruptions and ensure a smooth transition to alternative models or systems. Activities include identifying dependencies on the retired model, assessing risks associated with its removal, and devising strategies to mitigate these risks. By conducting thorough impact analysis, organizations can minimize downtime and maintain continuity in their AI-driven operations.

Documentation Update: Clear and comprehensive documentation is essential for maintaining organizational knowledge and ensuring compliance with regulatory requirements. The objective of updating documentation related to the retired model is to accurately record its retirement process, final performance evaluations, and any recommendations for replacement models if applicable. Activities involve documenting reasons for retirement, detailing the model's performance history, and outlining steps taken during the retirement process for future reference. The records and information management (RIM) team should be consulted to assist with maintaining documentation records.

Data Management: Effective management of data associated with the retired model is crucial for maintaining data integrity and compliance with privacy regulations. The objective here is to identify and manage relevant datasets used for training and evaluation, ensuring secure archiving of necessary data while responsibly deleting unnecessary information. Activities include identifying datasets linked to the retired model, implementing archival procedures, and securely deleting data that no longer serves a purpose. Including the data governance and privacy teams in this evaluation will help to ensure it is conducted thoroughly.

Communication and Notification: Transparent communication with stakeholders and affected teams is vital to ensure understanding and alignment throughout the retirement process. The objective is to provide necessary information for planning and decision-making related to the model's retirement. Activities include notifying stakeholders of the retirement plan, explaining reasons and implications, and offering support for transitioning to alternative models or systems.

Transition Planning: Planning for a seamless transition from the retired model to alternative solutions or newer versions is essential for maintaining operational continuity. The objective is to minimize disruptions and ensure that the organization can effectively adapt to the change. Activities include developing a detailed transition strategy, training users on new models or systems, and monitoring performance during the transition period to address any issues promptly.

Final Review and Approval: Conducting a final review of the retirement process ensures compliance with organizational policies and regulatory requirements. The objective is to verify the completeness of transition activities and obtain necessary approvals from relevant stakeholders. Activities include reviewing documentation related to the retirement process, assessing the effectiveness of transition plans, and obtaining approvals to finalize the retirement of the AI model.

Archiving and Retention: Archiving relevant documents, code, and configurations associated with the retired model is critical for preserving institutional knowledge and facilitating potential reevaluation or reactivation in the future. The RIM team and possibly a corporate archivist should be actively involved. The objective is to maintain organized and secure storage of materials related to the retired model. Activities include securely storing documentation, organizing code repositories, and maintaining access controls in accordance with organizational policies.

Monitoring and Feedback: Monitoring the impact of model retirement and gathering feedback from stakeholders provides valuable insights for continuous improvement. The objective is to identify lessons learned and opportunities for enhancing future model retirement processes. Activities include collecting feedback from users and stakeholders, assessing the effectiveness of transition strategies, and updating practices based on insights gained to optimize future retirement efforts.

By diligently following these steps in the Model Retirement phase, organizations can ensure responsible management of AI models throughout their lifecycle, from deployment to retirement, fostering adaptability and sustainability in AI-driven operations.

By governing these key phases of the AI software development life cycle, organizations can mitigate risks, ensure compliance, and foster the responsible and ethical use of artificial intelligence applications. Effective AI Governance throughout the lifecycle promotes transparency, accountability, and the overall success of AI projects.

Key Points

- The **Problem Definition and Project Initiation** phase is a crucial component of the AI software development life cycle, playing a pivotal role in shaping the trajectory of the project.
- **KPIs** are critical to measuring progress in an AI program or project.
- Establishing governance structures, roles, and responsibilities is critical during the Project Initiation phase.
- **Data acquisition and preparation** is a critical AI lifecycle phase, including data sourcing, cleansing, and structuring to ensure its relevance, quality, and ethical usage.
- A **Data Governance Framework** outlines policies, procedures, and responsibilities for managing data throughout its lifecycle. Key components include: Data Ownership, Data Quality Standards, and Compliance Requirements.
- **Data Cataloging and Metadata Management** involves creating a centralized data catalog that provides metadata information for each dataset. Metadata should include Data Origin, Data Schema, and Data Lineage.
- **Data Quality Assessment** evaluates quality using tools and processes to identify anomalies and address data bias: profile data (analyze data distribution and statistical characteristics to understand its nature).
- **Data Privacy and Security Measures** include Data Encryption, Access Controls, and Anonymization.
- **Ethical Data Collection Guidelines** address concerns related to Informed Consent, Data Minimization, and User Privacy.
- Processes to detect and mitigate biases in the dataset include **Bias Audits** and **Fairness Metrics**.
- **Transparent Data Usage Policies** can be maintained through Data Usage Agreements and communication with stakeholders.
- Policies are required for the retention and deletion of data, stating **Data Retention Periods**, and the process for **Secure Data Deletion**.
- Conduct regular ethical audits to assess compliance with ethical data usage practices.
- The **Data Exploration and Preprocessing** phase in the AI lifecycle is crucial for understanding the characteristics of the dataset and preparing it for model development.

- Data Exploration and Preprocessing involves sourcing, cleansing, and structuring data to ensure its relevance, quality, and ethical use.
- Ethical considerations are paramount in the **data acquisition and preparation** phase.
- Organizations should establish ethical guidelines for data collection, addressing informed consent, data minimization, and user privacy.
- Organizations need to establish policies, in consultation with the **records and information management (RIM)** departmental function, for data retention and deletion.
- **Algorithm Selection and Model Development** phase involves defining criteria for algorithm and model selection based on business requirements and implementing version control to track changes in algorithms and models.
- Algorithm selection criteria are established by analyzing the nature of the problem, scalability requirements, interpretability versus complexity trade-offs, and computational resource considerations.
- For code and algorithm versioning, practitioners use **tagging** to mark specific releases, major milestones, or experimental features.
- The **Training and Validation** phase involves training machine learning models on data and validating output to ensure their effectiveness and generalizability.
- Performance metrics and validation procedures should be implemented to assess model performance.
- Techniques to mitigate overfitting include: **Regularization, Dropout, Data Augmentation, and Early Stopping.**
- Cross-validation techniques, such as **k-fold cross-validation**, are employed for robust evaluation, particularly for smaller datasets.
- **K-fold cross-validation** is used for robustly evaluating model performance and improving the reliability of the results.
- Examples of **hyperparameters** include the learning rate, regularization strength, the number of hidden layers in a neural network, or the depth of a decision tree.
- **Hyperparameter tuning** is conducted to optimize model parameters, and a validation set is introduced for iterative model improvement during training.
- The **Training and Validation** phase is iterative, involving continuous experimentation and improvement.
- The **Interpretability and Explainability** phase is essential for ensuring that ML models are not black boxes and that their decisions can be explained.
- Explainable AI methods, such as **LIME** or **SHAP**, generate interpretable explanations for individual predictions, shedding light on the model's decision-making process.
- Both **LIME** and **SHAP** are valuable tools for model-agnostic interpretability, allowing stakeholders to gain insights into how specific models arrive at their predictions.
- Continuous model monitoring is established to update explanations and transparency measures as the model evolves, and a feedback loop is implemented for users.
- Documentation is crucial, maintaining records of testing protocols, identified defects, and resolution strategies for knowledge transfer and future consistency.
- The **User Training and Support phase** in the AI lifecycle is crucial for ensuring the effective adoption and ongoing operation of the deployed AI system.
- Organizations should begin user training by understanding user roles, identifying the specific needs of different user groups, and tailoring training programs accordingly.

- Code and model security are prioritized through **code signing** to verify code integrity, protecting trained models from tampering, and securing APIs with authentication and authorization mechanisms.
- Code signing is a fundamental security measure that helps maintain the integrity of AI systems during the deployment phase.
- In case of deployment issues, organizations develop both automated and manual **rollback procedures**.
- The **Post-Deployment Monitoring and Evaluation** phase involves continuous monitoring of AI applications and the evaluation of long-term performance and impact on users and stakeholders.
- The **Retirement** phase is the final phase where a model and its documentation, along with all associated data and outputs, are evaluated and ultimately archived.

Key Glossary Terms

Code Signing: A security practice that involves digitally signing software code to verify its integrity and authenticity.

Ethical Considerations Document: Outlines ethical guidelines and impact assessments.

Git: A distributed version control system (VCS) widely used for tracking changes in source code during software development.

Hyperparameter Tuning: The optimization of hyperparameters to enhance the performance of a machine learning model.

Hyperparameters: External configuration settings that are not learned from the data during the training process but are set prior to training.

K-fold Cross-validation: A technique used to assess the performance and generalization ability of an ML model. It involves splitting the dataset into k (the number of folds) subsets, called folds, and performing the training and validation process k times. In each iteration, one of the folds is used as the validation set, while the remaining k-1 folds are used for training the model.

Key Performance Indicators (KPIs): Quantifiable metrics used to assess the performance and success of an organization, project, or individual in achieving predefined objectives. They help track progress toward goals, facilitate decision-making, and improve performance and strategic planning.

L1 and L2 Regularization: Techniques used in ML to prevent overfitting and improve the generalization of models by adding a penalty term to the model's objective function.

LIME: A model-agnostic technique designed to explain the predictions of complex machine learning models by approximating their behavior locally.

Model Disgorgement: Also known as algorithmic disgorgement or algorithmic destruction, refers to the deletion or destruction of models and algorithms. This process is typically undertaken to eliminate "bad" data from a model, where bad data encompasses information that was illegally obtained, used without consent, found to be invalid, or otherwise impacts the validity and legality of the model.

Overfitting: Occurs when a model learns the training data too well, capturing noise and details that are specific to the training set but do not generalize well to new, unseen data.

Risk Register: Outlines identified risks, their impact, and mitigation plans.

Roles and Responsibilities Matrix: Details the duties of each team member.

SHAP (SHapley Additive exPlanations): SHAP values are *based on cooperative game theory* and aim to *fairly allocate contributions of each feature* to the prediction *across all possible feature combinations*. SHAP values provide a global perspective on feature importance and can be used for individual instance explanations as well.

SMART: Specific, Measurable, Achievable, Relevant, Time-Bound.

Notes

1 "Explaining Model Disgorgement," *Brandon Lalonde*, accessed January 16, 2024, https://iapp.org/news/a/explaining-model-disgorgement/.

2 Ibid.

4 The Role of Records and Information Management in AI Governance

The practice of Records Management goes back at least 4,000 years. In ancient Mesopotamia, merchants kept track of their business dealings by writing the details of their agreements on small clay tablets. These tablets recorded the details of what each merchant owed another, what income resulted, and what taxes they would subsequently owe to the king. These were the first contracts, and in turn, the first business records.

In some ways, how humans transact business has changed very little in those 4,000 years. Whether on a clay tablet or cryptographically encrypted onto a distributed blockchain, business records form the immutable reality of our business dealings. Without them, and the predictability, reliability, and memory they provide, our modern economy and society could not exist.

While a Mesopotamian merchant may need to keep track of many hundreds of tablets over their lifetime, a generative AI system of today needs to keep track of billions, if not trillions, of data points and variables. Further, those governing the AI must also deal with the fact that most of these tools are designed to learn through ongoing use. The answer provided today by a learning AI may be different from the answer it gives tomorrow, next week, or next year.

This then presents the great challenge of records management in the age of AI. Specifically, what constitutes a record, worthy of or necessitating retention, may constantly and purposefully change over time. Unless you specifically retain an output from an AI system today, you may not be able to recreate the same result in the future. This chapter will outline some of the specific challenges this presents and will offer specific actions to mitigate these challenges.

Records and information management *(RIM) plays a crucial role in AI Governance by maintaining control of records throughout their lifecycle* and providing a structured framework for handling and safeguarding data, which is fundamental to responsible and ethical AI practices. This is a key point: *AI Governance training programs that do not include training on the role of RIM are woefully incomplete.*

The International Organization for Standardization (ISO) defines (business) **records** as "information created, received, and maintained as evidence and information by an organization or person, in pursuance of legal obligations or in the transaction of business."[1] It further defines **records management** (RM) as "[the] field of management responsible for the efficient and systematic control of the creation, receipt, maintenance, use, and disposition of records, including the processes for capturing and maintaining evidence of and information about business activities and transactions in the form of records."[2] The field has expanded and adopted the moniker **records and information management** (RIM) to reflect its broadened role as the move to electronic records and information unfolded.

Organizations today are facing formidable challenges managing their records due to the complexity and diversity of technology employed, the rapid proliferation of data across departments, new and emerging regulations, and the need to derive insights from data to maintain a competitive edge. Records and information management principles and practices can be applied to the governance of data and artificial intelligence processes.

The Role of RIM in AI Governance

AI algorithms heavily depend on data for analysis, interpretation, insight derivation, and subsequent data generation. Managing this exponential data growth is a crucial challenge. This is where proficient RIM is key.[3]

RIM establishes the foundation for addressing the ingestion of data by ensuring accuracy, accessibility, and governance. *Well-defined RIM guidelines pertaining to data capture, protection, preservation, and defensible deletion once a data set has met its lifecycle requirements are essential to maintaining trusted and accurate records, and a complete audit trail. The goal is to assure that only high-quality, current data is ingested into AI systems for training and testing AI models. This, in turn, enhances the performance of AI systems*, helping to deliver more precise insights.

The strength of AI resides in its ability to discern patterns, trends, and correlations within extensive data sets. *Efficient records management plays a crucial role in ensuring that data is appropriately tagged and discoverable when needed by the AI system.* Well-managed records provide the groundwork for AI algorithms to extract valuable insights, thereby facilitating informed decision-making.[4]

AI's proficiency in extracting insights from data also comes with escalating concerns about data breaches and ransomware attacks. Through the **classification of sensitive data**, efficient records management enhances security by preventing AI technologies from accessing such data improperly, thereby reducing the risk of exposing sensitive business information.

Key aspects of the role of RIM in AI Governance include:

1. **Data Lifecycle Management:** Records management should oversee the entire lifecycle of data, from creation to disposal. This includes defining retention policies, ensuring proper data disposal, and managing archives. A well-defined data lifecycle is critical in preventing the accumulation of obsolete or unnecessary data that could pose risks in AI applications or cause them to render inaccurate insights.
2. **Data Quality Assurance:** Effective records management helps to ensure the accuracy, completeness, and reliability of data. This is essential for AI systems that heavily rely on high-quality data for training, analysis, and decision-making. By maintaining data integrity, records management contributes to the trustworthiness of AI outcomes.
3. **Data Accessibility and Transparency:** Records management establishes protocols for organizing and cataloging data, making it more easily accessible when needed. This accessibility enhances transparency in AI processes, allowing stakeholders to understand how data is gathered and used, ensuring accountability, and facilitating compliance with regulations.
4. **Security and Compliance:** Records management helps to define and enforce security measures for data classified as sensitive, preventing unauthorized access and mitigating the risk of data breaches. Compliance with regulations such as data protection laws is essential in AI Governance, and records management helps in establishing and maintaining the necessary controls.
5. **Risk Mitigation:** By implementing robust records management practices, organizations can identify and mitigate risks associated with AI applications. This includes risks related to data bias, discrimination, and unintended consequences. Records management helps in monitoring and addressing these risks throughout the AI development lifecycle.
6. **Ethical Considerations:** Records management contributes to the ethical use of AI by establishing guidelines for the collection, storage, and utilization of data. Ethical considerations, such as consent, privacy, and fairness, are integrated into records

management practices, aligning AI activities with ethical standards and societal expectations.

In summary, RIM is integral to AI Governance as it helps to ensure the responsible and ethical use of data, promotes transparency, enhances security, and helps organizations navigate the complexities of AI applications in compliance with regulations and ethical standards.

The Role of RIM in the AI Systems Lifecycle

The role of RIM in the lifecycle of a generative AI system is foundational and multifaceted, impacting each of the eight stages of the generative AI system lifecycle. This role ensures that AI operates within a framework of data integrity, security, and governance, which is critical for developing trustworthy and effective AI solutions. Below is a detailed exploration of the role of the RIM department at each stage:

1. **Problem Definition and Project Initiation**

   At the inception phase, where problems are defined and AI solutions are conceptualized, RIM plays a strategic role by working with data governance teams to ensure that the data governance policies are aligned with the objectives of the AI initiative. It involves identifying the types of data required, understanding the legal and compliance implications, and ensuring that there is a clear understanding of the data lifecycle. *RIM ensures that the problem definition includes considerations for data privacy, security, and ethical use.*

2. **Data Collection**

   During data collection, *RIM helps to ensure that data acquisition follows established guidelines for data quality, privacy, and ethical considerations.* This includes overseeing the collection methods to ensure they are legal and ethical, ensuring data accuracy and relevance, and managing consent where necessary. *RIM frameworks provide the structure needed to collect data responsibly and sustainably.*

3. **Data Preparation**

   In the data preparation stage, *RIM considerations are critical for organizing, cleaning, and annotating data effectively*. It involves establishing protocols for data classification, metadata management, and data curation practices. By doing so, RIM enhances the quality and usability of data for AI processing, ensuring that datasets are reliable and ready for analysis.

4. **Model Selection and Training**

   When selecting and training models, RIM contributes by assisting in managing the datasets used for training and validation, ensuring they are well-documented and preserved. This includes tracking dataset versions, managing data drift, and ensuring the reproducibility of AI models. *RIM practices ensure that the data used in training models remains consistent, secure, and in compliance with regulatory requirements.*

5. **Model Evaluation**

   For model evaluation, RIM ensures **transparency and accountability** by maintaining detailed records of evaluation processes, criteria, and outcomes. This involves *documenting the datasets used for testing, the performance metrics, and the evaluation results.* Such documentation supports the validation of model effectiveness and facilitates the auditing of AI systems.

6. **Model Deployment**

   During model deployment, RIM oversees the transition of AI models into operational environments, ensuring that data used in deployment is managed according to governance standards. This includes *providing input to the IT and cybersecurity teams and helping to manage access controls, data encryption, and secure data transfer processes*. RIM practices ensure that deployed models operate with data integrity and security.

7. **Monitoring and Maintenance**

   RIM is essential in the ongoing monitoring and maintenance of AI systems, *by providing frameworks for logging system performance, managing updates, and archiving obsolete data.* It helps to ensure that monitoring tools comply with data governance policies and that maintenance activities are documented for accountability and continuous improvement.

8. **Retirement**

   Finally, when an AI system reaches its end of life, *RIM assists in managing the decommissioning process, ensuring that data is securely archived or deleted according to retention policies and legal requirements.* This stage involves conducting a thorough audit of the data and AI system, ensuring that sensitive information is protected during disposal, and documenting the retirement process.

   Through these stages, RIM ensures that AI systems are built and operated on a foundation of data integrity, security, and governance. *By embedding RIM principles across the AI system lifecycle, organizations can mitigate risks, ensure compliance, and enhance the trustworthiness of AI applications.*

Records Management Business Rationale

Historically, highly regulated industries, such as banking, energy, and pharmaceuticals, have had the greatest need to implement RIM programs due to their compliance and reporting requirements. However, over the past decade or so, increased regulation and changes to legal statutes and rules have made RIM a business necessity for nearly every enterprise (beyond very small businesses).

Notable industry drivers fueling the growth of RIM programs include:

- ***Increased Government Oversight and Industry Regulation***: Government regulations that require enhanced reporting and accountability were early business drivers that fueled the implementation of formal RM programs. This is true at the federal and state level. In the United States, the Sarbanes-Oxley Act of 2002 (SOX) created and enhanced standards of financial reporting and transparency for the boards and executive management of public corporations and accounting firms. It also addressed auditor independence and corporate governance concerns. SOX imposes fines or imprisonment penalties for noncompliance and requires that senior officers sign off on the veracity of financial statements. It states clearly that pertinent business records cannot be destroyed during litigation or compliance investigations. Since SOX was enacted, Japan, Australia, Germany, France, and India have also have adopted stricter "SOX-like" governance and financial reporting standards. Newer legislation, such as the European Union GDPR, and global privacy concerns have further driven the need for updated and expanded RM programs. This has given the RM profession a boost in visibility and vitality.
- ***Changes in Legal Procedures and Requirements During Civil Litigation:*** In 2006, the need to amend the U.S. Federal Rules of Civil Procedure (FRCP) to contain specific rules for handling electronically generated evidence (versus paper) was addressed. The

changes included processes and requirements for legal discovery of **electronically stored information** (ESI) during civil litigation. *Today, email is the leading form of evidence requested in civil trials.* The changes to the US FRCP in 2006 and its update in 2015 (where proportionality was addressed) had a pervasive impact on American enterprises and required them to gain control over their ESI and implement formal records management (RM) and electronic discovery (e-discovery) programs to meet new requirements. Although they have generally been ahead of the United States in their development and maturity of RM practices, Canadian, British, and Australian law is closely tracking that of the United States in legal discovery. The United States is a more litigious society, so this is not unexpected.

- ***IG Awareness***: IG, in sum, is the set of rules, policies, and business processes used to manage and control the totality of an organization's information. *IG programs aim to minimize information risks and costs while maximizing information value.* Monitoring technologies are required to enforce and audit IG compliance. Beginning with SOX in 2002 and continuing with the massive US FRCP changes in 2006 and 2015, along with the introduction of the far-reaching GDPR legislation in 2018, have forced enterprises to become more IG aware and have spurred ramped-up efforts to control, manage, and secure their information. *A significant component of any IG program is implementing an RM program that specifies the retention periods and disposition (e.g., destruction, transfer, archive) of formal business records.* This program, for instance, allows enterprises to destroy records once their required retention period (based on external regulations, legal requirements, and internal IG policies) has been met and allows them to legally destroy records with no negative impact or lingering legal liability. This practice, if consistently implemented, allows for the elimination of information that has aged and is of low value to make room for new information that has higher business value. Think of it as "information digestion."
- ***Business Continuity Concerns:*** In the face of real disasters, such as the 9/11 terrorist attacks, Hurricane Katrina, Superstorm Sandy, and the Covid-19 pandemic, executives now realize that disaster recovery and business resumption are something they must plan and prepare for. Disasters really happen, and businesses that are not well prepared don't survive. The focus is on **vital records** (also known as "essential records"), which are the most mission-critical records that are needed to resume operations in the event of a disaster, and managing those records is part of an overall RM program.

Detailed RIM Role in AI Governance

Here's a detailed description of the role of RIM in AI Governance:

Data Classification and Access Controls

Classification: RIM, often working with IT, the data governance team, and/or the cybersecurity team, helps classify data based on its sensitivity, importance, and regulatory requirements, guiding appropriate handling within AI systems.

Data classification is a crucial component of AI Governance, ensuring that data is handled appropriately based on its sensitivity, importance, and regulatory requirements.

The first step involves defining clear data classification objectives in the context of AI Governance and aligning them with organizational goals, regulatory requirements, and privacy considerations.

To establish a robust foundation, standards and protocols for data classification are developed, defining criteria based on sensitivity, importance, and regulatory requirements.

Collaboration across cross-functional teams, including RIM professionals, data scientists, legal teams, compliance officers, and other stakeholders, must be fostered to ensure diverse perspectives in the classification process.

A comprehensive **data inventory** is conducted to identify the types, sources, and locations of organizational data, categorizing it based on its nature, purpose, and potential impact. **Sensitivity levels** for different types of data are defined, taking into account factors such as personal information, financial data, intellectual property, and the potential harm from unauthorized access.

Guidelines for handling data based on its classification are developed, specifying security measures, access controls, and encryption requirements for each level of access. The exploration of automated tools for data classification, such as machine learning or rule-based systems, is considered to ensure efficient and consistent classification.

Legal counsel is engaged to **conduct compliance checks** related to data classification, ensuring alignment with data protection laws and industry regulations. A data classification policy is developed and documented, communicated to relevant stakeholders, emphasizing the importance of adhering to data classification guidelines.

User training programs are conducted—(sometimes reinforced during an annual "Records Day")—to educate employees on data classification principles and procedures, ensuring awareness of their responsibilities. Integration of data classification mechanisms into AI systems is crucial, ensuring that AI models and applications are designed to handle data according to its classification.

Periodic reviews and updates of data classification criteria should be made, adapting them to changing business needs, technological advancements, and regulatory updates. A classification register is established to maintain a record of classified data, including details such as classification level, handling guidelines, and additional metadata.

Integration of data classification into data retention policies is emphasized, defining retention periods based on the sensitivity and importance of classified data. Further, the integration of data retention policies with existing records retention policies should be explored. **Ethical considerations** are brought into the classification process, evaluating the potential impact on individuals, and ensuring fair treatment.

Roles and responsibilities for **data stewardship** are documented, defining the responsibilities of individuals or teams overseeing classified data. Regular audits of data classification practices are conducted to ensure consistent classification according to established criteria.

By following these steps, organizations can leverage the role of RIM to establish effective data classification strategies. This approach ensures that data is handled appropriately within AI systems, promoting compliance with regulatory requirements, protecting sensitive information, and contributing to a robust AI Governance framework.

Access controls aligned with data classification levels are implemented, restricting access to classified data based on user roles and permissions, using the **principle of least privilege** (whereby only the minimum amount of information needed for employees to do their job is provided, also known as on a "need to know" basis). RIM works with IT and core business units to establish access controls to limit and monitor access to sensitive information, ensuring that only authorized personnel can interact with data used in AI processes. Developing access controls is a critical aspect of AI Governance, especially when it comes to protecting sensitive information used in AI processes. The role of RIM is essential in establishing and enforcing access controls.

Staying informed about emerging technologies for data classification is essential, with periodic assessments conducted to evaluate the feasibility of incorporating new tools or techniques to enhance efficiency and accuracy. In this holistic approach, RIM professionals contribute significantly to the ethical and effective management of data within the AI Governance framework.

Record Retention and Disposition

RIM establishes retention policies and develops a **records retention schedule** (RRS) that lists the records or file series being managed, cites the regulatory requirements applying to them, and establishes retention periods. This helps the organization comply with legal and regulatory requirements, which is critical, especially in industries with strict data retention laws.

Record retention is a critical aspect of AI Governance, especially in industries with strict data retention laws. RIM plays a key role in establishing and enforcing retention policies.

Engaging legal counsel specializing in data retention policies becomes key, ensuring ongoing guidance and compliance with evolving regulations. Seeking legal advice on specific retention practices, particularly in industries with complex regulatory environments, provides a strategic approach to compliance.

Monitoring changes in data retention regulations is a proactive measure, necessitating the establishment of processes to adapt retention policies promptly in response to regulatory updates. *Creating a comprehensive* ***records inventory*** *becomes foundational*, requiring the maintenance of a detailed record of all records, including data type, creation date, and sensitivity. Keeping this inventory up to date, with a constant update as new records are created and old ones disposed of, ensures accuracy and relevance.

Developing clear and comprehensive retention policies that align with legal and regulatory requirements is crucial, with a specific articulation of retention periods for different types of records based on their classification. Integrating record retention policies into the AI project lifecycle ensures that data used for training AI models and decision-making complies with established retention periods.

Implementing automated tools and systems for **retention management** is a practical step, ensuring consistency and efficiency. Automation can trigger alerts for records approaching the end of their retention period and coming due for disposition (normally destruction, but can also mean archiving or transfer to another unit, as is done with federal agencies sending records to the National Archives and Records Administration, NARA), facilitating timely actions. Allocating resources, including personnel and technology, to support compliance with record retention policies is imperative, ensuring the organization is equipped to manage records effectively.

Applying **data minimization** practices when creating records, ensuring only necessary information is captured and retained, and regularly reviewing records to identify and remove unnecessary data aligns with privacy-conscious operations.

Appointing **data stewards** responsible for providing input and overseeing record retention within business units in the organization, defining their roles and responsibilities, including monitoring compliance and addressing issues, enhances governance.

Developing and *documenting procedures for the secure destruction or disposal of records at the end of their retention period,* ensuring compliance with privacy and security requirements, is a crucial aspect of governance.

Providing training programs to educate employees on record retention policies and the importance of compliance ensures a workforce that is aware of its responsibilities in managing records.

Maintaining transparency in record retention practices by documenting policies, procedures, and compliance efforts, and documenting the rationale behind retention decisions and disposal actions contributes to a culture of accountability.

Fostering collaboration between business units, RIM professionals, legal teams, compliance officers, and AI development teams is a **cross-functional effort**. Retention policies are designed to consider legal, regulatory, and business requirements.

Conducting periodic **risk assessments** to identify potential risks associated with record retention and disposal and mitigating identified risks through adjustments to policies or processes ensures a proactive and adaptive governance approach. New records and risks introduced by the introduction of AI tools and techniques must be identified and addressed.

Regularly reviewing and updating **record retention policies** to reflect changes in regulations, technology, and business practices ensures policies remain relevant and effective over time. In this comprehensive and collaborative approach, RIM professionals play a central role in ensuring ethical and legally compliant record retention practices within the AI Governance framework.

By following these steps, organizations can leverage the role of RIM to establish and enforce effective record retention policies within the broader framework of AI Governance. This approach ensures that data used in AI projects is retained and managed in compliance with legal and regulatory requirements, and internal policies and standards.

Information Lifecycle Management

RIM implements **Information Lifecycle Management** (ILM) principles to manage data from creation to disposal, ensuring that AI systems are trained on relevant and current information.

Determining lifecycle phases is essential for ensuring that data is effectively managed from its creation to disposal. The role of RIM is crucial in aligning with ILM principles, especially in the context of AI Governance.

First and foremost, defining clear objectives for ILM within the scope of AI Governance is essential, ensuring alignment with organizational goals, regulatory requirements, and ethical considerations.

Fostering collaboration among cross-functional teams, including users, RIM professionals, data scientists, IT teams, legal teams, and compliance officers, is critical. This collaboration ensures that diverse perspectives are considered, addressing various concerns that may arise during the information lifecycle.

Conducting a **data sensitivity assessment** becomes a foundational step, allowing for the identification and classification of data based on its level of sensitivity. Distinguishing between public, internal, confidential, and highly sensitive data sets the stage for informed decision-making throughout the lifecycle.

Identifying critical phases in the information lifecycle that are particularly relevant to AI systems is crucial. Collaboratively considering phases such as data creation, acquisition, storage, processing, analysis, sharing, archiving, and disposal provides a comprehensive understanding of the entire data lifecycle.

Clear criteria for transitioning data between lifecycle phases are then defined, incorporating factors such as data relevance, accuracy, compliance requirements, and storage costs. Policies for data creation and collection are developed in alignment with ILM principles, specifying metadata requirements, data quality standards, and legal considerations during the data creation phase.

Development of archiving and retention policies that align with regulatory requirements and business needs is essential. Establishing criteria for moving data into the archive phase and defining retention periods are integral components of these policies. The integration of **metadata management** practices further enhances data discoverability and traceability.

Procedures for **data disposal**, considering the end of the information lifecycle, are developed. Secure and compliant methods for data destruction or anonymization are defined to ensure responsible disposal. Protocols for data migration between different storage systems or platforms are established, ensuring seamless movement while maintaining data integrity and relevance.

Periodic assessments of **data quality** throughout the information lifecycle are conducted, implementing checks and validations to identify and rectify data inconsistencies. Monitoring mechanisms to track changes made to data during its lifecycle are implemented, and changes are documented to ensure transparency and accountability.

Establishing processes for **legal holds** during the information lifecycle, including procedures for suspending the normal disposition of data in response to legal or regulatory requirements, adds a layer of compliance.

Integration of ILM principles into AI model training processes ensures that AI models are trained on relevant and current information, aligning with data lifecycle phases.

Documentation of instances of data movement through progressive lifecycle phases, maintaining records of transitions, including the reasons and outcomes, provides a comprehensive **audit trail**. Regular reviews of ILM policies are conducted to ensure their alignment with evolving organizational goals, regulatory changes, and technological advancements. In this integrated approach, RIM professionals play a central role in ensuring the ethical, secure, and compliant management of data within AI projects and programs.

By following these steps, organizations can leverage the role of RIM to effectively determine and manage lifecycle phases in ILM. *This approach ensures that AI systems are trained on relevant, accurate, and current information, contributing to a robust AI Governance framework.*

Compliance and Legal Requirements

Ensuring compliance with legal requirements and data privacy regulations is a critical aspect of AI governance. RIM plays a key role in this process, in consultation with legal staff and possibly outside experts.

Engaging legal counsel specializing in **data privacy** becomes paramount, providing ongoing guidance to ensure compliance with evolving regulations. Seeking legal advice on specific AI use cases with potential privacy implications is a proactive measure to navigate the intricate legal landscape.

Consultation with regulatory authorities and data protection agencies is a key strategy. Establishing open lines of communication and proactively engaging with regulators enables organizations to address inquiries or concerns promptly. *A comprehensive understanding of relevant legal and regulatory frameworks related to data privacy and security in the jurisdictions where the organization operates is essential.* Staying informed about updates and changes to privacy laws is crucial to adapting practices accordingly.

Mechanisms for staying abreast of legal developments in the field of data privacy are established, with a focus on monitoring legislative changes. Identifying applicable compliance standards, including ISO and IEEE standards, and understanding regulations such as GDPR, HIPAA, CCPA, CPRA, or sector-specific regulations are key steps. Tailoring data privacy practices to align with the specific requirements of each standard ensures a nuanced approach.

The appointment of **Data Protection Officers** (DPOs) to oversee data privacy compliance and defining their roles, responsibilities, and reporting lines within the organization is essential for effective governance. (The DPO is the only function explicitly mentioned in the GDPR.)

Organizations may also engage data privacy officers such as Chief Privacy Officers or Data Protection Managers to serve as the first line of defense when it comes to privacy and data protection matters.

Establishing comprehensive data privacy policies, in collaboration with the Privacy function, that align with applicable laws and regulations is a foundational step, clearly articulating how personal data will be handled, processed, and protected.

Creating and maintaining a comprehensive inventory of all data assets, classifying data based on sensitivity and privacy considerations, and implementing **Privacy Impact Assessments** (PIAs) for AI projects are vital components of a robust governance framework.

Integrating **privacy by design** principles into the development and deployment of AI systems, considering privacy implications throughout the AI lifecycle, ensures a proactive approach.

Developing and enforcing data retention policies aligned with legal requirements, including clear definitions for the duration of data retention and criteria for disposal, is a critical aspect of compliance. *Adopting* ***data minimization*** *practices, collecting only necessary data for specific purposes, and avoiding unnecessary processing of personal information* are integral to privacy-conscious operations.

Ensuring robust mechanisms for obtaining and managing user consent for data processing, with a focus on informed, specific, and easily withdrawable consent, is a fundamental element. Implementing **encryption mechanisms**, especially for sensitive personal data, both in transit and at rest, mitigates the risk of unauthorized access.

Monitoring and assessing the data privacy practices of third-party vendors and data processors, ensuring contractual inclusion of privacy and security obligations, is a vital aspect of comprehensive governance. Establishing procedures for handling **data subject rights** (DSR) requests and providing mechanisms for individuals to exercise their rights contributes to a privacy-centric approach.

Regular audits of data privacy practices to assess compliance with internal policies and external regulations, covering AI applications and data processing activities, are imperative. Offering regular training sessions to employees on data privacy best practices and compliance requirements, with a specific focus on the unique challenges posed by AI systems, enhances awareness.

Establishing and maintaining **records of processing** (ROP) activities, which document the lawful basis for data processing, data categories, and processing purposes, ensures transparency and accountability. Developing and regularly updating an **incident response plan** for addressing data breaches and privacy incidents, defining roles, responsibilities, and communication strategies, is a crucial aspect of proactive governance. In this comprehensive approach, RIM professionals, legal counsel, and AI development teams collaboratively navigate the intricate landscape of AI Governance, ensuring ethical and legally compliant practices in the development and deployment of AI systems.

By following these steps, organizations can leverage the role of RIM in ensuring compliance with legal requirements and data privacy regulations within the broader framework of AI Governance. This approach helps organizations build trust, mitigate risks, and demonstrate a commitment to responsible and ethical AI practices.

Data Quality and Integrity

Capture and Maintenance: RIM—working with Data Governance teams, including data stewards in business units—*ensures that data used for AI training and decision-making is accurately captured, stored, and maintained throughout its lifecycle. The idea is to capture the data accurately at the point of creation so that downstream analyses and reports are more accurate and reliable.*

Ensuring data quality and integrity in the context of AI Governance, particularly within the Capture and Maintenance function, involves meticulous management of records and information.

The initial step in this process is to define clear and comprehensive data quality standards that align with the organization's AI Governance goals. These standards encompass criteria for accuracy, completeness, consistency, and timeliness of data, establishing a robust foundation for data management.

Identifying critical data elements that significantly influence AI training and decision-making processes is the next imperative step. Prioritizing these elements allows for focused attention on aspects that have a pronounced impact on model performance and outcomes, ensuring that efforts are directed toward optimizing the most crucial components of the data.

To further enhance data quality, the establishment of **data stewardship roles** within the Capture and Maintenance function becomes essential. Appointing data stewards in business units—usually a business analyst type of professional—who are specifically responsible for overseeing data quality in their department ensures dedicated attention to this critical aspect. The roles and responsibilities of these data stewards are clearly defined, including their involvement in resolving data quality issues that may arise throughout the data lifecycle.

In collaboration with the Data Governance team and data stewards in business units, the implementation of a comprehensive data governance framework is the subsequent key step. This framework outlines roles, responsibilities, and processes for managing data quality across the organization. Importantly, it includes specific measures tailored for the Capture and Maintenance function, ensuring that data quality considerations are embedded seamlessly into the AI training and decision-making processes.

Through these systematic steps, the RIM team, in conjunction with the Data Governance team and data stewards, establishes a robust foundation for maintaining data quality and integrity throughout the data lifecycle. By defining standards, prioritizing critical elements, appointing dedicated stewards, and implementing a tailored governance framework, organizations can capture data accurately at the point of creation.

The next key step in this process involves *documenting the data capture processes* in detail. This documentation outlines the methods, tools, and procedures employed for capturing data, and includes comprehensive guidelines for data entry, validation, and verification. The emphasis here is on maintaining accuracy right from the point of data creation, laying a solid foundation for downstream analyses and reports to be inherently accurate and reliable.

To further reinforce the accuracy of captured data, training programs are offered to personnel involved in data capture. These programs underscore the importance of adherence to data quality standards, ensuring that individuals are well aware of the significance of their role in generating accurate and reliable data.

Requiring the use of **standardized data formats** is another essential practice to ensure consistency and interoperability across the data landscape. Defining and enforcing standards for data representation and structure helps maintain a cohesive and standardized approach to data capture.

The implementation of data validation checks is integral to the process, with a focus on identifying and rectifying errors promptly. Automated validation checks are integrated wherever possible to enhance efficiency and reduce the likelihood of human errors.

Version control mechanisms are instituted to track changes made to records over time, ensuring a clear version history for each dataset used for training and testing. This not only facilitates traceability but also provides a robust audit trail for comprehensive documentation and accountability.

Security measures are paramount in safeguarding data during capture, storage, and maintenance. Robust data security protocols, including **access controls, encryption**, and other security measures, are implemented to prevent unauthorized tampering and ensure the confidentiality and integrity of the captured data.

Regular **audits of captured data** are conducted to assess its quality and identify any discrepancies that may arise. This involves a combination of automated tools and manual checks to guarantee the accuracy and completeness of records, thereby reinforcing the commitment to data quality and integrity within the Capture and Maintenance function of AI Governance.

Additional steps:

1. **Implement Data Retention Policies**

   Define and enforce data retention policies to manage the lifecycle of records.

   Ensure timely deletion or archiving of obsolete or irrelevant data.

2. **Facilitate Data Traceability**

   Establish mechanisms for tracing the lineage of data from its origin through processing to decision-making.

   Maintain metadata that provides insights into data sources, transformations, and usage.

3. **Monitor Data Quality Metrics**

   Define key performance indicators (KPIs) related to data quality in the Capture and Maintenance function.

   Regularly monitor and report on these metrics to identify trends and areas for improvement.

4. **Enable Data Quality Reporting**

   Implement reporting mechanisms that enable stakeholders to access and understand data quality reports.

   Include visualizations and insights to facilitate decision-making.

5. **Document Data Maintenance Procedures**

   Document procedures for ongoing data maintenance, specifying how updates, corrections, and modifications should be handled.

   Ensure that these procedures align with data quality standards.

6. **Automate Routine Data Maintenance Tasks**

   Automate routine data maintenance tasks to improve efficiency and reduce the likelihood of human error.

   Implement scheduled checks and updates as part of automated workflows.

Collaboration with AI Development Teams

RIM professionals collaborate with AI development teams *to integrate records and information management practices seamlessly into the AI development lifecycle.*

To commence this collaboration, it is crucial to define clear objectives, aligning collaboration goals with AI Governance, regulatory compliance, and organizational information management standards.

Identifying key stakeholders within both the AI development teams and RIM professionals is the next step, ensuring representation from users, data scientists, AI developers, IT teams, and other relevant contributors. Creating collaboration frameworks involves the development of ongoing mechanisms, such as regular meetings, checkpoints, and collaborative platforms, to facilitate continuous communication.

Workshops or collaborative sessions can be organized to bring together AI development teams and RIM professionals, fostering open discussions to understand each other's roles, responsibilities, and expectations. Collaboration agreements and understandings are documented, specifying expectations, responsibilities, and deliverables from both sides.

Effective communication channels are established to ensure regular updates, feedback, and information sharing between RIM professionals and AI development teams. Clear roles and responsibilities for both parties are defined, outlining the expected contributions throughout the AI development lifecycle.

Decision-making processes within AI development teams are collaboratively documented, with a focus on integrating RIM principles into key areas like data selection, preprocessing, and model design. Opportunities to seamlessly integrate RIM practices into AI development processes are identified, covering data collection, preprocessing, model training, and deployment.

Guidelines for information management practices are developed to align with AI development processes, including standards for data documentation, metadata creation, version control, and model development documentation. Training programs and awareness sessions are conducted for AI development teams to ensure a comprehensive understanding of integrating RIM into their workflows.

Collaboration extends into broader data governance practices, aligning data stewardship roles, ownership, and accountability with RIM principles. Standards for documenting data used in AI development, metadata requirements, and data quality standards are established.

Version control practices for AI models are collaboratively aligned with RIM standards, ensuring consistent and transparent tracking of versioning information. Compliance checks related to information management and data protection are conducted in collaboration with legal counsel engaged to ensure adherence to relevant laws and regulations.

Integration of RIM practices into the evaluation and validation of AI models is a collaborative effort, documenting model performance, validation metrics, and any adjustments made during the validation phase. Audits and reviews of AI development processes are conducted regularly, ensuring adherence to information management and governance standards.

Celebrating successful collaborations and achievements, as well as sharing learnings and best practices, helps foster a culture of knowledge sharing between RIM professionals and AI development teams. This comprehensive and collaborative approach ensures that information management practices seamlessly integrate into the AI development lifecycle, promoting transparency, accountability, and compliance.

By following these detailed steps, organizations can ensure effective collaboration between RIM professionals and AI development teams, seamlessly integrating information management practices into the AI development lifecycle. This approach enhances transparency, governance, and the overall quality of AI processes within the organization.

Documentation and Auditing

The RIM function is involved in the documentation of the AI development and deployment processes, creating a comprehensive record of decisions, methodologies, and updates.

Documentation and auditing of AI processes are crucial components of AI Governance, ensuring transparency, accountability, and compliance with established standards. *The role of RIM is pivotal in creating comprehensive records of AI development decisions, acquisition of data sets, and deployment, which are called* ***paradata.*** **Paradata**, in the context of AI systems development, refers to *the metadata or auxiliary data that captures the process and context of how the initial system was set up, how and why data is collected, managed, and used throughout the lifecycle of an AI system.* Unlike traditional metadata that describes the basic characteristics of data (such as format, source, and date of creation), *paradata goes further to include information about how data is interacted with, including user interactions, data collection methodologies, processing decisions, and the usage patterns of the data itself.*

Organizations should establish clear and robust documentation standards for AI processes. This involves defining the types of information to be recorded, the required level of detail, and the format. These standards should be aligned with industry best practices and regulatory requirements to ensure thorough documentation.

Creating a centralized repository serves as a fundamental step in organizing and storing documentation related to AI processes. The selected platform should be secure and accessible, facilitating easy retrieval and sharing of information among relevant stakeholders.

The documentation process starts with recording the inception of AI projects, outlining objectives, scope, and expected outcomes. This includes crucial details about stakeholders, project sponsors, and any ethical considerations that need to be addressed.

For the data-centric phases, such as data collection and preprocessing, organizations need to precisely document the sources, methods, and criteria employed. The record should encompass preprocessing steps, including data cleaning, transformation, and any adjustments made to enhance data quality.

Similarly, detailed documentation of the model development process is crucial. This involves recording the algorithms, parameters, and techniques employed, along with any experimentation, adjustments, or iterations made during the development phase.

Feature selection and **engineering steps** should be specified in the documentation, including the rationale behind feature choices and any applied domain expertise.

Moving through the lifecycle, *organizations should document the model training and validation processes, capturing details about datasets used, hyperparameter tuning, and validation methodologies.*

Performance metrics, model accuracy, and any observed challenges or limitations should be included in the records.

Ethical considerations play a crucial role in AI Governance. Organizations should document decisions related to bias mitigation, fairness assessments, and steps taken to ensure ethical use of AI models.

Deployment and integration steps should be thoroughly documented, specifying the environment, tools, and infrastructure used. Furthermore, protocols for monitoring AI models in production and maintenance procedures, including updates and retraining schedules, should be recorded.

Explanations for model outputs, especially in cases where interpretability is crucial, should be detailed in the documentation. Techniques such as SHAP values, LIME, or other interpretability tools employed should be specified.

Decision-making processes throughout the AI model lifecycle, from model selection to deployment and updates, should be recorded, including any trade-offs made during these processes.

Implementing **version control** for models and associated code is essential. Organizations should document changes made over time, maintaining a clear version history for transparency and accountability.

Security measures implemented throughout the AI development and deployment lifecycle should be thoroughly documented. This includes specifications for encryption, access controls, and any measures taken to protect against adversarial attacks.

Also, compliance documentation should be recorded to ensure transparency regarding how AI processes comply with data protection laws, industry standards, and ethical guidelines. This comprehensive documentation approach within the realm of AI Governance facilitates transparency, accountability, and effective decision-making throughout the AI lifecycle.

Some additional steps include:

1. **Capture User Interaction and Feedback**

   Document user interaction with AI applications and systems.

   Record feedback, user experiences, and any adjustments made based on user input.

2. **Establish Change Management Processes**

   Define and document change management processes for AI models, algorithms, and code.

   Specify how changes are proposed, reviewed, approved, and implemented.

3. **Conduct Regular Audits**

   Schedule and conduct regular audits of AI process documentation.

   Ensure that documentation remains accurate, up to date, and aligned with organizational and regulatory requirements.

4. **Facilitate Cross-Functional Collaboration**

   Foster collaboration between RIM professionals, data scientists, developers, legal teams, and compliance officers.

   Ensure that documentation is comprehensive and reflects inputs from multiple stakeholders.

5. **Provide Training on Documentation Standards**

   Offer training programs to personnel involved in AI processes on documentation standards and best practices.

   Ensure that team members are aware of the importance of thorough and accurate documentation.

By following these detailed steps, organizations can leverage the role of RIM to create comprehensive documentation of AI processes. This approach ensures transparency, accountability, and compliance with regulatory and ethical standards throughout the AI development and deployment lifecycle.

Information Risk Management and Mitigation

RIM practitioners, in consultation with internal risk professionals and others on the AI Governance team, contribute to the establishment of controls and mitigation strategies to address risks related to the use of information in AI models. *(See the chapter on Risk Management for more details.)*

Audit Trails

RIM facilitates the creation of audit trails for AI systems, allowing for transparency and accountability in AI decision-making. This is especially important for regulatory compliance and internal reviews.

Creating audit trails in the context of AI Governance is crucial for transparency, accountability, and compliance. The role of RIM is pivotal in facilitating the creation and management of audit trails for AI systems. Establishing a robust audit trail is essential for ensuring transparency, accountability, and compliance in the development and deployment of AI systems.

Firstly, it's imperative to define the objectives of the audit trail, aligning them with both regulatory requirements and internal governance goals. This involves tracking decision-making processes, model updates, and user interactions. Once objectives are defined, *the next step is to identify key events and data to capture within the audit trail*, encompassing everything from data processing and model training to deployment and user interactions.

To maintain consistency and reliability, it's crucial to establish standards for recording and storing audit trail information, specifying the format, structure, and level of detail for each recorded event. Integration of the audit trail mechanism into the AI system's architecture is equally vital, ensuring coverage across the entire lifecycle, from data input to decision output.

Implementation of robust **time-stamping** mechanisms is essential to provide a chronological sequence of events. This involves synchronizing timestamps across different components of the AI system for accuracy. *User interactions should be thoroughly documented, capturing input data, queries, and user adjustments, along with roles, permissions, and contextual information.*

Furthermore, *the audit trail must encompass events related to model training and updates,* including datasets used, hyperparameter tuning, and rationale behind changes. Explanations for decision outputs should be captured, detailing interpretability methods, reasoning, and contextual information.

In the realm of data processing, *the audit trail needs to document steps such as data cleansing/scrubbing, transformation, and modifications to the dataset.* Logging changes to the configuration of the AI system, including updates to algorithms, parameters, or infrastructure, is vital for understanding the system's behavior.

Facilitating cross-functional collaboration is essential, ensuring that the audit trail captures events relevant to multiple stakeholders, including users, RIM professionals, data scientists, developers, and compliance officers. Access controls should be implemented to maintain the integrity and confidentiality of the audit trail, restricting access to authorized personnel with a need to know.

Security measures, including encryption of audit trail data in transit and at rest, are crucial for protecting against unauthorized access or tampering. Regular reviews and validation of audit trail data, including automated checks for anomalies or discrepancies, are necessary to ensure its accuracy and completeness.

Organizations should define a **retention period** for **audit trail data** based on regulatory requirements and internal policies, ensuring data is retained for an appropriate duration. Ethical considerations and bias mitigation measures should be thoroughly documented, including fairness assessments and actions taken to address biases.

Generating regular audit trail reports, including summary information and key insights, helps keep stakeholders and auditors informed. Engaging legal counsel for periodic compliance checks ensures alignment with legal and regulatory requirements.

In the event of incidents such as system failures or security breaches, incident response actions should be recorded in the audit trail, detailing the resolution process and any preventive measures implemented. Lastly, providing training programs on audit trail practices is essential to educate personnel involved in AI Governance, ensuring familiarity with standards and their role in maintaining transparency.

The RIM function should also work to ensure transparency and to ensure that AI systems address issues of ethics and potential bias.

Tracking Technological Changes

RIM evolves its practices to adapt to changes in information technology, ensuring that the governance framework remains effective in the context of advancing AI technologies.

Adapting to technological changes is essential for ensuring the continuous improvement of AI Governance practices within an enterprise.

Procedures must be in place to retire AI systems when no longer of use and to create and preserve a record of the process.

Education and Training

The RIM function provides input for education and guidance to AI teams on best practices for records management, documentation, and compliance with records management policies.

Developing education and guidance for collaboration with AI development teams is crucial for ensuring alignment with AI Governance principles. The role of RIM is essential in providing expertise on best practices. RIM teams should also provide education and guidance to user groups, perhaps periodically holding a "records management training update" to assess user knowledge and needs.

Ethics and Responsible AI

RIM practitioners provide input for developing ethical guidelines for the use of information in AI, including monitoring for bias and ensuring that ethical considerations are integrated into information management practices.

Developing ethical guidelines for the use of information in AI is crucial for responsible AI Governance.

Key Elements: Change Management, and Continuous Improvement

Implementation of **change order** processes is crucial for maintaining data accuracy and reliability. Establishing formal procedures for data modifications ensures that changes are documented, justified, and approved through a systematic process. This not only enhances transparency but also includes mechanisms for reviewing and validating changes, reinforcing the commitment to data integrity.

A fundamental aspect of sustaining data quality involves the establishment of a culture of continuous improvement. Organizations should embrace a mindset where feedback from data quality assessments, audits, and user experiences is actively used to enhance data capture and maintenance processes.

RIM teams should help the organization continuously improve by establishing **feedback loops** to enhance information management processes based on insights from AI deployments and evolving regulatory landscapes.

By regularly reviewing and updating procedures based on lessons learned, organizations can adapt to evolving needs and challenges, thereby promoting an environment of constant refinement in data management practices. This iterative approach ensures that data quality standards remain robust and aligned with the dynamic landscape of AI Governance.

Conclusion

By following these detailed steps, organizations can leverage the role of RIM to create comprehensive audit trails for AI systems. This approach ensures transparency, accountability, and compliance with regulatory requirements, facilitating internal reviews and external audits.

The Use of AI in Records Management

Although this chapter focuses on the application of AI principles and practices for responsible AI, it is important to note that the RIM professional can also benefit from the application of AI to improve RIM practices.

AI-driven solutions can potentially revolutionize the RIM field, empowering organizations to manage data, records, and information with minimal human involvement. Leveraging machine learning algorithms, *AI proficiently classifies, categorizes, and organizes information, obviating the necessity for manual tagging and filing.* This automated approach not only diminishes the time and effort invested in RIM tasks but also reduces the likelihood of errors and inconsistencies, ensuring greater accuracy and operational efficiency.

By harnessing the power of AI, the RIM function can unlock the full potential of data, extracting invaluable insights and patterns. Rapidly analyzing extensive datasets, AI algorithms can determine trends, correlations, and anomalies that might escape human analysts. These insights play a pivotal role in informed decision-making, process optimization, and identifying opportunities for growth. Additionally, AI-driven predictive analytics have the capability to anticipate future needs, providing organizations with the tools to embrace a more proactive approach in their RIM strategies.

Historically, the process of searching for specific information in structured, unstructured, and semi-structured information sources has been time-consuming and laborious. Yet, the advent of AI-driven search and retrieval systems has revolutionized this facet of RIM. Powered by AI algorithms, these systems can comprehend user queries and extract pertinent information, even when located across multiple systems. Consequently, users can quickly and precisely locate the information they need, fostering greater productivity and more informed and improved decision-making.

Data governance and **compliance** are key aspects of RIM, particularly in industries subject to stringent regulations. In this context, AI presents substantial progress by providing intelligent solutions for effective data governance and compliance management. Utilizing sophisticated algorithms, AI can scrutinize data repositories, identify sensitive or confidential information, find anomalies, and guarantee adherence to regulatory mandates. This capability not only diminishes the risk of data breaches and noncompliance but also empowers organizations to preemptively tackle emerging issues.

Retention and disposition schedules, also known as **records retention schedules** (RRS), play a key role in meeting compliance standards, discarding out-of-date files, and curbing storage expenses. AI proves invaluable in automating the determination of optimal retention periods for various record types, considering factors like legal obligations and business significance. Additionally, AI algorithms excel at pinpointing records or file series that have reached their disposition date, automating the secure and timely disposal of data. This automated approach streamlines the disposition process, alleviating administrative burdens and elevating overall compliance effectiveness.

Key Points

- RIM plays a crucial role in AI Governance by maintaining control of records throughout their lifecycle and providing a structured framework for handling and safeguarding data.
- Well-defined RIM guidelines pertaining to data capture, protection, preservation, and defensible deletion are critical to maintaining accurate records, and a complete audit trail.
- The goal is to ensure that high-quality, current data is ingested into AI systems for training and testing AI models. This enhances the performance of AI systems.
- Efficient records management plays a crucial role in ensuring that data is appropriately tagged and discoverable when needed by the AI system.
- Through the classification of sensitive data, efficient records management enhances security by preventing AI technologies from accessing such data improperly.
- Key aspects of the role of RIM in AI Governance include: Data Lifecycle Management, Data Quality Assurance, Data Accessibility and Transparency, Security and Compliance, Risk Mitigation, and Ethical Considerations.

- The role of RIM in the lifecycle of an AI system is foundational and multifaceted, impacting each of the eight stages of the AI system lifecycle.
- By embedding RIM principles across the AI system lifecycle, organizations can mitigate risks, ensure compliance, and enhance the trustworthiness of AI applications.
- RIM helps classify data based on its sensitivity, importance, and regulatory requirements, guiding appropriate handling within AI systems.
- Data classification is a crucial component of AI Governance, ensuring that data is handled appropriately based on its sensitivity, importance, and regulatory requirements.
- A comprehensive data inventory is conducted to identify the types, sources, and locations of organizational data, categorizing it based on its nature, purpose, and potential impact.
- Sensitivity levels for different types of data are defined, considering factors such as personal information, financial data, intellectual property, and harm from unauthorized access.
- Guidelines for handling data based on its classification are developed, specifying security measures, access controls, and encryption requirements for each level of access.
- The exploration of automated tools for data classification, such as machine learning or rule-based systems, should be considered to ensure efficient and consistent classification.
- Legal counsel is engaged to conduct compliance checks related to data classification.
- User training programs are conducted to educate employees on data classification principles and procedures, ensuring awareness of their responsibilities.
- Integration of data classification mechanisms into AI systems is crucial, ensuring that AI models and applications are designed to handle data according to its classification.
- Periodic reviews and updates of data classification criteria should be made, adapting them to changing business needs, technological advancements, and regulatory updates.
- Integration of data classification into data retention policies is emphasized.
- Ethical considerations are brought into the classification process, evaluating the potential impact on individuals, and ensuring fair treatment.
- Roles and responsibilities for data stewardship are documented, defining the responsibilities of individuals or teams overseeing classified data.
- Access controls aligned with data classification levels are implemented, restricting access to classified data based on user roles and permissions, using the principle of least privilege.
- Implementing automated tools for retention management ensures consistency and efficiency.
- Applying data minimization practices when creating records, ensuring only necessary information is captured and retained, and regularly reviewing records to identify and remove unnecessary data aligns with privacy-conscious operations.
- Appointing data stewards responsible for providing input and overseeing record retention within business units in the organization enhances governance.
- Developing and documenting procedures for the secure disposal of records at the end of their retention period is a crucial aspect of governance.
- Conducting periodic risk assessments to identify risks associated with record retention and disposal and mitigating identified risks, ensures a proactive governance approach.
- Regularly reviewing and updating record retention policies ensures policies remain relevant and effective over time.
- Identifying critical phases in the information lifecycle relevant to AI systems is crucial.

- Clear criteria for transitioning data between lifecycle phases are defined, incorporating factors such as data relevance, accuracy, compliance requirements, and storage costs.
- Development of archiving and retention policies that align with regulatory requirements and business needs is essential.
- The integration of metadata management practices further enhances data discoverability and traceability.
- Procedures for data disposal, considering the end of the information lifecycle, are developed.
- Periodic assessments of data quality throughout the information lifecycle are conducted, implementing checks and validations to identify and rectify data inconsistencies.
- A comprehensive understanding of relevant legal and regulatory frameworks related to data privacy and security in the jurisdictions where the organization operates is essential.
- Implementing encryption mechanisms, especially for sensitive personal data, mitigates the risk of unauthorized access.
- Monitoring and assessing the data privacy practices of third-party vendors and data processors is a vital aspect of comprehensive governance.
- Establishing and maintaining records of processing (ROP) activities, documenting the lawful basis for data processing, data categories, and processing purposes, ensures transparency and accountability.
- Developing and regularly updating an incident response plan for addressing data breaches and privacy incidents is a crucial aspect of proactive governance.
- RIM—working with Data Governance teams and data stewards in business units—ensures that data used for AI training is accurately captured, stored, and maintained.
- RIM professionals collaborate with AI development teams to integrate records and information management practices seamlessly into the AI development lifecycle.
- The role of RIM is pivotal in creating comprehensive records of AI development decisions, acquisition of data sets, and deployment, which are called paradata.
- Organizations should document the model training and validation processes, capturing details about datasets used, hyperparameter tuning, and validation methodologies.
- Explanations for model outputs, especially in cases where interpretability is crucial, should be detailed in the documentation.
- Decision-making processes throughout the AI model lifecycle, from model selection to deployment and updates, should be recorded.
- Implementing version control for models and associated code is essential.
- RIM facilitates the creation of audit trails for AI systems, allowing for transparency and accountability in AI decision-making.
- Implementation of time-stamping mechanisms is essential to provide a chronological sequence of events.
- User interactions should be thoroughly documented, capturing input data, queries, and user adjustments, along with roles, permissions, and contextual information.
- Implementation of change management processes is crucial for maintaining data accuracy and reliability.
- AI proficiently classifies, categorizes, and organizes information, obviating the necessity for manual tagging and filing. This reduces time, cost, and errors.

Key Glossary Terms

Metadata: Data that provides information about other data managed within the AI lifecycle. It is essentially "data about data." This can include a wide range of details such as the source of data, structure, content, format, quality, and condition.

Paradata: The metadata or auxiliary data that captures the process and context of how primary data is collected, managed, and used throughout the AI lifecycle.

Records and Information Management (RIM): Extends beyond records management to include information such as email, electronic documents, and reports.

Records Management: The field of management responsible for the efficient and systematic control of the creation, receipt, maintenance, use, and disposition of records.

Notes

1 "International Organization for Standardization," *ISO 15489-1: 2001 Information and Documentation—Records Management. Part 1: General* (Geneva: ISO, 2001), section 3.15.

2 Ibid., section 3.16.

3 Bivek Minj, "The Strategic Role of Records & Information Management in the Age of AI," *ZLTech*, September 26, 2023, https://www.zlti.com/blog/the-strategic-role-of-records-information-management-in-the-age-of-ai/.

4 Ibid.

5 Legal and Regulatory Challenges in AI Governance

Christopher Surdak, J.D.

Many industries and organizations adopt and adapt to technologies with ferocious speed. Telecommunications, Entertainment, and Information Technology are clear examples. Others have a more tempered approach to technology adoption. Here, Aerospace, Automotive, Utilities, Transportation, and Healthcare represent a more measured approach to technology adoption. Then, there is a category of industries that consistently lag far behind others in bringing new tools to bear. While Financial Services or Governments rank high on this list, it is perhaps the Legal industry that is most resistant to the adoption of new technologies.

This actually makes sense and generally benefits society and the economy. A highly dynamic, change-friendly legal or regulatory field would make our lives far too unpredictable for normalcy. If contract law changed every year or two, no one would be able to make long-term contracts. If prior case law could be overturned easily, no one would be able to make reasonable risk assessments for litigation. If regulations could change overnight, without a great deal of forethought and public discourse, organizations would be frozen into inaction, unsure of how to make reasonable business decisions in light of regulatory uncertainty.

With artificial intelligence (AI), there appears to be a relaxation of this temperance of oversight. Whether it is due to the extreme expense involved in AI investment, the extreme potential risks associated with an out-of-control AI, or the apparent need to get ahead of this technology before it's too late, there is a global explosion in regulation and law intended to rein in AI's social and legal impacts before it's too late.

The attention to this need is not misplaced, if it is somewhat hyperbolic. Certainly billions, if not trillions, of dollars of economic value stand to be created by AI over the coming decade, warranting some degree of regulatory trepidation. Will AI end the world? Not likely. Will it substantially change the world? Most certainly. The challenge for AI Governance professionals will be to maintain an even-keeled, measured approach to meeting legal and regulatory requirements for AI, even while the hype and fear, surrounding the technology have yet to peak.

Both of the authors have direct experience in releasing, revising, and responding to governance regulations and legislation; hence, this feedback comes from a place of understanding the regulatory process from the inside. There is, and will continue to be, a torrent of AI guidance and regulation being implemented by jurisdictions all over the world. This book seeks to provide a comprehensive list at the time of writing, but the list will continue to grow unabated.

The challenge for governance and risk professionals will be to seek out what is common in all of the applicable regulations and develop generic responses to these commonalities. Then, identify all of the unique characteristics, requirements, or challenges of applicable regulations to then create customized policies, procedures, or approaches to meeting these one-offs. Finally, AI Governance requires that professionals maintain a keen interest in those topics that regulators find interesting so that future requirements may be anticipated.

Introduction

Legal and regulatory compliance is central to AI Governance. Ensuring that the outcomes produced by AI meet the legal and regulatory structures established by society, these requirements must be integral to how these systems are defined, architected, built, operated, and retired. In this way, we may maximize the social and economic value and minimize the unintended risks associated with AI adoption.

Perhaps the key functional area that ***Information Governance*** *(IG) impacts most is legal functions,* since legal requirements are paramount. Failure to meet them can literally put an organization out of business or land executives in prison. Privacy, security, records management, information technology (IT), risk management, and business management functions are important—very important—but the most significant aspect of all of these functions relates to legality and regulatory compliance.

Key legal processes include information and record retention policies, electronic discovery (**e-discovery**) readiness and associated business processes, the **legal hold notification** (LHN) process, and legally **defensible disposition** practices.

The Revised 2006 and 2015 Federal Rules of Civil Procedure Changed Everything

Since 1938, the Federal Rules of Civil Procedure (FRCP) "have governed the discovery of evidence in lawsuits and other civil cases."[1] In law, ***discovery*** *is an early phase of civil litigation where plaintiffs and defendants investigate and exchange evidence and testimony to better understand the facts of a case and to make early determinations of the strength of arguments on either side.* Each side must produce evidence requested by the opposition or show the court why it is unreasonable to produce the information. As the Supreme Court stated in an early case under the Federal Rules, "Mutual knowledge of all the relevant facts gathered by both parties is essential to proper litigation" (*Hickman v. Taylor*, 329 US 495, 507 [1947]).

The FRCP applies to US district courts, which are the trial courts of the federal court system. The district courts have jurisdiction (within limits set by Congress and the Constitution) to hear nearly all categories of federal cases, including civil and criminal matters.[2]

The FRCP were substantially amended in 2006, specifically to address issues pertaining to the preservation and discovery of electronic records (versus paper) in the litigation process; and again in 2015 to address issues of proportionality (that is, evidentiary requests—and their associated costs—must be in reasonable proportion relative to the value litigated in the case).[3] These changes were a long time coming, reflecting the lag between the state of technology and the courts' ability to catch up to the realities of electronically generated and stored information.

After years of applying traditional paper-based discovery rules to e-discovery, amendments to the FRCP in 2006 were made to accommodate the modern practice of discovery of **electronically stored information** (ESI). *ESI is any information that is created or stored in electronic format.*

The goal of the 2006 FRCP amendments was to recognize the importance of ESI and to respond to the increasingly prohibitive costs of document review and protection of privileged documents. These amendments reinforced the importance of IG policies, processes, and controls in the handling of ESI.[4] Organizations must produce requested ESI reasonably quickly, and failure to do so, or failure to do so within the prescribed time frame, can result in sanctions. This requirement dictates that organizations put in place IG policies and procedures to be able to produce ESI accurately and in a timely fashion.[5] Following **the e-Discovery Reference Model (EDRM)** helps organizations posture for litigation by embedding repeatable processes for placing legal holds on documents, records, and emails, preserving them properly, and producing them when needed later in the e-Discovery process.

The E-Discovery Reference Model is a visual planning tool created by EDRM.net to assist in identifying and clarifying the stages of the e-discovery process. The figure below is the graphic depiction with accompanying detail on the process steps.

Notice that the Information Governance Reference Model is the first step in the EDRM, providing emphasis on proactive IG to clean up information stores and allow for more granular and accurate legal holds:

Information Governance: Getting your electronic house in order to mitigate risk and expenses should e-discovery become an issue, from the initial creation of electronically stored information through its final disposition.

Identification: Locating potential sources of ESI and determining their scope, breadth, and depth.

Preservation: Ensuring that ESI is protected against inappropriate alteration or destruction.

Collection: Gathering ESI for further use in the e-discovery process (processing, review, etc.).

Processing: Reducing the volume of ESI and converting it, if necessary, to forms more suitable for review and analysis.

Review: Evaluating ESI for relevance and privilege.

Analysis: Evaluating ESI for content and context, including key patterns, topics, people, and discussions.

Production: Delivering ESI to others in appropriate forms and using appropriate delivery mechanisms.

Presentation: Displaying ESI before audiences (at depositions, hearings, trials, etc.), especially in native and near-native forms, to elicit further information, validate existing facts or positions, or persuade an audience[6]

The Electronic Discovery Reference Model can assist organizations in focusing and segmenting their efforts when planning e-discovery initiatives.

Leveraging the IG Reference Model and e-Discovery Reference Model provide a foundational structure for AI Governance.

All types of litigation are covered under the FRCP, and all types of e-documents—most especially email—are included, which can be created, accessed, or stored in a wide variety of methods and on a wide variety of devices beyond hard drives. The FRCP applies to ESI held on all types of storage and communications devices: thumb drives, CDs/DVDs, smartphones, tablets, personal digital assistants (PDAs), personal computers, servers, zip drives, floppy disks, backup tapes, and other storage media. ESI content can include information from email, reports, blogs, social media posts (e.g., Twitter posts), voicemails, wikis, websites (internal and external), word processing documents, and spreadsheets, and includes the **metadata** associated with the content itself, which provides descriptive information.[7]

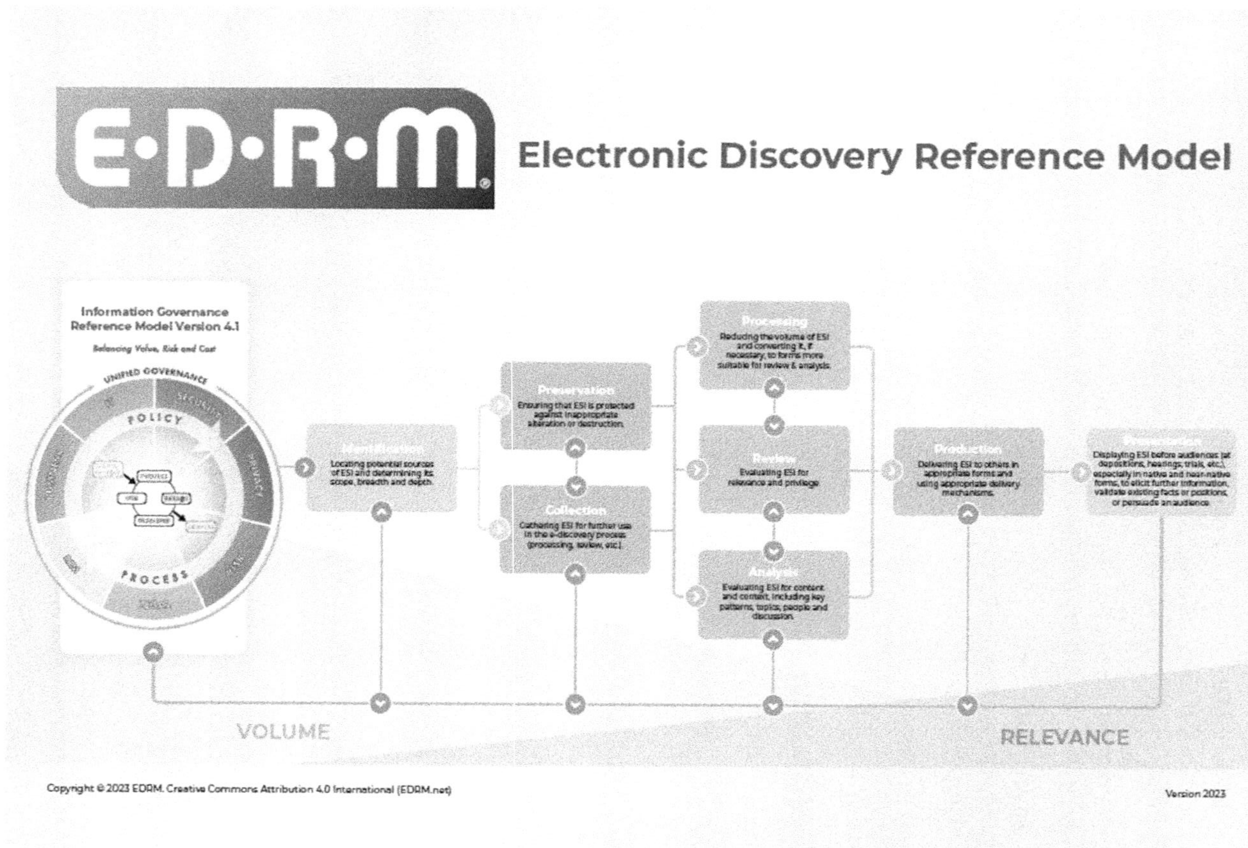

Figure 6.1 eDiscovery Governance Reference Model. EDRM.net; https://edrm.net/edrm-model/current/.

Under the FRCP amendments, corporations must proactively manage the e-discovery process to avoid sanctions, unfavorable rulings, and a loss of public trust. Corporations must be prepared for early discussions on e-discovery with all departments. Topics should include the form of production of ESI and the methods for preservation of information. Records management and IT departments must have made available all relevant ESI for attorney review.[8]

This new era of ESI preservation and production demands the need for cross-functional collaboration: records management, IT, and legal teams particularly need to work closely together. Legal teams, with the assistance and input of records management staff, must identify relevant ESI, and IT teams must be mindful of preserving and protecting the ESI to maintain its legal integrity and prove its authenticity.

Seven Basic Steps of the E-Discovery Process

In the e-discovery process, you must perform certain functions for identifying and preserving electronically stored information (ESI) and meet requirements regarding conditions such as relevance and privilege.[9] Typically, you follow this e-discovery process:

1. Create and retain ESI according to an enforceable electronic records retention policy and electronic records management (ERM) program. Enforce the policy and monitor compliance with it and the ERM program.
2. Identify the relevant ESI, preserve any so it cannot be altered or destroyed, and collect all ESI for further review.
3. Process and filter the ESI to remove the excess and duplicates. You reduce costs by reducing the volume of ESI that moves to the next stage in the e-discovery process.
4. Review and analyze the filtered ESI for privilege because privileged ESI is not discoverable unless some exception kicks in.
5. Produce the remaining ESI, after filtering out what is irrelevant, duplicated, or privileged. Producing ESI in native format is common.
6. Clawback [find and return] the ESI that you disclosed to the opposing party that you should have filtered out, but did not. Clawback is not unusual, but you have to work at getting clawback approved, and the court may deny it.
7. Present at trial if your case hasn't settled. Judges have little to no patience with lawyers who appear before them not understanding e-discovery and the ESI of their clients or the opposing side.

The Role of Legal Professionals in AI

Legal professionals identify the compliance landscape upon which AI solutions must operate. This includes:

Stakeholders: What parties hold an interest in the inputs, operations, and outputs of the system?

Assets: What items of value are consumed, transformed, or created by the operation of the system?

Title: What are the ownership interests in each of these assets? Who holds title, who obtains a license, and how are these interests defined and maintained?

Risks: Legal professionals are uniquely positioned to identify and mitigate risks that originate from legislation, regulation, and legal precedent.

Ensuring that legal compliance is obtained, retained, and protected throughout an organization requires coordination across all contributing parties. Legal professionals provide their deep expertise to this larger organizational goal.

AI Lifecycle and the Role of Legal

The AI lifecycle typically involves the following eight general steps. Each of these steps is crucial to developing an effective and reliable AI solution. It is also important to note that the AI lifecycle is iterative. Data Privacy provides the guardrails for AI adhering to privacy and data protection laws.

1. Problem Definition

Problem definition is the initial stage in the AI lifecycle where the specific problem that the AI system will address is identified and defined. This involves understanding the context of the problem, the stakeholders involved, and the desired outcomes.

From a legal perspective, problem definition involves:

- **Legal Impact Assessment (PIA):** Conducting an LIA to understand how the proposed AI system could be impacted by laws and regulations affecting its operations, the types of personal data that will be processed, the purposes for which it will be used, and the potential privacy risks. A related set of assessments specific to AI, sometimes **termed AI Impact Assessments** (AIIAs) or **Algorithmic Impact Assessments** (AIAs), is increasingly deployed to assess the potential risks of automated decision-making systems.
- **Jurisdictions:** Determining the jurisdictions in which the AI is maintained, where training data is sourced, and where users may reside, hold citizenship, or from which they are obtaining access. The applicability of jurisdictional rules is often context-dependent, hence defining the use cases ahead of time will ensure proper consideration of what laws and regulations apply. Legal should seek to apply the broadest possible jurisdictional definition to minimize unintended risks.
- **Interest Parties:** Determine via use cases, personas, and other agile development methods what actors may engage with the AI, in what roles, and under what conditions. Note that an "actor" may be any legal entity, including but not limited to persons, corporations, governments, and so on. As legal entities, each of these participants may have legal rights and responsibilities associated with their interaction with the AI and hence must be included in a comprehensive legal analysis.
- **Legal Rights:** For each actor, in each jurisdiction, in each use case, the legal rights must be considered, to ensure that the AI does not violate these rights.
- **Legal Responsibilities (Duty):** For each actor, in each jurisdiction, in each use case, the legal responsibilities or duties must be considered, to ensure that the AI does meet these legal obligations and does not put the organization at legal risk.
- **Risk Assessment:** A legal risk assessment should be generated that characterizes the likelihood of risk and potential magnitude of risk associated with the use cases provided. This should guide the business value assessment in determining if the AI is a good investment.

2. Data Collection

Data collection is the process of gathering and measuring information on variables of interest, in an established systematic fashion that enables one to answer stated research questions, test hypotheses, and evaluate outcomes. In the context of AI, data collection involves gathering the necessary data that will be used to train and test the AI model.

From a legal perspective, data collection involves:

1. **Data Types:** Identifying the data types that will be *used in and generated by* the AI's operations.
2. **Data Sources:** Identifying the sources from which the data will be procured.
3. **Data Owners:** Identifying the legal owners of data sources, which is often distinct from the data source. Note that owners may vary by jurisdiction.
4. **Data Access:** Obtaining rights to use data owned by others, by consent, title, or license. Note, the type of access may vary from jurisdiction to jurisdiction for a given source or owner.

3. Data Preparation

Data preparation is *the process of cleaning and transforming raw data prior to processing and analysis.* It is often considered one of the most time-consuming aspects of the AI lifecycle, but it's crucial for the success of AI models. In the context of AI, data preparation involves dealing with missing or inconsistent data, removing duplicates, and converting data into a format that can be used by AI models.

From a legal perspective, data preparation involves:

1. **Source Verification:** Sources should be authenticated to ensure that only data to which you have legal access is accepted. When collecting data from users, users should be authenticated so that chain of custody may be confirmed.
2. **Data Verification:** Data from authenticated sources should further be confirmed as authentic. Verified sources may provide data other than what was expected, authorized, or desired. Hence, it is important to ensure that what was received was what was expected and intended.
3. **Data Validity:** Data proven to be the type expected from the source should further be confirmed to be valid. Checks should be put in place to ensure validity on an ongoing basis.
4. **Data Security:** Throughout the data preparation process, robust security measures should be in place to protect the data from unauthorized access, use, disclosure, alteration, and/or destruction.

4. Model Selection and Training

Model selection and training is a crucial step in the AI lifecycle. It involves choosing the most appropriate machine learning algorithm for the problem at hand and training it on the prepared data to create an AI model. The choice of model and the quality of training can significantly impact the performance of the AI system.

From a legal considerations perspective, model selection and training involve:

1. **Intellectual Property Rights:** When selecting a model, it's important to consider the intellectual property (IP) rights associated with it. This includes ensuring that the use of the model does not infringe on the IP rights of others and understanding the licensing terms if the model is not developed in-house.
2. **Compliance with Anti-Discrimination Laws:** The selected AI model must not result in discriminatory outcomes. This is particularly important in applications like hiring, lending, and criminal justice. Models must be evaluated to ensure they do not inadvertently discriminate based on race, gender, age, or other protected characteristics.
3. **Transparency and Explainability:** Some jurisdictions can have significant impact and need to be understandable by humans. This is especially critical in sectors like healthcare, finance, and legal, where decisions need to be understandable by humans. Models that are inherently more interpretable may be favored to comply with these requirements.
4. **Data Privacy Compliance:** The model must be compatible with data privacy laws relevant to the application. For instance, if the model requires extensive personal data, it must align with laws like GDPR or CCPA, ensuring data minimization, consent, and the right to erasure.
5. **Security Considerations:** The model should be secure and resilient against attacks, such as adversarial attacks, which can manipulate the model's output. Ensuring security is not just a technical necessity but also a legal one, as a compromised AI system can have legal repercussions.
6. **Bias and Fairness Assessment:** The model should be assessed for bias. Even unintentional bias can lead to legal challenges, especially if the AI system's output affects individuals' rights or opportunities. It's important to conduct thorough testing and validation to identify and mitigate biases.
7. **Record-keeping and Documentation:** Maintaining detailed documentation of the model selection process, including why a particular model was chosen, the data used for training and testing, and the measures taken to ensure compliance with legal requirements, is essential. This documentation can be crucial for regulatory compliance and in case of legal scrutiny.
8. **Accessibility:** Ensuring the AI system is accessible to all users, including those with disabilities, might be a legal requirement in some jurisdictions. This includes considering the model's interface and output formats.
9. **International Regulations:** If the AI system is intended for use in multiple countries, the model must comply with international laws and regulations. Different countries may have different requirements regarding AI and data protection.
10. **Ethical Considerations:** While not strictly legal, ethical considerations are closely intertwined with legal ones. The chosen model should align with ethical AI principles, which can help preempt legal issues and maintain public trust.

5. Model Evaluation

Model evaluation is the process of assessing the performance of a trained AI model. It involves using various metrics to measure how well the model's predictions align with the actual outcomes. This step is crucial as it helps to ensure that the AI model is reliable, accurate, and effective.

From a legal consideration perspective, model evaluation involves:

1. **Predictability Metrics:** Evaluation metrics should be defined and should confirm predictable outcomes. This strengthens the argument that the legal duty of due diligence has been met.
2. **Rights Protections:** Outputs should reflect any constraints that may exist from the legal access provided by data sources and users. For example, licensed training data should not be replicable as an output unless specifically allowed by the license agreement.
3. **Transparency:** The results produced by the AI should be explainable and understandable by individuals with the same level of comprehension as users. This ensures that interaction with the AI is fair and the results are transparent to users.
4. **Bias and Fairness Assessment:** The evaluation process should also assess whether the model could lead to biased or unfair outcomes. This includes checking for potential biases in the model's predictions that could disadvantage certain groups of individuals. Care should be taken to identify bias and/or unfairness that shows up as a "disparate impact" on individual groups—such as the well-documented tendency of some facial recognition systems to misidentify people with darker skin—but which is not clear "on the face" of the system.

6. Model Deployment

Model deployment is the process of integrating a trained AI model into an existing production environment where it can provide predictions in real time. It is the stage where the model starts providing practical value by solving the problem it was designed to address.

From a legal consideration perspective, model deployment involves:

1. **Compliance with Relevant Laws and Regulations:** Ensure that the AI system complies with all relevant laws and regulations, which can vary depending on the industry and region. This includes data protection laws (like GDPR), consumer protection laws, sector-specific regulations (like healthcare or financial services), and international laws if the AI is used across borders.
2. **Data Privacy and Security:** Continuous adherence to data privacy regulations is crucial. This involves protecting user data from unauthorized access and breaches, and ensuring that data handling remains compliant with laws such as GDPR or CCPA. It's also important to regularly update security protocols to safeguard against new threats.
3. **Ongoing Monitoring for Bias and Fairness:** Regularly monitor the AI system for biases and ensure decisions are fair and non-discriminatory. This is particularly important in applications affecting people's lives, such as employment, credit scoring, or law enforcement. Failing to address bias can lead to legal challenges and reputational damage.
4. **Transparency and Explainability:** Depending on the jurisdiction and application, there might be legal requirements for transparency and explainability of AI decisions, especially in critical areas like healthcare, criminal justice, and finance. Users should be able to understand how and why a decision was made.
5. **Accountability and Liability:** Establish clear lines of accountability for the AI system's decisions. In case of errors or harmful outcomes, it should be clear who is responsible—whether it's the AI developer, the deploying organization, or another party. Understanding and planning for potential liabilities is crucial.

6. **Intellectual Property (IP) Considerations:** Ensure ongoing compliance with IP laws, including respecting the IP rights of others and understanding the implications of any open-source components used in the AI system.
7. **Consumer Protection Laws:** Adhere to consumer protection laws, which may require that AI systems do not mislead or harm consumers. This is especially important for AI systems involved in advertising, recommendation systems, or any form of consumer interaction.
8. **Accessibility Requirements:** Ensure that the AI system is accessible to all users, those with disabilities, to comply with relevant accessibility laws.
9. **Ethical Considerations:** Ethical deployment of AI, while not always legally mandated, is essential for public trust and social acceptance. This includes respecting user autonomy, preventing harm, and ensuring the AI system is used for socially beneficial purposes.
10. **Record-Keeping and Documentation:** Maintain thorough documentation of the AI system's performance, decisions made by the AI, and any issues or updates. This can be important for regulatory compliance and in case of legal disputes.
11. **Regular Audits and Compliance Checks:** Conduct regular audits to ensure the AI system remains compliant with all legal requirements, ethical standards, and internal policies. This includes checking for changes in laws and regulations that might affect the AI system's use.

7. Monitoring and Maintenance

Monitoring and maintenance are the stage in the AI lifecycle where the deployed model is continuously observed and updated as needed to ensure its performance remains optimal. This involves tracking the model's performance metrics, identifying and addressing any issues or changes in the underlying data, and retraining the model with new data if necessary.

From a legal perspective, monitoring and maintenance involve:

1. **Continuous Legal Impact Assessment:** *Regularly reassess the LIA* to account for any changes in the model or the data it uses.
2. **Compliance Audits**: Conduct regular audits *to ensure the model continues to comply with laws and regulations.*
3. **Anomaly Detection**: Implement anomaly detection mechanisms *to identify any unauthorized access* or use of the data.
4. **Compliance Training**: Provide *ongoing training* to all individuals who interact with the model to ensure *they understand and respect the legal issues related to its ongoing use.*

8. Retirement

Retirement is the final stage in the AI lifecycle, where an AI model is decommissioned and taken out of service. This could be due to various reasons, such as the model becoming obsolete, the problem it was designed to solve no longer existing, or a more efficient solution being developed.

From a legal consideration perspective, retirement involves:

1. **Decommissioning:** Once an AI model is retired, it is important to ensure that all data used by the model is securely deleted in accordance with data protection laws. This includes operational data, source data, metadata, and compliance reporting associated with the system's operational life.

2. **Preservation:** In some cases, records may need to be preserved for future reference or for compliance with certain regulations. It is crucial to ensure that these records are stored securely and continue to meet the operators' legal obligations.
3. **Audit Trails:** Maintain comprehensive audit trails documenting the retirement process. This includes when and why the model was retired, what data was deleted or preserved, and any other actions taken during retirement.
4. **Communication:** Notify relevant stakeholders, including individuals whose data was used by the model, generated by the model, or had a commercial or legal interest in the model about the retirement of the model and how their interest was handled. Pay particular attention to any jurisdictional requirements, such as notifying individuals of their proprietary rights.

The Responsibilities of the Legal Function in AI Systems Development

The Legal department plays a crucial role in overseeing AI systems development projects from an AI Governance perspective. The responsibilities of the Legal department, in summary, in this context include:

1. **Compliance with Laws and Regulations**

   Data Protection and Privacy Laws: Ensure that AI systems adhere to data protection and privacy regulations such as GDPR, HIPAA, or other applicable laws.

   Anti-discrimination Laws: Verify that AI models do not result in discriminatory outcomes, violating laws like the Fair Housing Act or Equal Credit Opportunity Act.

2. **Intellectual Property (IP) Management**

   Patent and Copyright Issues: Address and manage potential patent and copyright challenges associated with AI algorithms, ensuring that the organization's AI development doesn't infringe on existing patents or violate copyrights.

3. **Contractual Agreements**

   Vendor Agreements: Review and negotiate contracts with AI vendors to ensure compliance with legal standards, including data security, confidentiality, and performance obligations.

   User Agreements: Draft and review terms of service and user agreements to cover issues such as data ownership, liability, and user consent.

4. **Ethical and Responsible AI**

   Ethical Guidelines: Develop and enforce ethical guidelines for AI development to ensure responsible use and prevent the creation of AI systems that could be used unethically.

   Transparency and Explainability: Advise on transparency requirements to make AI systems more explainable and understandable, especially in cases where the decisions of AI models may have legal implications.

5. **Risk Management**

   Risk Assessment: Conduct risk assessments related to legal and regulatory compliance, potential liabilities, and reputational risks associated with AI projects.

   Liability Mitigation: Develop strategies to mitigate legal liabilities arising from AI system failures or unintended consequences.

6. **Data Governance**

   Data Use and Access Policies: Establish policies regarding the collection, use, and access to data, ensuring that AI projects comply with internal and external data governance standards.

   Data Security and Breach Response: Oversee legal aspects of data security, including the development of protocols for responding to data breaches involving AI systems.

7. **Audit and Monitoring**

   Audit Trails: Ensure that AI systems maintain accurate and comprehensive audit trails to facilitate accountability and compliance monitoring.

   Monitoring for Bias and Fairness: Implement mechanisms to monitor AI models for biases and fairness issues, with a plan for addressing and rectifying such issues.

8. **Regulatory Engagement**

   Communication with Regulatory Bodies: Engage with relevant regulatory authorities to stay informed about evolving regulations and contribute to the development of industry standards for AI Governance.

9. **Training and Awareness**

   Employee Training: Provide legal training and awareness programs for employees involved in AI development to ensure they are well-informed about legal requirements and risks.

10. **Incident Response Planning**

    Legal Response Protocols: Develop and implement legal response protocols for potential incidents involving AI, including breaches, biases, or other legal challenges.

By actively addressing these responsibilities, the Legal department helps organizations navigate the complex landscape of AI Governance, ensuring legal compliance, ethical use, and risk mitigation throughout the AI development lifecycle.

More Detail on the Role of Legal in AI Systems

AI systems development projects require compliance with laws and regulations, particularly focusing on Data Protection and Privacy Laws, as well as Anti-discrimination Laws.

In detail, these are the responsibilities of the Legal department in AI systems development:

Compliance with Data Protection and Privacy Laws

a. **Data Collection and Processing**

   Purpose Limitation: Ensure that AI systems only collect and process personal data for specified, explicit, and legitimate purposes, in accordance with the principles of data minimization.

   Consent Management: Develop protocols to obtain valid consent when necessary and ensure that the organization has clear records of consent for data processing activities associated with AI.

b. **Data Storage and Security**

   Data Security Measures: Oversee the implementation of robust security measures to protect the personal data processed by AI systems, considering encryption, access controls, and secure data storage practices.

Data Transfer Considerations: Address legal implications related to the cross-border transfer of data, ensuring compliance with applicable regulations and frameworks.

c. **Transparency and Accountability**

Privacy Policies: Collaborate in drafting and updating privacy policies that clearly communicate to users how their data will be processed by AI systems, including information about algorithms and decision-making processes.

Data Protection Impact Assessments (DPIAs): Work on conducting DPIAs for AI projects, assessing and mitigating potential risks to individuals' privacy, as required by regulations like GDPR.

d. **Data Subject Rights**

Access and Rectification: Establish mechanisms for data subjects to exercise their rights to access and rectify their personal data processed by AI systems.

Right to be Forgotten: Develop procedures for handling requests from individuals to erase their personal data, where applicable under relevant regulations.

Compliance with Anti-discrimination Laws

a. **Bias and Fairness Assessment**

Algorithmic Bias Analysis: Implement processes to assess and address biases within AI models to prevent discriminatory outcomes.

Fairness Metrics: Work on defining and monitoring fairness metrics to ensure that AI systems do not disproportionately impact certain groups, especially in contexts like hiring, lending, or housing.

b. **Model Explainability and Accountability**

Interpretable Models: Encourage the use of interpretable and explainable AI models to facilitate scrutiny and understanding of the decision-making process.

Accountability Frameworks: Develop frameworks for holding the organization accountable for discriminatory outcomes, ensuring transparency in how decisions are made by AI systems.

c. **Legal Risk Mitigation**

Risk Assessments: Conduct risk assessments to identify potential legal liabilities arising from discriminatory outcomes of AI systems.

Continuous Monitoring: Establish processes for continuous monitoring of AI systems to detect and address discriminatory patterns that may emerge over time.

d. **Compliance Documentation**

Documentation of Fair Practices: Maintain comprehensive documentation demonstrating the organization's commitment to fair and non-discriminatory AI practices.

Audit Trail: Keep detailed records and audit trails that can be used to demonstrate compliance with anti-discrimination laws in the event of legal scrutiny.

By actively addressing these aspects, the Legal department helps ensure that AI systems not only comply with data protection and privacy laws but also adhere to anti-discrimination laws, fostering responsible and ethical AI development within the framework of legal requirements.

Intellectual Property (IP) Management

a. **Patent Analysis and Clearance**

Prior Art Searches: Conduct thorough prior art searches to identify existing patents that may be relevant to the AI algorithms being developed.

Freedom-to-Operate (FTO) Analysis: Perform Freedom-to-Operate analysis to assess whether the organization's AI development would potentially infringe on existing patents.

b. **Patent Filing and Protection**

Patent Filings: Work closely with the AI development teams to identify innovative aspects of AI algorithms and strategize on filing patent applications to protect novel inventions.

Patent Portfolio Management: Develop and maintain a strategic patent portfolio to safeguard the organization's AI innovations and provide a competitive advantage.

c. **Copyright Compliance**

Code and Software Review: Scrutinize AI code and software components to ensure compliance with copyright laws, including proper licensing and adherence to open-source guidelines.

Authorship and Ownership: Clarify and document authorship and ownership of AI code and algorithms to avoid disputes related to copyright claims.

d. **Collaboration Agreements**

Collaborative Research Agreements: Negotiate and draft collaborative research agreements, clearly outlining intellectual property ownership, rights, and responsibilities when AI development involves collaborations with external entities.

Employee and Contractor Agreements: Ensure that employment contracts and agreements with contractors include provisions addressing the ownership and transfer of intellectual property rights related to AI creations.

e. **Licensing and Technology Transfer**

Licensing Strategies: Develop strategies for licensing AI technologies to third parties, if applicable, and negotiate licensing agreements that protect the organization's interests.

Technology Transfer Policies: Establish policies for internal technology transfers, defining how AI innovations developed within the organization can be shared among different business units or subsidiaries.

f. **IP Litigation Management**

Infringement Monitoring: Monitor the industry for potential infringements on the organization's AI-related patents and copyrights.

Enforcement Actions: Take legal action against entities infringing on the organization's intellectual property rights when necessary, to protect the AI innovations developed by the organization.

g. **Trade Secret Protection**

Trade Secret Policies: Develop and implement policies to protect trade secrets associated with AI algorithms, ensuring that sensitive information remains confidential and secure.

Employee Training: Provide training to employees on the importance of safeguarding trade secrets and confidential information related to AI development.

h. **Due Diligence for Mergers and Acquisitions**

IP Due Diligence: Conduct thorough intellectual property due diligence when the organization is involved in mergers, acquisitions, or partnerships, to assess the value and risks associated with the AI-related IP assets.

By addressing these responsibilities, the Legal department contributes to a comprehensive IP management strategy, ensuring that the organization's AI development is legally protected, and potential risks related to patent and copyright issues are proactively identified and managed.

Contractual Agreements

a. **Vendor Agreements**

i. Legal Compliance

Data Protection and Privacy: Ensure that vendor agreements comply with data protection and privacy laws, specifying how the vendor will handle and protect sensitive information, aligning with regulations such as GDPR or other applicable laws.

Intellectual Property: Clearly define the ownership and licensing terms of any intellectual property exchanged between the organization and the vendor, including any AI algorithms, code, or technology.

ii. Data Security

Security Standards: Establish contractual obligations for vendors to adhere to specific data security standards, including encryption, access controls, and incident response protocols.

Audit Rights: Include provisions granting the organization the right to audit the vendor's security measures to ensure ongoing compliance.

iii. Confidentiality and Non-Disclosure

Confidentiality Obligations: Define the scope of confidentiality obligations, specifying how confidential information, including AI-related innovations, will be handled and protected.

Non-Disclosure Agreements (NDAs): If necessary, negotiate and draft NDAs to provide additional legal protection for sensitive information shared with vendors.

iv. Performance Obligations

Service-Level Agreements (SLAs): Define clear performance metrics and service level agreements to ensure that the vendor meets specified standards for AI system development, maintenance, and support.

Remedies for Noncompliance: Establish remedies and penalties for noncompliance with contractual obligations, providing legal recourse in case of performance issues.

v. Indemnification and Liability

Indemnification Clauses: Negotiate indemnification clauses to protect the organization from potential legal and financial liabilities arising from the vendor's actions, such as data breaches or intellectual property infringement.

Limitation of Liability: Determine and negotiate the limitations of liability, setting caps on the vendor's financial responsibility for certain types of breaches or damages.

b. User Agreements

i. Data Ownership and Use

Data Ownership: Clearly define the ownership of data generated or processed by AI systems, outlining whether the organization or users retain ownership rights.

Data Use Restrictions: Specify how user data will be used, ensuring alignment with privacy policies and legal requirements.

ii. Liability and Risk Allocation

Limitation of Liability: Clearly articulate the limits of the organization's liability for issues such as system errors, data loss, or disruptions in service.

Assumption of Risk: Communicate to users any inherent risks associated with AI systems and clarify the extent to which users assume these risks.

iii. Consent and User Rights

Informed Consent: Draft provisions related to informed consent, particularly if the AI system involves sensitive data processing or decision-making that may impact users.

User Rights: Clearly outline the rights users have regarding their data, including access, rectification, and deletion rights in compliance with data protection laws.

iv. Dispute Resolution

Arbitration or Mediation Clauses: Include provisions for alternative dispute resolution mechanisms, such as arbitration or mediation, to efficiently handle legal disputes without resorting to lengthy court proceedings.

v. Regular Review and Updates

Periodic Review: Establish processes for periodic review and updates of user agreements to ensure they remain in compliance with evolving legal standards and industry best practices.

By actively managing Vendor Agreements and User Agreements, the Legal department helps mitigate legal risks, protects the organization's interests, and ensures that contractual relationships related to AI systems are governed by clear and enforceable terms.

Ethical and Responsible AI

a. Ethical Guidelines

i. Development and Review

Collaboration with Stakeholders: Collaborate with AI development teams, ethicists, and relevant stakeholders to develop comprehensive and context-specific ethical guidelines for AI development.

Regular Review: Periodically review and update ethical guidelines to ensure they align with evolving ethical standards, legal requirements, and societal expectations.

ii. Bias Mitigation

Bias Assessment Protocols: Implement procedures to assess and mitigate biases in AI algorithms during development to prevent discriminatory outcomes.

Fairness and Equity: Integrate considerations for fairness and equity into ethical guidelines, emphasizing the importance of avoiding disparate impacts on different demographic groups.

iii. Privacy Protection

Privacy by Design: Advocate for privacy-by-design principles, ensuring that ethical guidelines include measures to protect user privacy throughout the AI development lifecycle.

User Consent: Address the ethical implications of data use and processing, emphasizing the importance of obtaining informed and voluntary consent from users.

iv. Human Rights and Dignity:

Respect for Human Rights: Embed principles of respect for human rights and dignity within ethical guidelines, emphasizing the need to avoid AI applications that could violate fundamental rights.

Human-Centric Approach: Encourage a human-centered approach, ensuring that AI systems are developed to enhance human well-being and not compromise fundamental human values.

v. Stakeholder Inclusivity:

Engagement with Diverse Perspectives: Promote inclusivity by involving diverse stakeholders, including legal experts, ethicists, users, and affected communities, in the development and review of ethical guidelines.

Community Impact Assessment: Consider the potential impact of AI systems on communities and engage in community impact assessments to understand and address any ethical concerns.

b. Transparency and Explainability

i. Legal Compliance

Regulatory Guidance: Stay informed about regulatory requirements related to transparency and explainability in AI, providing legal guidance to ensure compliance with evolving standards.

Industry Standards: Advocate for the adoption of industry best practices in transparency and explainability, aligning with guidelines and standards set by relevant regulatory bodies.

ii. Decision-Making Processes

Explainability Requirements: Work with AI developers to define and implement mechanisms for explaining the decision-making processes of AI models, especially in cases where legal implications may arise.

User Understanding: Ensure that AI systems are designed to provide meaningful information to users about how decisions are made, fostering transparency and user understanding.

iii. Legal Implications

Liability Considerations: Advise on legal implications related to transparency, including considerations for potential liability in cases where a lack of transparency may result in harm or legal challenges.

Documentation and Records: Ensure that AI development processes include documentation and records that support the transparency and explainability of AI systems, which may be crucial in legal contexts.

iv. Public Communication

Public Disclosures: Work on legal aspects of public disclosures regarding the transparency of AI systems, ensuring that organizations communicate transparently about their AI technologies and practices.

Crisis Communication Protocols: Develop protocols for addressing public concerns related to transparency, especially during instances of controversy or public scrutiny.

v. Continuous Improvement

Feedback Mechanisms: Establish feedback mechanisms for ongoing improvement of transparency and explainability practices, integrating lessons learned from real-world applications and user interactions.

Ethical Audits: Explore the implementation of ethical audits or assessments to evaluate the organization's adherence to transparency and explainability commitments.

By focusing on these responsibilities, the Legal department contributes to the development of AI systems that not only comply with ethical standards but also meet transparency and explainability requirements, aligning with legal expectations and societal norms. This proactive approach helps mitigate legal risks and fosters trust in the responsible use of AI technologies.

Risk Management

a. Risk Assessment

i. Legal and Regulatory Compliance

Legal Landscape Analysis: Conduct a thorough analysis of the legal and regulatory landscape applicable to AI development, identifying potential compliance risks and ensuring adherence to relevant laws and regulations.

Regular Compliance Audits: Implement regular compliance audits to monitor changes in legal requirements and assess the organization's ongoing compliance with evolving standards.

ii. Data Protection and Privacy

Data Governance Review: Assess the organization's data governance practices, ensuring that AI projects comply with internal policies and external data protection and privacy laws.

Cross-Border Data Transfer: Evaluate the legal implications of cross-border data transfers associated with AI systems, addressing potential risks related to data sovereignty and jurisdictional differences.

iii. Intellectual Property Risks

IP Due Diligence: Conduct due diligence to identify and mitigate intellectual property risks, ensuring that AI development doesn't infringe on existing patents or violate copyrights.

Freedom-to-Operate Analysis: Assess the freedom to operate in the intellectual property landscape, identifying potential obstacles and risks associated with third-party patents.

iv. Ethical and Bias Risks

Ethical Risk Assessment: Evaluate ethical risks associated with AI algorithms, ensuring that AI systems are developed and used responsibly to avoid unintended consequences and ethical controversies.

Bias and Fairness Audits: Implement audits to assess and mitigate biases in AI models, reducing the risk of discriminatory outcomes.

v. Security and Cybersecurity

Security Vulnerability Assessments: Collaborate with cybersecurity experts to conduct security vulnerability assessments, identifying and addressing potential weaknesses in AI systems.

Incident Response Planning: Develop and refine incident response plans to address legal and reputational risks in the event of security breaches or cyberattacks targeting AI systems.

vi. Third-Party Relationships

Vendor Risk Management: Assess and manage risks associated with third-party vendors, ensuring that vendor agreements include provisions for data security, legal compliance, and performance obligations.

Contractual Protections: Negotiate contracts with vendors that include indemnification clauses and other provisions to protect the organization from potential risks associated with third-party relationships.

b. Liability Mitigation

i. Contractual Protections

Limitation of Liability: Negotiate and implement contractual clauses that define and limit the organization's liability in case of AI system failures, ensuring that the terms are fair and reasonable.

Indemnification Agreements: Establish indemnification agreements with vendors, collaborators, and other stakeholders to transfer or share potential liabilities arising from AI development.

ii. Insurance Strategies

Liability Insurance: Collaborate with insurance experts to assess the need for and secure liability insurance coverage specific to AI-related risks.

Policy Reviews: Regularly review and update insurance policies to ensure they align with the evolving risks and legal landscape associated with AI systems.

iii. Compliance Programs

Training Programs: Develop and implement training programs for AI developers, legal teams, and other stakeholders to enhance awareness of legal risks and compliance requirements.

Monitoring and Enforcement: Establish mechanisms for monitoring and enforcing compliance with internal policies and external regulations, ensuring a proactive approach to risk mitigation.

iv. Crisis Management

Crisis Response Plans: Develop and test crisis response plans to address legal and reputational fallout in the event of AI system failures or adverse consequences.

Communication Strategies: Work on strategies for transparent and effective communication with stakeholders, regulators, and the public during crisis situations.

v. Continuous Improvement

Post-Implementation Reviews: Conduct post-implementation reviews of AI projects to identify lessons learned, areas for improvement, and opportunities to enhance risk management strategies.

Adaptation to Emerging Risks: Stay abreast of emerging risks in the AI landscape, adapting risk management strategies to address new challenges and technologies.

By actively engaging in risk assessment and liability mitigation strategies, the Legal department plays a pivotal role in ensuring that AI systems are developed, implemented, and maintained in a manner that minimizes legal and reputational risks, fostering responsible and sustainable AI Governance.

Data Governance

a. Data Use and Access Policies:

i. Policy Development

Collaboration with Stakeholders: Work closely with data scientists, AI developers, and relevant stakeholders to develop comprehensive data use and access policies that align with the organization's AI Governance framework.

Legal Compliance: Ensure that data use policies comply with applicable laws and regulations, with a focus on data protection and privacy requirements.

ii. Purpose Limitation

Define Data Purposes: Clearly define the purposes for which data will be collected and used in the context of AI projects, ensuring adherence to the principle of purpose limitation.

Review and Approval Processes: Establish review and approval processes for data use cases, ensuring that proposed uses align with organizational goals and ethical considerations.

iii. User Consent and Transparency

Consent Mechanisms: Develop mechanisms for obtaining informed and valid consent from individuals whose data is used in AI projects, especially when such data involves personally identifiable information (PII).

Transparency Requirements: Include provisions in data use policies that emphasize transparency, ensuring that individuals are aware of how their data will be used in AI systems.

iv. Data Ownership and Rights

Ownership Clarification: Clearly articulate the ownership of data collected or generated by AI systems, addressing whether the organization, users, or other parties retain ownership rights.

User Rights Framework: Establish a framework for respecting and upholding the rights of individuals concerning their data, including the right to access, rectify, and delete personal information.

v. Data Sharing Agreements

Third-Party Data Sharing: If applicable, negotiate and draft data sharing agreements with third parties, ensuring that the terms align with data use policies and legal requirements.

Security and Confidentiality Clauses: Include clauses in data sharing agreements that address data security, confidentiality, and restrictions on further data sharing.

b. Data Security and Breach Response

i. Legal Compliance

Security Standards Adherence: Ensure that AI systems adhere to industry best practices and legal requirements related to data security, including encryption, access controls, and other protective measures.

Regulatory Compliance: Stay informed about evolving data security regulations and incorporate necessary measures to comply with standards such as GDPR, HIPAA, or other relevant laws.

ii. Protocols for Data Breach Response

Incident Response Plans: Collaborate with IT and cybersecurity teams to develop robust incident response plans specifically tailored for data breaches involving AI systems.

Legal Compliance in Breach Response: Ensure that breach response protocols comply with legal requirements, including timely notifications to affected individuals, regulatory bodies, and other stakeholders.

iii. Legal Analysis in Breach Incidents

Legal Implications Assessment: Conduct legal assessments of data breaches to determine potential liabilities, regulatory fines, and legal actions that may arise.

Communication Strategy: Work on legal aspects of communication strategies during and after a data breach, minimizing legal risks and maintaining transparency where necessary.

iv. Privacy by Design and Default

Embedding Privacy Measures: Advocate for the integration of privacy-by-design and default principles in AI system development, ensuring that data security measures are considered from the outset.

Continuous Monitoring: Implement ongoing monitoring of data security measures to identify and address potential vulnerabilities or risks before they escalate into breaches.

v. Compliance Documentation

Record-Keeping: Ensure that comprehensive records are maintained regarding data security measures, breach response activities, and any legal assessments conducted in the aftermath of a data breach.

Audit Trail: Establish and maintain an audit trail that documents security measures, data access activities, and responses to data breaches for compliance and accountability purposes.

By actively addressing these responsibilities, the Legal department contributes to robust data governance practices within AI systems development, fostering legal compliance, protecting data privacy, and enhancing the organization's overall risk management framework.

Audit and Monitoring

a. Audit and Monitoring

i. Requirement Definition

Collaboration with AI Teams: Work collaboratively with AI development teams to define the specific audit trail requirements based on legal, regulatory, and organizational needs.

Comprehensive Logging: Ensure that AI systems maintain comprehensive and accurate logs, capturing relevant information on data processing, model training, and decision-making processes.

ii. Legal Compliance

Adherence to Regulatory Standards: Establish audit trail practices that align with regulatory standards and legal requirements, ensuring that the organization can demonstrate compliance with applicable laws.

Data Retention Policies: Define data retention policies within audit trails to comply with data protection laws and other regulations governing the storage and handling of sensitive information.

iii. Accountability Mechanisms

User Accountability: Implement mechanisms in the audit trail to attribute actions and decisions to specific users or roles within the organization, promoting individual accountability.

Versioning and Change Tracking: Track changes to AI models, algorithms, and configurations within the audit trail, facilitating transparency and accountability in the development process.

iv. Regular Audits

Periodic Audits: Conduct regular audits of the audit trail itself to ensure its completeness, accuracy, and alignment with established standards.

Documentation of Audits: Maintain documentation of audit activities, findings, and any corrective actions taken to address identified issues.

v. Legal Reporting

Legal Reporting Requirements: Understand and comply with legal reporting requirements related to audit trails, ensuring that necessary information is available and accessible for legal and regulatory purposes.

Legal Discovery Readiness: Ensure that audit trail data is organized and stored in a manner that facilitates ease of access and retrieval during legal discovery processes.

b. Monitoring for Bias and Fairness

i. Bias Assessment Protocols

Integration with Development: Work closely with AI development teams to integrate bias assessment protocols within the development lifecycle, assessing potential biases during model training and testing phases.

Continuous Monitoring: Implement mechanisms for ongoing monitoring of AI models for biases, recognizing that biases may emerge or evolve over time.

ii. Fairness Metrics

Definition and Implementation: Collaborate on the definition and implementation of fairness metrics that align with organizational values and legal requirements.

Benchmarking Against Standards: Benchmark fairness metrics against industry standards and legal thresholds, ensuring that AI models meet or exceed established benchmarks.

iii. Explainability and Transparency

Explainability Monitoring: Advise on and implement monitoring mechanisms for the explainability of AI models, ensuring that decisions made by models are transparent and understandable.

User-Facing Transparency: Explore ways to provide transparency to end users regarding the functioning of AI models and the considerations taken to address bias and fairness.

iv. Bias Mitigation Strategies

Dynamic Adjustments: Work with AI teams to develop strategies for dynamically adjusting models to mitigate biases when identified, ensuring a proactive approach to bias reduction.

Continuous Improvement Plans: Establish plans for continuous improvement based on feedback from monitoring, audits, and assessments, with a focus on addressing bias and fairness issues.

v. Documentation and Reporting

Comprehensive Documentation: Ensure that comprehensive documentation is maintained regarding bias and fairness monitoring activities, including details on metrics used, assessment results, and actions taken.

Reporting to Stakeholders: Provide regular reports to stakeholders, including senior management, boards, and regulators, on the organization's efforts to monitor and address biases in AI systems.

By actively fulfilling these responsibilities, the Legal department contributes to the establishment of a robust framework for audit and monitoring within AI systems, promoting accountability, transparency, and adherence to ethical and legal standards. This approach helps mitigate risks associated with biases and ensures continuous improvement in the responsible development and deployment of AI technologies.

Regulatory Engagement

a. Communication with Regulatory Bodies

i. Monitoring Regulatory Landscape

Regular Surveillance: Establish mechanisms to regularly monitor and stay abreast of the evolving regulatory landscape related to AI and emerging technologies.

Subscription to Updates: Subscribe to regulatory newsletters, alerts, and official communications to ensure the Legal department is promptly informed about new developments.

ii. Regulatory Intelligence

Interpretation and Analysis: Interpret and analyze new or proposed regulations, translating legal language into actionable insights for AI development teams and other stakeholders.

Impact Assessments: Conduct impact assessments to understand the potential effects of new or updated regulations on ongoing and future AI projects within the organization.

iii. Communication Channels

Established Communication Channels: Develop and maintain established channels for communication with regulatory bodies, including designated points of contact.

Regular Interactions: Engage in regular interactions with regulatory authorities to foster a proactive and collaborative relationship.

iv. Compliance Advocacy

Regulatory Compliance Advocacy: Advocate for the organization's interests by engaging with regulatory bodies in discussions related to AI Governance, seeking clarity on compliance expectations, and contributing insights.

Participation in Consultations: Participate in regulatory consultations, providing the Legal department's perspective on proposed regulations and suggesting improvements or modifications as needed.

b. Contribution to Industry Standards

i. Industry Collaboration

Participation in Industry Forums: Actively participate in industry forums, working groups, and collaborative initiatives focused on developing AI Governance standards.

Networking with Peers: Network with legal professionals from other organizations to share insights, best practices, and contribute to the collective development of industry standards.

ii. Drafting Guidelines and Best Practices

Collaboration with Industry Stakeholders: Collaborate with industry stakeholders, including other legal professionals, AI developers, and ethicists, to draft guidelines and best practices for responsible AI development.

Alignment with Legal Standards: Ensure that any industry standards align with existing legal standards and contribute to the legal department's goals for compliance.

iii. Representation in Standardization Bodies

Participation in Standardization Bodies: Represent the organization in relevant standardization bodies or consortia dedicated to AI Governance, contributing legal expertise to the development of standards.

Advocacy for Ethical and Legal Considerations: Advocate for the inclusion of ethical and legal considerations in industry standards to promote responsible AI practices.

iv. Knowledge Dissemination

Internal Education: Disseminate knowledge gained from regulatory engagement and industry standardization activities internally, educating relevant teams on the legal landscape and industry best practices.

Training Programs: Develop training programs to enhance awareness within the organization about the importance of compliance with regulations and adherence to industry standards.

v. Continuous Monitoring for Changes

Dynamic Regulatory Environment Monitoring: Establish continuous monitoring processes to keep track of changes in the regulatory environment and promptly update internal policies and practices accordingly.

Agile Response: Develop agile response strategies to promptly address any legal or regulatory changes that may impact ongoing AI projects.

By actively engaging in regulatory communication and contributing to the development of industry standards, the Legal department ensures that the organization stays informed, compliant, and actively shapes the ethical and legal landscape surrounding AI Governance. This proactive approach supports the responsible and sustainable development of AI systems within the bounds of legal and regulatory frameworks.

Training and Awareness

a. Employee Training

i. Legal Framework Education

Overview of Legal Frameworks: Provide comprehensive training on the legal frameworks relevant to AI development, including data protection laws, intellectual property regulations, and other legal considerations.

Updates on Regulatory Changes: Regularly update employees on changes in the legal and regulatory landscape, emphasizing the impact on AI projects.

ii. Data Protection and Privacy

Data Governance Training: Educate employees on data governance principles, emphasizing compliance with data protection and privacy laws.

User Consent and Data Rights: Provide guidance on obtaining user consent, respecting data ownership, and ensuring compliance with data subject rights.

iii. Intellectual Property Rights

Understanding IP Laws: Offer training sessions to enhance employees' understanding of intellectual property laws, with a focus on patents, copyrights, and trade secrets.

Innovation Disclosure Processes: Educate on the proper processes for disclosing and protecting innovative AI developments within the organization.

iv. Contractual Awareness

Vendor Agreement Training: Train employees involved in vendor relationships on key legal aspects of vendor agreements, including data security, intellectual property considerations, and performance obligations.

User Agreement Awareness: Educate relevant teams on legal aspects of user agreements, ensuring that terms of service align with legal requirements and protect the organization's interests.

v. Ethical and Responsible AI

Ethical Guidelines Training: Communicate and reinforce ethical guidelines for AI development, emphasizing responsible AI practices and the avoidance of unethical applications.

Bias and Fairness Education: Provide awareness of the importance of monitoring and addressing biases in AI models, promoting fairness and equity in AI systems.

b. Continuous Training Programs

i. Periodic Refresher Courses

Regular Updates: Schedule periodic refresher courses to keep employees informed about changes in legal requirements and industry best practices related to AI Governance.

Interactive Workshops: Conduct interactive workshops to encourage discussions on legal challenges and foster a culture of legal compliance within the AI development teams.

ii. Scenario-Based Training

Real-world Scenarios: Develop scenario-based training sessions that simulate real-world legal challenges in AI projects, allowing employees to apply legal principles to practical situations.

Response Strategies: Train employees on appropriate responses to legal issues, including incident response protocols and collaboration with the Legal Department.

iii. Cross-Functional Collaboration

Interdepartmental Training: Facilitate cross-functional training sessions involving legal experts, AI developers, and other relevant teams to enhance mutual understanding and collaboration.

Legal and Technical Integration: Foster integration between legal and technical knowledge to empower employees to proactively address legal considerations during AI development.

iv. Certification Programs

Legal Certifications: Encourage and support employees in obtaining relevant legal certifications, enhancing their expertise in areas crucial to AI Governance. Legal professionals may also benefit from getting certified in AI Governance. The Certified Information Governance Officers Association (CIGOA.org) offers a comprehensive CIGO/AI training, mentoring, and testing program, where participants can earn that credential and stay engaged with attorneys and other professionals working in the field of AI Governance.

Recognition Programs: Establish recognition programs to acknowledge and reward employees who actively contribute to legal compliance and awareness within AI projects.

v. Accessibility of Resources

Resource Portals: Create accessible online portals or documentation repositories containing legal resources, guidelines, and training materials for easy reference by AI development teams.

Q&A Sessions: Organize regular Q&A sessions where employees can seek clarification on legal matters and receive guidance from legal experts.

c. Feedback Mechanisms

i. Employee Feedback Channels

Anonymous Reporting: Establish anonymous reporting channels for employees to raise concerns or seek clarification on legal matters without fear of reprisal.

Feedback Surveys: Conduct regular surveys to gather feedback on the effectiveness of training programs and identify areas for improvement.

ii. Continuous Improvement Initiatives

Adaptive Training: Use feedback and assessment data to adapt and improve training programs continuously, ensuring they remain relevant and effective.

Responsive Content Updates: Update training content promptly in response to changes in legal requirements, ensuring that employees are always well-informed.

By actively fulfilling these responsibilities, the Legal department contributes to creating a culture of legal compliance and awareness within AI development teams. This proactive approach helps mitigate legal risks, enhances ethical considerations, and fosters a collaborative environment where legal and technical expertise converge for the responsible development of AI systems.

Incident Response Planning

a. Legal Response Protocols

i. Scenario Identification

Risk Assessment: Collaborate with AI development teams to conduct risk assessments, identifying potential scenarios that could lead to legal incidents, such as data breaches, biases, or other challenges.

Categorization of Incidents: Categorize potential incidents based on severity, legal implications, and the impact on stakeholders.

ii. Cross-Functional Collaboration

Collaborative Approach: Work closely with cross-functional teams, including IT, cybersecurity, public relations, and other relevant departments, to develop integrated response protocols.

Legal and Technical Alignment: Ensure alignment between legal and technical aspects of incident response, with legal considerations embedded in technical response plans.

iii. Legal Incident Response Team

Establishment of Response Team: Form a legal incident response team with members possessing expertise in relevant legal areas, such as data protection, intellectual property, and regulatory compliance.

Roles and Responsibilities: Define roles and responsibilities within the legal incident response team, clarifying who is responsible for legal analysis, communication with regulators, and coordination with external legal counsel.

iv. Incident Categorization

Classification Framework: Develop a framework for categorizing incidents based on their legal nature, allowing for tailored legal responses depending on the type of incident.

Priority Assessment: Prioritize incidents based on their potential legal, regulatory, and reputational impact, ensuring a focused and efficient response.

b. Legal Analysis and Assessment

i. Immediate Legal Response

Immediate Legal Triage: Establish protocols for immediate legal triage, ensuring that legal experts are involved early in the incident response process to assess legal risks and obligations.

Advisory Communication: Provide immediate legal guidance to incident response teams on actions to be taken to minimize legal exposure.

ii. Data Breach Response

Legal Obligations Analysis: Conduct a swift analysis of legal obligations related to data breaches, including notification requirements to regulatory authorities and affected individuals.

Communication Strategy: Develop a legal communication strategy, ensuring that legal obligations are met while also managing reputational and regulatory implications.

iii. Bias and Fairness Incidents

Legal Implications Assessment: Assess the legal implications of bias and fairness incidents, determining whether they violate anti-discrimination laws or ethical guidelines.

Remediation Legal Guidance: Provide legal guidance on potential remediation measures and communication strategies to address bias incidents.

iv. Regulatory Interaction Protocols

Regulatory Notifications: Establish protocols for notifying relevant regulatory authorities in case of incidents that may trigger legal reporting obligations.

Legal Representation Coordination: Coordinate with external legal representation, if necessary, ensuring that legal counsel is engaged appropriately in discussions with regulatory bodies.

c. Communication and Transparency

i. Internal Communication Protocols

Communication Channels: Develop internal communication protocols to ensure that relevant stakeholders are informed promptly about legal incidents and the organization's response.

Legal Messaging: Provide guidance on the legal messaging within internal communications, ensuring accuracy, clarity, and compliance with legal requirements.

ii. External Communication Strategy

Public Relations Collaboration: Collaborate with the public relations team to develop an external communication strategy that balances legal obligations with transparency and reputation management.

Legal Approval Processes: Establish processes for legal review and approval of external communications to mitigate legal risks.

iii. Documentation and Record-Keeping

Incident Documentation: Ensure thorough documentation of the legal aspects of incidents, including legal analysis, decisions made, and communications exchanged.

Evidence Preservation: Develop protocols for preserving evidence related to legal incidents, facilitating potential legal investigations or audits.

iv. Post-Incident Legal Review

Legal Lessons Learned: Conduct a post-incident legal review to identify lessons learned, areas for legal process improvement, and opportunities for enhancing legal incident response protocols.

Documentation of Legal Response Effectiveness: Document the effectiveness of legal response strategies employed during incidents for continuous improvement.

d. Continuous Improvement Initiatives

i. Legal Training Integration

Incident Simulations: Integrate incident response simulations into legal training programs to ensure that legal teams are well-prepared for real-world incidents.

Feedback Incorporation: Gather feedback from incident response exercises to continually refine and enhance legal response protocols.

ii. Regulatory Updates Adaptation

Regulatory Changes Monitoring: Stay informed about changes in legal and regulatory requirements related to incident response, adapting legal protocols accordingly.

Training on Updated Protocols: Conduct training sessions to educate legal and incident response teams on any updates to legal response protocols.

By actively engaging in incident response planning, the Legal department ensures that the organization is well-prepared to address legal challenges associated with AI systems development, mitigating risks, and safeguarding legal compliance during potential incidents.

Compliance: The Structural Role of Legal in AI Deployment

While AI systems are poised to create tremendous business value over the coming decade, there exists an ever-growing landscape of laws and regulations that govern their use. These legal vehicles are used to protect individuals and organizations from the potentially negative impacts of the use of AI, both intended and unintended.

Legal and regulatory constraints on the use of AI stem from three areas of the law: Property Rights, Contracts, and Liability Law (Torts). For instance, the topic of data privacy entails elements of all three areas of the law in the following manner:

A user has property rights to their own data, and hence is able to trade those rights in return for something of value to them. (Property Law).

A user can enter a contract whereby they give up their rights to their data in exchange for something. (Contracts Law).

A user has a contractual expectation that if they provide you with their data, you will keep it private. (Contracts Law).

A user can claim damages if the privacy defined in the agreement is not maintained. (Liability Law).

Any legislation or regulation that governs the use of AI will derive from these three areas of the law. Hence, while the regulatory landscape surrounding AI may seem extremely complex, effective governance of AI solutions and services need not be. Instead, if we look at any law or regulation governing AI as some combination of these three areas of the law, we can reduce any law or regulation to some variation of the same set of core principles.

Due to the complexity of the regulatory landscape, the global nature of many AI solutions, the vast array of data sources, and then potential risks associated with data loss or hacking, the legal and regulatory challenges in AI Governance are critical considerations for organizations deploying artificial intelligence systems.

Incorporating Compliance into AI Governance Framework

The existing global economy has evolved to operate effectively, predictably, and controllably due to the highly evolved global regulatory and legal framework. AI stands to drive significant transformation of society and the economy, but this transformation must grow from this sound, structural foundation. The following categories outline the major themes of legal compliance that must be addressed by an AI Governance initiative.

Importance of Data Privacy in AI

As stated above, privacy is a key element of legal and regulatory controls pertaining to AI. An individual's right to privacy is codified in the legal systems of many countries, states, provinces, and so on. As such, personal privacy can be thought of as an asset that may be traded for something else of value under a contract. The value of obtaining the personal information of large numbers of individuals may be seen in the market values of those organizations that aggregate such information.

AI systems consist of two key inputs: Models/Algorithms and Training Data. As most of the data used in AI training is procured from third parties, their right to privacy under Property and Contracts Law must be ensured. While privacy rights may not be explicitly spelled out in user agreements, such rights have been enacted in legislation and regulation to ensure that these rights are maintained independent of the contracts that are executed with data owners.

This is an important issue to understand, as it is the basis for the language in many End User License Agreements (EULAs) that organizations have leveraged for many years. Online platforms such as social media sites, search engines, and online indexes such as Yahoo! or Wikipedia all use EULAs to govern their relationship with their users. Within these EULAs are the terms of service between the platform and its users, which form the contract between them.

Prior to the mid-2010s, nearly all EULAs provided online platforms with unlimited licenses to their users' data, and few guarantees of protection of users' rights to privacy. The large number of regulations enacted since then were in response to the absence of transparency about this arrangement and the need to provide consumers and users with legal protections.

Note that nearly every regulation related to safeguarding user privacy has a consent clause which states that the constraints placed upon data consumers by the privacy regulation are nullified if the end user waives their right to privacy and gives consent to the data consumer. Hence, properly managing user consent is a critical aspect of data and AI Governance.

Model Privacy

The second key input to AI systems, models, or algorithms, also falls under privacy law but represent and entirely different challenge for governance. Here, the mathematics, node values, tools, and techniques represent the intellectual property of their creators, which must be protected. This intellectual property converts inputs (user data) into useful outputs (products and services), which is the basis of the business proposition of these tools. Hence, ensuring their privacy, including the prevention of reverse-engineering, is a critical factor in protecting the value of AI investment.

Maintaining intellectual property rights to AI models is presenting a challenge to regulators as it represents a constraint upon oversight and enforcement. Regulators must balance the IP rights and interests of model developers and owners with the need to ensure safety, efficacy, and compliance of such tools. This drives the additional governance requirements under Bias, Fairness, Transparency, and accountability that follow.

Bias and Fairness

Biases in training data or algorithms can result in unfair treatment and discriminatory outcomes. Many jurisdictions have laws against individual discrimination, and there is a growing awareness that as AI systems generate outcomes for people, such biases must be identified and mitigated.

This challenge exists for the outcomes that AI solutions generate which, increasingly, means that they also apply to the data used for AI training. While this distinction has yet to be formalized in many regulatory frameworks, it is anticipated that this situation will change in the near future. As a result, AI Governance professionals should be prepared to identify, manage, and mitigate bias both in AI systems' results and in the data upon which those systems are trained.

In the United States, addressing biases in training data and mitigating potential discrimination in AI systems involves compliance with various regulations beyond Title VII of the Civil Rights Act. Similar regulatory frameworks exist in nearly every jurisdiction, which can represent a significant challenge for effective governance.

Organizations deploying AI systems in various domains, especially those impacting individuals' rights and opportunities, should conduct thorough assessments to ensure compliance with these legal requirements. Regular audits, transparency measures, and ongoing monitoring are essential components of effective AI Governance to address biases and discrimination.

AI Governance frameworks should consider these regulations, and organizations deploying AI systems in various domains, especially those impacting individuals' rights and opportunities, should conduct thorough assessments to ensure compliance with these legal requirements. Regular audits, transparency measures, and ongoing monitoring are essential components of effective AI Governance to address biases and discrimination.

Employment and Labor Laws

Guarding the impact of AI on employment, workforce dynamics, and potential legal implications. The intersection of AI systems and employment and labor laws involves considerations related to workforce management, privacy, discrimination, and intellectual property. While specific laws may vary by jurisdiction, here are some general areas of employment and labor laws that pertain to AI systems and development from a governance perspective

Algorithmic Accountability and Transparency

As dictated by Contracts and Liability Law, organizations that use end-user data to produce products and services that are then provided to consumers have a duty of good faith. In AI systems, such good faith manifests in the concept of transparency. Many AI systems are mathematical "black boxes," where the reason a result is generated is neither predictable nor explainable, making transparency a particular challenge. Many AI systems are trained on data sets that are curated across many sources, with varying degrees of transparency and validity, potentially calling into question the results they generate in the systems they've trained.

Lack of transparency and accountability in AI decision-making processes can be a legal concern. This may be true of both the results themselves and the process(es) that produce them. The challenge for those tasked with governing AI solutions is to maintain their organization's information property rights alongside their contractual obligation to deal in good faith with their counterparties.

Data Sovereignty

AI systems often require the transfer of data across borders, both for upfront training and for subsequent interaction with users. This is also true of ongoing model learning that occurs through use. This raises concerns about data protection laws across those jurisdictions in which the AI operates.

Addressing antitrust concerns in the AI sector requires ongoing scrutiny by antitrust authorities and regulatory bodies. Authorities may assess issues such as market dominance, anti-competitive agreements, and the impact of mergers and acquisitions on competition. Companies operating in the AI space should stay informed about changes in antitrust laws, cooperate with regulatory investigations, and adopt practices that promote fair competition.

Integrating Compliance into AI Systems — Compliance by Design

Integrating compliance into AI systems involves *embedding legal considerations into every stage of the AI lifecycle, from problem definition to retirement*. Seven principles are called for in the EU's General Data Protection Regulation (GDPR). While these seven principles are specifically aligned to issues of privacy, they apply equally to ensuring broad compliance with legal requirements. Here are the seven foundational principles of **Privacy by Design:**

1. **Proactive not Reactive; Preventative not Remedial:** Legal considerations, such as jurisdictions, title and ownership, and custody should be identified at the beginning of the development process, rather than added as an afterthought. This approach is both more efficient and provides great assurance that compliance will be achieved and maintained.
2. **Compliance as the Default Setting:** Design decisions should seek to create a compliant solution from the beginning, rather than redesigning for compliance later in the life cycle.
3. **Compliance Embedded into Design:** All aspects of systems design should be informed by compliance requirements.

4. **Compliance as Value-Add:** Compliance should be viewed as valuable in itself, rather than as a design trade-off. Compliance and ethics have inherent market value, as well as contributing significantly to goodwill.
5. **Full Lifecycle Compliance:** Designing compliance from the beginning of problem definition ensures that legal risk is minimized while also ensuring the maximum value retention of licensable intellectual property that results from the system's operation.
6. **Transparency:** Designing for and maintaining oversight minimizes the risks of unintended consequences from misuse, attacks, or other acts by bad actors.
7. **Stakeholder-Centricity:** Many legal conflicts arise when the interests of one or more stakeholders are not met. Whether perceived or real, such disconnects often prove to be extremely expensive in money, attention, and time. By defining and then enforcing the interests of all stakeholders, AI systems may generate their maximum positive return on investment.

The concentration of AI capabilities and power in a few large entities can raise antitrust concerns related to competition and market dominance. Various countries have antitrust laws and regulations in place to prevent anticompetitive practices and protect fair competition.

Conclusion

Addressing these legal and regulatory challenges requires a comprehensive approach, involving collaboration between legal experts, policymakers, and technologists to ensure that AI Governance frameworks align with existing and evolving legal landscapes. Organizations should stay informed about changes in regulations and adapt their AI Governance practices accordingly to maintain compliance and ethical standards.

Key Points

- Effective AI Governance requires active participation from Legal throughout the entire adoption lifecycle.
- Ensuring that legal compliance is obtained, retained, and protected throughout an organization requires coordination across all contributing parties.
- Legal Impact Assessment (PIA): Conducting an LIA to understand how the proposed AI system could be impacted by laws and regulations affecting its operations.
- Legal must ensure that training data is accurate, authentic, and legally usable.
- In model selection, Legal must ensure that the model complies with legal and regulatory requirements, including issues of property rights, bias, and privacy.
- In model evaluation, Legal must ensure that model results are predictable, accurate, and as free from bias as possible.
- In deployment, Legal must ensure compliance, efficacy, and accuracy of results.
- In retirement, Legal must ensure that records retention rules are followed for as long as regulations require.

Key Glossary Terms

Bias: Prejudice in favor of or against one thing, person, or group compared with another, usually in a way considered to be unfair.

Indemnification: Security against legal liability for one's actions.

Jurisdiction: The power to make legal decisions and judgments. Jurisdiction is often tied to a specific geography or may be domain-specific.

Liability: The state of being responsible for something, especially by law.

Transparency: The quality of being easy to perceive or detect. For AI, transparency refers to the need to understand where, why, and how an AI responds in the way that it does.

Notes

1 Linda Volonino and Ian Redpath, *e-Discovery For Dummies* (Hoboken, NJ: John Wiley & Sons, 2010), 9.

2 "New Federal Rules of Civil Procedure," United States Courts, accessed November 26, 2023.http://www.uscourts.gov/FederalCourts/UnderstandingtheFederalCourts/DistrictCourts.aspx.

3 Ibid.

4 Ibid.

5 Volonino and Redpath, *e-Discovery for Dummies*, p. 13.

6 ECM^2, "15-Minute Guide to eDiscovery and Early Case Assessment," accessed May 21, 2013, www.emc.com/collateral/15-min-guide/h9781-15-min-guide-ediscovery-eca-gde.pdf.

7 Ibid., p. 11.

8 "New Federal Rules of Civil Procedure."

9 *Source:* Linda Volonino and Ian Redpath, e-*Discovery For Dummies* (Hoboken, NJ: John Wiley & Sons, 2010), accessed December 5, 2023, https://www.dummies.com/business/e-discovery-for-dummies-cheat-sheet/. Used with permission.

6 Risk Management for AI Implementations

Risk management is one of the most important, and least popular, topics in the realm of AI Governance. There seems to be intense polarity in this discussion among professionals and laypersons alike. At one extreme lie those who embrace any new technology with open arms; the more disruptive the better, and AI is delightfully disruptive. At the other extreme lie those who believe that the risks of AI are world-ending.

As with most things in the real world, the reality of AI risk lies in the middle of, and far away from, these extreme views. If applied properly, organizations should experience a great deal of disruption (both good and bad) from the adoption of AI. Those who don't adopt the technology deeply will likely be outcompeted in short order; hence, the need to join the AI race with some gusto.

However, investing in and deploying AI rapidly, broadly, and deeply will almost certainly lead to a wide range of unanticipated and unintended consequences. So a "go slow" approach of piloting AI technology for use in low-risk internal applications is a prudent approach. For example, one major insurance company began by training a large language model on its internal policies to make queries on policy issues by agents easy and accessible (compare this to searching for answers in huge policy manuals).

Positive and Negative Risks

A major challenge in managing AI risk is identifying and characterizing positive risk in addition to negative risk. **Negative risk** is the risk that an organization takes by not adopting a new technology, like AI. Such risks include loss of competitiveness, loss of market share, loss of talent, and ultimately loss of business revenue. **Positive risk** consists of those risks that come with a successful adoption of a new technology such as AI. This includes the need to redeploy or eliminate skilled personnel, the risks of the system going down, the risk of the operating costs changing significantly, the risk of a more adverse regulatory environment.

Nearly all organizations evaluate the negative risk as part of their investment management process. This is fundamental to calculating the initial return on investment (ROI) of implementing a new technology like AI. Similarly, most organizations calculate the ongoing costs of operating their investments once deployed. However, few organizations assess the potential risks associated with an operational system failing, operating suboptimally, or where the necessary conditions of operation suddenly change.

With AI being viewed as a potential replacement for substantial portions of the human workforce, understanding positive adoption risks is a critical addition to an organization's risk profile management.

Managing Risk Through the AI Lifecycle

In the realm of AI Governance, risk management plays a pivotal role across the entire lifecycle of an AI solution. This lifecycle typically encompasses eight distinct phases:

1. Problem Definition
2. Data Collection
3. Data Preparation
4. Model Selection and Training
5. Model Evaluation
6. Model Deployment
7. Monitoring and Maintenance
8. Retirement

The systematic integration of risk management within these phases ensures the development of effective, reliable, and ethically compliant AI systems. Let's delve into the role of risk management within each of these stages.

1. Problem Definition and Program Initiation

In the initial phase of ***Problem Definition***, *risk management focuses on understanding the potential ethical, legal, and operational risks associated with the AI application.* This involves conducting a preliminary risk assessment to identify any adverse impacts the solution might have on various stakeholders. Risk managers work alongside project stakeholders to ensure that the AI's objectives align with ethical guidelines and legal requirements, mitigating risks of misuse or unintended consequences from the outset.

2. Data Collection

During the **Data Collection** phase, *risk management entails the identification and mitigation of risks related to data privacy, security, and provenance.* Ensuring the collection of data complies with relevant data protection regulations (such as GDPR in the European Union) is critical. Risk managers assess the sources of data for potential biases and the legality of their use, setting the stage for responsible AI development.

3. Data Preparation

The **Data Preparation** *stage involves cleaning and organizing the collected data for training the AI model.* Here, *risk management includes scrutinizing the dataset for biases, redundancies, inaccuracies, or missing values that could lead to skewed AI decisions.* Implementing robust data governance practices ensures data quality and fairness, reducing the risk of developing biased AI systems.

4. Model Selection and Training

In **Model Selection and Training**, *risk management assesses the suitability of various AI models for the task at hand, considering their transparency, interpretability, and potential for bias.* It involves evaluating the models' vulnerabilities to adversarial attacks and their performance across diverse demographic groups. By choosing models that are well understood and transparent, risk managers can mitigate the risks of unintended behavior or discrimination.

5. *Model Evaluation*

The **Model Evaluation** *phase is crucial for assessing the AI model's performance and its adherence to ethical standards. Risk management activities include thorough testing for fairness, accuracy, and reliability across a range of scenarios and populations.* This step ensures that the model's decisions do not disproportionately affect certain groups negatively and that it meets the predefined ethical and operational standards.

6. *Model Deployment*

Upon **Model Deployment**, *risk management shifts towards ensuring the AI system operates as intended in the real world. This includes continuous monitoring for operational risks such as system failures, security breaches, and compliance with regulatory standards.* Risk managers also prepare for incident response, developing protocols for addressing unexpected AI behavior or data breaches promptly.

7. *Monitoring and Maintenance*

The **Monitoring and Maintenance** stage *emphasizes the ongoing assessment of the AI system's performance and the evolving landscape of risks. This includes updating the system to adapt to new data, regulatory changes, or emerging threats.* Risk managers play a key role in implementing feedback loops that allow for the continuous improvement of the AI system, ensuring its long-term reliability and compliance.

8. *Retirement*

Finally, in the **Retirement** phase, *risk management involves ensuring a responsible phase-out of the AI system. This includes assessing the impact of decommissioning the system on stakeholders and managing the secure disposal of data and proprietary information.* Risk managers ensure that the retirement process complies with legal requirements and ethical standards, mitigating risks related to data breaches or loss of service.

In summary, *integrating risk management across the AI lifecycle is essential for the responsible development and deployment of AI systems.*

By systematically addressing potential risks at each stage, organizations can not only comply with regulatory requirements and ethical standards but also build trust with users and stakeholders. This comprehensive approach to AI Governance ensures that AI technologies achieve their intended benefits while minimizing negative impacts on society.

The Risk Identification, Evaluation, and Mitigation Process

Properly managing and mitigating risks in AI implementations involves a systematic and comprehensive approach. *Identifying and mitigating data risks*, including biases and inaccuracies in training data, *is a crucial step in managing the overall risks associated with AI* implementations for proper AI Governance.

Here are steps to consider during the risk identification process in the context of AI:

Risk Identification

The process begins by defining clear objectives and scope for the AI system and understanding its:

1. Use case
2. Target audience
3. Potential impact (on a business problem or society)

Identifying and documenting all ***data sources*** *used in the training process is crucial*, including internal datasets, external datasets, and third-party data. A thorough **audit** of the data collection process ensures alignment with ethical guidelines and legal requirements, evaluating its representativeness and relevance.

Assessing **data quality**, examining representation across demographic groups, and identifying biases and inaccuracies through statistical analysis are also key steps.

Additionally, a critical review of **data labels** and annotations, evaluation of historical data for contextual factors, and engaging diverse stakeholders in the risk identification process contribute to a comprehensive understanding of potential issues.

External audits by independent experts can provide an unbiased perspective, and their involvement in the process ensures a thorough review. *Documenting findings in a comprehensive report is essential*, detailing identified issues, potential impacts, and recommendations for mitigation.

The implementation of **mitigation strategies** to reduce identified risks involves developing and applying techniques such as data preprocessing, algorithmic adjustments, and fairness-aware machine learning methods.

Continuous monitoring of data risks throughout the AI system's lifecycle is critical, requiring regular updates and refinements to risk identification processes.

Transparency and **accountability** play a vital role in this process, fostering a culture of openness and collaboration with stakeholders. Communicating openly about identified risks and the steps taken to address them ensures ongoing awareness and facilitates a proactive approach to risk management in AI Governance practices.

Remember that *addressing biases and inaccuracies in training data* is an *iterative process*. Regularly reassess and update risk identification processes as the AI system evolves and new data becomes available.

- **Assess data quality, integrity, and security.**

To ensure effective AI Governance, *adopting a standardized, systematic, and comprehensive method for evaluating data quality, integrity, and security is crucial.* [1]

A detailed **audit** of the data collection process is vital to confirm it aligns with ethical guidelines, legal mandates, and industry benchmarks. This audit examines if the data meets high standards for quality, integrity, and security. Assessing data quality involves checking for completeness, accuracy, consistency, and timeliness, identifying any gaps or inaccuracies that could undermine the AI system's performance and dependability.

Integrity checks are crucial for maintaining data consistency and reliability, ensuring the data remains unaltered and intact throughout its collection, storage, and transmission. Moreover, a security evaluation is imperative to safeguard the data against unauthorized access, breaches, or cyber threats. This includes scrutinizing encryption methods, access controls, and security protocols to fortify data protection.

Examining **data governance** practices within the organization ensures clear policies, procedures, and responsibilities for managing and maintaining data quality, integrity, and security.

1. Checking compliance with relevant data protection and privacy regulations
2. Reviewing data lifecycle management
3. Evaluating data access controls is integral to the assessment

Assessing data documentation, including metadata and data dictionaries, enhances data quality and aids in understanding the context and structure of the data.

For **external datasets**, a risk assessment is conducted for third-party data sources, verifying their reliability, quality, and security practices.

Threat modeling is performed to identify potential security threats and vulnerabilities, considering both internal and external factors that could impact data quality, integrity, and security. *Engaging security experts in the risk identification process leverages their expertise* to identify risks and mitigation strategies.

Documenting findings in a comprehensive report detailing identified issues, potential impacts, and recommendations for mitigation is essential.

The implementation of mitigation strategies involves:

1. Improving data quality processes
2. Enhancing security measures
3. Implementing data integrity checks

Continuous monitoring of data quality, integrity, and security throughout the AI system's lifecycle, coupled with **transparency** and **accountability,** fosters a culture of openness and collaboration with stakeholders to maintain awareness of potential issues.

Addressing data quality, integrity, and security is an ongoing process, and organizations should continually reassess and update their risk identification processes as the AI system evolves and new data becomes available.

- Model Risks:
  - **Evaluate the robustness and reliability of AI models.**

In managing and mitigating risks in AI implementations, the identification of model risks is a critical and foundational step that requires a systematic and comprehensive approach. To ensure the robustness and reliability of AI models, it is essential to follow key principles.

The process begins with a clear definition of the objectives of the AI model and the scope of its application, understanding the specific use case, target audience, and desired outcomes.

Understanding the model's purpose involves articulating its intended functionality and role in decision-making within the broader system or process.

Assessing data quality and preprocessing techniques is crucial to identify potential biases, inaccuracies, or limitations in the training data that may impact the model's performance.

A thorough analysis of **feature engineering** *evaluates the relevance, representativeness, and significance of features contributing to the model's predictive capabilities.* The appropriateness of the chosen algorithm(s) is assessed, considering their strengths, weaknesses, and assumptions in relation to the given task. **Model complexity analysis** helps evaluate if the model is **overfitting** or **underfitting** the training data and whether its complexity aligns with the available data.

Examining **hyperparameter**[2] choices and tuning them systematically enhances the model's robustness. In the context of AI systems, *hyperparameters are external configuration settings that are not learned from the data but are set prior to the training process.* They are parameters that govern the overall behavior of the learning algorithm and have a significant impact on the model's performance. Unlike **model parameters**, which are learned during training, hyperparameters are set by the machine learning engineer or researcher.

Model interpretability is assessed to ensure transparency and understanding, especially in applications where interpretability is crucial. Tools such as LIME or Shapley values can assist in simplifying complex models to gain insights into their inner workings. Assessing model performance on unseen data is evaluated using validation and test datasets.

Addressing bias and fairness issues involves analyzing the model for disparate impacts on different demographic groups and taking steps to mitigate biases. Robustness to adversarial attacks is assessed to ensure stability and reliability when exposed to intentionally manipulated inputs. Sensitivity to input variability is evaluated under different conditions and variations in input features.

*Analyzing **model output and confidence levels** helps evaluate the reliability of predictions and the model's ability to provide accurate uncertainty estimates.* Monitoring and assessing **model drift** (where the statistical properties of the target variable or the input features change over time, leading to a degradation in the performance of a machine learning model) over time ensures continued performance as the distribution of input data changes. Identifying external factors that may impact the model's performance, such as changes in the environment or regulatory requirements, is crucial.

Engaging with **domain experts** to validate and interpret model outputs leverages their expertise to identify potential risks and refine the model accordingly.

Documenting findings related to model risks, including potential weaknesses, uncertainties, and areas for improvement, is essential. Implementing **mitigation strategies** may involve model retraining, algorithm adjustments, or the introduction of additional features to enhance robustness.

Establishing a system for **continuous monitoring** of model performance, coupled with a culture of transparency and accountability, ensures ongoing collaboration with stakeholders to maintain awareness of potential issues and facilitates the communication of identified model risks and the steps taken to address them.

Addressing model risks is an ongoing process, and organizations should continually reassess and update their risk identification processes as the AI model evolves and new data becomes available.

- **Identify potential biases and fairness issues in model outputs.**

Effectively managing and **mitigating risks** in AI implementations requires *a comprehensive approach to identifying potential biases and ensuring fairness in model outputs.*[3]

To systematically address biases, it is essential to define **fairness metrics**, such as demographic parity, equalized odds, and disparate impact, tailored to the context of the application. Identifying relevant protected *attributes* (such as race, gender, or age) plays a crucial role, and considerations of the legal and ethical implications of using such attributes should be taken into account.

An in-depth analysis of the training data is necessary to evaluate biases. This involves examining the distribution of sensitive features and addressing imbalances or disparities that may lead to biased model outputs. **Fair data preprocessing techniques**, such as *re-sampling and re-weighting, can be applied to mitigate biases in the training data.*[4]

During the model training phase, *fairness evaluation should be integrated, monitoring the model's performance across different demographic groups.* Evaluating model outputs across subgroups and checking for disparate impact ensures fairness and consistency. Assessing the model on unseen data, considering intersectional biases, and engaging domain experts for their insights are crucial steps in the process.

Explainability *techniques (e.g. LIME and SHAP) can be leveraged to understand how the model arrives at decisions, shedding light on potential biases* rooted in its features and decision-making processes. User feedback and the implementation of bias detection tools provide additional perspectives on fairness concerns. Documenting findings related to potential biases and fairness issues is crucial for transparency and accountability.

Mitigation strategies, *such as adjusting model parameters and retraining with augmented data, are implemented based on the documented findings.* Continuous monitoring is established to adapt to the evolving nature of the model and incoming data. *Transparency and accountability are fostered by openly communicating about identified biases and fairness issues and the steps taken to address them.*

*Legal and ethical compliance considerations*_ensure that the model's outputs align with established standards related to fairness, non-discrimination, and equal opportunity.

Addressing biases and fairness issues in model outputs is an ongoing process, and organizations should continually reassess and update their risk identification processes as the AI model evolves and new data becomes available.

- Operational Risks
  - **Consider risks associated with system integration and deployment.**

Effectively managing operational risks associated with system integration and deployment is crucial for the governance of AI implementations. *Key integration points,* (where the AI system interfaces with other systems, databases, or external services, *should be identified, and dependencies and data flows at these points thoroughly understood.*

Evaluation of **data transfer protocols** for security, reliability, and efficiency, as well as compatibility assessments with existing software, hardware, and infrastructure, are critical steps in risk identification.

Assessing system interdependencies and the scalability of the AI system ensures its ability to handle increased data volumes, user loads, or additional functionalities without compromising performance. Resource availability, including computing power, storage, and network bandwidth, must be checked to support the AI system during deployment. **Diversity in deployment environments**, such as cloud, on-premises, or hybrid setups, should be considered, and compatibility and performance across these environments assessed.

Thorough testing of the integrated system, including functional, performance, and stress testing, is imperative to identify potential operational issues before deployment.

Security protocols and compliance with regulatory requirements, including data protection and privacy, must be evaluated to address vulnerabilities and ensure legal adherence.

Assessing failover mechanisms, redundancy strategies, and implementing robust monitoring and logging mechanisms contribute to the seamless operation of the system during deployment. Evaluation of user authentication and authorization mechanisms helps ensure secure access control and mitigate risks associated with unauthorized access or data breaches.

Considering user training needs and support mechanisms is vital to ensure end users understand how to interact with and interpret the outputs of the AI system.

Change order management processes for updates, patches, or modifications to the AI system should be evaluated to ensure smooth implementation without causing disruptions.

Backward compatibility checks, collaboration with stakeholders, and documentation of findings related to operational risks are integral to transparency and accountability. *Mitigation strategies, involving adjustments to system configurations, improvements in monitoring, or changes to deployment procedures, are crucial for addressing identified operational risks.*

Continuous monitoring of operational risks throughout the AI system's lifecycle and ongoing communication about identified risks and mitigation steps help maintain awareness and foster a culture of transparency and accountability.

Addressing operational risks in AI system integration and deployment is an ongoing process, and organizations should continually reassess and update their risk identification processes as the AI system evolves and new data becomes available.

- **Assess the impact of AI failures on business operations.**

Identifying operational risks associated with the impact of AI failures on business operations is a fundamental aspect of ensuring effective governance in AI implementations.

To mitigate risks related to AI failures, it is crucial to understand the ***system architecture****, integration points, and dependencies.* By assessing data transfer protocols and compatibility with existing infrastructure, potential issues that might disrupt business operations can be identified early in the implementation process. Evaluating the **scalability** of the AI system ensures its ability to handle increased workloads without compromising performance.

Thorough testing, including functional and stress testing, provides insights into potential operational issues that may arise during AI failures. Assessing the robustness of security protocols and compliance with regulatory requirements helps safeguard against data breaches or other security-related challenges that could impact business operations.

To mitigate the impact of AI failures on business operations, *organizations should establish* **failover mechanisms** *and* **redundancy strategies**.[5]

Monitoring and logging mechanisms should be implemented *to promptly detect anomalies and facilitate swift troubleshooting.* Regular evaluations of user authentication and authorization mechanisms contribute to secure access control, preventing unauthorized access and potential disruptions.

Considering user training needs and support mechanisms is essential to ensure that employees can effectively interact with AI systems and understand their outputs. **Change management** processes for updates, patches, or modifications to the AI system should be in place to prevent disruptions to ongoing business operations.

Continuous monitoring of operational risks associated with AI failures throughout the system's lifecycle is crucial. This involves ongoing collaboration with stakeholders, including IT teams, system administrators, and end users, to gather insights and feedback on potential risks. Transparent communication about identified risks and the steps taken to address them fosters a culture of accountability.

In summary, effective governance in AI implementations necessitates a proactive and systematic approach to identify, assess, and mitigate operational risks associated with AI failures. This includes a holistic understanding of the AI system's objectives, robust testing, security assessments, and continuous monitoring, all while fostering transparency and collaboration across the organization.

Addressing operational risks related to the impact of AI failures on business operations is an ongoing process, and *organizations should continually reassess and update their risk identification processes* as the AI system evolves and new data becomes available.

Risk Assessment

- Quantitative Assessment

  - **Use metrics to quantify the impact and likelihood of identified risks.**

Developing metrics to quantify the impact and likelihood of identified risks in a **quantitative assessment** involves a systematic and comprehensive approach. Here are steps to consider when creating such metrics:

The process begins with clear **risk identification** (see previous section), documenting specific risks associated with the AI implementation, covering aspects like data, model, and operations. Subsequently, categorizing these risks into groups based on their nature (such as data quality or operational risks) is essential.

To create a robust quantitative assessment, *defining impact and likelihood criteria is crucial.*

Impact criteria should encompass factors such as financial losses, operational disruptions, and reputational damage, while likelihood criteria may include probability, frequency, or historical occurrence data. Numerical values are then assigned to represent the potential impact and likelihood of each risk, typically on a scale from 1 to 10.

The development of a ***risk matrix****, combining impact and likelihood scores, aids in visualizing and prioritizing risks based on their severity.* Weightings are assigned to different risk factors based on their significance, emphasizing risks that have a more substantial impact on critical business processes. **Overall risk scores are calculated by multiplying the impact score by the likelihood score,** providing a quantitative measure of each risk's severity.

Although risk can be quantified and risk scores calculated, it is often helpful for executives to establish thresholds and to categorize risk scores into different levels (e.g., low, medium, high), setting boundaries for acceptable and unacceptable risk levels.

Collaboration with stakeholders, including business leaders and risk management professionals, is crucial to validate the developed metrics and ensure alignment with organizational goals and risk tolerance.

Documentation of the entire metrics framework, including numerical values, weightings, and calculation methods, serves as a reference for ongoing risk assessments and updates. Incorporating external benchmarks or industry standards provides context and helps organizations gauge their risk levels relative to industry norms.

Continuous improvement is a key principle, necessitating regular reviews and updates to the metrics based on feedback, changes in the business environment, or evolving risk profiles. Automation tools can streamline the calculation process, reducing the likelihood of errors and ensuring consistency. Integrating the metrics into the organization's overall risk management system facilitates ongoing monitoring, reporting, and decision-making related to identified risks.

Training relevant personnel on how to use and interpret the risk metrics, coupled with effective communication about the significance of the metrics in contributing to overall risk governance, is essential.

Regular updates to the metrics, feedback mechanisms, and alignment with business objectives ensure that the quantitative assessment remains a dynamic and effective tool in the ongoing management of AI system risks.

Quantifying the impact and likelihood of identified risks through a quantitative assessment provides organizations with a structured and data-driven approach to risk management. It enables informed decision-making, resource allocation, and the prioritization of risk mitigation efforts.

- **Prioritize risks based on their severity and potential consequences.**

In prioritizing risks based on their severity and potential consequences in a quantitative assessment for AI implementations, several key steps are integral to effective risk management.

To begin, reviewing the risk assessment data is essential. This involves gathering and comprehensively reviewing data collected during the risk identification and quantitative assessment phases, including information on the impact and likelihood of each identified risk. The established metrics are then utilized to quantify the impact and likelihood, assigning numerical values based on predefined criteria within the risk assessment framework.

High-risk scenarios are prioritized, focusing on those with the highest potential impact and likelihood. Interdependencies between different risks are considered, examining how the occurrence of one risk may influence others. Weighted analysis comes into play, assigning weights to different risk factors based on their significance and relevance to organizational objectives.

The evaluation of identified **risk mitigation strategies** is key at this stage, with a focus on prioritizing risks that may require immediate attention or more intensive mitigation efforts. Stakeholder consultation, involving business leaders, subject matter experts, and risk management professionals, helps gather insights and ensures alignment with organizational goals and risk tolerance.

Additional considerations in the risk prioritization process include:

1. Legal and regulatory implications
2. Reputational impact
3. Alignment with business objectives

Scenario analysis is conducted to understand potential outcomes of high-priority risks, considering different scenarios and their impact on various aspects of the organization.

Documentation of the prioritization results is a crucial step, articulating the prioritized risks, their associated scores, and the rationale behind the decisions. Transparent communication is vital, as it fosters a shared understanding of the risks and facilitates informed decision-making among stakeholders.

Allocating resources accordingly, including budget and efforts, is guided by the prioritized risks. Establishing **monitoring mechanisms** helps track changes in risk levels over time, facilitating regular reassessment and updates to the risk prioritization. Continuous improvement of the risk prioritization framework is emphasized, ensuring it remains dynamic and relevant to evolving circumstances.

Lastly, *integrating the prioritized risks into the organization's decision-making processes ensures that risk prioritization is a fundamental consideration* in strategic, operational, and tactical decisions related to the AI implementation. This comprehensive approach ensures that risk management is an ongoing, informed, and integral part of the AI implementation lifecycle.

- Qualitative Assessment
  - **Consider the subjective factors and expert opinions in assessing risks.**

In a qualitative risk assessment for AI implementations, considering subjective factors and expert opinions is crucial for capturing nuanced aspects of risks that may not be easily quantifiable.

Expert selection is a critical first step, involving the identification and engagement of a diverse group of subject matter experts (SMEs) with relevant domain knowledge, including AI practitioners, ethicists, legal experts, data scientists, and representatives from impacted stakeholder groups.

Stakeholder engagement is equally vital, as involving key stakeholders, including end users, customers, and those affected by the AI system, provides valuable insights into the system's potential impact.

Defining assessment criteria is essential for qualitative evaluation, encompassing factors such as ethical considerations, societal impacts, fairness, interpretability, and other subjective aspects that experts can evaluate based on their expertise.

Facilitating workshops and discussions with experts becomes a dynamic method to explore potential risks, utilizing structured frameworks or open-ended discussions to elicit diverse viewpoints. Scenario analysis and ethical impact assessments, conducted with input from ethicists and experts in ethical considerations, help uncover risks that may not be immediately apparent.

Cultural sensitivity assessments, involving experts with knowledge of cultural nuances, offer insights into how cultural factors may influence the perception and consequences of AI-related risks.

Legal and regulatory expertise is engaged to assess risks related to compliance with laws and regulations, considering how legal frameworks may impact the development, deployment, and use of the AI system. Encouraging experts to provide qualitative narratives describing potential risks, along with subjective ratings or rankings, helps in prioritizing risks in a qualitative manner.

The **Delphi method**,[6] *involving iterative rounds of surveys or discussions with experts, facilitates the convergence of opinions over multiple rounds, providing a refined understanding of risks.*

Consensus building among experts is pursued through open communication and collaboration, seeking areas of agreement and disagreement for a comprehensive view of potential risks. Public and stakeholder consultation is considered, providing diverse perspectives and highlighting concerns that may not be evident to experts alone.

Systematic documentation of expert inputs is crucial for transparency and future reference, capturing the reasoning behind assessments, including any disagreements or uncertainties. Collecting feedback from experts on the risk assessment process and outcomes allows for iteration and refinement of the qualitative assessment methodology for continuous improvement.

Developing a **risk matrix** that incorporates qualitative descriptions of risks, along with expert input, aids in communicating the severity and characteristics of risks to stakeholders in a nuanced way.

Cross-disciplinary collaboration is fostered between experts from different disciplines, enriching the assessment by considering diverse viewpoints and identifying risks that may be overlooked by a single discipline.

Encouraging experts to use ***storytelling techniques*** *to convey the narrative of potential risks makes the risks more relatable and understandable to a broader audience.*

Peer review within the expert group subjects expert opinions and qualitative assessments to scrutiny, ensuring robustness and validity in the qualitative evaluation process. Finally, *integrating qualitative assessments with quantitative approaches,* where feasible, results in a more *comprehensive risk management strategy leveraging both types of insights.*

By following these steps, organizations can effectively integrate subjective factors and expert opinions into the qualitative risk assessment process for AI implementations. This approach enhances the understanding of complex and nuanced risks, leading to more informed decision-making and proactive risk mitigation strategies.

- **Evaluate the reputational and regulatory implications of identified risks.**

Evaluating the reputational and regulatory implications of identified risks in a qualitative assessment for AI implementations is critical for comprehensive risk management.

The process begins by identifying and documenting the relevant regulatory frameworks and compliance requirements applicable to the AI implementation. Legal and regulatory experts are engaged to provide insights into how identified risks may impact compliance and regulatory requirements.

A **regulatory impact assessment** is conducted for each identified risk, evaluating how noncompliance or adverse events associated with the risk may affect the organization's standing with regulatory bodies. Understanding enforcement mechanisms and potential consequences, fines, or penalties for noncompliance is essential information sought in this evaluation.

Special attention is given to risks related to **data protection and privacy**, ensuring that the AI system adheres to privacy regulations such as GDPR in Europe or CPRA/CCPA (and other relevant state privacy laws) and HIPAA in the U S healthcare sector. The impact of identified risks on stakeholder trust is assessed, recognizing that reputational damage often correlates with the erosion of stakeholder trust.

Historical precedents and industry case studies are reviewed to learn from similar risks that led to regulatory scrutiny or reputational damage.

Communication strategies are evaluated to assess the organization's preparedness in communicating with regulatory bodies and stakeholders in the event of a risk materializing. Clear and transparent communication is recognized as a key element to mitigate reputational damage.

The potential perception of identified risks by the media and the public is analyzed, anticipating potential narratives and reactions. **Mitigation strategies** are developed in collaboration with legal and regulatory experts, involving adjustments to policies, procedures, or the technical aspects of the AI system.

Incident response planning is emphasized, with the development or review of plans that specifically address regulatory and reputational risks. Clear protocols are established for reporting incidents to regulatory bodies and responding to media inquiries. The impact of each identified risk on the organization's brand image and reputation is assessed, considering the potential long-term consequences on customer loyalty and market standing.

Public relations experts are engaged to assess and contribute insights on the potential reputational fallout from identified risks, informing communication strategies and brand management. Surveys or focus groups with key stakeholders are considered to understand their perceptions of the organization and the potential impact of identified risks on trust and confidence.

Continuous monitoring of the regulatory landscape is established to stay informed about changes in regulations that may affect the organization's risk profile. **Scenario planning exercises** specifically focused on reputational risks are conducted, anticipating potential scenarios that could damage the organization's reputation and devising strategies for mitigation.

Periodic legal compliance audits are conducted to ensure ongoing adherence to relevant regulations, with adjustments made as needed to address emerging risks. Open and transparent communication with regulatory authorities is fostered to proactively address concerns and demonstrate a commitment to compliance.

Key performance indicators (KPIs) are developed to measure and monitor reputational and regulatory risks over time, including metrics such as media sentiment analysis, customer satisfaction, and regulatory compliance.

Finally, the documentation of the evaluation of reputational and regulatory implications for each identified risk is emphasized. Clear documentation is essential for internal use, reporting to stakeholders, and, if necessary, communication with regulatory authorities.

Legal and Ethical Considerations

(Note: more on this in the Legal chapter)

- Data Privacy and Compliance:
  - **Ensure compliance with relevant data protection laws (e.g., GDPR).**

Ensuring compliance with relevant data protection laws, such as the General Data Protection Regulation (GDPR), involves a combination of legal and ethical considerations. Here are key steps to address legal and ethical considerations and achieve compliance:

1. **Understand Applicable Laws**

   Conduct a thorough review of the relevant data protection laws applicable to your organization, such as GDPR in the European Union. Familiarize yourself with the principles, requirements, and obligations outlined in these laws.

2. **Appoint a Data Protection Officer (DPO)**

   Designate a Data Protection Officer if required by the applicable laws. A DPO is responsible for overseeing data protection strategy, ensuring compliance, and serving as a point of contact for data protection authorities.

3. **Data Mapping and Inventory**

   Conduct a comprehensive data mapping exercise to identify and document the types of personal data your organization processes, where it is stored, and how it flows within the organization.

4. **Legal Basis for Data Processing**

   Clearly identify and document the legal basis for processing personal data. Ensure that processing activities are justified under one of the lawful bases defined in data protection laws, such as the necessity of processing for the performance of a contract or compliance with legal obligations.

5. **Transparency and Privacy Notices**

   Provide clear and concise privacy notices to individuals about how their data is collected, processed, and used. Ensure transparency regarding the purpose of processing, the legal basis, and individuals' rights.

6. **Data Subject Rights**

   Establish processes to respect and fulfill data subject rights, including the right to access, rectify, erase, restrict processing, and data portability. Respond promptly to data subject requests and provide mechanisms for individuals to exercise their rights.

7. **Data Minimization and Purpose Limitation**

   Implement data minimization principles, ensuring that you collect and process only the data necessary for the specified purposes. Avoid using data for purposes beyond the original intent without obtaining additional consent.

8. **Consent Management**

   If relying on individuals' consent for data processing, ensure that consent is freely given, specific, informed, and unambiguous. Provide mechanisms for individuals to withdraw consent easily.

9. **Data Security Measures**

   Implement robust data security measures to protect personal data from unauthorized access, disclosure, alteration, and destruction. This includes encryption, access controls, and regular security assessments.

10. **Cooperate with Data Protection Authorities**

    Cooperate with data protection authorities in case of inquiries or investigations. Demonstrate a willingness to engage in dialogue and address any concerns raised by regulatory bodies

11. **Data Protection Impact Assessments (DPIAs)**

    Conduct Data Protection Impact Assessments for high-risk processing activities. Assess the potential risks to individuals' rights and freedoms and implement measures to mitigate those risks.

12. **Cross-Border Data Transfers**

    If your organization transfers personal data across borders, ensure compliance with the legal mechanisms for international data transfers, such as Standard Contractual Clauses (SCCs) or Binding Corporate Rules (BCRs).

13. **Vendor and Third-Party Assessments**

    Assess the data protection practices of third-party vendors and service providers. Ensure that they comply with data protection laws and have adequate safeguards in place for the data they process on your behalf.

14. **Incident Response Plan**

    Develop and maintain an incident response plan to address data breaches promptly. Comply with legal requirements for notifying data protection authorities and affected individuals in the event of a breach.

15. **Record-Keeping and Documentation**

    Maintain detailed records and documentation of data processing activities, risk assessments, and compliance measures. This documentation serves as evidence of your organization's commitment to data protection.

16. **Training and Awareness**

    Train employees and raise awareness about data protection principles, legal requirements, and the organization's policies. Ensure that staff members understand their responsibilities and the importance of protecting personal data.

17. **Ethical Considerations and Accountability**

    Foster an ethical culture within the organization that prioritizes the protection of individuals' privacy. Promote a sense of accountability for data protection throughout all levels of the organization.

18. **Regular Audits and Assessments**

    Conduct regular internal audits and assessments of data protection practices to identify areas for improvement. Stay proactive in ensuring ongoing compliance with evolving legal requirements.

19. **Legal Consultation**

    Seek legal advice from privacy and data protection experts to ensure that your organization's policies and practices align with the latest legal interpretations and precedents.

20. **Continuous Monitoring and Adaptation**

    Stay informed about developments in data protection laws and regulations. Continuously monitor changes in the legal landscape and adapt your organization's practices to remain compliant.

By combining legal and ethical considerations and following these steps, organizations can establish a strong foundation for compliance with data protection laws and demonstrate a commitment to protecting individuals' privacy rights.

- **Address ethical concerns related to AI, such as transparency and accountability.**

Addressing ethical concerns related to AI, particularly issues such as transparency and accountability, involves a *multifaceted approach that combines legal compliance, ethical considerations, and proactive measures* to ensure responsible AI development and deployment.

From a legal perspective, organizations should thoroughly understand and *comply with existing and emerging laws and regulations related to AI,* data protection, and privacy in the jurisdictions where they operate. This includes adherence to anti-discrimination laws to prevent biased treatment based on protected characteristics and alignment with consumer protection laws to ensure transparency, fairness, and disclosure in AI applications impacting consumers.

Ethical considerations play a pivotal role in fostering responsible AI practices. Establishing an ethical framework for AI development and deployment is crucial, emphasizing principles such as fairness, transparency, accountability, and the protection of user privacy. Organizations should consider setting up **ethical review boards** or committees to assess potential ethical implications, particularly in sensitive domains.

Promoting **diversity and inclusion** *in AI teams is essential to reduce biases in algorithmic decision-making, as diverse teams bring varied perspectives* that can help identify potential biases. Adopting human-centered design principles ensures that AI systems prioritize the needs, values, and experiences of users.

Transparency is a key element in addressing ethical concerns. AI systems should be designed to be explainable and interpretable, allowing users and affected individuals to understand how decisions are made. Providing clear documentation and transparency about the algorithms used, including information on training data, model architecture, and decision-making processes, is vital. The *use of **explainable AI** techniques enhances transparency* and provides insights into decision-making processes. User interfaces should be designed to communicate the capabilities and limitations of AI systems transparently.

Accountability is fundamental to responsible AI. Organizations should establish clear lines of responsibility for the development, deployment, and monitoring of AI systems, ensuring accountability at every stage of the AI lifecycle.

Enabling **auditability** of AI systems allows for tracking and reviewing system behavior, aiding in the identification and rectification of issues.

Conducting **ethical impact assessments** before deploying AI systems helps evaluate potential risks and ethical implications associated with the technology. Organizations should acknowledge and address biases in AI systems, implementing mechanisms to detect and rectify biases while establishing accountability for bias-related issues. A robust governance structure for AI projects ensures that decision-making processes are transparent, and ethical considerations are integrated into organizational practices.

Continuous improvement is integral to ethical AI practices. Fostering a culture of continuous learning and improvement allows organizations to learn from mistakes and use insights to enhance future AI development practices. Establishing **feedback mechanisms** for users and stakeholders to report concerns or provide feedback related to the ethical implications of AI systems promotes ongoing improvement. Industry collaboration is encouraged, as organizations should collaborate with others, researchers, and industry stakeholders to share best practices and collectively address ethical challenges in AI. This collaborative approach contributes to the development of ethical standards and guidelines for the responsible use of AI technology.

By combining legal compliance with ethical considerations and adopting these proactive steps, organizations can contribute to the responsible development and deployment of AI systems, addressing concerns related to transparency and accountability. This approach not only helps meet regulatory requirements but also fosters trust among users and stakeholders.

Documentation and Transparency

- Document AI Processes

    - **Maintain comprehensive documentation of the AI development lifecycle.**

Maintaining comprehensive documentation of the AI development lifecycle is crucial for effective AI Governance. This documentation helps ensure transparency, accountability, and the ability to address regulatory requirements. The documentation process should occur at various stages of the AI project:

In the project initiation phase, document the **problem statement, goals**, and **objectives**, specifying the intended impact of the AI system on business processes or outcomes. Identify and document key stakeholders involved in the project, including sponsors, data owners, legal and compliance teams, and end users. Document ethical considerations and compliance requirements, aligning the project with ethical principles and legal obligations, including data protection laws.

Detail the process of collecting and preprocessing data for training and testing the AI model, including data sources, cleaning procedures, and transformations applied.

Document the selection and engineering of features, explaining the rationale behind choices and any domain expertise applied. Specify the criteria for selecting the AI model architecture, compare different models, state the reasons for the chosen model, and discuss potential trade-offs.

In the training process, detail **hyperparameter** tuning, validation procedures, and techniques to enhance model performance. Document algorithms used and their configurations. Describe model validation and testing methods, including datasets, evaluation metrics, and adjustments based on results. Document efforts to make the model explainable and interpretable, detailing techniques employed for transparency.

Specify how bias in the AI model is detected and mitigated, documenting strategies for addressing bias in training data and model outcomes, along with fairness considerations. For model deployment, document the process, deployment environments, integration with existing systems, and scalability considerations. Detail the monitoring and maintenance plan for the deployed system, specifying KPIs, monitoring intervals, and procedures for addressing production issues.

Incorporate documentation of security measures implemented throughout the AI development lifecycle, covering data encryption, access controls, and protection against security threats. Implement and document a **version control system** for tracking changes to code, data, and model versions, ensuring reproducibility and collaboration. Provide comprehensive documentation for the codebase and algorithms, including comments, function explanations, and dependencies.

Document collaboration processes and communication channels among team members, specifying how knowledge sharing, updates, and feedback are managed. Develop documentation for training new team members and transferring knowledge about the AI system, including tutorials and best practices. Ensure that all steps in the AI development lifecycle are auditable and traceable, documenting changes, decisions, and outcomes.

Establish a **feedback loop** for **continuous improvement**, documenting how feedback from end users, stakeholders, and monitoring mechanisms is collected, analyzed, and incorporated.

Finally, *maintain compliance documentation demonstrating adherence to ethical guidelines, legal requirements, and industry standards*, including records of audits, assessments, and actions taken to address noncompliance. This comprehensive documentation serves as a foundational element for robust AI Governance.

- **Document decision-making processes, including model selection and parameter choices.**

Documenting decision-making processes in AI development is a fundamental practice for fostering transparency, reproducibility, and accountability. A systematic documentation approach should characterize various aspects of the decision-making journey:

Begin by providing a project overview, offering a high-level perspective on the AI project's goals, objectives, and the context of deployment. *Clearly articulate the* ***problem statement*** *and the intended impact of the AI system.*

Identify **key stakeholders** involved in decision-making processes, including project sponsors, data owners, domain experts, and members of the AI development team. Document their roles and responsibilities in the decision-making process.

Explicitly document ethical considerations related to the AI project, focusing on how ethical principles, fairness, and potential biases are considered in decision-making, especially during model selection and parameter tuning. Outline how the AI project complies with relevant regulations and standards, documenting legal considerations influencing decision-making and ensuring alignment with data protection laws and industry-specific regulations.

Define decision criteria clearly, including metrics, benchmarks, and objectives guiding decisions related to model selection and parameter choices. Document the rationale behind selecting a specific model architecture, explaining considerations such as complexity, interpretability, and performance. List alternative models considered during the decision-making process and provide reasons for selecting the chosen model over others, including advantages and limitations.

Document choices made regarding hyperparameters, training procedures, and validation and testing strategies. Clearly describe the strategy for model validation and testing, specifying datasets, evaluation metrics, and acceptance or rejection criteria. Discuss how considerations for model explainability and interpretability influenced decision-making and efforts made to enhance transparency.

Address how biases in the training data and potential fairness issues were handled during decision-making. Document preprocessing steps, fairness metrics used, and adjustments made to mitigate bias. Consider model robustness and generalization, documenting strategies to ensure the model's performance on diverse datasets and in real-world scenarios.

Discuss decisions related to model scalability and deployment, considering different environments and scale requirements.

Establish **feedback mechanisms** for gathering input on decision-making processes from team members, stakeholders, and end users. Document how collaboration and communication occur within the team regarding decision-making, specifying channels and documentation methods.

Provide detailed documentation for the code related to model selection, including scripts or notebooks used for experimentation. Implement **version control** *for code, data, and models, documenting the versioning process and maintaining version history for reproducibility.* Ensure traceability of decision-making processes by documenting the trail of decisions, adjustments, and iterations made during the model development lifecycle.

Finally, establish review and audit processes to ensure regular assessments of decision-making documentation for compliance, transparency, and adherence to governance principles. This comprehensive documentation approach ensures that decision-making in AI development is well documented and accountable at every stage of the project.

Model Validation and Testing

- Validation Procedures
    - **Conduct rigorous testing and validation of AI models.**

Rigorous testing and validation of AI models are paramount in AI Governance, serving as the foundation for ensuring their reliability, accuracy, and ability to generalize.

This multifaceted process begins with **data splitting**, dividing the dataset into training, validation, and test sets. The **training set** is instrumental in building the model, the **validation set** aids in tuning hyperparameters and mitigating overfitting, while the **test set** is crucial for the final evaluation of the model's efficacy.

Cross-validation, (particularly methods like **k-fold cross-validation)**, *plays a critical role in evaluating the model's performance across diverse data subsets.* This strategy enhances the robustness of the estimation of the model's generalization power.

Defining evaluation metrics is another essential step, selecting standards such as accuracy, precision, recall, **F1 score**, and the area under the **receiver operating characteristic** (ROC) **curve** to gauge model performance.

Establishing a baseline model or benchmark is vital for comparison, setting a minimal acceptable performance level. A structured train-validation-test workflow ensures that the data across these sets remains distinct, preventing data leakage. **Hyperparameter tuning** then systematically refines these parameters, employing techniques like grid or random search to optimize model performance.

Model training proceeds with these hyperparameters, closely monitoring performance on the validation set to detect any overfitting or underfitting. **Early stopping mechanisms** halt training if model performance plateaus or declines, avoiding **overfitting**. The trained model undergoes evaluation on the test set to simulate real-world application and ensure unbiased generalization capability.

Exploration of ensemble methods, such as **bagging** or **boosting**, can further strengthen model robustness and generalization by aggregating predictions from multiple models. (**Bagging** is an ensemble method that involves training multiple instances of the same learning algorithm on different subsets of the training data. **Boosting** is another ensemble technique, but instead of training models independently, it focuses on training a sequence of models where each new model corrects the errors of its predecessor.) It's also critical to assess and document uncertainties in model predictions, employing techniques like **dropout** during inference for accurate uncertainty estimates. Ensuring model fairness and mitigating bias are imperative, assessing performance across various subgroups to guarantee equitable outcomes.

Robustness testing evaluates the model's resilience against adversarial attacks and input variations, ensuring consistent performance under diverse conditions. External validation, using datasets from varied sources or conditions, bolsters the model's credibility and generalizability. Documenting the entire validation process enhances transparency, reproducibility, and regulatory adherence.

Comparing the developed model against alternatives or benchmarks contextualizes its effectiveness. If performance falls short, an iterative testing and improvement process revisits training and validation procedures. A **comprehensive testing plan** anticipates various scenarios, including edge cases, to identify vulnerabilities. Involving cross-functional teams in the validation process ensures a holistic and informed review.

Finally, **continuous monitoring** of the model in production detects deviations from expected behavior, facilitating timely re-evaluation or retraining. This exhaustive approach to testing and validation is indispensable for deploying robust, accurate, and fair AI systems, embodying best practices in AI Governance.

By following these validation procedures, organizations can establish a robust and accountable process for testing and validating AI models, ensuring that they meet performance expectations, adhere to ethical standards, and comply with governance principles.

- **Use diverse datasets to identify and mitigate biases.**

*Ensuring the use of diverse datasets is paramount for building fair and unbiased AI models*_during the validation and testing process.

To achieve this, it is crucial to start by clearly defining **demographic variables** relevant to the application domain, such as age, gender, and ethnicity. Diverse data collection strategies, including the adoption of various sources, regions, and contexts, help capture a broad spectrum of experiences. Techniques like **data augmentation** and **synthetic data generation** play a vital role in artificially increasing diversity, aiding the model in generalizing across a wide range of scenarios.

Data augmentation is a technique commonly used in machine learning and deep learning to *artificially increase the size of a dataset* by applying various transformations to the existing data. The *goal is to diversify the dataset*, introducing variations that help improve the generalization and robustness of machine learning models. In natural language processing, variations of sentences can be generated through paraphrasing or introducing synonyms. In audio processing, variations in pitch or speed can be applied. Overall, data augmentation is a powerful tool to enhance model performance, reduce overfitting, and create more robust models that can handle a wider range of inputs.

Synthetic data generation involves creating artificial data that simulates the characteristics of real-world data, yet maintaining its statistical validity. This technique is commonly used in machine learning and data science when the available amount of real data is insufficient or when privacy concerns limit access to sensitive information. Synthetic data aims to replicate the statistical properties, patterns, and structures found in real data, allowing machine learning models to learn and generalize effectively.

Stratifying the dataset during splitting ensures that each subset maintains a representative distribution of demographic variables, preventing skewness in any particular subgroup. The use of **bias detection tools and metrics**, such as **Fairness Indicators** or **AI Fairness 360**, allows for quantitative assessments of biases across different groups. Fair sampling techniques and manual review and annotation of the dataset, performed by domain experts, further contribute to identifying potential biases and nuances.

Fairness Indicators in AI systems refer to tools and metrics designed to assess and measure the fairness of machine learning models, particularly in terms of their impact on different demographic groups.

AI Fairness 360 (AIF360)[7] is an open-source toolkit developed by IBM to help developers, data scientists, and researchers assess and mitigate bias in machine learning models. It provides a comprehensive set of tools and algorithms designed to address fairness and transparency concerns across various stages of the machine learning lifecycle. AI Fairness 360 is implemented in Python and is designed to be compatible with popular machine learning frameworks such as scikit-learn and TensorFlow. It is intended to be an accessible and practical resource for researchers and practitioners working on machine learning fairness.

Integrating external data sources cautiously enhances diversity, while soliciting user feedback provides valuable insights that automated analyses may miss.

Adversarial testing, involving intentional bias or perturbations in inputs, tests the model's robustness and sensitivity. Regular data audits track changes in demographic distributions and uphold the dataset's diversity over time.

Ethical considerations are integral, requiring guidelines for responsible data collection and respecting the rights and privacy of individuals.

Transparency and documentation of dataset collection practices, along with diversity metrics like demographic parity and equalized odds, ensure clarity and accountability. Collaborating with communities and organizations representing diverse perspectives fosters inclusivity, and an iterative approach to dataset improvement, along with ongoing education and training, promotes awareness and continuous enhancement.

Compliance with legal and ethical standards, including regulations governing sensitive demographic information, is essential. External audits or third-party reviews provide an additional layer of scrutiny, validating the dataset's diversity and mitigating potential biases. Collectively, these measures contribute to the development of AI models that are fairer, more fair, transparent, and representative of the diverse world they aim to serve.

By incorporating these methods and steps, organizations can enhance the diversity of their datasets, identify potential biases, and take proactive measures to mitigate biases during the validation and testing of AI models.

- **Identify vulnerabilities and implement defenses against potential exploits.**

Identifying vulnerabilities and implementing defenses against potential exploits is crucial for robust AI model validation and testing in the context of AI Governance.

Securing AI models through robust validation and testing is a fundamental aspect of AI Governance, ensuring the reliability and trustworthiness of these systems.

To accomplish this, organizations must adopt a multi-faceted approach, beginning with **threat modeling**—a process that involves analyzing the system architecture and data flow to anticipate potential vulnerabilities and attack vectors.

Adversarial testing, which simulates real-world attacks, is essential for identifying weaknesses that malicious actors may exploit. **Penetration testing**, conducted by ethical hackers, provides a proactive means to expose vulnerabilities in the security architecture. **Code reviews**, encompassing a thorough examination of the implementation, are crucial for identifying common issues like input validation errors and insecure dependencies.

Static and dynamic analysis of the source code, along with regular dependency scanning, help identify vulnerabilities before and during runtime. Implementing **secure coding practices** and enforcing these among developers further mitigates potential security pitfalls. **Secure data handling practices**, including encryption, access controls, and secure storage, are needed to protect sensitive data from unauthorized access. Robust **user authentication and authorization** mechanisms, along with **secure model deployment** in a protected environment, ensure that only authorized individuals can access sensitive functions and data.

Continuous efforts such as regular security audits, the development of an incident response plan, and compliance with data privacy regulations, such as GDPR, HIPAA, and various US state privacy laws contribute to an organization's overall security posture.

Ensuring the security of **API endpoints** *by safeguarding against common vulnerabilities is crucial when the AI system exposes APIs.* Robust monitoring and logging mechanisms aid in detecting and tracking suspicious activities, allowing for a prompt response to potential security incidents.

Encryption of data in transit and at rest, secure mechanisms for model updates, ongoing employee training in cybersecurity best practices, and effective security **patch management** processes further fortify AI systems against potential exploits.

Finally, collaborating with the broader security community, engaging with security researchers, and participating in responsible disclosure programs contribute to staying informed about emerging threats and best practices in AI security. This comprehensive approach enhances the resilience of AI systems and aligns with governance principles to ensure the responsible development and deployment of AI technologies.

By systematically addressing these methods and steps, organizations can enhance the security of their AI systems, reduce the risk of exploits, and establish a robust governance framework for model validation and testing.

- **Privacy Controls** (See Chapter 7 on Privacy's role in AI Gov)

Employee Training and Awareness

- Training Programs
    - **Provide training to employees on AI ethics, risks, and responsible use.**

Providing comprehensive training to employees on AI ethics, risks, and responsible use is indispensable for reducing risks and fostering ethical AI program development.

To begin, it's *essential to assess the audience, understanding their knowledge levels, roles, and responsibilities related to AI.* Tailoring the training program to address the specific needs and concerns of different employee groups ensures maximum relevance and impact. Clear learning objectives should be defined, encompassing key topics such as AI ethics, associated risks, responsible development practices, and the broader impact of AI on various stakeholders.

The training program should commence with an introduction to AI concepts and technologies, ensuring that employees have a foundational understanding of what AI is, how it operates, and its potential applications. *Emphasizing AI ethics principles, including fairness, transparency, accountability, privacy, and inclusivity, should be a focal point.* The significance of these principles in guiding responsible AI practices should be illustrated through real-world examples and case studies, demonstrating instances of both responsible AI use and ethical concerns that have arisen.

Addressing biases and fairness issues in AI algorithms is crucial, and strategies for identifying and mitigating bias throughout the AI development lifecycle should be discussed. Privacy concerns related to AI, particularly when handling personal data, should also be a key focus, accompanied by guidelines for compliance with data protection laws and best practices for protecting user privacy. Exploring potential risks and challenges associated with AI, such as unintended consequences, security vulnerabilities, and societal impacts, encourages employees to think critically about the implications of AI technologies.

Introducing employees to regulatory compliance is vital, providing an overview of relevant regulations and standards governing AI, depending on the industry. This may include GDPR, HIPAA, or other sector-specific regulations, along with explanations of the legal obligations associated with AI development. Highlighting the importance of explainability and transparency in AI systems is key, emphasizing how to communicate AI decisions to users and stakeholders to foster trust and accountability.

Interactive learning elements, including quizzes, case studies, and group discussions, should be incorporated to promote engagement and enable employees to apply ethical principles to practical scenarios. Creating an environment for open dialogue is crucial, encouraging employees to ask questions, share insights, and express concerns related to AI ethics. Offering practical guidelines, including checklists, best practices, and decision-making frameworks, helps guide responsible AI practices.

Providing additional resources for further learning, such as recommended readings, online courses, and industry guidelines, ensures that employees have the opportunity to delve deeper into AI ethics. Facilitating cross-functional collaboration among different departments, including AI developers, legal teams, and business stakeholders, ensures a holistic approach to AI ethics. Tailoring training content based on specific roles and responsibilities ensures that developers, data scientists, managers, and legal teams receive insights and guidance tailored to their needs.

Implementing assessments to gauge understanding and retention of key concepts, along with providing certifications upon completion of the training, recognizes employees' commitment to responsible AI practices.

Regularly updating the training program to reflect emerging trends, new regulations, and best practices in AI ethics is essential, considering the evolving nature of technology and ethical considerations. Seeking external expertise, such as bringing in external experts in AI ethics for specialized workshops or training sessions, can provide valuable insights and broaden employees' understanding. Finally, implementing mechanisms to measure the impact of the training program, assessing changes in employee behavior, awareness, and the incorporation of ethical considerations into AI development projects, ensures ongoing effectiveness and improvement.

By following these steps, organizations can develop a comprehensive and effective training program on AI ethics, risks, and responsible use, fostering a culture of ethical AI development and deployment within the workforce.

Crisis Response Plan

- Incident Response Plan
  - **Develop a comprehensive incident response plan for AI-related failures.**

Developing a comprehensive incident response plan for AI-related failures is crucial for effectively managing crises and mitigating potential negative impacts. Here are steps to create an incident response plan specifically tailored for AI programs:

1. **Establish an Incident Response Team**
   Form a dedicated incident response team consisting of key stakeholders, including AI developers, data scientists, IT personnel, legal experts, and communications professionals. Define roles and responsibilities within the team.
2. **Define Incident Categories**
   Identify and categorize potential incidents related to AI failures. These may include bias-related issues, security breaches, data breaches, performance degradation, ethical concerns, or unintended consequences.
3. **Conduct Risk Assessments**
   Perform risk assessments to understand the potential impact and likelihood of different AI-related incidents. Prioritize incidents based on their severity and potential consequences.

4. **Establish Incident Severity Levels**

   Define severity levels for different types of incidents. Classify incidents based on their impact, and determine the appropriate level of response for each severity level.

5. **Develop Incident Response Procedures**

   Create detailed incident response procedures for each identified incident category. Clearly outline the steps to be taken during detection, analysis, containment, eradication, recovery, and lessons learned phases.

6. **Set Response Time Objectives**

   Define response time objectives for each incident severity level. Establish realistic timelines for acknowledging, investigating, and mitigating incidents based on their criticality.

7. **Implement Continuous Monitoring**

   Deploy continuous monitoring mechanisms to detect AI-related incidents promptly. Use monitoring tools and alerts to identify abnormal behavior, performance issues, or security breaches in real time.

8. **Integrate with Existing Security Protocols**

   Ensure that the incident response plan integrates seamlessly with existing organizational security protocols. Align AI incident response with broader cybersecurity practices and policies.

9. **Define Communication Protocols**

   Establish clear communication protocols for notifying stakeholders about AI incidents. Define the internal and external communication channels, and identify spokespersons responsible for conveying information to the media, customers, and internal teams.

10. **Legal and Compliance Considerations**

    Include legal and compliance considerations in the incident response plan. Understand and comply with relevant data protection laws, industry regulations, and contractual obligations associated with AI programs.

11. **Data Breach Response**

    Develop specific response procedures for AI-related data breaches. Include steps for notifying affected parties, conducting forensic analysis, and coordinating with legal teams to manage potential regulatory requirements.

12. **Engage External Experts**

    Identify and establish relationships with external experts, such as AI ethicists, legal advisors, and cybersecurity consultants, who can provide guidance and support during incident response.

13. **Training and Simulation Exercises**

    Conduct regular training sessions and simulation exercises to ensure that the incident response team is familiar with the procedures. Simulate different incident scenarios to test the effectiveness of the response plan.

14. **Document Lessons Learned**

    After each incident, document lessons learned and areas for improvement. Use these insights to enhance the incident response plan continuously.

15. **Coordinate with Public Relations**

    Collaborate with public relations and communications teams to prepare messaging in the event of a public-facing incident. Develop strategies for managing the public perception of AI-related failures.

16. **Establish Post-Incident Review Processes**

    Implement post-incident review processes to analyze the effectiveness of the response. Evaluate the timeliness of actions, the accuracy of decisions, and the overall impact on the organization.

17. **Continuous Improvement**

    Foster a culture of continuous improvement in incident response. Regularly update the plan based on emerging threats, changes in AI technologies, and lessons learned from previous incidents.

18. **Legal and Ethical Oversight**

    Integrate legal and ethical oversight into incident response activities. Ensure that actions taken during incident response align with legal requirements and ethical considerations.

19. **Secure Backup and Recovery**

    Implement secure backup and recovery mechanisms for AI models and datasets. Ensure that backup copies are regularly tested for restoration effectiveness.

20. **Regularly Update Contacts and Resources**

    Maintain an up-to-date list of contacts, resources, and external experts who may be needed during incident response. Ensure that the incident response team has access to the necessary support.

By following these steps, organizations can develop a robust incident response plan specifically tailored to address AI-related failures. This proactive approach helps minimize the impact of incidents, enhance organizational resilience, and promote responsible AI development practices.

- **Define roles and responsibilities in the event of a crisis.**

Defining roles and responsibilities is a crucial aspect of developing an effective **Incident Response Plan** for AI programs. Assigning clear roles ensures that the incident response team works cohesively to address crises promptly.

The formation of an **Incident Response Team** (IRT) is crucial, comprising individuals with diverse expertise such as AI developers, data scientists, IT personnel, legal experts, RIM professionals, privacy, security, information risk, and communication professionals, and relevant department heads. *Leadership roles within the IRT should be clearly defined*, including an **Incident Commander** or **Team Leader** responsible for overseeing the overall response efforts and making critical decisions during a crisis. Technical experts in AI, data security, and system operations serve as incident responders, while data stewards are designated to oversee data handling, protection, and integrity.

Legal and compliance experts play a vital role in addressing legal and regulatory aspects, ensuring compliance with data protection laws, and managing legal implications. Communication and public relations specialists are crucial for managing external and internal communications during a crisis, disseminating messages to stakeholders, the media, and the public. Additionally, AI ethicists or subject matter experts can provide insights into ethical considerations associated with AI failures. Incident coordination roles are established to facilitate communication between different teams, ensuring effective information flow and decision-making processes.

Roles such as technical support, liaison roles for external entities, decision-making authority, and backup roles are also clearly defined within the IRT. Detailed role descriptions, training sessions, and simulation exercises are conducted to familiarize team members with their responsibilities, the incident response plan, and overall goals. Regular reviews and updates of role assignments, coupled with the establishment of secure communication channels and reporting procedures, contribute to the IRT's effectiveness. Ultimately, promoting a collaborative culture within the incident response team, emphasizing teamwork, effective communication, and shared responsibility, is essential for managing AI-related crises effectively.

By following these steps, organizations can effectively define roles and responsibilities within the Incident Response Plan for AI programs, ensuring a well-coordinated and organized response to crises. This collaborative approach helps mitigate the impact of incidents and enhances the organization's resilience in the face of AI-related challenges.

- Communication Strategy
  - **Develop a communication strategy to address stakeholders in the event of a significant AI-related incident.**

Developing a communication strategy is a critical aspect of an Incident Response Plan for AI programs, as it plays a pivotal role in building trust with stakeholders and mitigating potential reputational damage. In the preparatory phase, the identification and categorization of key stakeholders, both internal and external, are crucial. Understanding the information needs and concerns of different stakeholder groups allows for tailoring communication messages based on specific interests and expectations. *Drafting initial messages in advance ensures a rapid response during the early stages of an incident, assuring stakeholders that the situation is being addressed and committing to regular updates.*

Establishing communication channels involves identifying primary channels such as press releases, official statements, social media platforms, email notifications, and direct communication with key individuals or groups. Designating official spokespeople who are trained in crisis communication and ensuring the security and reliability of communication channels are paramount. Timely notification procedures, both internal and external, must be defined, with specific timelines based on the severity and nature of the incident. Internal communication protocols should be in place to disseminate information efficiently within the organization.

Crafting messages with transparency, clarity, and empathy is essential. Acknowledging the impact of the incident on stakeholders and providing actionable information, including steps being taken to resolve the issue, fosters a sense of understanding. Clearly outlining the organization's planned actions and future steps establishes a roadmap for resolution, remediation, and prevention of similar incidents.

Consistent messaging across all communication channels and prompt addressing of rumors and speculation contribute to a unified front and counter misinformation. Compliance with legal considerations, including a legal review of communication messages, is vital to avoid compromising the organization's legal position. Considering data protection and privacy laws when communicating about incidents involving personal or sensitive data is crucial.

Engaging stakeholders through two-way communication and establishing feedback mechanisms demonstrates transparency and openness. Post-incident communication involves providing updates on recovery and remediation efforts, sharing lessons learned, and communicating the organization's commitment to continuous improvement. Effective media relations include defining procedures for handling media inquiries, preparing press releases, and controlling the dissemination of information.

Documenting communication activities is essential for post-incident analysis and reporting. Evaluation of communication effectiveness during and after the incident helps identify areas for improvement. Continuous improvement involves regular review and updating of the communication strategy based on emerging trends, stakeholder expectations, and organizational changes. Training and drills ensure the incident response team and spokespersons are well prepared for potential incidents.

Engaging public relations and crisis communication experts, as well as providing media coaching for spokespersons, enhances communication skills and effectiveness during high-profile incidents.

By following these steps, organizations can develop a robust communication strategy for addressing stakeholders in the event of a significant AI-related incident. This proactive approach contributes to maintaining trust, managing perceptions, and mitigating reputational risks during crises.

Continuous Monitoring

- Real-time Monitoring

    - **Implement systems for real-time monitoring of AI applications.**

Implementing **real-time monitoring** *of AI applications is pivotal in safeguarding performance, security, and compliance, enabling organizations to quickly identify and address issues, respond* to anomalies, and uphold the integrity of AI applications within the framework of AI Governance.

This begins with clearly defined monitoring objectives, understanding the **key performance indicators** (KPIs), security metrics, and compliance requirements essential for continuous oversight. Aligning these objectives with the organization's goals and the specific needs of the AI application sets the foundation for effective monitoring.

Selecting relevant metrics is the next step, identifying those that best reflect the AI application's health and performance, such as model accuracy, inference time, resource utilization, and error rates.

A comprehensive monitoring plan is then developed, detailing the metrics to be monitored, monitoring frequency, and the stakeholders involved. This plan also defines acceptable metric ranges or thresholds and criteria for triggering alerts.

Choosing the right monitoring tools is critical, selecting solutions that align with the organization's infrastructure and the AI application's unique needs. *Tools may include application performance monitoring (APM) solutions, logging frameworks, and specialized AI monitoring platforms.* Instrumenting the AI application with monitoring code or agents enables the collection of pertinent data, integrating monitoring libraries and logging mechanisms to capture essential metrics in real time.

Real-time alerting mechanisms are implemented based on predefined thresholds to notify relevant personnel when metrics deviate from expected values, with clearly defined severity levels to prioritize responses. An **incident response plan** is crucial, outlining the actions to be taken in response to alerts, defining roles and responsibilities, communication channels, and escalation procedures.

Security monitoring measures are integrated to detect potential threats, alongside monitoring for data quality issues that could impact model performance. Scalability monitoring ensures the AI application can handle varying workloads, identifying potential bottlenecks and optimizing resource allocation. Compliance monitoring ensures adherence to regulatory standards, while user experience monitoring gauges how end users interact with the application, addressing any issues that affect satisfaction.

Model performance metrics are continuously tracked to ensure reliability and relevance, and infrastructure monitoring ensures the supporting systems are robust and capable. For AI systems involving continuous learning, monitoring for model drift and degradation is vital, with processes in place for timely retraining.

Documentation of the monitoring setup, regular reviews for optimization, and education and training for teams on monitoring data interpretation and tool usage are essential. A culture of **continuous improvement** encourages regular reassessment and updating of monitoring practices, and staying informed about emerging technologies enhances monitoring capabilities, contributing to effective AI Governance.

By following these steps, organizations can establish an effective real-time monitoring system for their AI applications, enabling proactive detection of issues, ensuring compliance, and optimizing the overall performance of AI systems.

- **Set up alerts for deviations from expected behavior.**

Setting up alerts for deviations from expected behavior is a crucial aspect of continuous monitoring in AI Governance. Alerts enable organizations to respond promptly to anomalies, ensuring the integrity, performance, and security of AI applications. Here are methods and steps to set up alerts for deviations from expected behavior:

1. **Define Monitoring Objectives**

   Clearly define the monitoring objectives and identify the key performance indicators (KPIs) or metrics that need to be monitored. Understand the baseline or expected behavior for each metric.

2. **Establish Thresholds**

   Set thresholds for each monitored metric to define acceptable ranges of behavior. These thresholds serve as benchmarks against which deviations will trigger alerts. Thresholds can be based on historical data, industry standards, or predefined performance goals.

3. **Define Alert Triggers**

   Determine the conditions that trigger alerts. Define specific rules or conditions that, when met, indicate a deviation from expected behavior. This may include exceeding a threshold, a sudden change in trend, or reaching a critical level.

4. **Severity Levels**

   Establish severity levels for alerts to prioritize responses. Classify alerts based on their impact and urgency. For example, critical issues may require immediate attention, while lower-severity alerts may be addressed during regular monitoring reviews.

5. **Real-Time Alerting**

   Implement real-time alerting mechanisms to notify relevant stakeholders or teams when a deviation occurs. Utilize alerting systems that support real-time notifications through channels such as email, SMS, or integration with collaboration platforms.

6. **Automated Alerting**

   Automate the alerting process to minimize response time. Implement automated workflows that trigger alerts and initiate predefined responses, reducing the reliance on manual intervention.

7. **Escalation Procedures**

   Define escalation procedures to ensure that alerts are appropriately addressed. Specify the individuals or teams responsible for responding to different severity levels of alerts. Establish clear communication channels and escalation paths.

8. **Incident Response Plan**

   Integrate alerting into the incident response plan. Clearly document the steps to be taken in response to alerts, including the roles and responsibilities of team members, communication protocols, and resolution procedures.

9. **Continuous Review and Adjustment**

   Regularly review alerting configurations to ensure their relevance and effectiveness. As the AI application evolves, update thresholds and alert triggers based on changes in system behavior or performance goals.

10. **Feedback Loops**

    Establish feedback loops to continuously improve alerting. Collect feedback from incidents, assess the effectiveness of alerts, and use this information to refine alert configurations. Consider the feedback of those who respond to alerts for process improvement.

11. **Contextual Alerts**

    Implement contextual alerts that provide additional information about the nature of the deviation. Include relevant context, such as the affected component, potential root causes, and recommended actions to streamline the response process.

12. **Integration with Monitoring Tools**

    Integrate alerting mechanisms with monitoring tools and platforms. Leverage application performance monitoring (APM) tools, logging frameworks, or specialized AI monitoring solutions to facilitate seamless alerting and monitoring workflows.

13. **User-Friendly Notifications**

    Ensure that alert notifications are user-friendly and actionable. Clearly communicate the nature of the deviation, the affected component, and any recommended steps for resolution. Make alerts comprehensible to both technical and non-technical stakeholders.

14. **Multichannel Alerts**

    Implement alerts across multiple communication channels to reach stakeholders effectively. Use a combination of email, messaging apps, dashboards, and other channels to ensure that alerts are noticed promptly.

15. **Adaptive Alerting**

    Implement adaptive alerting that adjusts to changes in system behavior. Avoid unnecessary alerts due to temporary fluctuations or expected variations by incorporating adaptive algorithms or statistical methods.

16. **Periodic Review Meetings**

    Conduct periodic review meetings to assess the performance of alerting mechanisms. Gather feedback from monitoring teams, incident responders, and other stakeholders to identify areas for improvement and refinement.

17. **Documentation**

    Document the alerting configurations, including the thresholds, triggers, and response procedures. Maintain documentation for reference, audits, and to facilitate knowledge transfer among team members.

18. **Training and Awareness**

    Provide training and awareness sessions for relevant teams on how to interpret alerts and respond effectively. Ensure that team members are familiar with the alerting system and understand their roles in the incident response process.

19. **Simulation Exercises**

    Conduct simulation exercises to test the effectiveness of alerting and incident response. Simulate scenarios where deviations from expected behavior occur and evaluate how well the alerting system and response procedures perform.

20. **Compliance Monitoring**

    Integrate alerting mechanisms with compliance monitoring efforts. Ensure that alerts are configured to notify relevant stakeholders of any deviations from regulatory or organizational compliance requirements.

By following these methods and steps, organizations can establish a robust alerting system for deviations from expected behavior, enabling timely responses to anomalies and contributing to effective AI Governance.

Key Points

- Risk management plays a key role in AI Governance, across the lifecycle of an AI system.
- Integrating risk management across the AI lifecycle is essential for the responsible development and deployment of effective, reliable, and ethically compliant AI systems.
- Identifying and mitigating data risks, including biases and inaccuracies in training data, is a crucial step in managing the overall risks associated with AI systems.
- Identifying and documenting all data sources used in the training process is crucial, including internal datasets, external datasets, and third-party data.
- Assessing data quality, examining representation across demographic groups, and identifying biases and inaccuracies through statistical analysis are also key steps.
- For external datasets, a risk assessment is conducted for third-party data sources, verifying their reliability, quality, and security practices.
- Engaging security experts in the risk identification process leverages their expertise to identify risks and mitigation strategies.
- In managing and mitigating risks in AI implementations, the identification of model risks is a critical and foundational step that requires a systematic and comprehensive approach.
- A thorough analysis of feature engineering evaluates the relevance, representativeness, and significance of features contributing to the model's predictive capabilities.
- Model complexity analysis helps evaluate if the model is overfitting or underfitting the training data and whether its complexity aligns with the available data.
- Documenting findings related to model risks, including potential weaknesses, uncertainties, and areas for improvement, is essential.
- Implementing risk mitigation strategies may involve model retraining, algorithm adjustments, or the introduction of additional features to enhance robustness.
- To address biases, it is essential to define fairness metrics, such as demographic parity, equalized odds, and disparate impact, tailored to the context of the application.
- Key integration points, (where the AI system interfaces with other systems) should be identified, and risks, dependencies, and data flows at these points thoroughly understood.
- Thorough testing of the integrated system, including functional, performance, and stress testing, is imperative to identify potential operational issues and risks before deployment.

- Security protocols and compliance with regulatory requirements, including data protection and privacy, must be evaluated to address vulnerabilities and ensure legal adherence.
- Considering user training needs and support mechanisms is vital to ensure end users understand how to interact with and interpret the outputs of the AI system.
- The development of a risk matrix, combining impact and likelihood scores, aids in visualizing and prioritizing risks based on their severity.
- Overall risk scores are calculated by multiplying the impact score by the likelihood score, providing a quantitative measure of each risk's severity.
- High-risk scenarios are prioritized, focusing on those with the highest potential impact and likelihood.
- In a qualitative risk assessment, considering *subjective factors and expert opinions is crucial for capturing nuanced aspects of risks that may not be easily quantifiable.*
- The Delphi method, involving iterative rounds of surveys or discussions with experts, facilitates the convergence of opinions over multiple rounds.
- Encouraging experts to use storytelling techniques to convey the narrative of potential risks makes the risks more relatable and understandable to a broader audience.
- Integrating qualitative assessments with quantitative approaches results in a more comprehensive risk management strategy leveraging both types of insights.
- Evaluating the reputational and regulatory implications of identified risks in a qualitative assessment for AI implementations is critical for comprehensive risk management.
- Risk mitigation strategies are developed in collaboration with legal and regulatory experts, involving adjustments to policies, procedures, or the technical aspects of the AI system.
- Conduct a comprehensive data mapping exercise to identify and document the types of personal data processed, where it is stored, and how it flows within the organization.
- Organizations should establish a strong foundation for compliance with data protection laws and demonstrate a commitment to protecting individuals' privacy rights.
- Addressing ethical concerns related to AI, particularly transparency and accountability, involves a multifaceted approach that combines legal compliance and ethical considerations.
- Ethical considerations play a pivotal role in fostering responsible AI practices.
- Maintaining comprehensive documentation of the AI development lifecycle is crucial for effective AI Governance.
- Documenting decision-making processes in AI development is a fundamental practice for fostering transparency, reproducibility, and accountability.
- Document choices made regarding hyperparameters, training procedures, and validation and testing strategies.
- Early stopping mechanisms halt training if model performance plateaus or declines, avoiding overfitting.
- Securing AI models through robust validation and testing is fundamental to AI Governance.
- Ensuring the security of API endpoints by safeguarding against common vulnerabilities is crucial.
- Implementing robust data governance practices is crucial for ensuring high-quality training data in AI systems.
- The designation of data stewards is key to ensuring the quality of training data, enforcement of data governance policies, resolution of data quality issues, and compliance.

- Establishing data lineage and traceability mechanisms helps to track the origin and transformations applied to training data.
- Providing comprehensive training to employees on AI ethics, risks, and responsible use is indispensable for reducing risks and fostering ethical AI program development.
- Tailoring the training program to address the specific needs will make it more effective.
- Developing a comprehensive Incident Response Plan for AI-related failures is crucial for effectively managing crises and mitigating potential negative impacts.
- Developing a communication strategy is a critical aspect of an Incident Response Plan.
- Implementing real-time monitoring of AI applications is pivotal in safeguarding performance, security, and compliance.

Key Glossary Terms

Adversarial testing: The process of evaluating the robustness and resilience of AI systems by intentionally presenting them with challenging or deceptive inputs. It aims to identify vulnerabilities and weaknesses in AI models.

AI Fairness 360 (AIF360): An open-source toolkit developed by IBM to help developers, data scientists, and researchers assess and mitigate bias in machine learning models.

Bagging: An ensemble method that involves training multiple instances of the same learning algorithm on different subsets of the training data.

Boosting: Another ensemble technique, but instead of training models independently, it focuses on training a sequence of models where each new model corrects the errors of its predecessor.

Cross-validation: A statistical method used to evaluate the performance and generalizability of AI models by partitioning the data into subsets, training the model on some of these subsets, and validating it on the remaining ones.

Data augmentation: The process of artificially expanding a dataset by creating modified versions of existing data or generating new synthetic data. This technique is employed to enhance the diversity and volume of training data available.

Data profiling: The systematic examination of datasets intended for use in AI models to understand their structure, quality, and potential issues. This process involves analyzing the data to uncover patterns, anomalies, inconsistencies, missing values, and other characteristics that could impact the performance and fairness of AI systems.

Data splitting: The practice of dividing a dataset into distinct subsets to train, validate, and test AI models in a manner that ensures their reliability, generalizability, and fairness.

Ethical impact assessment: A structured evaluation designed to identify, analyze, and address the ethical implications and consequences of deploying AI technologies.

Explainability: The ability to describe or present the workings of an AI model in understandable terms to humans. It can be seen as a bridge between complex AI models and human users who seek to understand how these models arrive at their conclusions.

F1 score: A critical metric used to evaluate the precision and recall balance of a predictive model, providing a single measure of a model's accuracy in classifying cases, especially in imbalanced datasets.

Fair data preprocessing techniques: Methods applied to data before it is used to train AI models, aiming to mitigate biases in training sets that could lead to unfair outcomes.

Fairness indicators: Tools and metrics designed to assess and measure the fairness of machine learning models, particularly in terms of their impact on different demographic groups.

Fairness metrics: Quantitative measures used to assess the fairness of AI algorithms and models. These metrics help identify and mitigate biases that may exist in AI systems.

Hyperparameters: External configuration settings that are not learned from the data but are set prior to the training process.

K-fold cross-validation: A method used to evaluate the performance and generalizability of AI models across different subsets of a dataset, ensuring that the model is reliable and performs consistently under various conditions.

Model degradation: A decline in the performance of a machine learning model over time, even in the absence of external changes in the data distribution.

Model drift: Where the statistical properties of the target variable or the input features change over time, leading to a degradation in the performance of a machine learning model.

Overfitting: When a model learns the training data too well, akin to memorizing the training data rather than learning the underlying relationships. As a result, an overfitted model may perform very well on the training data but fail to generalize to new, unseen examples.

Receiver Operating Characteristic (ROC) curve: A graphical representation used to evaluate the diagnostic ability of binary classifiers, a type of AI model that categorizes instances into one of two groups (e.g., positive or negative). The ROC curve plots the true positive rate (TPR, or sensitivity) against the false positive rate (FPR, or 1-specificity) at various threshold settings.

Regulatory impact assessment: A systematic process to evaluate the potential effects of proposed regulations or policies on the development, deployment, and use of AI.

Root cause analysis (RCA): A systematic process aimed at identifying the underlying reasons for faults, failures, or undesired outcomes in AI systems.

Rule-based validation: The systematic application of predefined rules and criteria to verify the integrity, quality, and appropriateness of data used in AI systems, and to ensure that the behavior of AI models aligns with ethical standards, regulatory requirements, and organizational policies.

Synthetic data generation: The creation of artificial data that mimics the statistical properties of real-world data but does not directly correspond to any real individual events or entities. It is utilized to overcome challenges related to privacy, data scarcity, and imbalanced datasets.

Notes

1 "Drive Trust in AI with Data Observability & Data Quality," Informatica Incorporated, accessed May 2, 2025. https://www.informatica.com/lp/roadmap-to-trustworthy-ai-a-cdos-blueprint-for-data-quality-and-observability_5010.html.

2 "What is the Difference Between a Parameter and a Hyperparameter?" *Machine Learning Mastery*, accessed May 1, 2025. https://machinelearningmastery.com/difference-between-a-parameter-and-a-hyperparameter/.

3 Ferrara, "Fairness and Bias in Artificial Intelligence: A Brief Survey of Sources, Impacts, and Mitigation Strategies," University of Southern California, Thomas Lord Department of Computer Science, December 26, 2023, https://www.mdpi.com/2413-4155/6/1/3.

4 "How to Mitigate Bias in Machine Learning Models," Encord Incorporated, accessed May 12, 2025, https://encord.com/blog/reducing-bias-machine-learning/.

5 "Guide for Cybersecurity Event Recovery," NIST Special Publication 800-184, National Institute of Standards and Technology, accessed May 10, 2025, https://nvlpubs.nist.gov/nistpubs/specialpublications/nist.sp.800-184.pdf.

6 "What Is the Delphi Method, and How Is It Useful in Forecasting?" *Investopedia*, accessed May 8, 2025, https://www.investopedia.com/terms/d/delphi-method.asp.

7 "Introducing AI Fairness 360," IBM Incorporated, accessed May 13, 2025, https://research.ibm.com/blog/ai-fairness-36

7 The Role of Privacy in AI Governance

Dr. Pieter Van der Walt and Robert F. Smallwood

Introduction to AI and Privacy

Issues of data privacy have been at the forefront of technology for nearly four decades. The Internet has always been an insecure place. The arrival of Web 2.0, with e-commerce, personalization, and vast revenue opportunities, made it even more so.[1] The social media revolution further compounded the challenges of privacy, as people revealed ever-deepening wells of their most intimate thoughts, which were then monetized to the tune of several trillions of dollars through the 2010s. The coming of Web 3.0 is intended to strengthen privacy controls for individuals.

The second generation of the Web brought with it a Privacy Paradox, where consumers wanted to maintain their personal privacy and anonymity online while simultaneously receiving personalized offers based on one's geolocation. It is impossible to have both deep personalization and privacy; they are mutually exclusive.

A wide range of privacy legislation began to be implemented in the mid-2010s, as governing bodies came to recognize the value and power of vast quantities of personal data. While these laws attempted to curtail some of the negative aspects of users surrendering their personal data in order to gain context-specific benefits, nearly all regulations contain a consent clause. These clauses allow platform providers to continue to collect and leverage personal data so long as the customer consents to this collection and consumption. This is naturally a Faustian bargain, as one must consent to the data collection if one is to access the platform.

Artificial intelligence (AI) brings several new challenges to the issue of privacy. Generative AI makes use of trillions of documents, videos, and data records collected from the Internet, each of which has an author and hence someone with associated privacy rights. Several AI platforms have demonstrated the ability to recreate, on demand, entire pieces of original training data, completely removing any controls on that data's privacy. In neural networks with tens of thousands of nodes, such an ability to recreate original training data is likely inevitable.

Further, in reinforcement training, an AI model is taught to distinguish between acceptable and unacceptable responses. Again, this is in the eye of the trainer, and it is inevitable that an AI so trained will take on the attitudes, biases, and beliefs of its trainer or training team.

Finally, nearly all AI systems are designed to continue to learn from ongoing use. Inasmuch as user interactions with the AI are associated back to the user in question, a whole new range of privacy and proprietary rights questions arise due to these interactions.

As with other aspects of the use of data analytic tools, AI takes issues that already existed and amplifies both their positive and negative consequences. Regarding privacy, organizations that adopt AI must be vigilant about the training, use, and ongoing development of these platforms, ensuring ongoing compliance with an ever-growing set of rules and regulations.

AI is a transformative technology with the potential to significantly benefit society, the economy, and the environment. However, it also presents numerous challenges and risks, including bias, discrimination, and misuse. Therefore, it's crucial that AI is developed and used responsibly and ethically. This necessitates a comprehensive approach to AI Governance, incorporating data privacy, data governance, ethics, information security, risk management, and more.. These elements are vital for protecting the rights and interests of those affected by AI and for ensuring the quality, reliability, and accountability of AI systems.

Data privacy must be central to AI Governance. Indeed, data privacy is one of the five rights given in the US Office of Science and Technology Policy's "AI Bill of Rights,"[2] which states that data subjects "should be protected from abusive data practices via built-in protections and [. . .] should have agency over how data about [them] is used" (2023). While privacy is notoriously difficult to define, *we can state that AI privacy, then, involves the protection of personal data that is collected, stored, processed, and shared by AI systems.* Given that AI technologies often depend on large volumes of data, including personal and sensitive information, robust data privacy measures are essential. These measures respect individuals' privacy rights and ensure that their data is used lawfully, fairly, and transparently. They also involve implementing suitable technical and organizational safeguards to protect data from unauthorized access, use, disclosure, alteration, and destruction. Furthermore, they provide individuals with control over their data, including the rights to access, correct, delete, and transfer their data. *Prioritizing data privacy in AI Governance helps build trust in AI systems, encourages responsible data practices, and shields individuals and society from potential harm.*

For businesses aiming to thrive and sustain in the AI market, integrating privacy controls into their AI systems is a must. Privacy professionals have long been managing AI risk, helping clients ensure that automated decision-making, biometrics, Internet of Things, and other AI-driven processing activities comply with privacy and data protection laws.

Data Privacy: The Bedrock of AI Governance

Data privacy in AI involves the protection of personal data that is collected, stored, processed, and shared by AI systems. Given *that AI technologies often depend on large volumes of data, including personal and sensitive information, robust data privacy measures are essential.* These measures respect individuals' privacy rights and ensure that their data is used lawfully, fairly and transparently. They also involve implementing suitable technical and organizational safeguards to protect data from unauthorized access, use, disclosure, alteration and destruction. Furthermore, they provide individuals with control over their data, including the rights to access, correct, delete and transfer their data. *Prioritizing data privacy in AI Governance helps build trust in AI systems, encourages responsible data practices and shields individuals and society from potential harm.*

A set of principles—the **Fair Information Practice Principles** (FIPPs)[3]—has been foundational in data and information privacy since at least 1973, when the US Department of Health, Education, and Welfare released its seminal report on "Records, Computers, and the Rights of Citizens." Those same principles have remained central to data privacy governance right through to the current moment, forming the foundations of the EU's General Data Protection Regulation and a slew of privacy regulations, standards, and solutions. In the context of AI, the following principles are particularly relevant:

- **Lawfulness, Fairness, and Transparency:** AI systems must process personal data lawfully, fairly, and in a transparent manner. This involves clearly informing individuals about how their data will be used and ensuring that the data is used for legitimate purposes.
- **Purpose Limitation:** Personal data collected and consented to be used for specific purposes should not be used for other purposes without the individual's consent. This principle is crucial for maintaining trust in AI systems.

- **Data Minimization:** AI systems should only collect and process the minimum amount of personal data necessary for their purposes. This helps reduce the risk of the impact of data breaches and misuse.
- **Accuracy:** AI systems must ensure that the personal data they process is accurate and up to date. Inaccurate data can lead to incorrect AI outputs and decisions.
- **Storage Limitation:** Personal data should not be kept longer than necessary. This principle is important for managing the lifecycle of data within AI systems.
- **Integrity and Confidentiality:** AI systems must ensure the security of personal data. This involves implementing appropriate technical and organizational measures to protect data against unauthorized or unlawful processing and accidental loss, destruction, or damage.
- **Accountability:** The organization responsible for the AI system must be able to demonstrate compliance with all of these principles. This involves keeping records of data processing (ROP) activities and implementing data protection impact assessments for high-risk processing.

Each of these measures has a significant impact on AI. For instance, they influence the design and operation of AI systems, the *types* of data that AI systems can use, and the *ways* in which AI systems can use that data. They also shape the responsibilities of those involved in the development and use of AI systems, including data scientists, engineers, and decision-makers. Activities related to these measures include developing and implementing data protection policies, conducting data protection impact assessments, training staff on data protection requirements, and responding to data subject requests (DSR).

The Role of Privacy Professionals in AI

Privacy professionals have long been managing data and information-related risk, including AI risk, helping businesses to comply with privacy and data protection laws. *Many AI-related harms can be traced back to AI failures, some of which can be linked to privacy requirements.* For instance, obligations for **transparency** and "**explainability**" compel organizations to understand how AI systems operate and evaluate decision quality. Data minimization requires AI developers to use data that is relevant, necessary, and adequate, while the principle of accuracy may warrant more, not less, quality data to enhance statistical accuracy.

Privacy professionals play a pivotal role in managing AI risk, ensuring that AI-driven processing activities, such as automated decision-making, biometrics, Internet of Things, and other AI-driven processing activities, comply with privacy and data protection laws. They are responsible for:

- **Transparency and Explainability:** Ensuring organizations understand how AI systems operate and evaluate decision quality. This involves making the AI's decision-making process understandable and transparent to users and stakeholders.
- **Data Minimization:** Guiding AI developers to use data that is relevant, necessary, and adequate. This principle ensures that only the minimum necessary data is processed for each specific purpose.
- **Accuracy:** Advocating for the use of higher-quality data to enhance statistical accuracy. This helps improve the performance and reliability of AI systems.

Privacy professionals work closely with various stakeholders such as ethics, compliance, legal, information security, procurement, data stewards, developers, IT, risk, actuaries, marketing, data governance, audit, and so on. Each stakeholder plays a unique role in working with privacy professionals in the context of AI:

- **Ethics:** Ensures AI systems are designed and used in a manner that respects societal norms and values.
- **Compliance:** Helps meet regulatory requirements related to AI and data privacy.
- **Legal:** Provides advice on legal matters related to AI, such as intellectual property rights and contractual obligations.
- **Information Security:** Implements technical and organizational measures to protect AI systems and data from security threats.
- **Procurement:** Assists in sourcing and purchasing AI-related services and products that comply with privacy requirements.
- **Data Stewards:** Manage and oversee the organization's data assets to ensure they are used responsibly and ethically in AI systems.
- **Developers and IT:** Responsible for the technical development and maintenance of AI systems.
- **Risk and Actuaries:** Assess and manage risks associated with the use of AI, including privacy and security risks.
- **Marketing:** Ensures that AI-driven marketing activities respect privacy rights and comply with relevant laws.
- **Data Governance:** Establishes policies and procedures for data management in AI systems.
- **Audit:** Conducts audits to verify control effectiveness and compliance with privacy and other requirements in AI systems.

Ensuring that data privacy is protected throughout an organization requires that privacy professionals be able to coordinate with and leverage the strengths of their counterparts in a variety of disciplines and to communicate the strategic importance of privacy.

Engagement with Authorities on Data Privacy

Engaging with authorities on data privacy is a critical aspect of AI Governance. Privacy professionals often liaise with regulatory authorities to ensure compliance with data privacy laws. They may also participate in consultations on new regulations, contribute to industry guidelines, and engage in dialogue with authorities on privacy issues related to AI. This engagement helps shape the regulatory landscape, promotes best practices, and ensures that the organization's—or even the entire profession's—voice is heard in policy debates. It also helps the organization stay abreast of regulatory developments and understand how they may impact its AI activities.

AI Lifecycle and the Role of Data Privacy

The generative AI lifecycle typically involves the following eight steps. Each of these steps is crucial to developing an effective and reliable AI solution. It is also important to note that *the AI lifecycle is iterative*. Data privacy provides the guardrails for AI adhering to privacy and data protection laws.

1. Problem Definition

Problem definition is the initial stage in the AI lifecycle where the specific problem that the AI system will address is identified and defined. This involves understanding the context of the problem, the stakeholders involved, and the desired outcomes. Potential use cases are fleshed out and evaluated.

From a data privacy perspective, problem definition involves:

Privacy Impact Assessment (PIA): Conducting a PIA *to understand how the proposed AI system could impact individuals' privacy.* This includes identifying the types of personal data that will be processed, the purposes for which it will be used, and the potential privacy risks. A related set of assessments specific to AI, sometimes termed **AI Impact Assessments** (AIIAs) or **Algorithmic Impact Assessments** (AIAs), is increasingly deployed to assess the potential risks of automated decision-making systems.

Data Necessity: Determining the necessity of the personal data for solving the problem. This involves *ensuring that only the minimum necessary data is collected and used,* in line with the principle of data minimization.

Consent Management: Establishing mechanisms for obtaining individuals' consent for data processing where required. This includes *providing clear and transparent information about how their data will be used.*

Privacy Goals: Setting privacy goals for the AI system. This could involve *ensuring that the system respects individuals' privacy preferences*, implements robust data security measures, and provides transparency about its data processing activities.

2. Data Collection

Data collection is the process of gathering and measuring information on variables of interest, in an established systematic fashion that enables one to answer stated research questions, test hypotheses, and evaluate outcomes. In the context of AI, data collection involves gathering the necessary data that will be used to train and test the AI model.

From a data privacy perspective, data collection involves:

1. **Data Minimization:** Collecting only the data that is necessary for the AI system to function properly. Consider alternatives to using data that could raise privacy concerns, such as **synthetic data**, which is data that is artificially generated or altered, rather than being based on real-life people and/or events, which helps to protect private data, yet retains statistical reliability.
2. **Transparency:** Informing individuals about the data being collected, the purpose of the data collection, and how the data will be used. This is part of the principle of transparency, which requires organizations to be open about their data practices.
3. **Consent:** Obtaining individuals' consent for data collection where required. This involves providing clear and transparent information about the data collection and giving individuals the opportunity to opt in or opt-out.
4. **Anonymization:** Implementing measures to anonymize the collected data, where possible, to protect individuals' privacy. This could involve techniques such as **data masking** or **pseudonymization**. It is important to differentiate between anonymizing and pseudonymizing solutions, especially in AI-based systems, as the latter may not be sufficient to protect data in all circumstances and/or jurisdictions.

3. Data Preparation

Data preparation is *the process of cleaning and transforming raw data prior to processing and analysis. It is often considered one of the most time-consuming aspects of the AI lifecycle, but it's crucial* for the success of AI models.[4] In the context of AI, data preparation involves dealing with missing or inconsistent data, removing duplicates, checking and balancing inherent bias, and converting data into a format that can be used by AI models.

From a data privacy perspective, data preparation involves:

1 **Data Anonymization**: Before any data preparation begins, it's important to anonymize the data to protect individuals' privacy. This could involve techniques such as data masking or pseudonymization.

2 **Data Minimization**: During data preparation, it's crucial to ensure that only the necessary data is processed. This is in line with the principle of data minimization, which states that only the minimum necessary data should be collected and processed.

3 **Data Accuracy**: Ensuring the accuracy of the data is also a key aspect of data privacy. Incorrect data can lead to inaccurate AI predictions, which can have serious implications for individuals' privacy.

4 **Data Security**: Throughout the data preparation process, robust security measures should be in place to protect the data from unauthorized access, use, disclosure, alteration, and/or destruction.

5 **Eliminating bias**: By balancing data sets to achieve statistical representation that is fair.

4. Model Selection and Training

Model selection and training are a crucial step in the AI lifecycle. They involve *choosing the most appropriate machine learning algorithm for the problem at hand and training it on the prepared data to create an AI model.* The choice of model and the quality of training can significantly impact the performance of the AI system.

From a data privacy perspective, model selection and training involves:

1. **Privacy-Preserving Algorithms:** Some machine learning algorithms can inherently protect privacy better than others. For instance, **differential privacy** introduces noise to the data or computations to prevent the disclosure of individual data points.
2. **Secure Multi-party Computation:** In situations where data is distributed across multiple parties, secure multi-party computation can be used to train a model without sharing raw data.
3. **Data Usage Transparency:** It's important *to clearly document and communicate how and why data is used in model training.* This transparency helps ensure compliance with data privacy laws and builds trust with users. It is particularly important to ensure that the use of data as training data conforms to the **purpose limitation principle**, and that there is a lawful basis, such as consent, to use said data to train the model.
4. **Bias and Fairness:** Care should be taken to avoid training data that could lead to biased or unfair outcomes. This includes being mindful of potential biases in the data collection process that could be reflected in the AI model. Keeping in mind the iterative nature of AI development, ensuring data usage transparency is key to responding effectively to later identified bias and/or unfairness.

5. Model Evaluation

Model evaluation is the *process of assessing the performance of a trained AI model.* It involves using various metrics to measure how well the model's predictions align with the actual outcomes. This step is crucial as it helps to ensure that the AI model is reliable, accurate, and effective.

From a data privacy perspective, model evaluation involves:

1. **Privacy-Preserving Evaluation Metrics:** Evaluation metrics should be *designed in a way that they do not reveal sensitive information*. For instance, aggregated metrics can be used instead of individual-level metrics.
2. **Data Anonymization:** If the evaluation involves using personal data, such data should be anonymized to protect individuals' privacy.
3. **Evaluation Transparency:** Similar to model training, it's important to document and communicate how the model evaluation was conducted and what data was used. This transparency helps ensure compliance with data privacy laws and builds trust with users.
4. **Bias and Fairness Assessment:** The evaluation process should also assess *whether the model could lead to biased or unfair outcomes*. This includes checking for potential biases in the model's predictions that could disadvantage certain groups of individuals. Care should be taken to identify bias and/or unfairness that shows up as a "disparate impact" on individual groups—such as the well-documented tendency of some facial recognition systems to misidentify people with darker skin—but which is not clear "on the face" of the system.

6. Model Deployment

Model deployment is the process of integrating a trained generative AI model into an existing production environment where it can provide predictions or answers to prompts in real time. It is the stage where the model starts providing practical value by solving the problem it was designed to address.

From a data privacy perspective, model deployment involves:

1. **Privacy Impact Assessment (PIA):** Before deploying the model, conduct a PIA to *identify and mitigate any potential privacy risks*. Also consider Algorithmic Impact Assessment if appropriate.
2. **Data Minimization:** Only use the minimum amount of personal data necessary for the model to function effectively.
3. **Secure Data Transfers:** Ensure that any data used by the model during deployment is transferred securely to prevent unauthorized access. Personal data should be secured both in transit and at rest.
4. **Access Controls:** Implement strict access controls to ensure that only authorized individuals can interact with the deployed model and the data it uses.
5. **Transparency:** Be transparent about how the model uses data and how it makes decisions. This can help build trust with users and comply with data privacy regulations.

7. Monitoring and Maintenance

Monitoring and maintenance is the stage in the AI lifecycle where the deployed model is continuously observed and updated as needed to ensure its performance remains optimal. This involves tracking the model's performance metrics, identifying and addressing any issues or changes in the underlying data, and retraining the model with new data if necessary.

From a data privacy perspective, monitoring and maintenance involve:

1. **Continuous Privacy Impact Assessment:** Regularly reassess the PIA to account for any changes in the model or the data it uses.

2. **Data Quality Checks:** Regularly check the quality of the data used by the model to ensure it remains accurate and up-to-date and that it respects the principles of data minimization and purpose limitation.
3. **Privacy Audits:** Conduct regular privacy audits to ensure the model continues to comply with data privacy laws and regulations.
4. **Anomaly Detection:** Implement anomaly detection mechanisms to identify any unauthorized access or use of the data.
5. **Privacy Training:** Provide ongoing privacy training to all individuals who interact with the model to ensure they understand and respect data privacy principles.

8. Retirement

Retirement is *the final stage in the generative AI lifecycle, where an AI model is decommissioned* and taken out of service. This could be due to various reasons, such as the model becoming obsolete, the problem it was designed to solve no longer existing, or a more efficient solution being developed.

From a data privacy perspective, retirement involves:

1. **Data Deletion:** Once an AI model is retired, it is important to *ensure that all personal data used by the model is securely deleted* in accordance with data protection laws.
2. **Preservation:** *In some cases, data may need to be preserved for future reference* or for compliance with certain regulations. It is crucial to ensure that this archived data is stored securely and continues to respect individuals' privacy rights. Consultation with the **records and information management** (RIM) department will help in determining preservation methods and retention periods.
3. **Audit Trails:** Maintain comprehensive audit trails documenting the retirement process. This *includes when and why the model was retired, what data was deleted or preserved,* and any other actions taken during retirement.
4. **Communication:** *Notify relevant stakeholders*, including individuals whose data was used by the model, about the retirement of the model and how their data was handled. Pay particular attention to any jurisdictional requirements, such as notifying individuals of their data subject rights.

Incorporating Data Privacy into an AI Governance Framework

In the rapidly evolving landscape of AI, the integration of data privacy into the AI Governance framework has become a critical necessity. This integration *ensures that AI systems are designed and operated in a manner that respects and safeguards individual privacy rights.* As organizations strive to balance innovation with ethical considerations, it is imperative to adopt robust mechanisms that not only protect sensitive information but also comply with global privacy regulations. This approach fosters trust among end users and paves the way for a responsible and ethical use of AI technology.

Importance of Data Privacy in AI

The importance of data privacy in AI cannot be overstated. AI systems often rely on vast amounts of data, often including personal and sensitive information, to function effectively. This data is used to train AI models, make predictions, and provide personalized services. However, ***the large size of the training data sets and the specific nature of some algorithms can increase the risk that personal data and information can be leaked or publicized by AI.***

In December 2023, researchers at Indiana University successfully bypassed the privacy restrictions in GPT-3.5 Turbo, a generative AI, and revealed personal information that had been used to train the model (White, 2023).[5] The misuse of this data can lead to serious privacy violations and potential harm to individuals and society. This is part of the reason that many data protection laws, including the EU GDPR and the California CCPA and CPRA, specify this, so it is crucial to prioritize data privacy in the development and use of AI systems.

Data privacy in AI is not just about compliance with laws and regulations. It is also about respecting individuals' rights and freedoms, maintaining trust in AI systems, and ensuring ethical and responsible data practices. By prioritizing data privacy, organizations can mitigate risks, protect individuals' rights, and build trust in their AI systems. This, in turn, can enhance the acceptance and adoption of AI, drive innovation, and create value for both organizations and society. Therefore, the importance of data privacy in AI should be a key consideration in any AI Governance framework.

Role of Data Privacy in Building Trust

Data privacy plays a crucial role in building trust in AI systems. It reassures users that their personal data is being handled responsibly and ethically, and that their rights are being respected. Here are some ways in which data privacy contributes to trust in AI:

1. **Transparency:** Transparency about how personal data is used, including the purposes for which it is used, the types of data collected, and the third parties with whom it is shared, helps to build trust. In the context of AI, transparency can also extend to providing explanations of how models make decisions. Activities related to AI include developing clear privacy policies and providing explanations of AI decisions.
2. **Accountability:** Accountability ensures that organizations are responsible for their AI systems and that they can be held accountable for any harm caused. This includes ensuring compliance with data privacy laws and regulations and implementing measures to prevent and respond to data breaches. Activities related to AI include implementing robust data governance frameworks and establishing clear lines of responsibility for AI systems.
3. **User Control:** Providing users with control over their data, including the rights to access, correct, delete, and transfer their data, helps to build trust. In the context of AI, user control can also involve providing users with options to opt out of certain AI functionalities. Activities related to AI include developing user-friendly privacy settings and providing clear instructions on how users can exercise their data rights.
4. **Security:** Implementing robust security measures to protect personal data from unauthorized access, use, disclosure, alteration, and destruction is crucial for building trust. In the context of AI, security also involves protecting the integrity of AI models and systems. Activities related to AI include implementing secure coding practices, conducting regular security audits, and providing training on data security.

5. **Fairness:** Ensuring that AI systems operate in a fair and non-discriminatory manner is key to building trust. This involves using unbiased data, implementing fair algorithms, and regularly testing AI systems for bias. Activities related to AI include conducting fairness assessments, implementing bias mitigation techniques, and providing training on AI ethics.

By prioritizing data privacy and incorporating these measures into AI systems, organizations can build trust, encourage responsible data practices, and shield individuals and society from potential harm. These measures should be considered essential components of any AI Governance framework.

Trust, Data Subject Rights, and Consent Management

All AI systems are fundamentally data systems, reliant upon substantial corpuses of training data to train algorithms which then act upon new data. To ensure that AI systems are indeed **fair, accountable, transparent, and ethical** (sometimes termed **FATE AI/ML**) and build trust, a number of regulatory requirements and best practices should be implemented regarding individual data subjects' privacy rights and the management of consent.

Informed Consent and Data Usage

Informed consent—explicit consent that is freely given with a clear understanding of what the person is consenting to—is the cornerstone of the lawful and ethical use of personal information. Data should not be used in ways that individuals have not consented to unless there exists some other lawful basis for processing (such as the "phone book" exceptions for publicly available information that exist in many data privacy laws).

Clearly define the purposes for which the data will be used.

Consent cannot be informed if the data subject does not understand what they are consenting to and the likely consequences. Before developing any form of privacy notice or consent form for the use of personal data by an AI system, the organization must clearly understand the purpose(s) for which the data will be used.

Develop Clear and Concise Privacy Notices

A well-known problem with privacy consents is the "**transparency paradox**": to provide people with enough information that they can make meaningful decisions about their privacy, *it is often necessary to provide so much information that people cannot read or absorb it all.* While this is improving with a more certain regulatory landscape, *many privacy notices still contain page after page of dense legal jargon.* To ensure meaningful privacy notices, which advance the transparency and accountability of their AI systems, organizations should:

- *Create clear and concise privacy notices* that explain the scope and purpose of data processing in language that is easily understandable by the average person—it's recommended that consents be written at a sixth- to eighth-grade reading level unless the audience is known to read a significantly higher or lower level.
- *Present information in a user-friendly format*, such as bullet points or short paragraphs. Ensure that consents are fully accessible (e.g., compatible with screen readers).

Implement Consent Management

It is important to implement mechanisms for obtaining informed consent from individuals before collecting and processing their data, and to ensure the organization has systems, policies, and processes in place for consent management. As consent must be given for specific purposes, it is necessary to have ways to track the purposes for which each person has consented to their data being used, if the consent has been revoked, and to enable the organization to respond to **data subject access requests** (DSARs) and other rights assertions efficiently and effectively.

Privacy Rights — Data Access and Control

Individuals should—and in many jurisdictions legally do—have the *right to access their data, correct inaccuracies, and request deletion or transfer of their data.* Furthermore, and of particular importance to AI Governance, many modern data privacy regulations provide rights related to automated decision-making.

Enable Data Subject Rights

Organizations must provide for the assertion of data subject rights in all systems in which they process personal data, including AI systems. In addition to solid RIM (covered in the "Role of RIM in AI Governance" chapter) and excellent information security practices (covered in the Cybersecurity chapter):

- Implement mechanisms for data subjects to exercise their rights, such as the right to access, rectification, and deletion of their personal data.
- Provide clear instructions on how individuals can exercise their rights.

Data Sharing and Disclosure

Define policies for sharing data with third parties. Ensure third parties adhere to the same data privacy standards.

By considering these aspects of data privacy, the **AI Governance framework** can help ensure that AI systems respect individuals' privacy rights and operate in a trustworthy manner.

Integrating Privacy into AI Systems — Privacy by Design

Integrating privacy into AI systems involves *embedding privacy considerations into every stage of the AI lifecycle, from problem definition to retirement.* This approach is often referred to as "**Privacy by Design**" and is a key aspect of the General Data Protection Regulation (GDPR). Here are the seven foundational principles of Privacy by Design:

1. **Proactive not Reactive; Preventative not Remedial:** The Privacy by Design approach is characterized by proactive rather than reactive measures. It anticipates and prevents privacy-invasive events before they happen. In the context of AI, this could involve conducting privacy impact assessments before deploying AI systems.
2. **Privacy as the Default Setting:** Privacy by Design seeks to deliver the maximum degree of privacy by ensuring that personal data is automatically protected in any given IT system or business practice. In the context of AI, this could mean implementing strong data access controls and encryption methods.
3. **Privacy Embedded into Design:** Privacy by Design is embedded into the design and architecture of IT systems and business practices. It is not bolted on as an add-on, after

the fact. For AI, this could involve integrating privacy considerations into the initial design of AI algorithms.

4. **Full Functionality—Positive-Sum, not Zero-Sum:** Privacy by Design seeks to accommodate all legitimate interests and objectives in a positive-sum "win-win" manner. It avoids the pretense of false dichotomies, such as privacy vs. security. In the context of AI, this could mean developing AI systems that respect privacy while still delivering valuable insights.
5. **End-to-End Security—Full Lifecycle Protection:** Privacy by Design, having been embedded into the system prior to the first element of information being collected, extends securely throughout the entire lifecycle of the data involved. In the context of AI, this could involve secure data storage, use, and deletion practices.
6. **Visibility and Transparency—Keep It Open:** Privacy by Design seeks to assure all stakeholders that whatever the business practice or technology involved, it is, in fact, operating according to the stated promises and objectives, subject to independent verification. In the context of AI, this could involve clear communication about how AI systems use and protect data.
7. **Respect for User Privacy—Keep It User-Centric:** Above all, Privacy by Design requires architects and operators to keep the interests of the individual uppermost by offering such measures as strong privacy defaults, appropriate notice, and empowering user-friendly options. In the context of AI, this could involve providing users with control over their data, including the ability to access, correct, and delete their data.

Compliance with Privacy and Data Protection Laws

Compliance with privacy and data protection laws is a critical aspect of AI Governance. It involves ensuring that AI systems adhere to relevant legal requirements, which can vary across different jurisdictions. While a number of new data privacy (and the closely related data protection) regulations have come into force in recent years, some of the major laws include:

1. **General Data Protection Regulation (GDPR):** This EU regulation provides robust privacy protections and gives individuals control over their personal data. In the context of AI, it requires transparency about how AI systems process personal data, and it mandates data minimization and purpose limitation. The impact on AI is extensive; for example, GDPR's requirements that data processors and controllers provide clear communication about data usage and restrict unnecessary data collection apply to AI systems that process personal data. GDPR also provides individuals with a right "not to be subject to a decision based solely on automated processing, including profiling, which produces legal effects concerning him or her or similarly significantly affects him or her" (Article 22). Even where individuals consent to such processing, they must have recourse to human intervention—which requires that the data processor have sufficient control over the AI system that a human can understand, explain, and either support or correct the automated decision. Activities related to AI could include implementing mechanisms to ensure transparency and limiting the data used by AI systems. It is also worth noting that GDPR applies to organizations that process data outside of the European Union if those organizations are processing the personal data of people within the EU and the data is being processed to (1) offer goods or services to people within the EU, or (2) monitor the behavior of people within the EU.
2. **California Consumer Privacy Act (CCPA):** This US law gives California residents the right to know what personal information is collected about them and how it is used

and shared. For AI, this could involve disclosing how AI systems use personal data and providing individuals with the ability to opt out of data selling. The impact on AI is that it requires explicit disclosure of data usage and provides individuals with more control over their data. Activities related to AI could include developing clear privacy policies and implementing mechanisms for individuals to opt out of data selling. The California Privacy Protection Agency, as of December 2023, has proposed automated decision-making technology regulations that include artificial intelligence and will provide rights including consumer opt-out of the use of automated decision-making, consumer rights to access information about an organization's use of these technologies, and rights to an explanation of how consumers can exercise their privacy rights vis-à-vis such systems. Given that many other data privacy laws contain similar language about automated decision-making technologies, organizations should ensure that they have sufficient control over their AI systems to meet the requirements in such regulations.

3. **Health Insurance Portability and Accountability Act (HIPAA):** This US law protects sensitive patient health information from being disclosed without the patient's consent or knowledge. In the context of AI, this could involve ensuring that AI systems used in healthcare maintain the confidentiality and integrity of patient data. The impact on AI is that it imposes strict requirements for handling health data, which is often used in AI applications in healthcare. Activities related to AI could include implementing strong data security measures and obtaining patient consent before using their data.
4. **AI-Specific Regulations:** There are ongoing developments around specific AI laws, such as the EU's Artificial Intelligence Act, which aims to regulate AI systems to mitigate risks and respect fundamental rights. The impact on AI is that it could impose additional requirements for high-risk AI systems, such as biometric identification. Activities related to AI could include staying updated on these developments and adapting AI systems to comply with new regulations. By ensuring strong AI privacy governance and adhering to the principles and best practices discussed in this module, one can help "future-proof" one's AI systems as regulatory control imposes higher levels of control.

To familiarize oneself with these requirements and remain compliant in a sustainable way, consider the following:

- **Stay Updated:** *Regularly monitor changes in privacy and data protection laws*, especially those that directly impact AI. This could involve subscribing to legal updates or working with legal professionals.
- **Training:** *Provide training for employees on privacy and data protection laws*, especially those involved in developing and managing AI systems.
- **Privacy Impact Assessments (PIAs):** *Conduct PIAs to identify and mitigate privacy risks in AI projects*; in some cases, an AI Impact Assessment may be a necessary complement to the PIA for high-risk or highly novel systems.
- **Data Protection Officer (DPO):** *Consider appointing a DPO* to oversee data protection strategy and implementation to ensure compliance with relevant laws. In some jurisdictions this is a legal requirement.
- **Consultation:** *Consult with legal professionals to understand the implications of privacy and data protection laws* on your AI projects.

Link between AI Failures and Privacy Requirements

AI failures often have a direct link to privacy requirements. Here are some examples:

1. **Reidentification and Deanonymization:** This refers to the process of identifying individuals from anonymized data. In the context of AI, this could lead to privacy breaches if sensitive data is mishandled. Activities related to AI could include implementing strong anonymization techniques and conducting regular privacy audits. An example of a failure could be a data breach where anonymized data is reidentified, leading to privacy violations.
2. **Discrimination, Unfairness, Inaccuracies, and Bias:** These issues can arise when AI systems make decisions based on biased or inaccurate data. Activities related to AI could include implementing fairness checks and bias mitigation techniques. An example of a failure could be an AI system that discriminates against certain groups due to biased training data.
3. **Opacity and Secrecy of Profiling:** *This refers to the lack of transparency in how AI systems use data for profiling.* Activities related to AI could include implementing transparency measures and providing clear explanations of profiling practices. An example of a failure could be a lack of understanding of how profiling decisions are made, leading to mistrust and potential misuse of the system.
4. **Data Exploitation:** *This refers to the misuse of data for unauthorized purposes.* Activities related to AI could include implementing strong data governance measures and obtaining explicit consent before using data. An example of a failure could be the unauthorized use of personal data, leading to privacy breaches and noncompliance with data protection laws.
5. **Prediction:** *This refers to the use of AI to predict future outcomes based on data.* Activities related to AI could include implementing measures to ensure the accuracy and fairness of predictions. An example of a failure could be inaccurate or unfair predictions, potentially causing harm to individuals or businesses.
6. **Handling of Personal Data:** This refers to the collection, storage, processing, and sharing of personal data. Activities related to AI could include *implementing strong data security measures and privacy policies*. An example of a failure could be a data breach, leading to privacy violations and noncompliance with data protection laws.
7. **Potential for AI Systems to Be Hacked or Manipulated:** This refers to the risk of unauthorized access or manipulation of AI systems. Activities related to AI should include *implementing strong cybersecurity measures and regular system audits.* An example of a failure could be a cyberattack on an AI system, leading to data breaches and potential misuse of the system.
8. **Inappropriate Use of Facial Recognition:** This refers to the misuse of facial recognition technology, which can lead to privacy violations and discrimination. Activities related to AI could include *implementing strict usage policies and obtaining explicit consent.* An example of a failure could be the unauthorized use of facial recognition technology, leading to privacy breaches and potential misuse.
9. **False Accusations by AI:** This refers to situations where AI systems incorrectly accuse individuals based on inaccurate or biased data. Activities related to AI could include implementing robust validation and verification processes. *An example of a failure could be an AI system falsely accusing an individual of a crime due to biased training data.*
10. **Inference of Sensitive Information:** This refers to situations where AI systems infer sensitive information from seemingly innocuous data. Activities related to AI could

include *implementing strict data usage policies and conducting regular privacy audits.* An example of a failure could be an AI system inferring an individual's health status from their shopping habits, leading to potential privacy violations.

While these harms are rightfully understood in terms of their impact on the person whose privacy has been breached, it is important to remember that each of these failures risks significant harm to the responsible organization(s) as well. *When AI failure leads to a data privacy breach, it can undermine organizational trust and/or reputation, as well as lead to liability.* Failures that don't rise to the level of public attention or legal action can still lead the organization to rely on flawed or faulty decision-making, making AI tools less effective or even fully ineffective for their intended purpose. As an example, AI systems have been implemented to assist in hiring decisions, with the goal of reducing implicit human bias in the process. However, because bias mitigations had not been implemented in these systems, and because the training data reflected the biased hiring practices of the past, the system served to retrench the hiring bias that it was meant to mitigate.

Data Privacy Breaches in AI

Data privacy breaches occur when unauthorized individuals gain access to confidential data. *In the context of AI, these breaches can have severe consequences, given the large volumes of personal and sensitive data that AI systems often handle.*

Many modern data protection regulations have breach-related requirements, including requirements for incident response plans, breach notification requirements for both affected individuals and data protection authorities, and mitigation requirements. Even in jurisdictions without a data protection regulation, a breach notification statute may exist independently; all fifty states in the United States have breach notification laws. While the hope, of course, is that no breach will ever occur, responsible *AI Governance requires being prepared to respond both effectively and efficiently should a breach happen.*

1. **Definition:** A data privacy breach in AI refers to an incident where an unauthorized entity accesses, discloses, alters, or destroys data used by an AI system. This could be due to weak security measures, human error, or malicious attacks.
2. **Impact of Privacy Breaches:** Privacy breaches can lead to the exposure of sensitive personal information, resulting in potential harm to individuals. They can also undermine trust in AI systems and the organizations that deploy them and lead to legal and regulatory penalties for non-compliance with data protection laws.
3. **Prevention Measures:** To prevent data privacy breaches, organizations should implement robust security measures, including encryption, access controls, and regular security audits. To mitigate the damage of a potential breach, the organization should have solid records and data governance, including a robust retention schedule, excellent classification practices, and they should also provide training to staff on data protection and privacy practices.
4. **Response Measures:** In the event of a breach, organizations should have a response plan in place. This includes identifying and closing the security loophole, notifying affected individuals and regulatory authorities, and taking steps to mitigate the impact of the breach.
5. **Learning from Breaches**: Organizations should learn from each breach to improve their data privacy and security measures. This includes conducting a post-breach analysis to identify the cause of the breach and implementing measures to prevent similar incidents in the future.

By considering these aspects, organizations can better protect the data used by their AI systems, thereby enhancing trust in AI and ensuring compliance with data protection laws. This is crucial for realizing the full potential of AI while safeguarding individuals' privacy rights.

Summary

The importance of data privacy in AI cannot be overstated. *As generative AI systems often rely on large volumes of data, including personal and sensitive information, robust data privacy measures are essential*. These measures not only respect individuals' privacy rights but also ensure that their data is used lawfully, fairly and transparently. Furthermore, they provide individuals with control over their data, including the rights to access, correct, delete, and transfer their data.

Data privacy forms the bedrock of AI Governance, helping to build trust in AI systems, encourage responsible data practices, and shield individuals and society from potential harm. It also plays a crucial role in AI's lifecycle, providing the guardrails for AI to adhere to privacy and data protection laws.

Incorporating data privacy into an AI Governance framework involves considering various factors, including the importance of data privacy in AI, essential data privacy measures, the role of data privacy in building trust, integrating privacy into AI systems, compliance with privacy and data protection laws, the link between AI failures and privacy requirements, and data privacy breaches in AI.

In conclusion, prioritizing data privacy in AI is crucial for realizing the full potential of AI while safeguarding individuals' privacy rights. It is a key aspect of responsible and ethical AI development and use, and it is a critical component of a comprehensive approach to AI Governance.

Detailed Guidance: Privacy and AI Data Control

A complete privacy management program requires a full-organization commitment. While this chapter presents the major elements of a privacy management program in a linear fashion, *in practice, there will often be overlap and portions may be done simultaneously*. For example, ensuring legal compliance is an aspect of many different program controls, including the data inventory and the development of policies; it makes sense to identify as many of the legal questions up front to maximize the return on the investment in legal counsel. Furthermore, *effective privacy and AI Governance require well-coordinated collaboration across organizational functions*; data classification should include IT, RIM, and legal, incorporating everything from security and sensitivity to retention schedules.

Conduct a Thorough Inventory of the Data Used in AI Systems.

You cannot control or protect data that you don't know about. ***Conducting a thorough inventory of the data used in AI systems is a critical first step in ensuring data privacy and responsible AI Governance.*** Here are the steps, along with the role of data privacy, in conducting such an inventory:

1. *Define the purpose and scope, clarifying the objectives, such as understanding data flows, identifying privacy risks, and ensuring compliance. Engage key stakeholders from diverse*

backgrounds, including data scientists, privacy officers, legal experts, records managers, and representatives from business and IT departments, ensuring a holistic understanding of data usage.

2. *Document all data sources* comprehensively, detailing origin, ownership, and purpose, followed by classifying data into categories like personal, sensitive, non-sensitive, and metadata, assigning appropriate protection measures.
3. *Map the flow of data throughout the AI system, documenting collection, processing, analysis, and storage to identify potential privacy risks and vulnerabilities*. Document specific processing activities for each data type, including transformations, aggregations, and applied algorithms. Assign ownership responsibilities for each dataset to specific individuals or teams, clearly defining their roles in managing, securing, and ensuring data privacy. Assess legal and regulatory compliance, reviewing alignment with laws such as GDPR, CCPA, or industry standards.
4. Conduct **Data Privacy Impact Assessments** (DPIAs) to *identify and mitigate potential risks, and implement access controls, encryption, and authentication mechanisms.* Ensure secure data storage through encryption, pseudonymization, and anonymization, as appropriate, protecting data at rest against unauthorized access.
5. Working with the records management team, *establish and implement data retention policies aligned with legal requirements, minimizing unnecessary storage*. Implement mechanisms for data subjects to exercise their rights and ensure transparency in communication about data usage, processing, and protection.
6. Create monitoring and auditing mechanisms to track data usage, detect unauthorized access, and conduct regular privacy audits for ongoing compliance.
7. *Document the data inventory* in a centralized repository, including details on data types, sources, processing activities, access controls, and relevant privacy measures. Conduct regular reviews and updates to reflect changes in data processing activities promptly.
8. *Provide training to personnel involved in data management and processing to ensure awareness of privacy considerations and compliance* requirements, fostering a privacy-aware culture within the organization.

Classify data based on sensitivity and privacy implications.

Classifying data based on sensitivity and privacy implications is a crucial aspect of responsible AI Governance, and the following detailed steps are essential for a systematic approach.

First, *define clear criteria for data classification, taking into account sensitivity, confidentiality, and privacy implications*. Identify key factors such as **personally identifiable information** (PII), financial data, and health information. Familiarize yourself and your team with relevant data protection regulations and industry-specific standards to align classification criteria with legal requirements.

Collaborate with key stakeholders, including data owners, legal experts, privacy officers, and domain experts, to ensure a comprehensive understanding of the data landscape. Develop a comprehensive data inventory (see previous section on Inventorying), documenting the purpose, origin, and ownership of each dataset. Establish clear data classification levels (e.g., Public, Internal Use Only, Restricted, Confidential) based on the defined criteria, along with articulated restrictions and handling guidelines.

Where possible, implement automated tools and technologies, including machine learning algorithms or data discovery tools, to assist in the classification process. Provide training and awareness programs to individuals handling data, empowering them to make informed decisions based on data classification. *Develop clear and concise guidelines for handling data at each classification level, specifying access controls, encryption requirements, and other security measures.*

Enforce robust access controls based on data classification, regularly reviewing and updating access permissions. Utilize **encryption** to protect sensitive data during storage and transmission, and consider anonymization or pseudonymization techniques.

Implement monitoring mechanisms to track data usage and access patterns, set up alerts for unusual or unauthorized activities, and conducting regular audits.

Regularly review and update data classifications to account for changes in data usage, regulations, or organizational priorities. Integrate data classification into broader data governance policies, ensuring alignment with other governance practices such as data quality management and data lifecycle management. Perform **Privacy Impact Assessments** for projects involving personal or sensitive data, assessing potential privacy risks and proposing mitigation strategies.

Establish a ***Data Classification Committee*** *responsible for overseeing the process, including representatives from different departments to ensure diverse perspectives.* Document the rationale behind data classification decisions, maintaining a record for transparency and accountability. ***Communicate data classification policies regularly to all relevant stakeholders, ensuring employees are aware of their responsibilities*** and the importance of data protection. Periodically review and audit the effectiveness of the data classification process, identifying areas for improvement and refining the criteria based on lessons learned.

Data Minimization and Purpose Limitation

Only collect and use data that is necessary for the intended purpose.

Implementing data minimization and purpose limitation is crucial for responsible AI Governance and safeguarding data privacy. The *process begins by clearly defining the purpose for data collection, ensuring alignment with organizational goals and legal requirements.* Identify and document specific data elements necessary to fulfill the defined purpose, distinguishing between essential and non-essential information. Conduct **Data Impact Assessments** (DIA) to evaluate the potential impact of data processing activities on privacy, assessing the necessity of each data element.

Establish a legal basis for processing each category of data, ensuring compliance with data protection laws requiring a legal basis for processing personal data. *Obtain informed consent* from individuals before collecting their personal data, transparently communicating the purpose of data collection and any involved third parties. *Restrict data collection to the minimum necessary, avoiding the collection of excess data irrelevant to the defined goal.*

Implement and enforce data collection policies that mandate adherence to data minimization and purpose limitation principles, communicating these policies clearly to relevant employees. Explore anonymization and pseudonymization techniques to protect privacy, considering whether the intended purpose can be achieved without directly identifying individuals. Develop data retention policies aligned with the purpose and legal requirements, conducting regular reviews to purge or anonymize unnecessary data.

Enforce access controls based on job responsibilities and the necessity for the defined purpose, regularly reviewing and updating access permissions.

Implement encryption for data in transit and at rest to enhance security, protecting sensitive data from unauthorized access. Provide training to employees involved in data collection, raising awareness about data minimization and purpose limitation principles.

Conduct periodic audits to ensure ongoing compliance with these principles, assessing alignment with organizational policies and legal requirements. *Maintain clear documentation* of data processing activities, including purpose, data elements collected, and relevant approvals, using documentation for accountability and transparency. Involve **Data Protection Officers** (DPOs) or privacy experts in decision-making, seeking guidance on compliance with privacy regulations and best practices.

Continuously monitor changes in the business environment, regulatory landscape, and technological advancements, adapting data minimization and purpose limitation practices accordingly. Communicate the organization's commitment to data privacy to customers, stakeholders, and the public, building trust through responsible data handling practices.

Informed Consent

Obtain explicit and informed consent before processing personal data.

Obtaining informed consent is a fundamental requirement for responsible AI Governance and data privacy. Here are the steps required to obtain explicit and informed consent before processing personal data:

1. **Clearly Define the Purpose**

   Clearly articulate and define the specific purpose for which the personal data will be processed.

   Ensure that the purpose aligns with legal requirements and is communicated in a transparent manner.

2. **Use Clear and Simple Language**

   Present information in clear and simple language that is easily understandable by the average person.

   Avoid using complex technical terms or legal jargon that may confuse individuals.

3. **Provide Detailed Information**

   Offer comprehensive information about the data processing activities, including the types of data collected, the purposes of processing, and any third parties involved.

   Specify the duration for which the data will be retained.

4. **Specify Data Processing Methods**

   Clearly explain how the personal data will be processed, including any automated decision-making processes or profiling.

   Disclose if the data will be shared with external parties or used for targeted advertising.

5. **Communicate Risks and Consequences**

   Inform individuals about any potential risks and consequences associated with the data processing activities.

   Clearly articulate the impact on individuals' rights and freedoms.

6. **Enable Granular Consent Options**

   Provide granular consent options that allow individuals to choose the specific types of data processing activities to which they agree to.

   Avoid bundling multiple purposes under a single consent request.

7. **Implement Opt-In Mechanisms**

   Use opt-in mechanisms that require individuals to actively provide their consent.

   Pre-checked boxes or assumed consent should be avoided.

8. **Offer the Right to Refuse or Withdraw Consent**

   Clearly communicate individuals' right to refuse consent without facing negative consequences.

   Provide an easy and accessible way for individuals to withdraw their consent at any time.

9. **Ensure Freely Given Consent**

   Ensure that consent is freely given and not obtained through coercion, undue pressure, or manipulation.

   Avoid making consent a precondition for accessing services when it is not necessary.

10. **Use Layered Consent Notices**

    Implement layered consent notices, providing concise information upfront with the option for individuals to access more detailed information if desired.

    Ensure that essential information is prominently displayed.

11. **Consider Age and Capacity**

    Take into account the age and legal capacity of individuals when obtaining consent.

    For minors, ensure that consent is obtained from a parent or legal guardian as required by applicable laws.

12. **Implement Confirmation Mechanisms**

    Include confirmation mechanisms to ensure that individuals understand and actively agree to the terms.

    Send confirmation emails or notifications to document the consent process.

13. **Regularly Review and Update Consent**

    Regularly review and update consent mechanisms to reflect changes in data processing activities, purposes, or legal requirements.

    Promptly communicate changes to individuals and seek renewed consent if necessary.

14. **Document Consent Records**

    Maintain detailed records of individuals' consent, including the date, time, and specific terms agreed upon.

    Document the information provided to individuals during the consent process.

15. **Provide Contact Information**

    Include contact information, such as a dedicated email address or phone number, for individuals to reach out with questions or concerns regarding consent.

    Facilitate a communication channel for data subjects to exercise their rights.

16. **Educate Data Handlers**

    Provide training to individuals involved in obtaining consent to ensure awareness of privacy principles and compliance requirements.

    Foster a culture of respecting individuals' privacy rights.

17. **Monitor Compliance**

    Implement monitoring mechanisms to ensure ongoing compliance with consent-related practices.

    Conduct regular audits and reviews to assess the effectiveness of the consent process.

18. **Promote Transparency**

    Communicate transparently with individuals about how their data will be processed, stored, and protected.

    Build trust through openness and honesty in all interactions.

By following these steps, organizations can establish a robust and ethical process for obtaining informed consent, promoting transparency, respecting individuals' privacy rights, and adhering to data protection regulations.

Data Security Measures

- Implement robust security measures to protect personal data from unauthorized access or breaches.

Implementing robust data security measures is imperative for AI Governance and data privacy to shield personal data from unauthorized access or breaches. A comprehensive data security framework involves several essential steps. *Begin with a* ***risk assessment*** *to identify potential vulnerabilities and assess the impact of security incidents on personal data. Develop a thorough data security policy outlining principles, practices, and standards, and communicate it clearly to all stakeholders.*

Classify personal data based on sensitivity and criticality, applying different security measures accordingly.

Encrypt sensitive personal data in transit and at rest using strong encryption algorithms. Enforce strict access controls, limiting access based on job roles and responsibilities, and regularly review and update permissions. Implement robust authentication mechanisms, including multi-factor authentication, to verify user identity and secure password policies.

Monitor and audit data access with mechanisms that track modifications and raise alerts for suspicious activities. Securely store personal data in databases or storage systems with built-in security features, ensuring regular updates and patches. *Employ network security measures* like firewalls and intrusion detection/prevention systems, and secure wireless networks. Keep all software and systems up to date with the latest security patches.

Secure data transmission with encrypted communication channels, and implement endpoint security solutions for computers, laptops, and mobile devices.

Provide comprehensive training to employees on data security best practices and raise awareness about cybersecurity threats. *Control physical access* to data storage facilities, data centers, and server rooms, implementing security measures like access cards, biometric authentication, and surveillance.

Deploy **Data Loss Prevention** (DLP) solutions *to prevent unauthorized data exfiltration and conduct regular security audits to identify and address potential vulnerabilities.* Develop a comprehensive **incident response plan**, including procedures for notifying affected individuals and authorities. ***Implement regular data backups and establish a robust disaster recovery plan.***

Assess the security measures of third-party vendors handling personal data, ensuring compliance with security standards and contractual obligations. Stay informed about and comply with data protection laws, regularly reviewing and updating security measures to align with changing legal requirements.

Continuous improvement *within the security function is essential for ensuring robust AI Governance.* One key aspect is the implementation of corrective actions, driven by the findings of regular security assessments. These assessments help identify vulnerabilities and weaknesses in the security infrastructure, providing insights into areas that require immediate attention. A proactive approach is crucial in addressing these issues promptly, employing remediation measures to strengthen the overall security posture. This iterative process ensures that security mechanisms are not static but adaptive, evolving to effectively counter emerging threats.

Another vital element in continuous improvement is the regular review and update of security policies and procedures. Lessons learned from security assessments and audits contribute valuable insights into the efficacy of existing policies. Regular reviews enable organizations to identify areas for improvement and adjust policies to align with evolving threats and technologies. It is essential to ensure that security policies remain up to date, reflecting the current threat landscape and incorporating best practices to mitigate emerging risks. This dynamic approach to policy management enhances the organization's ability to adapt to new security challenges and maintain a resilient security framework in the realm of AI Governance.

Documenting training records is a critical component of effective AI Governance, particularly in the context of security functions. To ensure a comprehensive record-keeping system, organizations should meticulously maintain training records that capture personnel participation in security training initiatives. This involves documenting details such as the specific training modules undertaken, the dates of completion, and any certifications obtained by individuals. These detailed records not only serve as a historical account of training efforts but also enable organizations to track the proficiency and skill levels of their personnel in security-related domains.

Moreover, the significance of **training records** extends beyond internal tracking; they play a pivotal role in demonstrating compliance with industry regulations and standards. By leveraging these records, organizations can provide tangible evidence of their commitment to adhering to security protocols mandated by regulatory frameworks and industry best practices. These records serve as a valuable resource during audits or assessments, showcasing the organization's proactive efforts to enhance security awareness among its workforce. The integration of training records into compliance strategies not only fosters a culture of accountability but also reinforces the organization's dedication to maintaining a robust and well-informed security posture in the realm of AI Governance.

Data Subject Access Rights

- ***Ensuring individuals have mechanisms to access, correct, or delete their data is integral to effective data privacy management within AI systems.***

To establish a robust process, organizations should first understand the applicable regulations, such as GDPR, CCPA, or CPRA, familiarizing themselves with the data access and control rights granted to individuals. Clear data access policies should then be developed, specifying procedures for accessing personal data and outlining the information required for identity verification.

To enable data access requests, organizations should establish multiple channels, such as online forms, email, or dedicated portals, and educate individuals about their rights through easily understandable informational material published on relevant platforms. Secure identity verification processes, including multi-factor authentication, should be implemented to ensure the authenticity of requests.

For data correction requests, mechanisms should be provided for individuals to submit requests to rectify inaccurate or incomplete personal data, specifying the types of corrections that can be requested. Similarly, clear procedures should be established for data deletion requests, communicating the conditions under which deletion requests will be honored.

Centralized request handling ensures consistency, with a designated team or point of contact responsible for managing these requests. Defined response timelines, adhering to legal mandates, should be communicated to individuals submitting requests. Self-service portals can be developed to allow individuals direct access and management of their data, ensuring security and user-friendliness.

Maintaining detailed records of data access, correction, and deletion requests is crucial for accountability, and a review process should be implemented to verify the validity of these requests, avoiding disclosure or changes based on fraudulent or unauthorized submissions. Transparent communication about data collection, processing, and retention policies, along with training for personnel handling requests, enhances overall understanding.

The implementation of encryption mechanisms ensures secure data handling during access, correction, or deletion processes, safeguarding data in transit and at rest.

Regular audits are necessary to monitor compliance with procedures, detecting any unauthorized access or changes to personal data. Clear communication of outcomes to individuals, including reasons if requests cannot be fulfilled, is essential, fostering transparency.

Collaborating with data protection authorities, particularly in complex or contentious cases, and staying informed about changes in data protection laws are critical elements. Lastly, organizations should seek continuous improvement by soliciting feedback from individuals, using this input to identify areas for enhancement in their data access, correction, or deletion processes.

- **Educate individuals about their rights and how to exercise them.**

Educating individuals about their data privacy rights and how to exercise them is a pivotal aspect of responsible AI Governance and data privacy practices. Begin by thoroughly familiarizing yourself with the specific rights granted to individuals under relevant data protection regulations, such as GDPR or CCPA. Develop clear and comprehensive informational material that explains individuals' data privacy rights, including the right to access, correct, delete, and object to the processing of personal data.

Ensure the accessibility of this material by publishing it prominently on your organization's website, privacy policy, and other relevant platforms. Utilize multiple communication channels, including social media, newsletters, and email, to disseminate information about data privacy rights and reach a wider audience. Present information using simple and clear language that caters to individuals with varying levels of familiarity with legal terms, avoiding jargon and technical language.

Enhance comprehension by incorporating visual aids such as infographics to make the material more engaging. Provide practical examples and scenarios to illustrate how individuals can exercise their data privacy rights in real-world situations. Clearly explain the process of submitting requests to access, correct, delete, or object to the processing of personal data, offering step-by-step instructions for each type of request.

Detail the identity verification procedures individuals need to undergo when exercising their data privacy rights, specifying the types of documentation or information required. Clearly highlight the expected timelines for responses to data privacy requests, emphasizing the organization's commitment to timely and transparent communication. Provide easily accessible contact information for individuals to reach out if they have questions or need assistance.

Consider hosting educational sessions, such as privacy workshops or webinars, to provide in-depth information about data privacy rights and allow for interactive sessions where individuals can ask questions. Develop FAQs and help guides that address common queries related to data privacy rights and make these resources readily available on your website.

Utilize periodic email updates to summarize key information about data privacy rights and encourage individuals to revisit educational material. Launch awareness campaigns, particularly during Data Privacy Awareness Months or relevant observances, using various channels to promote awareness. Measure the effectiveness of your educational efforts by implementing surveys or quizzes to gauge individuals' understanding of their data privacy rights and use feedback to identify areas for improvement.

Engage with user communities and forums to address questions and concerns related to data privacy, fostering an open dialogue with individuals. Collaborate with non-governmental organizations (NGOs) or privacy advocates to amplify educational efforts and leverage external expertise to enhance content. Stay informed about changes in data protection laws and regulations, regularly updating educational material to reflect the latest information. Promote a culture of privacy within the organization and among its users, emphasizing the shared responsibility of both the organization and individuals in protecting personal data.

Employee Training on Data Privacy

Establishing an effective data privacy training program specific to AI projects is essential for fostering a culture of responsibility and compliance within an organization. The initial step involves providing comprehensive training to employees, ensuring they are well-versed in data privacy laws, internal policies, and industry best practices relevant to AI initiatives. This training should cover key aspects such as the principles of data protection, the legal frameworks governing personal information, and specific considerations related to AI data processing.

To promote a privacy-aware culture, organizations should conduct regular awareness campaigns that go beyond basic training sessions. These campaigns can take various forms, including workshops, webinars, and interactive modules tailored to the unique aspects of AI projects. Emphasis should be placed on the ethical considerations surrounding AI, the responsible use of algorithms, and the implications of data processing on individuals' privacy. By incorporating real-world scenarios and case studies specific to AI applications, employees can better understand the practical implications of data privacy principles within their work context.

In addition to formal training, organizations should implement ongoing communication strategies to reinforce data privacy awareness. Regular newsletters, internal communications, and updates can serve as reminders of the importance of maintaining data privacy standards in the context of AI projects. These communications can also highlight any updates or changes in relevant regulations, ensuring that employees stay informed about evolving legal requirements.

To enhance engagement and knowledge retention, organizations can introduce interactive elements into their training programs, such as quizzes, discussion forums, or scenario-based exercises. This approach encourages active participation and allows employees to apply data privacy principles to specific AI scenarios they may encounter in their roles.

By investing in a comprehensive and continuous data privacy training program specific to AI projects, organizations not only equip employees with the necessary knowledge but also instill a sense of responsibility and ethical consideration in their AI-related activities. This proactive approach contributes to a privacy-conscious workforce and aligns with the broader goals of responsible AI Governance.

Regular Audits and Assessments

- **Conduct regular audits to assess compliance with data privacy regulations**.

Conducting regular audits is an indispensable element of effective AI Governance and data privacy practices, ensuring ongoing compliance with relevant regulations. To initiate this process, organizations must establish a systematic approach to auditing that focuses on privacy compliance related to data access and control procedures. This involves regular reviews and assessments of internal systems and processes to verify adherence to established privacy policies, as well as compliance with data protection regulations such as GDPR or CCPA.

During audits, particular attention should be paid to monitoring for any unauthorized access or changes to personal data. Implementing robust monitoring mechanisms is essential to track user activities and system logins, enabling the identification of any irregularities or suspicious behavior. Automated tools and technologies can be employed to streamline the auditing process and detect unauthorized access promptly. *Regular reviews should encompass a thorough examination of user permissions, ensuring that access rights align with job responsibilities and that any changes are documented and authorized.*

The audit process should also include an assessment of data storage and transmission practices to guarantee the security of personal data both at rest and in transit. Encryption mechanisms should be in place to protect sensitive information from unauthorized access. ***Regularly updating and (security) patching systems is crucial*** *to address potential vulnerabilities that could be exploited for unauthorized access during audits.*

Additionally, organizations should engage in periodic assessments of their data access and control policies, making adjustments as needed to align with evolving regulations and technological advancements. This proactive approach ensures that privacy measures remain effective in the face of dynamic threats and changing compliance landscapes. The audit findings should be documented comprehensively, including any identified areas of improvement or noncompliance, and communicated transparently within the organization.

By conducting regular audits, organizations not only demonstrate their commitment to data privacy but also proactively identify and address potential issues, contributing to the establishment of a robust privacy framework within the broader context of responsible AI Governance.

Continuous Improvement

Ensuring continuous improvement in data privacy compliance for AI systems is essential to adapt to the dynamic landscape of technology, regulations, and business processes. Organizations should institute a systematic approach to regularly review and update privacy policies and governance structures. This involves conducting periodic assessments of existing policies, taking into account feedback from stakeholders, changes in regulations, and emerging best practices. By fostering a culture of ongoing evaluation, organizations can identify gaps, anticipate potential risks, and refine their privacy policies to align with evolving standards.

Adapting to changes in technology, regulations, and business processes is another critical aspect of continuous improvement. As technology evolves, organizations must stay abreast of advancements and assess their impact on data privacy. Regularly engaging with updates in privacy regulations and legal requirements is paramount, as it ensures that privacy policies remain compliant with the latest standards. This proactive approach involves assigning dedicated personnel or teams to monitor regulatory changes and integrating these updates into the organization's privacy framework promptly.

Furthermore, continuous improvement should extend to accommodating changes in business processes. As organizations evolve and adopt new technologies or alter their operational workflows, these changes can have implications for data privacy. Therefore, a dynamic governance structure that can flexibly adapt to shifts in the business environment is crucial. Organizations should establish mechanisms for regular assessments, seeking input from relevant stakeholders to ensure that the privacy governance framework remains effective and responsive.

Implementing a robust feedback loop, including incident response analyses and lessons learned from privacy-related incidents, is integral to the continuous improvement process. By learning from past experiences, organizations can enhance their privacy controls, update protocols, and fortify defenses against potential vulnerabilities.

In summary, embracing continuous improvement for data privacy compliance in AI systems requires a commitment to regular policy reviews, an agile response to technological and regulatory changes, and an adaptable governance structure that aligns with evolving business processes. This iterative approach ensures that organizations not only meet current privacy standards but also proactively anticipate and address emerging challenges in the dynamic landscape of AI and data protection.

Conclusion

Effectively managing data privacy in AI Governance involves a holistic and ongoing effort that integrates legal, technical, and organizational measures. Adhering to specific laws and regulations, such as GDPR, CCPA, and HIPAA, is crucial for organizations operating in different jurisdictions. Continuous monitoring, transparency, and a commitment to ethical data handling practices are essential components of a robust data privacy framework for AI implementations.

Key Points

- Data privacy must be central to AI Governance, from Problem Definition to Retirement.
- AI privacy involves the protection of personal data that is collected, stored, processed, and shared by AI systems.
- Conducting a thorough inventory of the data used in AI systems is a critical first step in ensuring data privacy and responsible AI Governance.
- Prioritizing data privacy in AI Governance helps build trust in AI systems, encourages responsible data practices, and shields individuals and society from potential harm.

- Many AI-related harms can be traced back to AI failures, several of which can be linked to privacy requirements.
- Privacy professionals play a pivotal role in managing AI risk, ensuring that AI-driven processing activities comply with privacy and data protection laws.
- Engaging with authorities on data privacy is a critical aspect of AI Governance.
- Data privacy provides the guardrails for AI adhering to privacy and data protection laws throughout the entire lifecycle of AI systems development.
- Conducting a Privacy Impact Assessment (PIA) to understand how the proposed AI system could impact individuals' privacy is crucial in the Problem Definition phase.
- Regularly reassess the PIA to account for any changes in the model or the data it uses.
- The Privacy function must insist on Data Minimization: collecting and processing only the data that is necessary for the AI system to function properly.
- Privacy professionals should see that measures to anonymize the collected data are implemented, where possible, to protect individuals' privacy.
- Data preparation is the process of cleaning and transforming raw data prior to processing and analysis.
- Conduct regular privacy audits to ensure the model continues to comply with data privacy laws and regulations.
- Provide ongoing privacy training to all individuals who interact with the model to ensure they understand and respect data privacy principles.
- Once an AI model is retired, it is important to ensure that all personal data used by the model is securely deleted in accordance with data protection laws.
- The large size of the training data sets and the specific nature of some algorithms can increase the risk that personal data and information can be leaked or publicized by AI.
- Data privacy contributes to trust in AI through transparency, accountability, user control, security, and fairness.
- Privacy professionals must ensure that AI systems are fair, accountable, transparent and ethical (sometimes termed FATE AI/ML) and build trust.
- When providing people with enough information about their privacy, it is often necessary to provide so much information that people cannot read or absorb it all, known as the "transparency paradox."
- It is important to implement mechanisms for obtaining informed consent from individuals before collecting and processing their data.
- The principles of Privacy by Design should be followed throughout the AI lifecycle.
- Consider appointing a DPO to oversee data protection strategy and implementation to ensure compliance with relevant laws. In some jurisdictions this is a legal requirement.
- Even in jurisdictions without a data protection regulation, a breach notification statute may exist independently; all fifty states in the US have breach notification laws.
- Establish and implement data retention policies aligned with legal requirements, minimizing unnecessary storage.
- Utilize encryption to protect sensitive data during storage and transmission, and consider anonymization or pseudonymization techniques.
- Integrate data classification into broader data governance policies, ensuring alignment with other governance practices.

- Establish a Data Classification Committee responsible for overseeing the process, including representatives from different departments to ensure diverse perspectives.
- Communicate data classification policies regularly to all relevant stakeholders, ensuring employees are aware of their responsibilities.
- Classify personal data based on sensitivity and criticality, applying different security measures accordingly.
- Obtaining informed consent is a fundamental requirement for responsible AI Governance and data privacy.
- Begin data security planning with a risk assessment to identify potential vulnerabilities and assess the impact of security incidents on personal data.
- Deploy Data Loss Prevention (DLP) solutions to prevent unauthorized data exfiltration and conduct regular security audits to identify and address potential vulnerabilities.
- Implement regular data backups and establish a robust disaster recovery plan.
- Assess the security measures of third-party vendors handling personal data.
- Continuous improvement within the security function is essential for ensuring robust AI Governance.
- Ensuring individuals have mechanisms to access, correct, or delete their data is integral to effective data privacy management within AI systems.
- For data correction requests, mechanisms should be provided for individuals to submit requests to rectify inaccurate or incomplete personal data.
- Maintaining detailed records of data access, correction, and deletion requests is crucial for accountability.
- Educating individuals about their data privacy rights and how to exercise them is a pivotal aspect of responsible AI Governance and data privacy practices.
- Regularly updating and (security) patching systems is crucial to address potential vulnerabilities that could be exploited for unauthorized access during audits.
- Ensuring continuous improvement in data privacy compliance for AI systems is essential.

Key Glossary Terms

Anonymization: The process of removing personally identifiable information from data sets so that the individuals whom the data describe remain anonymous. This is done to protect individuals' privacy by making it impossible to identify them.

Bias and fairness assessment: Involves evaluating algorithms and data sets for biases that could lead to unfair or discriminatory outcomes when AI systems are deployed. Biases can arise from various sources, including the data used to train AI models.

Data anonymization: Involves processing personal data to remove or modify personal identifiers, making it difficult to associate the data with a specific individual. Techniques such as masking, pseudonymization (replacing identifiers with pseudonyms), and aggregation are used to protect individuals'' identities.

Data Loss Prevention (DLP): Strategies and tools used to prevent unauthorized access to, exposure of, or theft of sensitive information. In the context of AI Governance, DLP is crucial for protecting the vast amounts of personal and proprietary data used in AI systems against breaches, leaks, or inadvertent sharing. DLP solutions can monitor, detect, and block sensitive data.

Deanonymization: The deliberate attempt to reverse the process of anonymization to re-identify individuals from anonymized data.

Privacy-preserving algorithms: Privacy-preserving algorithms are designed to protect the privacy of individuals' data while allowing for the analysis and processing of that data. These algorithms enable AI models to learn from data without exposing sensitive information.

Privacy-preserving evaluation metrics: Privacy-preserving evaluation metrics are methods used to assess the effectiveness of privacy-preserving techniques without compromising the privacy of the data itself. These metrics help evaluate how well a system maintains data utility while protecting privacy.

Pseudonymization: A related but distinct process where personal identifiers in a data set are replaced with artificial identifiers, or pseudonyms. This allows the data to be matched with its source without revealing the actual source.

Reidentification (or **de-anonymization**): The process of matching anonymous data with external information in order to discover the identity of the individuals to whom the data belongs. This can occur even when data has been anonymized, if enough information is available from other sources to allow cross-referencing of data points.

Notes

1 "Security, Privacy and Web 2.0," IBM Global Innovation Outlook, accessed May 22, 2025. ibm_gio_web2point0_brochure_hi.pdf.

2 "Blueprint for an AI Bill of Rights," The White House Office of Science and Technology Policy, issued June 24, 2022, accessed May 28, 2025. ibm_gio_web2point0_brochure_hi.pdf.

3 "The Fair Information Practice Principles," United States Department of Homeland Security, issued August 10, 2015, accessed May 21, 2025. https://www.dhs.gov/sites/default/files/2024-01/Fair%20Information%20Principles_12_2008.pdf.

4 Liang, Tadesse, et al., "Advances, Challenges, and Opportunities in Creating Data for Trustworthy AI," *Nature Portfolio Journal*, Issue 669-677, 2022, accessed May 24, 2025. https://www.nature.com/articles/s42256-022-00516-1.

5 "Generative AI and Your Privacy," *White*, Indiana University, December 2023, accessed June 23, 2025, https://datamanagement.iu.edu/news/archive/2023/generative-ai.html.

8 The Role of Cybersecurity in AI Governance

Michael Esola and Robert F. Smallwood

Artificial Intelligence (AI) systems and applications are being rapidly adopted across industries and use cases. As the utilization of AI grows, it becomes *increasingly important to ensure these systems remain secure, ethical, and trustworthy throughout their lifecycle.* AI Governance plays a key role in providing oversight and guidance for developing, deploying, and managing AI responsibly. A fundamental component of robust AI Governance is cybersecurity.

Cybersecurity *involves the policies, procedures, technologies, and practices focused on protecting data and documents from threats that could undermine reliability and trust.* Because AI relies extensively on data, predictive models, complex software, and broad connectivity, vulnerabilities can provide opportunities for malicious actors to manipulate models, steal sensitive data, interrupt critical services, and cause other forms of harm. Successful cyberattacks targeting AI systems can have serious consequences given the expanding role of AI in areas like healthcare, financial services, energy, transportation, manufacturing, and defense.

This chapter examines the indispensable role of cybersecurity as part of holistic AI Governance. It outlines practical steps and processes for organizations to implement cybersecurity measures tailored to AI and connected systems. Guidance ranges across various stages of the AI and general software lifecycle. Cybersecurity frameworks like the **National Institute of Standards and Technology (NIST) Cybersecurity Framework**[1] provide globally recognized best practices and structure for cybersecurity programs.

Specific capabilities and controls also address emerging risks unique to AI—like **model manipulation** or **adversarial data poisoning** (more on that later)—as well as more foundational risks related to data management, infrastructure exposures, software vulnerabilities, and insider threats. Key aspects of cybersecurity include threat modeling, data encryption and access management.

Identity and Access Management (IAM), continuous monitoring, third-party risk assessments, forensic readiness, security team skills development, fostering an organizational culture vigilant to cyber risks, and maintaining alignment and compliance with evolving laws and regulations. *Whew!* That's a lot, but we will unpack it step by step.

When properly secured and governed, AI systems can deliver tremendous value to organizations, their customers, and society as a whole—improving decision-making, increasing efficiency, personalizing services, revealing insights from data, and automating repetitive tasks. Becoming knowledgeable about core cybersecurity principles will help AI Governance professionals play an indispensable role in securing our integrated AI-powered future.

The Role of Cybersecurity in the AI System Development Lifecycle

The integration of cybersecurity within the lifecycle of AI system development is vital for ensuring the security, integrity, and trustworthiness of AI applications. Cybersecurity teams play a crucial role in each phase of this lifecycle, providing expertise and implementing measures to mitigate risks. Here's a summary look at their roles across the eight phases:

1. **Problem Definition**

   Risk Assessment: Cybersecurity teams help identify potential security risks related to the AI project, considering the data involved, the application's context, and potential threat vectors.

   Security Requirements Specification: They contribute *to setting security and privacy requirements*, ensuring that security considerations are integrated from the outset.

2. **Data Collection**

   Secure Data Sourcing: *Ensuring that data is collected from secure, reliable sources* and that the collection process complies with relevant data protection regulations (e.g., GDPR).

   Data Privacy: Implementing measures to *protect personal and sensitive information,* including anonymization or pseudonymization where necessary.

3. **Data Preparation**

   Data Cleaning and Security: *Assessing and mitigating risks in data preprocessing*, such as ensuring data integrity and preventing the injection of malicious data.

   Access Control: *Establishing strict access controls and authentication mechanisms to ensure only authorized personnel can access sensitive data.*

4. **Model Selection and Training**

   Secure Development Practices: *Guiding the development process to use secure coding practices and to select frameworks and tools that are robust against vulnerabilities.*

   Model Security: Evaluating potential vulnerabilities in chosen models, such as susceptibility to adversarial attacks and applying countermeasures.

5. **Model Evaluation**

   Security Evaluation: *Assessing the model for security weaknesses*, including testing for vulnerabilities to various types of attacks (e.g., adversarial, poisoning).

   Validation of Data Privacy: Verifying that the model does not expose or infer sensitive information about individuals in the training data.

6. **Model Deployment**

   Deployment Security: Ensuring *secure deployment practices*, including the use of secure servers and environments, encryption of data in transit and at rest, and implementing robust authentication mechanisms.

   Threat Monitoring and Response: *Setting up systems to monitor for and respond to threats in real time*, including intrusion detection systems and automated response mechanisms.

7. **Monitoring and Maintenance**

   Ongoing Risk Assessment: *Continuously assessing the security posture* of the AI system, considering evolving threats and vulnerabilities.

   Patch Management: Regularly updating AI applications, libraries, and frameworks to *address security vulnerabilities.*

8. **Retirement**

   Secure Decommissioning: *Ensuring that the AI system and its data are securely decommissioned,* with all sensitive data properly deleted or archived according to policy.

   Post-Mortem Analysis: *Conducting a security review to identify lessons learned* and improve security practices for future projects.

Throughout these phases, the cybersecurity team works closely with other stakeholders, including AI researchers, developers, legal and compliance teams, and business leaders, to ensure that AI systems are developed, deployed, and maintained in a manner that upholds security and trust. This collaborative approach is essential for addressing the complex and evolving security challenges associated with AI technologies.

Threat Modeling

As AI systems are increasingly deployed in real-world settings across various industries, securing these systems against cyber threats has become a crucial concern. ***AI Governance*** *refers to the frameworks, policies, controls, and processes needed to ensure AI systems are trustworthy, safe, reliable, and compliant.* As part of a comprehensive AI Governance strategy, cybersecurity plays a vital role in identifying, assessing, and mitigating risks.

Threat modeling is one of the key cybersecurity techniques used to systematically evaluate the security risks associated with AI systems. *It enables organizations to understand threats, prioritize defenses, and implement appropriate safeguards.*

Fundamentals of Threat Modeling

Threat modeling refers to the structured process of identifying, categorizing, and mitigating vulnerabilities in a system. The core objectives are to:

- Identify assets, entry points, and trust boundaries.
- Determine potential threats, attacks, vulnerabilities, and impacts.
- Define security controls to detect, prevent, or mitigate risks.

Threat modeling produces artifacts documenting threats, severity ratings, mitigations, and open risk issues. The output guides design improvements and resource allocation to strengthen defenses.

As systems evolve over time, threat modeling must be an ongoing activity integrated across the development lifecycle — not just a one-time activity. Regular reviews and updates are essential.

Unique Security Considerations for AI

While traditional threat modeling frameworks provide a foundation, AI systems have distinctive features warranting tailored assessments:

Data Dependency: The accuracy and reliability of AI applications rely heavily on the quality and integrity of the data used. Threats related to data poisoning, model evasion, adversarial samples, and so on must be addressed.

Complexity: Components like dynamic neural networks and autoencoders add layers of complexity. Lack of explainability compounds risks.

Interconnectivity: AI systems frequently have integrations with external data sources, third-party models, and backend services. More connection points increase the attack surface.

Adaptability: Systems based on **machine learning** (ML) continuously "learn" and change behavior by examining new data. While enhancing functionality, this also introduces potential emerging risks that must be monitored.

To fully evaluate an AI system's threat landscape, the analysis must encompass the entire data pipeline or lifecycle—including data collection means, preprocessing and cleansing steps, the selected model architecture, post-processing of outputs, connectivity with other systems, and ultimately how humans interact with the application.

Best Practices for AI Threat Modeling

Organizations using AI should adopt these practices as part of their cyber risk management:

- Maintain thorough documentation covering system architecture, data flows, technologies used, trust boundaries, and security mechanisms implemented.
- Build a comprehensive **inventory of assets and access points** across all layers of the AI pipeline, updating whenever changes occur.
- Incorporate adversarial AI techniques like evasion attacks, data poisoning, model extraction, and cloning attacks into regular testing procedures to uncover hidden flaws.
- Leverage automation and orchestration tools to continually monitor data quality, model performance metrics, software dependencies, and infrastructure security posture.
- Establish **incident response plans** tailored to AI, with emphasis on gracefully downgrading functionality when anomalies are detected.
- Implement **access controls**, behavior monitoring, rotation policies, and separation of duties aligned with zero trust principles, especially for privileged users.
- Train all stakeholders on secure coding practices, ethical sourcing of training data, and risks associated with uncontrolled model sharing.
- Maintain full transparency within legal bounds related to data provenance, model development methodology, and performance benchmarks to build trust.

For large enterprises, formal threat modeling exercises should be conducted regularly throughout the AI application lifecycle by engaging experts from information security, privacy, and legal teams along with the technical staff. For smaller projects, lightweight questionnaires and checklists may suffice to identify high-risk areas. In either case, threat modeling directly enables organizations to develop robust defenses for reliable and trustworthy AI systems aligned to governance standards.

Data Security

AI systems are being rapidly adopted across various industries and use cases. As these AI systems handle sensitive and confidential data, data security has become a critical concern, especially from a governance perspective.

Securing Data in AI Systems

AI systems ingest, process, generate, and transmit various forms of data throughout the AI lifecycle. This data can range from sensitive personal information to confidential commercial data to proprietary algorithmic models. *Safeguarding such critical digital assets is crucial.* The core practices for securing AI data include data encryption, access management, infrastructure protection, continuous threat detection monitoring, and compliance.

Data Encryption

The process of data encryption involves encoding (or "scrambling") data in a way that only authorized parties can access it. *Encrypting sensitive AI data is fundamental for ensuring confidentiality and preventing unauthorized access.* The major aspects related to encryption include:

1. **Encryption Algorithms:** Industry-standard algorithms like the Advanced Encryption Standard (**AES**) and **RSA** (named after its inventors Ron Rivest, Adi Shamir, and Leonard Adleman) should be used for encrypting AI data. They provide strong protection efficiently.
2. **Encryption Keys:** Encryption keys are used alongside algorithms to encode data. Secure generation, storage, and rotation of encryption keys are vital to prevent keys from being compromised.
3. **Data-at-Rest Encryption:** Data persisted in storage systems should be encrypted. Database encryption and file/folder encryption methods must be implemented.
4. **Data-in-Transit Encryption:** Data flowing across networks and systems should be encrypted. Secure communication protocols like Transport Layer Security (TLS) must be enforced.
5. **End-to-End Encryption:** Encrypting data throughout the entire data pipeline prevents intermediate system compromise. Where viable, organizations can explore mechanisms for end-to-end AI data encryption.

Access Management

The accessibility to AI data and related infrastructure must be restricted only to authorized users and processes. Key mechanisms include:

- **Authentication:** Users must be validated before being granted access to AI resources via strong multi-factor authentication.
- **Authorization:** User roles and access levels that align with organizational policies must be configured on AI components. The principle of least privilege should be followed.
- **Network Security:** Firewalls, intrusion prevention systems, and strict connectivity policies limit network-level access to AI environments hosting sensitive data.

Infrastructure Protection

The infrastructure underpinning AI platforms must be secured in depth to prevent data compromise:

1. **OS-Level Security:** AI servers should be hardened at the **operating system** level, according to security standards to prevent intrusions and malicious takeovers.

2. **Application Security:** Any software vulnerabilities must be addressed through testing and remediation to mitigate data exfiltration paths.
3. **Operational Security:** Infrastructure OS and applications must be configured for high availability, resilient disaster recovery, and automated security patching for robust data protection.
4. **Physical Security:** Data center physical access controls secure stored AI data against theft and tampering attempts.

Continuous Threat Detection Monitoring

This process involves the *continual monitoring, logging, and reviews of access patterns, user activities, infrastructure configurations and data flows which are necessary for detecting threats* to AI data:

- **System Logging:** Centralized logging from all infrastructure components aids security monitoring and incident forensics.
- **Behavioral Analytics:** AI/ML can be applied to system logs to dynamically flag anomalies that potentially signify threats.
- **Data Loss Prevention (DLP):** Organizations can implement data loss prevention programs tailored to securing confidential AI data.
- **Security Operations Center:** A dedicated SOC team undertakes monitoring, rapid threat alerting, and incident response coordination.

Compliance

Governing AI security requires organizational policies, standards, and oversight processes to be aligned with the technical measures undertaken. Key connections between cybersecurity and AI Governance include:

- **Compliance Mandates:** Legal/regulatory compliance directives around data protection and privacy impose security obligations that AI Governance frameworks must enforce.
- **Security Policies:** Enterprise security policies and AI-specific policies must mandate that confidentiality controls are embedded within AI systems as per governance directives.
- **Risk Assessments:** Both technology-focused and business-centric risk evaluation of AI data flows is imperative for holistic security governance.
- **Vendor Oversight:** Third-party vendor security practices must be evaluated by procurement teams and continuously validated by AI Governance leads through audits.
- **Incident Response:** AI data breach response protocols must be defined with cross-department coordination to align with organizational incident response procedures.
- **Training and Awareness:** Governance leads must conduct security awareness programs for AI teams to foster a culture focused on data protection.

Key Takeaways: *Safeguarding sensitive data used in AI systems via strong cybersecurity controls bolsters trust and facilitates oversight over data flows.* Encryption, access management, and infrastructure hardening provide multilayered data security. Continuous monitoring and testing enable threat visibility.

An integrated governance approach that connects leadership-driven policies and compliance directives with system-level security measures is key to maximizing AI data integrity. With robust data security foundations guided by risk-aware governance, organizations can ethically operate AI safely and responsibly.

Access Controls for AI Systems

Information Governance, risk management, and cybersecurity professionals play a pivotal role in governing AI systems. A crucial responsibility is implementing strong access controls to restrict unauthorized access to the data that fuels AI systems. *Without rigorous access controls, sensitive datasets can be exposed to compromise or abuse.*

Key Concepts

Access Control: Restricting user access to sensitive AI training data, models, and processed outputs.

Zero Trust (ZT) Security: Verifying identity for every user and device trying to access resources, regardless of inside or outside of the network perimeter.

Encryption: The process of encoding data to prevent unauthorized access.

Role-Based Access Control (RBAC): Permissions assigned based on user roles.

Multi-Factor Authentication (MFA): Authentication using two or more verification factors, like passwords and a one-time code sent to a mobile device.

Data Classification — Organizing data by sensitivity/criticality levels to determine security controls

Governance Considerations

AI systems present new challenges related to data security and access controls, necessitating heightened attention from governance teams. *The training datasets used for AI often include highly sensitive information such as personal data, healthcare records, and financial information. The compromise of such data could have severe consequences, affecting privacy and eroding trust in AI systems.*

Moreover, the **algorithms** that power AI systems hold significant commercial value, making them attractive targets for unauthorized access. Unauthorized entry could result in the theft of valuable intellectual property, emphasizing the importance of robust security measures.

Another concern arises from the potential manipulation of ML models by malicious actors, who may attempt to skew outputs in their favor. This manipulation poses a threat to the integrity and reliability of AI-generated results, raising questions about the trustworthiness of these systems.

Additionally, as AI automation enhances the capabilities of systems, the criticality and impact of potential malicious access become more pronounced. This escalation in risk emphasizes the need for comprehensive security protocols to safeguard against unauthorized activities that could compromise the functionality and integrity of AI systems.

To govern these risks, cybersecurity and information governance leaders must partner closely with AI development teams to implement preventive access controls aligned with the sensitivity of data and systems. Failing to restrict access could undermine trust in AI through harmful data exposures.

Access Control Methods

There are three main types of security access controls, including:

1. technical
2. administrative
3. physical

1. Technical Controls

Technical controls are the **system-based**, automated mechanisms, tools, and safeguards used to manage access, protect data, and defend infrastructure against threats. Key technical access controls include:

Authentication

- Leverage **single sign-on** systems to simplify and strengthen user authentication.
- Enforce **multi-factor authentication** for all users.
- **Block access** after X failed login attempts.

Role-Based Access Control (RBAC)

- It restricts system access to authorized users based on the roles, responsibilities, and attributes assigned to a user account rather than specific lists of what resources each user can access.
- For example, users in an "analyst" role can only access certain datasets or capabilities, while an "administrator" role has elevated permissions.
- Permissions are managed centrally through directories and access management tools rather than being individually assigned.

Attribute-Based Access Control (ABAC)

- Leverage **ABAC** to enhance traditional role-based access controls for AI resources. With ABAC, access decisions consider attributes like time, location, device state, authentication method, and more.
- The heightened sensitivity of AI training data merits the extra granularity of attribute-based dynamic access evaluations.

Access Control Lists (ACLs)

- For authorization, apply finely tuned ACLs to access attempts at the dataset, ML model artifact, compute instance, and storage volume levels.
- Allow only specified users or processes to interact with specific AI assets, with predefined permissions.

Network Security

- Place AI systems within secured virtual private cloud environments with firewalls.
- Limit communication between AI resources and broader networks.
- Monitor traffic for anomalies.

Encryption

- Encrypt network traffic flowing between AI components.
- Encrypt stored data, including datasets, ML models, logs, and processed data.

Operating System Controls

- Harden operating systems that support AI workflows according to security baselines.
- Apply system updates on a regular basis (to patch security holes/weaknesses).
- Restrict users to standard accounts without administrative privileges.

2. Administrative Controls

Enable the oversight, auditing, and policy enforcement of information systems.

Data Classification

- Classify datasets and AI models based on sensitivity to guide access requirements.
- Define protection standards aligned with the internal data classification taxonomy.

Access Control Policies

- Document policies specifying formal access control rules for data and systems.
- Outline provisioning processes, authorized user duties, access review cadence, and audit procedures.

Access Provisioning and Reviews

- Integrate AI systems within central IAM infrastructure.
- Provision access after approval from resource owners according to documented access policies.
- Review entitlements quarterly, as well as during employee offboarding.

Access Policy Enforcement

- Leverage access control systems and identity platforms to enforce defined policies.
- Centrally manage access and closely monitor activity for security events.

Zero Trust Security

- This is both an administrative and technical control approach.
- Never automatically trust users, devices, or applications inside or outside the network.
- **Requires secure verification and authenticating all access.**
- Enforces strict identity verification and least privilege access to resources.

Least Privilege Access

- Adhere to the **Principle of Least Privilege** discipline by restricting all personnel and production systems to only the datasets, ML pipelines, and integrations strictly necessary for their roles.
- Set predefined access timeframes. Require re-approval for continued access after initial access period expires.

Temporal Access Controls

- Establish time-based constraints permitting access to sensitive training data or ML ops functions only during scheduled periods, such as normal business hours.
- Promptly revoke access when it is no longer needed.

Emergency Access Procedures

- Define procedures for emergency access to AI resources required for high-severity incident responses or time-sensitive mitigations.
- Log and audit all emergency access. Require multiple senior personnel approvals.

Regulatory Compliance

- Adjust controls to adhere to all compliance obligations across jurisdictions.
- Conduct gap assessments between access controls for AI systems and data protection mandates within GDPR, CCPA, CPRA, HIPAA, FERPA, and other relevant regulations.

Training and Awareness

- Train employees and contractors on security policies and access control discipline.
- Increase awareness of escalation channels for suspicious access attempts.

Audits

- Routinely audit access controls through internal teams or third parties.
- Identify policy gaps, investigate violations, and refine controls accordingly.

3. Physical Controls

The third control group that is an important component of a defense-in-depth access control strategy for AI systems are physical controls. Here are some key points on implementing physical controls:

- *Restrict physical access to facilities* housing AI systems using card readers, biometrics, reception areas, and security personnel.
- *Designate areas with sensitive AI components as secure zones* with additional access screening. Limit access to essential personnel.
- *Log all physical access requests and entry/exit events.* Revoke promptly when they are no longer needed.
- *Deploy mantraps, barriers, intrusion detection, and video surveillance* to detect and delay unauthorized access.
- *Control access to AI model production environments* to prevent tampering or theft.
- *For AI edge devices, implement tamper defenses such as enclosures and monitoring.*
- *Securely grant temporary supervised access to third parties according to time-bound policies.*

Robust physical security controls and cybersecurity measures provide overlapping protections for critical AI infrastructure. Governing physical access is essential, as breaching perimeters often enables wider unauthorized system access.

Proactively addressing risks and implementing preventive controls across the AI lifecycle facilitates balancing innovation with responsible data use, reduced exposures, and trustworthy outcomes.

Cryptographic Best Practices for Protecting Sensitive Data in AI Systems

As AI systems are increasingly entrusted with sensitive and confidential data, implementing robust cybersecurity controls, including cryptography, has become an imperative for responsible and ethical AI Governance. **Cryptography** refers to techniques for securing information through mathematical functions called ciphers.[2]

When properly implemented, cryptography can ensure the confidentiality, integrity, and availability of sensitive data utilized in AI systems. *This section provides an overview of cryptographic best practices that Information governance and cyber professionals overseeing AI systems should be aware of, even if they do not have specialized expertise in cybersecurity.* Adopting these practices allows organizations to embed security into the design and deployment of AI systems from the ground up.

Identifying and Classifying Sensitive Data

The first step is to identify sensitive data like **personally identifiable information** (PII), financial information, intellectual property, or proprietary algorithms that require encryption or other protection measures per governance requirements or organizational policies. Clear **data classification** allows for appropriately protecting data depending on its sensitivity level. Data custodians should classify data into categories based on Impact Levels so that commensurate protections can be applied.

Choosing Strong Encryption Algorithms

Standardized and well-tested symmetric encryption algorithms like the AES or asymmetric encryption methods like RSA should be utilized as the foundation of the cryptographic approach.

Emerging areas like **homomorphic encryption** (which allows computations on encrypted data and quantum-resistant cryptographic algorithms)[3] can also be evaluated. Integration with reputable cryptographic modules and libraries is recommended over building proprietary solutions.

Implementing Secure Key Management

A centralized key management strategy should generate, distribute, rotate, back up, and destroy keys to reduce the risks from compromised, weak, or reused keys over time. **Hardware security modules** (HSMs) provide high assurance secure key storage and cryptographic processing. *Key management interconnects with IAM systems to link keys with authorized users and applications.*

Applying Data-at-Rest and Data-in-Transit Encryption

Encryption *must extend across all data lifecycle stages including transmission, processing, and storage.* **Data-at-rest** encryption applies ciphers to data persisted in databases, logs, file shares, and cloud object storage via file system/volume encryption, database encryption, or application-level encryption. **Data-in-transit** encryption, such as TLS protocol, should be enforced for all internal and external communication channels.

Documenting Cryptographic Configurations and Training Personnel

Detailed **topology diagrams** showing **encryption usage at different layers** (storage, database, network, application) should be maintained with configurations documented in a central repository. Training programs should educate data stewards, application developers, and IT administrators on properly implementing the organization's prescribed cryptographic designs, policies, and key management procedures.

Conducting Cryptographic Audits and Seeking External Expertise

Independent cryptographic audits should periodically assess encryption efficacy, key management robustness, algorithm viability, and personnel competency against industry standards—identifying backdoors, expired keys, weak ciphers, or TLS misconfigurations. External consultants can advise particularly for sophisticated use cases like homomorphic or zero-knowledge encryption.

Cryptographic Controls for Responsible AI Governance

Cryptography aligns with Trustworthy AI principles around safety and reliability per frameworks like the **EU Ethics Guidelines for Trustworthy AI**.[4] Encrypting training data, models, and algorithms maintains provenance while authentication seals integrity. As biases or attacks can violate fairness or accountability, encryption prevents unauthorized visibility, enabling responsible AI Governance. Fundamental cryptographic controls facilitate robust cyber protection and ethical AI lifecycle management.

Establishing a Robust Data Access Monitoring Methodology for AI Systems

As AI sees rapidly expanding adoption, securing AI systems and data has become a major concern. AI systems are powered by data—they learn from vast volumes of data and derive insights that drive automated decisions. Safeguarding this data is critical for ethical AI Governance.

Cyberattacks on AI data stores or supply chains can severely undermine AI reliability and trustworthiness. Malicious actors could manipulate training data to skew algorithmic outputs or steal sensitive personal information used by AI applications. As such, cybersecurity is integral to responsible AI Governance in organizations.

A core aspect of securing AI environments entails monitoring and controlling access to AI data and training pipelines. By logging and auditing data access, security teams can detect unauthorized activities and cyber threats early. This allows a prompt response to prevent impacts on AI systems or products.

This section provides Information Governance and cyber professionals with an overview of key steps in implementing robust data access monitoring frameworks to ensure AI security. It covers critical monitoring capabilities, technologies, and processes—from storage to analytics to response.

Defining Data Access Monitoring

Data access monitoring refers to the processes of recording, tracking, and analyzing access to data by users and applications over time. It involves:

- Capturing data access events such as view, edit, delete, or copy actions.
- Logging relevant contextual details like user IDs, timestamps, and data objects.
- Identifying anomalous patterns that may signify cyber threats.
- Enabling analysis to uncover risk trends across datasets.

For AI, access patterns to training data lakes, model-building environments, and AI application data *require monitoring to detect abnormalities.*

Governance Considerations

While strong technical measures enable lower-level monitoring, *governance sets the vision for what must be safeguarded and why.* Key considerations for governance leaders overseeing AI monitoring programs include:

- **Cataloging Sensitive Assets:** *Classify datasets containing proprietary formulas, personal data, or other sensitive information* that specifically require access controls and auditing.
- **Defining Protection Priorities:** *Clarify which data types, pipelines, or AI applications warrant deeper, more advanced monitoring* based on impact severity.
- **Developing Risk Metrics:** *Establish quantitative metrics* calibrated to business impact that feed into executive dashboards and allow risk-based comparisons across AI domains.
- **Communicating Objectives:** *Clearly convey the goals* of balancing open data sharing needed for innovation with controls that sustain reliability and trust.

- **Instituting Accountability:** *Ensure roles and responsibilities for providing, protecting, and monitoring access are explicitly defined and enforced* through processes like **access certification.**

Looking Ahead

In collaboration with IT and Security, Information Governance leaders play an indispensable role in nurturing a culture focused on responsible data usage rather than just availability. Careful oversight, measured transparency, and principled accountability ultimately build confidence in AI systems both within and outside the organization.

As AI assumes greater importance in products and operations, adversaries are incentivized to attack weaknesses in AI data supply chains. *Robust monitoring combined with vigilant governance offers a strong safeguard.* It expands visibility into access patterns enterprise-wide while supporting swift, decisive responses to early indicators of compromise. Over time, insights uncovered help continuously refine policies and controls. By putting proper guardrails around AI, organizations can advance innovations confidently in line with their values.

Version Control for AI Model Reproducibility and Security

As AI integration grows across applications, ensuring security, fairness, and reliability is crucial for Information Governance and cyber professionals. *Since AI systems learn behaviors from statistical models and large datasets, tracking* **data provenance** *and development changes matters. Undetected errors, biases, or misconfigurations can severely impact production environments.*

Comprehensive **version control** *provides audit trails* and enables reproducibility by capturing code, data, and dependencies. It facilitates collaboration while enforcing access controls. For oversight of organizational AI, mandating version control instruments and important cyber risk **control is essential.**

Version Control Systems Overview

Version control systems (VCS) record changes in files or directories over time so that specific versions can be recalled later. Key concepts in version control include:

- **Repository**: Central database storing all file versions. Enables team collaboration.
- **Commit**: Bundling updates into the repository as a logical single unit.
- **Branch**: Diverging workflows from the mainstream to allow concurrent work.
- **Merge**: Combining changes across branches. Requires resolving conflicts between parallel edits.
- **Tag**: Marking significant releases or project milestones for easy future reference.

Popular version control systems include Git, GitHub, Subversion (SVN), and Mercurial. Of these, ***Git has become a de facto standard*** *for tracking updates to code and data.* Hosted web platforms like **GitHub, GitLab, and Bitbucket** provide collaboration capabilities on top of core Git versioning functions.

Benefits for AI Systems

1. **Model Reproducibility**

   In applied AI, reproducing the exact software environment used to train ML models is vital for continuity and avoiding **data drift** if re-training is needed. By committing dependency manifests, containerization configurations, OS/hardware details, and other relevant parameters to version control, data scientists can recreate environments precisely. This facilitates reproducibility, debugging, and adaptations of the modeling pipeline.

2. **Audit Trail of Changes**

   Examining the incremental changes made throughout an AI project provides useful oversight into the development life cycle. Governance teams can analyze **commit logs** and **model artifacts** to ensure best practices were followed by data scientists as models progressed from prototypes to production systems.

3. **Collaboration Enablement**

   Centralized repositories allow multiple data scientists to concurrently edit code and assets associated with an AI project in a managed way. **Branching** isolates streams of work until ready to be integrated via peer code reviews. Access controls also restrict unwanted changes by those unauthorized.

4. **Disaster Recovery**

   In the event of catastrophic failures, *entire AI model repositories can be restored thanks to the comprehensive version histories maintained.* This is invaluable if retraining is needed from a previous state.

Leveraging Version Control for AI Governance and Security

Cybersecurity leaders have an important responsibility in advising governance committees and data science teams on technology safeguards for AI assets. *Version control acts as a foundational data lineage tracking mechanism that, when implemented effectively, can mitigate several security and compliance risks inherent to complex model development.*

Specifically, **Chief Information Security Officers** (CISOs) should champion policies and practices requiring:

- Use of *access-controlled version control repositories by AI teams rather than informal shared drives or* notebooks restricts exposure to proprietary algorithms and training data.
- *Routine auditing of version control commit histories* to ensure best practices around branching, peer reviews, testing, and deployment workflows was adhered to per internal protocols.
- *Enablement of authentication mechanisms, access controls, and encryption to secure both repositories and CI/CD pipeline components.* Vulnerabilities in the orchestration stack could allow unauthorized model or data access.
- *Development of disaster recovery runbooks for reconstructing repositories and orchestration infrastructure* in the event of destructive malware or ransomware incidents.

Advising governance working groups on version control requirements provides CISOs another touchpoint to instill cybersecurity best practices. The reproducibility and oversight version control confers will directly translate to more secure, responsible, and compliant AI systems.

Key Takeaways

Implementing comprehensive version control procedures provides a critical foundation enabling AI Governance over ethics, algorithmic fairness, and reliability. By mandating the use of version control's use across data science teams, organizations can track model provenance, changes, environments, inputs, and mitigating several security and compliance risks inherent to AI. Governance leaders should work closely with cybersecurity leaders to institute policies ensuring that version control repositories are securely implemented and routinely audited.

Machine Learning Framework Updates and Patches for Security

As AI and **ML** systems grow in sophistication and integration into business processes, the cybersecurity practices surrounding them have become a critical component of overall Information Governance and **risk management**. Organizations must take a proactive and ongoing approach to securing their AI environments in alignment with cyber risks. *One key element is the implementation of robust software* **patch management** *(updates to improve security, integrity) for ML frameworks and libraries.*

What Are Machine Learning Frameworks and Libraries?

ML ***frameworks and libraries provide reusable components for developing AI models and applications***. This includes code for data preprocessing, model architectures (e.g., neural networks), training algorithms, deployment mechanisms, visualizations, and more. Common open-source Python frameworks used by data scientists are TensorFlow, PyTorch, Keras, scikit-learn, Pandas, and NumPy.

Why Patch Management Matters for AI Systems

Like all software, the ML frameworks and libraries used in *AI systems require regular security updates from vendors. However, data science teams often prioritize innovation over keeping components patched.* Reasons include a focus on modeling rather than operations, concern about impacts to existing models, and a lack of processes. *This exposes significant cyber risks,* as attackers actively exploit vulnerabilities in AI libraries to steal data, manipulate models, or evade fraud detection.

Recent examples include backdoors discovered in OpenCV and Foolbox. By collaboratively establishing patch management practices for ML infrastructure, cybersecurity, and data science teams can balance innovation with appropriate risk management. Keeping AI systems patched allows for pursuing innovation while upholding security, reliability, and compliance standards.

Secure AI Model Deployment

This section provides an overview of cybersecurity best practices for one key aspect of the AI lifecycle—the deployment of AI models. **Model deployment** *is the stage where trained AI models are integrated into applications and made available for practical* use. Secure deployment establishes a resilient foundation for delivering reliable AI predictions and decisions.

Containerization

Containerization *encapsulates AI models, along with their frameworks, libraries, and other dependencies, into standardized units for deployment and execution.* Popular container platforms include Docker and Red Hat OpenShift.

Benefits of containerization:

- **Portability**: Containers can run uniformly on any infrastructure.
- **Agility**: Containerized models can be quickly updated or redeployed.
- **Consistency**: Containers ensure models function the same across environments.
- **Isolation**: Containers isolate models and minimize interdependencies across systems.

To secure containers, organizations should scan container images for vulnerabilities, enable runtime protections, restrict network traffic between containers, and implement user access controls.

Identity and Access Management (IAM)

Strict **access controls** must govern all users and systems interacting with AI deployments. IAM enforces authentication, authorization, and auditing.

Multi-factor authentication ensures only verified users gain access. **Role-based access** controls restrict user permissions to only necessary actions. API keys authorize external services while security protocols like OAuth 2.0 and OpenID Connect federate access.

Continuous monitoring of access patterns detects anomalies and attempted misuse. Session management limits sessions to guard against hijacking.

Deployment Pipelines

Modern systems rely on **continuous integration/continuous delivery** (CI/CD — see detailed definition in Glossary at the end of chapter) *to automate building, testing, and deployment of code changes*. Security must be baked into these pipelines.

Steps include static and dynamic analysis to catch bugs and misconfigurations early, container image scanning at all stages, blocking unsafe registries, and policy enforcement before releases.

Post-deployment, practices like immutable infrastructure and blue-green deployments help reduce downtime from patching vulnerabilities.

Encryption

Data encryption protects information generated by or supporting AI systems from unauthorized access and tampering.

- Encrypt data in transit using TLS, HTTPS, SSL, and IPsec VPNs.
- Encrypt data at rest via file/disk encryption and database encryption.
- Carefully manage keys and crypto parameters.
- Hashed signatures, data masking, and tokenization also help secure sensitive datasets.

Monitoring, Logging, and Auditing

Robust behavioral monitoring, analysis of logs, and regular audits are crucial for swift detection and response to attacks on AI deployments. Key capabilities include:

- Asset management provides real-time visibility, while performance monitoring tracks unusual resource usage, and network analysis detects anomalous traffic patterns.
- Log centralization enables investigation of detailed audit trails produced by the above monitoring systems.
- Frequent audits check overall security posture and policy compliance.
- Alert notifications and automatic mitigations stem the impact while teams investigate triggers.

Responsible AI Governance

While comprehensive technical measures are indispensable, ethical oversight mechanisms are also vital for Trustworthy AI aligned to principles around accountability, reliability, and safety. Organizations require adaptable governance strategies encompassing continuous control assessment, specialized talent development, executive engagement, and collaboration with external groups establishing frameworks and standards guiding responsible innovation.

Securing AI APIs and External System Integrations

Application Programming Interfaces (APIs) enable communication between software systems and applications, playing a crucial role in external AI interactions. However, *APIs present cyber risks that require security.* Likewise, third-party integrations provide capabilities but introduce potential vulnerabilities that can be exploited to compromise AI.

As AI Governance evolves across disciplines, cybersecurity is indispensable for ensuring safety, security, ethics, and compliance. Guidance on securing APIs and integrations supports robust AI Governance frameworks.

Securing AI APIs

APIs allow AI systems and components to communicate with other applications and compute resources. However, attackers frequently target APIs as a doorway into backend systems and data assets. Hence, comprehensive API security is critical. **Multi-factor authentication** provides additional assurance by requiring multiple credentials. API credentials should have short expiry periods and frequent rotation to limit the impact if compromised.

Authorization controls like **role-based access** and **fine-grained permissions** restrict access to only vetted identities. This minimizes insider risks from credential misuse.

API Gateways

API gateways centralize authentication, access control, encryption, etc. for consistent policy application. They also enable monitoring, logging, alerting, and other security capabilities. Input validation blocks common attacks like code injection or unauthorized data access attempts.

Encryption

Transport Layer Security (TLS) encrypts API communication channels. Additionally, sensitive data should be encrypted in transit and at rest through cryptographic schemes like **AES-256.** This protects confidentiality and integrity throughout the data **lifecycle**.

Logging, Monitoring, and Auditing

Comprehensive logging captures administrative, user, and system activities involving APIs. Logs enable real-time monitoring systems to detect anomalies and trigger alerts. Regular audits and penetration testing identify vulnerabilities to address.

Secure Development

Adhering to **secure coding practices** and conducting peer code reviews minimizes weaknesses in API application logic. API versioning also supports iterating security improvements while maintaining compatibility.

Third-Party Integration Security

In addition to proprietary APIs, *many AI systems integrate with online services via third-party APIs for added capabilities*. However, the external ownership of such connections warrants additional due diligence**.**

Vendor Assessments

Thorough assessments of a vendor's data security controls, compliance, and general security posture are necessary for risk-based decisions on integration viabilities or contractual obligations. *Continuous monitoring also provides ongoing assurance.*

Audits and Incident Planning

Contracts should require vendors to regularly audit security controls and collaborate on incident response plans. Vendors are responsible for meeting contracted security expectations.

As vendors evolve their offerings, important security-impacting changes must be closely tracked to re-evaluate integration risks.

Wrapping Up

While APIs and third-party integrations enable interfacing AI systems with additional capabilities, *these connections also risk infiltration*. Securing interfaces is thus critical to preserve confidentiality, integrity, availability, and accountability across interconnected systems.

Comprehensive API security controls deter external threats and insider misuse by locking down ingress and egress channels. Due diligence ensures vendors meet security obligations. *Multilayered defenses across integration touchpoints enhance AI functionality without compromising resilience.*

Developing an Incident Response Plan for AI Systems

As organizations adopt AI to drive decisions, products, and automation, *attack surfaces grow.* Like any software, AI systems have vulnerabilities requiring incident plans to quickly detect, respond, and recover when exploited. A comprehensive response plan tailored to ML security challenges is key. Incident response capabilities enable responsible AI Governance across the lifecycle.

Key Challenges in Responding to AI Incidents

The complexity and opacity of many AI algorithms make investigating incidents extremely difficult. The key challenges include:

- **Lack of Model Explainability:** Understanding why models make certain predictions or decisions is critical for analysis but is not straightforward for many AI models.
- **Data Dependencies:** Training data, feature engineering, and other data-related issues can contribute to incidents. Tracing these lineages presents challenges.
- **Detection Difficulty:** Subtle changes in model behavior or adversarial attacks may not trigger alerts. Sensitive anomaly detection is needed.
- **Short System Lifecycles:** Frequent model updates complicate containment strategies relying on versioning rollbacks.

Developing an AI Incident Response Plan

Organizations need customized plans for responding to the unique risks AI systems manifest. Key steps include:

1. **Define AI Incident Response Team and Roles**

   Cross-functional team across IT, Privacy, InfoSec, AI Engineering, Legal, and Communications and other relevant functions

   Clearly define responsibilities.
2. **Document AI System Architectures**

   Comprehensive documentation of components and data flows

   Understand dependencies and integration touchpoints
3. **Identify Critical AI Assets**

   Prioritize high-impact AI models, data, and systems
4. **Develop AI-Focused Response Procedures**

   Model versioning and rollback strategies

   Containing compromised data

   Managing model degradation
5. **Implement Anomaly Monitoring**

   Monitor for deviations in model inputs, behaviors, and outputs.

   Tuned detection thresholds
6. **Conduct AI-Specific Incident Analysis**

   Forensic analysis of model decision-making

   Reconstructing data provenance and lineages

7. **Ensure Compliance Requirements Met**
   Work with legal and compliance teams
   Understand reporting obligations
8. **Provide Ongoing Team Training**
   AI security vulnerabilities and risks
   Response plan execution
9. **Test and Update Response Plans Regularly**
   Simulate incident scenarios
   Update based on learnings

By developing AI-tailored incident response plans, organizations can better prepare for, detect, mitigate, and recover from incidents that may profoundly impact business functions dependent on AI systems. Cybersecurity functions play a fundamental role in protecting AI assets and upholding reliability.

Continuous Monitoring and Auditing for AI System Security

As AI and ML are deployed in mission-critical systems, effectively governing these technologies requires implementing comprehensive cybersecurity defenses. Continuous monitoring and routine auditing of AI systems provide ongoing visibility into security risks and vulnerabilities. *By establishing rigorous continuous monitoring and auditing practices tailored to AI environments, organizations can rapidly detect and respond to threats, minimizing potential impacts.*

Defining Continuous Monitoring and Auditing

Continuous monitoring refers to the *ongoing awareness of information security risks and controls using automated data feeds and tools.* It enables prompt identification and addressing threats. Auditing examines the effectiveness of security controls through periodic in-depth inspections, assessments, and formal testing.

For AI systems, key focus areas for continuous monitoring and audits include:

- Access controls and activity logging
- Monitoring model behavior and performance metrics
- Malicious input detection
- Infrastructure and supply chain integrity
- Vulnerability management
- Incident response preparedness

Implementing a Comprehensive Program

Organizations should design continuous monitoring and auditing initiatives specifically for their AI environments while integrating into enterprise-wide programs. Essential elements include:

A *risk-based approach* is essential in managing AI systems effectively, necessitating initial risk assessments to guide the prioritization, scope, and frequency of monitoring and audits. To ensure robust AI security and governance, it is crucial to establish comprehensive policies addressing continuous monitoring, auditing, and third-party assessment requirements.

The implementation of **detection rules** and **data science** techniques is key to analyzing logs and indicators from AI systems, facilitating the rapid detection of anomalies and potential threats. This proactive approach is further enhanced by leveraging AI-specialized security tools, combined with centralized log analysis and security orchestration platforms, to automate monitoring processes and streamline audits.

Appointing skilled personnel is integral to the success of continuous monitoring and audits. Competent staff with applied expertise in AI, cybersecurity, data analysis, and risk assessment contribute to the effective execution of these processes. Additionally, integrating continuous monitoring alerts with incident response playbooks tailored for AI assets and associated risks enhances the organization's ability to respond swiftly to potential incidents.

Transparent communication is vital, and leadership and stakeholders should be kept informed through dashboards, notifications, and documentation that present the security posture, identified risks, events, and corresponding responses. Regular maintenance and updating of detection rules, controls, auditing procedures, and monitoring scope are necessary to adapt to evolving threats and changes in AI systems. This periodic fine-tuning ensures the continued effectiveness of security measures in the dynamic landscape of AI development and deployment.

Sustaining Effective Continuous Monitoring and Auditing

Maintaining robust continuous monitoring and auditing for AI involves:

- Providing training to involve staff in maintaining high awareness of risks and controls.
- Conducting **tabletop exercises** to validate response plans for security incidents.
- Performing **after-action reviews** following major incidents to identify monitoring and control gaps.
- Benchmarking against industry practices and seeking regular guidance from third-party AI and security experts.
- Allocating dedicated budgets and cross-functional staff committing time to support the program is essential for its success.
- Documenting all architectures, controls, processes, analytics, and dashboards to facilitate oversight.

By establishing rigorous continuous monitoring combined with regular audits and adaptations, organizations can secure AI assets against escalating cyber threats while demonstrating diligent governance.

Regulatory Compliance and Cybersecurity Best Practices for AI Systems

As AI systems grow in capabilities and adoption across industries, developing robust governance practices, including regulatory compliance and cybersecurity, has become imperative. AI

Governance refers to the operational frameworks, policies, controls, and processes needed to ensure AI systems are ethical, unbiased, secure, and compliant throughout their lifecycle.

Staying Informed About AI Cybersecurity Regulations

Given the nascent yet growing adoption of AI across business verticals, *cybersecurity regulations applicable to AI systems are still evolving and vary across different jurisdictions.* Organizations leveraging AI need systematic processes for tracking regulatory changes and ensuring continuous compliance. Key steps include:

1. **Regulatory Intelligence System:** Establish mechanisms to identify and monitor cybersecurity regulations governing AI in relevant geographies. Engage legal teams for interpretive guidance.
2. **Industry Participation:** Actively participate in industry associations focused on AI security to stay abreast of emerging compliance trends.
3. **Regular Assessments:** Conduct periodic assessments comparing current security policies and controls against updated regulations.
4. **Training Programs:** Educate AI developers and governance teams on evolving compliance obligations.

Industry and Regional Cybersecurity Standards

In addition to tracking AI cybersecurity regulations, *organizations need to comply with industry-specific frameworks and regional data protection laws based on their sectors and operating jurisdictions.* For example, healthcare companies in the United States deploying AI need to conform to HIPAA while European entities need to comply with GDPR. Steps for ascertainment include:

1. **Gap Analysis:** Perform a gap analysis comparing the organization's current security posture versus requirements stated in relevant industry and regional standards.
2. **Risk-based Prioritization:** Create a roadmap to close identified gaps, prioritizing higher-risk areas first.
3. **Control Implementation:** Progressively implement technical, administrative, and physical controls to achieve compliance with applicable standards.
4. **Continuous Monitoring:** Utilize tools to automate the monitoring of compliance controls across the infrastructure.

Cybersecurity Best Practices for AI Systems

The following cybersecurity best practices can help enhance the security posture of AI systems:

Data Security: Since AI systems are data-driven, securing the training datasets and AI models built on top requires implementing robust data security controls, including:

1. **Data Encryption:** Encrypt AI training data and model artifacts both at rest and in transit to prevent unauthorized access.
2. **Access Controls:** Enforce least privilege and need-to-know-based access for AI data using role-based access controls, attribute-based access control, or similar mechanisms.

3. **Data Lifecycle Protection:** Protect AI data across its lifecycle, right from sourcing, labeling, storage, model development, to dissemination and retirement, as per defined retention policies.

Infrastructure Protection: Safeguarding the underlying IT infrastructure, including clouds, containers, middleware, and pipelines used to support AI systems, is critical, specifically:

1. **Secure Configuration:** Harden IT infrastructure per security benchmarks - disable unnecessary ports/services, implement account lockouts, and so on.
2. **Continuous Monitoring:** Actively monitor infrastructure components, APIs, and communications for vulnerabilities, misconfigurations, intrusion attempts, etc.
3. **Patch Management:** Establish mechanisms to rapidly roll out remedial patches for detected vulnerabilities across components.

Identity and Access Management: With a wide range of internal and external stakeholders collaborating on AI systems, managing identities and enforcing privileged access management is vital:

1. **Principle of Least Privilege:** Provision just enough user privileges based on defined responsibilities.
2. **Multifactor Authentication:** Enforce additional factors for authentication including biometrics before granting access to sensitive AI resources.
3. **Session Management:** Configure fixed duration for user sessions post which reauthentication needs to be performed to access AI systems.

Threat Modeling and Detection: AI systems have unique vulnerabilities that can be exploited if not identified and mitigated early on through:

1. **Threat Modeling:** Adopt techniques like STRIDE to methodically identify threats associated with AI components.
2. **Anomaly Detection:** Leverage User and Entity Behavior Analytics (UEBA) tools to detect anomalous user behavior indicative of insider threats across AI systems.
3. **Attack Simulations**: Routinely simulate known attack scenarios like data poisoning and model evasion etc. to assess the effectiveness of deployed security controls.

Continuous Validation: Periodically evaluating security controls and responding to evolving attack vectors is key for sustained protection.

1. **Bug Bounties:** Launch bug bounty programs inviting external security researchers to identify vulnerabilities in AI systems.
2. **Blue Team Exercises:** Conduct scheduled blue team exercises to test deployed AI cybersecurity use cases and incident response plans.
3. **Patching Cadence:** Maintain regular patching cycles for AI systems synchronized with the vulnerability disclosure timelines of components.

Wrapping Up

As AI adoption spreads, robust governance guiding ethics, security, and compliance is imperative. Organizations must implement data, infrastructure, identity, and threat detection controls while regularly training developers and assessing protections against evolving regulations, frameworks, and attack techniques. Comprehensive governance sustains resilience.

Employee Cybersecurity Training for AI Systems

As organizations increasingly adopt AI to automate processes and gain insights from data, securing these systems from cyber threats has become imperative. However, *technical controls alone are insufficient—the actions and behaviors of people interacting with AI systems can also*[5] *introduce vulnerabilities*. This section will focus on recommended practices for strengthening the human element, which is pivotal for holistic AI security and governance.

Cultivating Employee Cybersecurity Awareness

Formal training programs are imperative to educate all employees on handling AI security risks responsibly. Core aspects include:

CISO-Led Assessments: CISOs need to assess employees' baseline cyber risk knowledge through surveys, interviews, and simulated phishing. This highlights where additional training is warranted.

Customized Content: For relevance, training should cover the organization's specific AI policies, infrastructure, and use cases using relatable real-world examples. This makes abstract AI threats more tangible.

AI Security Focus: While crucial, basic concepts like passwords warrant less emphasis than emerging AI-specific risks like model vulnerabilities, data poisoning, insider theft, software supply chain compromise, and adversarial attacks.

Role-Based Specialization: AI developers require secure coding training. Data scientists need guidance on anonymization. Incident responders require AI-specific breach containment training.

Comprehension Assessments: Quick quizzes during and after training, plus periodic refreshers, instill accountability and indicate program ROI via metrics assessing retained comprehension.

Fostering an AI Security-Focused Culture

Leadership Messaging: Business leaders must communicate that security enables, not hinders, AI innovation. Employees take cues from the top—when leadership prioritizes cyber protection, all teams internalize that mandate.

Shared Responsibility: Every employee should recognize that AI security is not just the CISO's duty alone. Their individual actions collectively contribute to the overall risk posture. Carelessness introduces weaknesses that attackers exploit.

Encouraging Secure Behaviors: Positive recognition of actions reflecting security awareness helps incentivize sustaining those behaviors. If an executive spots and reports a phish, they deserve public praise.

Enabling Transparent Dialogue: Employees should feel comfortable asking questions when unsure about AI security standards. Healthy discourse fosters mutual trust in leadership's intentions.

Sustaining Momentum: While training and culture provide foundations, progress requires continued nurturing. Remain patient and steadfast in improving secure behaviors through positive reinforcement over time.

The Way Forward

Ultimately, *technology alone cannot safeguard systems from the ramifications of human decisions and behaviors. Organizations must continually invest in their people while strengthening technical controls.* Training and awareness programs that factor in AI risks equip employees to become the first line of defense. Coupling education with positive reinforcement produces shared ownership of AI security. Get these elements right, and the human element ceases to become the weakest link. Instead, it evolves into the most durable shield.

Conclusion

Safeguarding AI systems requires holistic cybersecurity strategies spanning across regulations, industry standards, technologies, and teams. Information Governance leaders need to coordinate with cybersecurity groups to implement data-centric protections and continuously validate controls amid dynamic threats. Adopting the cybersecurity best practices outlined in this chapter can help strengthen the resilience of AI investments against adverse security events.

Key Points

- Cybersecurity is a fundamental component of robust AI Governance.
- Cybersecurity teams play a crucial role in each phase of the AI system development lifecycle.
- Threat modeling is used to systematically evaluate security risks associated with AI systems.
- AI systems rely extensively on data, predictive models, complex software, and broad connectivity.
- Successful cyberattacks on AI systems can have serious consequences.
- AI Governance plays a key role in providing oversight and guidance for developing, deploying, and managing AI responsibly.
- Cybersecurity frameworks like NIST provide globally recognized best practices for cybersecurity programs.
- Cybersecurity measures should be tailored to AI and connected systems.
- Securing data used by AI systems requires data encryption, access management, infrastructure protection, continuous threat monitoring, and compliance with regulations.
- Access controls are critical for restricting unauthorized access to sensitive AI data and systems.
- Zero Trust Security verifies identity for every user and device trying to access resources.
- Role-Based Access Control (RBAC) assigns permissions based on user roles.
- Multi-Factor Authentication (MFA) uses two or more verification factors for authentication.
- Data classification organizes data by sensitivity/criticality levels to determine security controls.
- Cryptography best practices for AI include using strong encryption algorithms, secure key management, encrypting data at rest and in-transit, and documenting configurations.
- Logging and monitoring access patterns to AI data and training pipelines allow detecting unauthorized activities and cyber threats early.

- Version Control Systems (VCS) enable reproducibility, collaboration, audit trails, and recovery for AI model code and artifacts.
- Access-controlled repositories mitigate risks in AI development.
- Deploying AI models securely involves containerization, identity and access management, secure CI/CD pipelines, encryption, and continuous monitoring.
- APIs and third-party integrations with AI systems require rigorous security assessments, access controls, encryption, monitoring, and vendor management.
- AI incident response plans define cross-functional teams, architectures, procedures, anomaly monitoring, and analysis methods customized for investigating AI security events.
- Continuous monitoring and auditing of AI systems enable rapid threat detection and demonstrate diligent governance.
- A risk-based approach is essential in managing AI systems effectively.
- Regulatory compliance for AI security requires tracking evolving regulations and conducting assessments against industry standards.
- Implementing data, infrastructure, identity, and detection controls helps achieve compliance with applicable standards.
- Gap analysis compares an organization's current security posture versus requirements stated in relevant industry and regional standards.
- Employee training and awareness programs covering AI-specific security risks are essential for improving the human element of AI security.
- Securing AI training datasets and model artifacts requires data encryption, access controls, and data lifecycle protection.
- Safeguarding IT infrastructure supporting AI systems involves secure configuration, continuous monitoring, and patch management.
- Identity and Access Management for AI systems should follow the Principle of Least Privilege, enforce MFA, and configure session management.
- Threat modeling techniques like STRIDE help identify threats associated with AI components.
- User and Entity Behavior Analytics (UEBA) tools detect anomalous user behavior indicative of insider threats across AI systems.
- Simulating known attack scenarios like data poisoning and model evasion helps assess the effectiveness of deployed security controls.
- Continuous validation of AI security controls involves bug bounties, blue team exercises, and maintaining regular patching cycles.
- Leadership must communicate that security enables, not hinders, AI innovation.
- Every employee should recognize that AI security is a shared responsibility.
- Encouraging secure behaviors and enabling transparent dialogue fosters a culture of AI security.
- Technology alone cannot safeguard systems from the ramifications of human decisions and behaviors.
- Coupling education with positive reinforcement produces shared ownership of AI security.
- Adopting cybersecurity best practices can help strengthen the resilience of AI investments against adverse security events.

Key Glossary Terms

Access control: Restricting user access to sensitive AI training data, models, and processed outputs.

Adversarial attack: An attempt to fool or misguide ML models by providing deceptive input.

API gateway: A server that acts as a single entry point into a system, used to handle requests by routing them to the appropriate backend service or by invoking multiple backend services.

Auditing: The examination of the effectiveness of security controls through periodic in-depth inspections, assessments, and formal testing.

Continuous delivery (CD): The practice of automating the deployment process, making every code change deployable to production environments automatically.

Continuous integration (CI): The practice of regularly integrating code changes from multiple contributors into a shared repository and running automated tests.

Continuous monitoring: The ongoing awareness of information security risks and controls using automated data feeds and tools.

Data classification: Organizing data by sensitivity/criticality levels to determine security controls.

Data encryption: The process of encoding data using a cryptographic algorithm or cipher so that it is unintelligible to unauthorized parties.

Data poisoning: A type of attack where an attacker manipulates the training data of a ML model, often by injecting malicious or misleading data points, in order to compromise the model's performance or cause it to learn incorrect patterns.

Homomorphic encryption: A type of encryption that allows computation to be performed directly on encrypted data without requiring access to a secret key.

Multi-factor Authentication (MFA): Authentication using two or more verification factors, like passwords and a one-time code sent to a mobile device.

Role-based access control (RBAC): Permissions assigned based on user roles.

Threat modeling: A structured process of identifying, categorizing and mitigating vulnerabilities in a system.

Version control systems (VCS): Systems that record changes in files or directories over time so that specific versions can be recalled later.

Zero trust (ZT) security: Verifying identity for every user and device trying to access resources, regardless of inside or outside of the network perimeter.

Notes

1 Feretzakis, et al. "Privacy-Preserving Techniques in Generative AI and Large Language Models: A Narrative Review," Hellenic Open University, November 4, 2024, last visited June 2, 2025, https://www.mdpi.com/2078-2489/15/11/697.

2 Barker, "Guideline for Identifying an Information System as a National Security System," National Institute for Standards and Technology, Special Publication 800-59, August 2003, last visited June 1, 2025, https://nvlpubs.nist.gov/nistpubs/Legacy/SP/nistspecialpublication800-59.pdf.

3 "What is Homomorphic Encryption?" IEEE Digital Privacy, last visited June 1, 2025, https://digitalprivacy.ieee.org/publications/topics/what-is-homomorphic-encryption/.

4 "Ethics Guidelines for Trustworthy AI," The European Commission, Published April 8, 2019, last visited June 1, 2025, https://digital-strategy.ec.europa.eu/en/library/ethics-guidelines-trustworthy-ai.

5 Brundage et al, "The Malicious Use of Artificial Intelligence: Forecasting, Prevention, and Mitigation," Oxford University and OpenAI, published February 2018, last visited June 2, 2025, https://arxiv.org/pdf/1802.07228.

9 The Role of IT in AI Governance

Historically, the information technology (IT) department has played a leading role in the selection, design, implementation, and maintenance of IT platforms. As such, the efficacy of IT's relationship with the businesses it supported was a critical factor in success.

More modernly, in the era of cloud computing, subscription-based IT usage, and multi-tenant platforms, an ever-increasing proportion of technology support has been outsourced to third parties, leaving many IT organizations focused on infrastructure, security, and connectivity.[1]

While AI platforms will continue this outsourced trend (indeed, the scale of generative AI largely precludes the use of dedicated platforms, although there are efforts to build "AI Super Data Centers" with hundreds of thousands of **graphical processing units** (GPU), which provide the hardware horsepower to handle complex AI computations), the technical skills required to properly assess and manage AI are far greater than with earlier platforms. Their inherent complexity, coupled with their relative newness, means that the talent and experience required to properly design and manage these systems is extremely rare and hence difficult to procure and retain.

While the last few generations of IT automation focused on reducing or even eliminating the involvement of technology professionals, success with AI once again demands high technical proficiency. As more and more of an organization's outcomes are dependent on these platforms, the need to be intimately aware of their design, operation, and functioning is paramount. IT must be intimately involved in all aspects of engaging with AI, and technical proficiency with these tools will be critical to operational success.

In the evolving landscape of artificial intelligence (AI), the IT department emerges as a pivotal entity, orchestrating the lifecycle of AI systems to align with organizational objectives, security mandates, and technical prerequisites. This critical involvement spans various phases, from inception through deployment to continuous improvement, ensuring AI technologies not only meet current needs but are also poised for future demands. Below is an explanation of the IT department's key responsibilities in the AI systems lifecycle.

Infrastructure Planning

The cornerstone of effective AI implementation lies in meticulous infrastructure planning. The IT department is tasked with designing, provisioning, and maintaining the computing infrastructure essential for AI systems. This encompasses a broad array of hardware, software, and networking resources. ***The department must keenly assess the computational demands of AI algorithms and models, ensuring the infrastructure is not just available but is also scalable*** and efficient enough to handle processing needs. This foundational step guarantees that the AI systems operate smoothly and are capable of scaling in response to evolving computational requirements.

Data Management

A robust data management strategy is crucial for the success of AI applications. *The IT department ensures the establishment and upkeep of systems for data storage, processing, and retrieval, tailored to support AI functionalities.* This involves setting up data pipelines, storage solutions, and databases that are optimized for AI workloads, emphasizing **data quality**, accessibility, and security. Through effective data management, AI systems can access high-quality data, a critical factor for the accuracy and reliability of AI insights.

Integration with Existing Systems

Integrating AI systems with the existing IT landscape is a complex but necessary endeavor. The *IT department facilitates this integration, ensuring AI systems seamlessly connect with existing infrastructure, databases, and applications*. This collaborative effort with other IT teams ensures data flows smoothly across systems, maintaining compatibility and enhancing the overall value delivered by AI technologies.

Security and Compliance

In the realm of AI, where data is both a valuable asset and a potential liability, security and compliance are paramount. The IT department implements *comprehensive security measures to safeguard AI systems and data, aligning with relevant regulations and standards.* Employing *encryption, access controls, and secure coding* practices, alongside regular vulnerability assessments, helps protect sensitive information and maintain trust in AI applications.

Model Deployment and Monitoring

Deploying trained AI models into production and establishing robust monitoring mechanisms are key responsibilities. The IT department works closely with data scientists and AI developers to ensure models are deployed effectively and perform as expected. *Monitoring systems are put in place to detect any operational issues, performance degradation, or security breaches*, ensuring the AI systems remain reliable and secure over time.

Scalability and Performance Optimization

As AI systems grow in complexity and usage, ensuring scalability and optimizing performance becomes critical. *The IT department monitors system performance, identifies bottlenecks, and implements optimizations* to improve efficiency and responsiveness. This ongoing process ensures AI systems can handle increasing workloads and deliver insights promptly.

System Updates and Maintenance

Regular updates, security patches, and maintenance are essential for the longevity and security of AI systems. The IT department manages these tasks, ensuring AI technologies remain up to date and operate without disruptions. This includes scheduling maintenance activities and coordinating updates to AI models or algorithms, thereby maintaining the operational excellence of AI systems.

User Training and Support

Ensuring end users can effectively interact with AI systems requires comprehensive training and support. *The IT department develops training materials, conducts workshops, and provides technical assistance, enabling users to leverage AI applications* to their full potential. This not only enhances user experience but also fosters an environment where AI can deliver maximum value.

Collaboration with Data Science Teams

The synergy between IT and data science teams is vital for the seamless deployment and operation of AI systems. Collaborating closely, the IT department understands technical requirements and addresses challenges, ensuring the infrastructure supports AI workflows and model deployment efficiently.

Backup and Disaster Recovery

Robust backup and disaster recovery plans are crucial safety nets. The IT *department ensures that AI systems and data are backed up and that contingency plans are in place in an Incident Response Plan to recover functionality in the event of failures* or disasters. This preparedness is key to maintaining continuity and resilience in AI operations.

Ethical and Responsible AI Implementation

Embedding AI systems within an ethical framework that reflects organizational values is a shared responsibility. *The IT department plays a crucial role in ensuring AI practices adhere to principles of transparency, fairness, and accountability, collaborating with governance and legal teams to uphold responsible AI deployment.*

This comprehensive approach to managing the AI systems lifecycle underscores the IT department's pivotal role in navigating the complexities of AI technology, ensuring systems are secure, efficient, and aligned with ethical standards, thus driving forward organizational objectives in an increasingly AI-driven world.

By fulfilling these responsibilities, the IT department contributes to the successful development, deployment, and maintenance of AI systems while addressing technical challenges and ensuring alignment with organizational goals and ethical standards.

Bias: Detailed Description and Definition

The IT department must be cognizant of, and develop strategies to counter, various forms of bias, which can skew results in queries made to the AI model, and can even lead to legal liabilities.

Sources of Bias

- **Data Bias:** This arises when the dataset used to train an AI model is not representative of the real-world scenario it is intended to address. It can occur due to overrepresentation, underrepresentation, or misrepresentation of certain groups within the data. For instance, a facial recognition system trained predominantly on images of people from a specific ethnic background may perform poorly on individuals from other backgrounds.
- **Algorithmic Bias:** Sometimes, the design of the algorithm itself can introduce bias. This may be due to the assumptions, simplifications, or choices made by developers during the model development process. For instance, an algorithm might prioritize certain outcomes based on the way it was programmed, irrespective of the data it's trained on.
- **Prejudice Bias:** Prejudice or cultural biases reflect societal stereotypes or prejudices that can be embedded in AI systems. For example, if historical hiring data reflects a gender bias in certain job roles, an AI system trained on this data might perpetuate this bias by favoring male candidates over female candidates for those roles.

Manifestations of Bias

- **Direct Bias:** Directly correlates to explicit characteristics in the data, such as race, gender, age, or socioeconomic status, leading to discriminatory outcomes against certain groups.
- **Indirect Bias:** Refers to bias that occurs through variables indirectly related to sensitive attributes. For instance, zip codes might serve as proxies for racial demographics, inadvertently introducing racial biases into AI decisions.
- **Feedback Loops:** AI systems can exacerbate initial biases over time through feedback loops. For example, a predictive policing tool that dispatches more police to neighborhoods it identifies as high-risk can lead to more arrests in those areas, reinforcing the tool's perception of those neighborhoods as high-risk and perpetuating a cycle of biased enforcement.

Mitigating Bias

Mitigating bias in AI systems involves a multifaceted approach, including:

- **Diverse and Representative Data:** Ensuring training datasets are diverse and representative of all relevant groups and scenarios can help reduce data biases.
- **Bias Detection and Correction Techniques:** Employing statistical techniques and algorithms designed to identify and correct bias in datasets and model predictions.
- **Ethical and Inclusive Design:** Involving stakeholders from diverse backgrounds in the AI development process can help identify potential biases and ethical concerns early on.
- **Transparency and Accountability:** Making AI systems transparent (explainable AI) and holding developers accountable for the outcomes of their AI systems can foster trust and facilitate the identification and correction of biases.
- **Continuous Monitoring:** Regularly assessing AI systems in real-world applications to identify and mitigate emerging biases over time.

Addressing bias in AI systems is not only a technical challenge but also an ethical imperative, requiring ongoing vigilance, interdisciplinary collaboration, and a commitment to fairness and inclusivity.

IT Failures in AI Systems Development and Deployment

While AI systems have shown great promise, there have been instances of failures and challenges in development and deployment, often involving the IT department. Here are some examples of failures in AI systems development and deployment:

1. **Bias in Facial Recognition Systems**

   Failure: Facial recognition systems have faced criticism for exhibiting bias, particularly in misidentifying individuals from certain demographic groups. This bias is often linked to inadequate representation in training data and flawed algorithms.

   Cause: Incomplete or biased training data, lack of diversity in the development team, and insufficient consideration of ethical implications.

2. **Facial Recognition Privacy Concerns**

   Failure: Widespread adoption of facial recognition technology has raised privacy concerns. Instances of misuse, unauthorized surveillance, and the creation of databases without consent have led to public backlash.

   Cause: Lack of clear regulations, insufficient privacy safeguards, and the potential for misuse by governments or private entities.

3. **Autonomous Vehicle Accidents**

   Failure: Incidents involving autonomous vehicles, such as accidents or collisions, have highlighted the challenges in the development of self-driving technology. Failures in real-world scenarios indicate limitations in the AI models' ability to handle complex and dynamic environments.

   Cause: Insufficient testing under diverse conditions, limitations in perception algorithms, and challenges in addressing unpredictable scenarios on the road.

4. **Chatbot Miscommunications**

   Failure: Chatbots, designed for customer interactions, have faced instances of providing inaccurate or inappropriate responses, leading to misunderstandings and dissatisfaction.

   Cause: Inadequate natural language processing capabilities, lack of contextual understanding, and insufficient training on diverse conversational patterns.

5. **Algorithmic Trading Glitches**

   Failure: Algorithmic trading systems have experienced glitches leading to financial losses. Flash crashes, where markets experience sudden and significant drops in value, have been attributed to flaws in automated trading algorithms.

   Cause: Insufficient testing and risk management procedures, overly complex algorithms, and a lack of safeguards to prevent cascading failures.

6. **Invasion of Privacy with Voice Assistants**

   Failure: Voice assistants, such as smart speakers, have faced concerns related to unintentional activation and recording of private conversations. Instances of devices recording and sending sensitive information without user consent have raised privacy issues.

   Cause: Inadequate user awareness, insufficient privacy controls, and flaws in the wake-word detection algorithms.

7. **Healthcare Diagnosis Errors**

   Failure: AI systems used for medical diagnosis have been involved in cases where incorrect diagnoses were provided, potentially leading to inappropriate treatments or delayed interventions.

Cause: Insufficient training data representing diverse patient populations, lack of interpretability in complex medical decision-making, and challenges in explaining model decisions.

8. **Automated Hiring Biases**

   Failure: AI systems used in recruitment processes have been criticized for perpetuating biases in hiring decisions. Models trained on biased historical data may unfairly favor or disfavor certain demographics.

   Cause: Unconscious bias in training data, lack of diversity in recruitment datasets, and inadequate measures to ensure fairness and transparency.

These examples underscore the importance of thorough testing, diverse and representative training data, ongoing monitoring, and ethical considerations in AI systems development and deployment. The failures often result from a combination of technical, ethical, and regulatory challenges that need careful consideration throughout the AI system lifecycle.

The Role of IT in the AI Systems Lifecycle

In the dynamic realm of AI system development, the IT department plays an indispensable role at each juncture, ensuring that the process unfolds effectively, securely, and in compliance with established regulations. This role is multifaceted, spanning the entirety of the AI system development lifecycle, from the initial conception of the project to the retirement of AI systems. Below is a synthesized narrative that covers the contributions of the IT department across the eight pivotal steps of this lifecycle: (1) problem definition; (2) data collection; (3) data preparation; (4) model selection and training; (5) model evaluation; (6) model deployment; (7) monitoring and maintenance; and (8) retirement.

1. Problem Definition

The inception of an AI system begins with a clear understanding of the problem it aims to solve, a process in which IT professionals engage deeply. *Collaborating with domain experts and stakeholders, they harness their technical acumen to assess the feasibility of proposed AI solutions, identifying potential challenges and ensuring that the AI system's objectives align seamlessly with broader business goals.* This foundational step guarantees that the development trajectory of the AI system is both technically sound and strategically focused.

2. Data Collection

As the backbone of any AI system, *the data collection phase is meticulously orchestrated by IT professionals. They are tasked with establishing robust data collection mechanisms that prioritize the relevance, reliability, and ethical provenance of data sources.* With an acute awareness of the sensitivities surrounding data privacy and security, the IT department enacts stringent measures to safeguard sensitive information, all while rigorously adhering to compliance standards and regulatory mandates, ensuring the data collection process upholds the highest ethical and legal standards.

3. Data Preparation

Transforming raw data into a format amenable for AI model training is a complex undertaking, where the IT department's expertise is paramount. *Through rigorous data cleaning, preprocessing, and transformation practices, IT professionals work to elevate data quality,* ensuring consistency and integrity across datasets, as well as to root out bias.[2] Collaborating closely with data scientists, they architect and refine data pipelines that are both robust and scalable, laying a solid foundation for the AI system's learning processes.

4. Model Selection and Training

In the model selection and training phase, *IT professionals lend their support to data scientists in choosing the most suitable machine learning models and computational frameworks.* They provision the necessary infrastructure and computing resources, optimizing for both scalability and efficiency, to accommodate the intensive computational demands of model training. This ensures that the AI system is built on a technologically sound and resource-efficient platform.

5. Model Evaluation

The evaluation of AI models is a critical step where IT contributes significantly. By developing and applying rigorous evaluation metrics and methodologies, *IT helps in assessing model performance, with a keen eye on addressing potential biases, ensuring fairness, and enhancing model interpretability.* Their involvement guarantees that the evaluation process remains both transparent and reproducible, upholding the integrity of the AI system's performance assessment.

6. Model Deployment

Deploying AI models into production environments is a critical juncture managed by the IT department. They not only *ensure the secure integration of AI models with existing systems but also establish comprehensive monitoring mechanisms to oversee the deployed models' performance* continuously. This phase underscores the IT department's role in safeguarding the operational deployment of AI systems, ensuring they deliver on their intended outcomes securely and effectively.

7. Monitoring and Maintenance

Post-deployment, the IT department's focus shifts to the continuous monitoring and maintenance of AI systems. *By tracking real-world performance and developing protocols for regular updates and retraining, IT professionals ensure that the AI systems remain dynamic and responsive to emerging challenges.* Their efforts underpin the sustained reliability, efficiency, and relevance of AI applications in ever-changing operational contexts.

8. Retirement

The lifecycle of an AI system culminates in its retirement, a process adeptly managed by the IT department. *From decommissioning obsolete models and infrastructure to ensuring data is handled and disposed of in compliance with regulatory standards, IT coordinates closely with all stakeholders* (including Records and Information Management and possibly a corporate archivist) to mitigate any adverse impacts on existing processes. This final phase reflects the IT department's comprehensive stewardship over the AI system's lifecycle, ensuring a responsible and strategic conclusion to its deployment.

Through this detailed exposition, it becomes evident that the IT department's involvement is not just supportive but central to the AI system development lifecycle, embodying a commitment to technological excellence, security, and ethical responsibility. Their work ensures that AI systems are not only aligned with organizational goals but are also adaptable, secure, and ethically grounded, ready to meet the challenges of tomorrow.

Here's a summary of key points regarding the role of the IT department in each of the eight key steps:

1. **Problem Definition**

   IT professionals collaborate with domain experts and stakeholders to understand the problem that the AI system aims to solve.

   They assess the technical feasibility and potential challenges in implementing a solution.

   IT ensures alignment between the business objectives and the proposed AI system.

2. **Data Collection**

   IT is responsible for designing and implementing data collection processes, ensuring data sources are relevant, reliable, and ethical.

   They consider data privacy and security issues, implementing measures to protect sensitive information.

   Compliance with data regulations is a key focus, and the IT department helps establish and maintain these standards.

3. **Data Preparation**

   IT plays a crucial role in data cleaning, preprocessing, and transformation to make the data suitable for training AI models.

   They implement **data governance** practices to ensure data quality, consistency, and integrity.

   IT teams collaborate with data scientists to create a robust data pipeline.

4. **Model Selection and Training**

   IT professionals assist data scientists in selecting appropriate machine learning models and frameworks.

   They set up the infrastructure and computing resources required for model training.

   IT ensures scalability and efficiency in model training processes.

5. **Model Evaluation**

   IT contributes to the development of evaluation metrics and methodologies.

   They help assess the performance of AI models, addressing issues like bias, fairness, and interpretability.

   IT ensures that the evaluation process is transparent and reproducible.

6. **Model Deployment**

   IT is responsible for deploying AI models into production environments.

   They implement security measures and ensure the integration of the model with existing systems.

   Monitoring mechanisms are set up to track the performance of the deployed model.

7. **Monitoring and Maintenance**

   IT establishes continuous monitoring systems to track the model's performance in real-world scenarios.

They develop protocols for handling model updates, retraining, and addressing any issues that may arise.

IT ensures the ongoing reliability and efficiency of the deployed AI system.

8. **Retirement**

   IT manages the retirement process of AI systems, including the decommissioning of models and related infrastructure.

   They ensure proper data handling and disposal in compliance with data protection regulations.

   IT collaborates with relevant stakeholders to assess the impact of retiring the AI system on existing processes.

Throughout these steps, the IT department also plays a critical role in establishing and maintaining ethical AI practices, cybersecurity measures, and compliance with relevant regulations and policies.

IT Departmental Responsibilities in the AI Lifecycle — in Detail

I. The **Problem Definition** phase is a critical starting point in AI system development, and the role of the IT department is pivotal in several aspects:

1. **Collaboration with Domain Experts and Stakeholders**

   Understanding the Problem: IT professionals work closely with domain experts and stakeholders from various departments to gain a comprehensive understanding of the problem or challenge the AI system is intended to address. This collaboration involves discussions, workshops, and knowledge-sharing sessions to gather insights into the specific domain requirements and nuances.

   Requirements Gathering: IT teams actively engage with stakeholders to gather and document their requirements, ensuring that the AI system aligns with the organization's goals and objectives. This collaboration helps in defining clear and achievable objectives for the AI project.

2. **Assessment of Technical Feasibility**

   Technology Assessment: IT professionals assess the technical landscape, evaluating the existing infrastructure, hardware, software, and other technological components within the organization. This assessment helps determine the compatibility of the proposed AI solution with the existing technology stack.

   Resource Evaluation: IT teams analyze the availability of resources, including computational power, storage, and personnel. They assess whether the organization has the necessary expertise or if additional training or hiring is required for successful AI implementation.

   Risk Analysis: IT plays a crucial role in identifying potential technical challenges and risks associated with implementing the AI solution. This includes considerations such as data availability, data quality, regulatory compliance, and ethical implications. The goal is to anticipate and mitigate potential roadblocks early in the project.

3. **Alignment with Business Objectives**

   Strategic Alignment: IT ensures that the proposed AI system aligns with the broader strategic goals and objectives of the organization. This involves understanding the business context, market dynamics, and competitive landscape to ensure that the AI solution contributes meaningfully to the organization's success.

ROI Assessment: IT collaborates with business stakeholders to assess the potential **return on investment** (ROI) of the AI project. This involves estimating the economic benefits, cost implications, and potential efficiency gains that the AI system could bring to the organization.

Scalability and Flexibility: IT considers the scalability and flexibility of the proposed solution to accommodate future business needs and changes. This includes evaluating whether the AI system can adapt to evolving requirements and technological advancements.

In summary, during the Problem Definition phase, the IT department acts as a bridge between technical feasibility and business objectives. They facilitate collaboration, gather requirements, assess technical aspects, and ensure that the proposed AI solution aligns strategically with the organization's goals. This collaborative approach sets the foundation for a well-defined and purposeful AI development process.

Scalability – in Detail

Scalability ensures that an AI system remains efficient, reliable, and responsive under varying loads and can expand to meet the requirements of larger datasets, more complex models, or increased user demand without a significant drop in performance or usability. Below are key aspects of scalability in AI systems:

Horizontal and Vertical Scalability

- **Horizontal Scalability (Scaling Out/In):** This involves adding more machines or nodes to a system to manage increased load. For AI systems, this might mean distributing data processing and inference tasks across multiple servers or cloud resources to manage larger datasets or serve more users simultaneously.
- **Vertical Scalability (Scaling Up/Down):** This refers to adding more power (e.g., CPU, GPU, memory) to an existing machine to improve its capacity. For an AI system, scaling up can enhance the ability to train more complex models or reduce the time required for data processing and model training.

Data Scalability

As the volume of data that an AI system needs to process or analyze grows, the system must be able to efficiently handle this increase. This includes the ability to store, retrieve, and process large datasets without significant delays or bottlenecks, ensuring timely and relevant outputs.

Model Scalability

AI systems must also scale in terms of model complexity. As models become more sophisticated *to improve accuracy or address more complex problems, the system should support increased computational demands.* This might involve more advanced algorithms, larger neural networks, or more intensive computational processes.

Performance Scalability

The *system should maintain or improve performance as it scales up and expands.* This includes ensuring that response times remain low and that the accuracy of AI models is maintained or enhanced as the system scales up to handle more data or more complex problems.

Cost-Effective Scalability

Scalability should be cost-effective, meaning that the system can grow without prohibitive increases in costs. This involves optimizing resource utilization and leveraging cloud resources or other technologies to achieve the most efficient scaling in terms of both performance and cost.

Scalability Challenges

Addressing scalability involves overcoming various challenges, including managing data storage and processing requirements, ensuring the parallel processing of tasks, and maintaining model accuracy and performance. It also requires careful planning and resource management to ensure that scaling efforts are efficient and effective.

In conclusion, scalability is a fundamental attribute of AI systems that ensures they can adapt and grow to meet increasing or evolving demands. It encompasses the system's ability to extend its processing capabilities, handle larger datasets, support more complex models, and maintain or improve performance and accuracy, all while managing costs. Effective scalability strategies are essential for the sustainable and efficient deployment of AI technologies across different domains and applications.

II. In the **Data Collection** phase of AI system development, the IT department plays a crucial role in ensuring that data is collected in a responsible, ethical, and secure manner. Here are the key points related to the IT department's role in this phase:

1. **Designing and Implementing Data Collection Processes**

   System Architecture: IT professionals are responsible for designing the overall architecture of the data collection process. This involves determining how data will be collected, stored, and processed throughout its lifecycle.

   Data Pipeline Development: IT teams develop and implement data pipelines to efficiently collect and transport data from various sources to storage and processing environments. This includes designing processes for data ingestion, transformation, and integration.

2. **Ensuring Data Relevance, Reliability, and Ethics**

   Data Quality Assurance: IT ensures that the data collected is relevant and reliable for the intended use. This involves implementing measures to verify and validate the quality of the data, addressing issues such as completeness, accuracy, and consistency.

   Ethical Considerations: IT professionals collaborate with data ethics experts and legal teams to ensure that data collection practices align with ethical standards. They work to prevent biases in the data and establish protocols for handling sensitive information responsibly.

3. **Data Privacy and Security Measures**

   Privacy Compliance: IT is responsible for implementing measures to protect individuals' privacy during the data collection process. This includes anonymizing or pseudonymizing data, obtaining necessary consents, and ensuring compliance with privacy regulations such as GDPR or HIPAA.

Security Protocols: IT establishes robust security protocols to safeguard collected data from unauthorized access, breaches, or cyber threats. This involves encryption, access controls, and regular security audits to identify and address vulnerabilities.

4. **Compliance with Data Regulations**

   Regulatory Awareness: The IT department stays informed about relevant data protection regulations and privacy laws applicable to the organization's operations. This includes understanding regional and industry-specific compliance requirements.

   Policy Development: IT contributes to the development of data governance policies that ensure compliance with regulations. They establish guidelines for data usage, retention, and sharing, emphasizing transparency and accountability.

5. **Establishing and Maintaining Standards**

   Data Standards: IT professionals help establish and enforce standards for data collection, ensuring consistency across the organization. This includes defining data formats, naming conventions, and metadata standards to enhance data interoperability.

   Documentation and Auditing: The IT department maintains comprehensive documentation of data collection processes and conducts regular audits to ensure adherence to established standards. This documentation aids transparency and accountability.

By actively participating in the Data Collection phase, the IT department contributes to the foundation of a reliable and ethical dataset, setting the stage for subsequent steps in the AI system development lifecycle. Their role in designing secure, compliant, and efficient data collection processes is essential for the overall success and ethical implementation of AI systems.

III. In the **Data Preparation** phase of AI system development, the IT department is instrumental in refining and shaping the raw data into a format suitable for training AI models. Here are the key points related to the IT department's role in this phase:

1. **Data Cleaning, Preprocessing, and Transformation**

   Data Cleaning: IT professionals are responsible for identifying and addressing inconsistencies, errors, and missing values in the dataset. Software tools can assist. They implement cleaning procedures to improve the overall quality of the data.

   Data Preprocessing: IT plays a crucial role in preprocessing tasks such as normalization, standardization, and feature scaling. These steps are essential for ensuring that the data is in a suitable format for training machine learning models.

   Data Transformation: IT teams collaborate with data scientists to implement transformations, such as encoding categorical variables or handling outliers. These transformations are designed to enhance the robustness and effectiveness of the machine learning models.

2. **Implementing Data Governance Practices**

   Data Quality Assurance: IT establishes and enforces data governance practices to ensure high-quality data. This involves defining standards for data quality, consistency, and accuracy. It implements measures to monitor and maintain these standards throughout the AI system's lifecycle.

   Metadata Management: IT professionals oversee the creation and management of metadata, providing context and documentation for the data. Metadata helps ensure understanding and traceability of the data preparation process.

3. **Collaboration with Data Scientists**

   Communication and Collaboration: IT teams work closely with data scientists to understand the specific requirements for training AI models. Effective communication between IT and data science teams is crucial to align data preparation activities with the goals of the machine learning models.

   Infrastructure Support: IT provides the necessary infrastructure and computing resources for data scientists to carry out complex data preparation tasks efficiently. This includes optimizing data processing pipelines for performance and scalability.

   Tooling and Platforms: IT selects, configures, and maintains the tools and platforms used for data preparation. This may involve implementing data processing frameworks, databases, or other technologies that support the data preparation pipeline.

4. **Creating a Robust Data Pipeline**

   Pipeline Design and Optimization: IT professionals collaborate with data scientists to design and optimize data processing pipelines. These pipelines automate the flow of data from raw sources to a format suitable for model training, ensuring efficiency and repeatability.

   Scalability: IT ensures that the data pipeline is scalable to handle large volumes of data efficiently. This involves selecting appropriate technologies and architectures that can accommodate the growth of data over time.

By actively participating in the Data Preparation phase, the IT department contributes to the creation of a high-quality, well-structured dataset that forms the basis for effective machine learning model training. Their role in implementing data governance practices and collaborating with data scientists ensures that the prepared data meets the necessary standards for accuracy, consistency, and suitability for AI model development.

IV. In the **Model Selection and Training** phase of AI system development, the IT department plays a crucial role in supporting data scientists in choosing the right machine learning models, setting up the necessary infrastructure, and ensuring scalability and efficiency. Here are the key points related to the IT department's role in this phase:

1. **Assisting Data Scientists in Model Selection**

   Understanding Technical Requirements: IT professionals collaborate closely with data scientists to understand the technical requirements of the AI project. This includes discussions on the nature of the data, complexity of the problem, and specific objectives of the machine learning models.

   Selection of Models and Frameworks: IT assists data scientists in selecting appropriate machine learning models and frameworks based on the requirements. This involves evaluating the strengths and weaknesses of different algorithms and frameworks, considering factors such as accuracy, interpretability, and computational efficiency.

2. **Setting Up Infrastructure and Computing Resources**

   Infrastructure Planning: IT is responsible for planning and setting up the necessary infrastructure to support model training. This includes selecting hardware, such as GPUs or TPUs, and configuring servers or cloud-based resources to meet the computational demands of the chosen models.

   Environment Configuration: IT ensures that the development environment is properly configured with the required software libraries, dependencies, and frameworks needed for model training. This may involve using containerization technologies like Docker to create reproducible and consistent environments.

3. **Scalability and Efficiency in Model Training Processes**

   Scalable Architecture: IT professionals design and implement a scalable architecture to handle the training of machine learning models, particularly when dealing with large datasets or computationally intensive algorithms. This involves considerations for distributed computing and parallel processing.

   Resource Optimization: IT focuses on optimizing the utilization of computing resources during model training. This may include load balancing, resource allocation, and monitoring to ensure efficient use of available hardware.

   Performance Tuning: IT collaborates with data scientists to fine-tune the performance of the training process. This may involve optimizing hyperparameters, adjusting batch sizes, and employing techniques to enhance convergence speed.

4. **Ensuring Data Security and Compliance**

   Data Access Controls: IT establishes access controls to ensure that only authorized personnel have access to sensitive data used during model training. This helps in maintaining data security and preventing unauthorized use.

   Compliance with Regulations: IT ensures that the model training process adheres to relevant regulations and compliance standards. This includes handling sensitive information in accordance with data protection laws and industry-specific regulations.

5. **Monitoring and Logging**

   Monitoring Training Processes: IT implements monitoring systems to keep track of the progress and performance of model training. This includes monitoring resource usage, identifying bottlenecks, and ensuring that the training process is running smoothly.

   Logging and Auditing: IT establishes logging and auditing mechanisms to capture relevant information about the model training process. This documentation is essential for troubleshooting, auditing, and maintaining a record of model development activities.

By actively participating in the Model Selection and Training phase, the IT department ensures that data scientists have the necessary infrastructure, resources, and support to train machine learning models effectively. Their role in infrastructure setup, scalability planning, and maintaining data security contributes to the overall success and reliability of the AI system.

V. In the **Model Evaluation** phase of AI system development, the IT department plays a crucial role in contributing to the development of evaluation metrics, assessing model performance, and ensuring transparency and reproducibility in the evaluation process. Here are the key points related to the IT department's role in this phase:

1. **Contribution to Evaluation Metrics and Methodologies**

   Collaborative Approach: IT professionals collaborate with data scientists, domain experts, and stakeholders to define appropriate evaluation metrics and methodologies. This involves understanding the specific objectives of the AI system and selecting metrics that align with the desired outcomes.

   Defining Performance Indicators: IT helps in defining key performance indicators (KPIs) that reflect the effectiveness, efficiency, and reliability of the AI models. These metrics may include accuracy, precision, recall, F1 score, area under the curve (AUC), among others, depending on the nature of the problem.

2. **Assessment of Model Performance**

   Performance Analysis: IT assists in analyzing the performance of AI models across different datasets, scenarios, and use cases. This involves conducting comprehensive evaluations to assess how well the models generalize to unseen data and perform in real-world conditions.

Addressing Bias and Fairness: IT professionals work with data scientists to identify and address biases in the AI models. They help implement fairness-aware evaluation techniques to mitigate biases related to sensitive attributes such as gender, race, or socioeconomic status.

Interpretability and Explainability: IT contributes to evaluating the interpretability and explainability of AI models. They help assess the transparency of model predictions and identify methods to enhance interpretability, making it easier to understand and trust the decisions made by the AI system.

3. **Ensuring Transparency and Reproducibility**

   Documentation Standards: IT establishes documentation standards to ensure that the evaluation process is well documented and transparent. This includes documenting evaluation methodologies, parameters, and results in a clear and accessible format.

   Version Control: IT implements version control systems to track changes to models, datasets, and evaluation procedures. This helps ensure reproducibility by enabling researchers to replicate experiments and compare results across different iterations.

   Open Science Practices: IT promotes open science practices by making evaluation methodologies, datasets, and code publicly available whenever possible. This fosters transparency, collaboration, and peer review within the AI research community.

4. **Adherence to Ethical Guidelines**

   Ethical Review: IT facilitates ethical review processes to ensure that the evaluation of AI models adheres to ethical guidelines and standards. This includes considering ethical implications related to privacy, consent, and potential societal impacts.

   Compliance Checks: IT ensures that the evaluation process complies with relevant regulations and policies, such as data protection laws and industry-specific guidelines. They implement measures to safeguard sensitive information and protect the rights of individuals involved in the evaluation.

By actively participating in the Model Evaluation phase, the IT department contributes to the credibility, reliability, and accountability of AI systems. Their role in defining evaluation metrics, assessing model performance, and ensuring transparency and reproducibility helps build trust in the AI systems and promotes responsible AI Governance.

VI. In the **Model Deployment** phase of AI system development, the IT department plays a crucial role in transitioning the developed models from a development environment to production. Here are the key points related to the IT department's role in this phase:

1. **Deployment of AI Models**

   Infrastructure Setup: IT professionals are responsible for setting up the necessary infrastructure to deploy AI models into production environments. This involves configuring servers, cloud resources, or edge devices to support the operational deployment of the models.

   Deployment Pipeline: IT establishes a deployment pipeline that facilitates the smooth and automated deployment of AI models. This pipeline ensures consistency and reliability in pushing models to production, reducing the risk of errors and discrepancies.

2. **Security Measures**

   Access Controls: IT implements access controls to restrict access to deployed models, ensuring that only authorized users and systems can interact with them. This helps protect the models from unauthorized use and potential security threats.

Data Encryption: IT incorporates encryption mechanisms to secure data during model deployment, especially when handling sensitive information. This prevents unauthorized access to data during transit and storage.

Secure APIs: If the model is accessed through APIs (Application Programming Interfaces), IT ensures the implementation of secure API practices, including authentication and authorization mechanisms, to protect against potential security vulnerabilities.

3. **Integration with Existing Systems**

   System Integration: IT professionals integrate deployed AI models with existing systems and workflows within the organization. This involves ensuring compatibility with databases, data storage systems, and other applications that may interact with or consume the model's predictions.

   Interoperability: IT ensures that the deployed models can seamlessly communicate with other software components and services in the broader IT ecosystem. This facilitates a smooth integration of AI capabilities into the existing infrastructure.

4. **Monitoring Mechanisms**

   Performance Monitoring: IT establishes monitoring mechanisms to track the performance of the deployed AI models in real-world scenarios. This includes monitoring key performance indicators, such as prediction accuracy, response time, and resource utilization.

   Anomaly Detection: IT implements anomaly detection systems to identify and address any unexpected behavior or deviations from the expected model performance. This helps in detecting issues promptly and maintaining the reliability of the deployed models.

   Logging and Auditing: IT ensures that comprehensive logging and auditing are in place to capture relevant information about the interactions with the deployed models. This information is crucial for troubleshooting, performance optimization, and compliance purposes.

5. **Scalability and Resource Management**

   Scalability Planning: IT professionals plan for the scalability of deployed models to handle increased workloads or growing user demands. This involves optimizing resource allocation and ensuring that the deployed infrastructure can scale horizontally or vertically as needed.

   Resource Optimization: IT continuously monitors resource usage and optimizes the allocation of computing resources to ensure efficient operation. This includes adjusting configurations, optimizing algorithms, and upgrading hardware when necessary.

6. **Documentation and Knowledge Transfer**

   Documentation: IT creates comprehensive documentation for the deployed AI models, including configuration details, dependencies, and integration points. This documentation aids in troubleshooting, maintenance, and future updates.

   Knowledge Transfer: IT facilitates knowledge transfer to operational teams, ensuring that those responsible for maintaining and supporting the deployed models have the necessary skills and understanding. This may involve training sessions, documentation reviews, and collaboration with data scientists and developers.

By actively participating in the Model Deployment phase, the IT department ensures the successful transition of AI models into operational environments while prioritizing security, integration, and ongoing performance monitoring. Their role is critical in maintaining the reliability, scalability, and security of deployed AI systems, contributing to effective AI Governance.

VII. In the **Monitoring and Maintenance** phase of AI system development, the IT department plays a vital role in ensuring the ongoing reliability, performance, and effectiveness of the deployed AI system. Here are the key points related to the IT department's role in this phase:

1. **Continuous Monitoring Systems**

   Performance Metrics Tracking: IT establishes and maintains continuous monitoring systems to track key performance metrics of the deployed AI models in real-world scenarios. This includes monitoring accuracy, latency, throughput, and other relevant indicators.

   Anomaly Detection: IT implements anomaly detection mechanisms to identify unusual patterns or deviations in model performance. This enables prompt identification and response to any issues that may arise during the system's operation.

   Resource Utilization Monitoring: IT monitors the utilization of computational resources to ensure efficient operation. This involves tracking CPU usage, memory consumption, and other resource metrics to identify potential bottlenecks or inefficiencies.

2. **Handling Model Updates and Retraining**

   Update Protocols: IT develops and follows protocols for handling model updates. This includes defining processes for deploying new versions of models, ensuring minimal disruption to the system, and handling rollbacks in case of issues.

   Retraining Strategies: IT collaborates with data scientists to establish retraining schedules and strategies. This involves determining when and how often models should be retrained based on changes in the data distribution or evolving requirements.

   Version Control: IT maintains version control for both models and associated code, allowing for easy tracking of changes, comparisons between model versions, and efficient management of updates.

3. **Issue Resolution and Troubleshooting**

   Incident Response: IT establishes incident response protocols to address any issues or anomalies detected during monitoring. This includes defining escalation procedures, communication plans, and response times to minimize the impact of issues on system performance.

   Root Cause Analysis: In the event of performance issues or failures, IT conducts thorough root cause analyses to understand the underlying reasons. This analysis helps in implementing corrective measures and preventing similar issues in the future.

4. **Documentation and Knowledge Transfer**

   Maintenance Documentation: IT creates and maintains documentation outlining the ongoing maintenance procedures. This includes details about monitoring tools, incident response processes, and protocols for model updates and retraining.

   Knowledge Transfer: IT facilitates knowledge transfer to operational teams, ensuring that those responsible for system maintenance have the necessary skills and understanding. This may involve training sessions, documentation reviews, and collaboration with data scientists and developers.

5. **Ensuring Reliability and Efficiency**

   Performance Optimization: IT continuously works on optimizing the performance of the deployed AI system. This involves identifying areas for improvement, implementing efficiency measures, and addressing any bottlenecks in the system.

Scalability Planning: IT revisits scalability considerations and plans for accommodating increased workloads or changes in user demands. This may involve upgrading infrastructure, adjusting configurations, or optimizing resource allocation.

6. **Security Measures**

   Ongoing Security Monitoring: IT maintains continuous security monitoring to detect and respond to potential security threats or vulnerabilities in the deployed AI system. This includes implementing intrusion detection systems and staying vigilant against evolving cybersecurity risks.

   Security Updates: IT ensures that security measures, including patches and updates, are regularly applied to all components of the AI system to protect against known vulnerabilities.

By actively participating in the **Monitoring and Maintenance** phase, the IT department plays a critical role in the long-term success and sustainability of the deployed AI system. Their responsibilities encompass continuous monitoring, effective incident response, and collaboration with data scientists to ensure that the AI system remains reliable, efficient, and aligned with evolving business needs. This proactive approach is essential for effective AI Governance and ongoing system optimization.

VIII. In the **Retirement** phase of AI system development, the IT department plays a crucial role in the decommissioning process, data handling, and collaboration with stakeholders to assess the impact of retiring the AI system. Here are the key points related to the IT department's role in this phase:

1. **Decommissioning of Models and Infrastructure**

   Model Decommissioning: IT is responsible for managing the retirement process of AI models. This includes the decommissioning of outdated or obsolete models, ensuring that they are no longer used in production.

   Infrastructure Decommissioning: IT oversees the decommissioning of infrastructure and resources that were specifically allocated for the retired models. This involves releasing computational resources, stopping servers or instances, and optimizing the overall IT environment.

2. **Data Handling and Disposal**

   Data Retention Policies: IT ensures adherence to data retention policies during the retirement process. They identify and handle the data associated with the retired models, making decisions on whether to archive, delete, or anonymize the data based on organizational policies.

   Data Disposal in Compliance with Regulations: IT professionals work in compliance with data protection regulations to ensure proper data disposal. This includes implementing secure data erase methods and documenting the disposal process to demonstrate compliance with relevant laws.

3. **Collaboration with Stakeholders**

   Stakeholder Assessment: IT collaborates with relevant stakeholders, including business leaders, data scientists, and users of the AI system, to assess the impact of retiring the system on existing processes. This involves understanding how the retirement may affect workflows, dependencies, and overall business operations.

   Communication and Transition Planning: IT facilitates transparent communication with stakeholders about the retirement process. They work collaboratively to plan and execute a smooth transition, minimizing disruptions and ensuring that stakeholders are well-informed about the changes.

Knowledge Transfer: IT ensures that knowledge about the retired system is appropriately transferred to relevant stakeholders. This may involve documenting procedures, sharing insights, and providing necessary training to personnel who will be working with alternative systems or processes.

4. **Documentation and Compliance**

   Retirement Documentation: IT creates comprehensive documentation detailing the retirement process, including steps taken for decommissioning models, handling data, and collaborating with stakeholders. This documentation serves as a record for auditing purposes and ensures transparency in the retirement process.

   Compliance Checks: IT conducts compliance checks to ensure that the retirement process aligns with legal and regulatory requirements. This includes verifying that data handling practices comply with data protection laws and that the retirement process adheres to organizational policies.

5. **Security Measures**

   Security Considerations: IT incorporates security measures during the retirement process to protect against potential risks. This includes ensuring that any sensitive information is securely handled and that access controls are in place to prevent unauthorized access to retired systems or data.

   Security Audits: IT may conduct security audits to assess the overall security posture during the retirement phase. This helps identify and address any vulnerabilities that could pose risks during the decommissioning process.

By actively participating in the Retirement phase, the IT department ensures a well-managed and secure conclusion to the AI system's lifecycle. Their responsibilities include decommissioning models and infrastructure, handling data in compliance with regulations, collaborating with stakeholders, and documenting the retirement process for transparency and accountability. This approach contributes to responsible AI Governance and effective management of AI system lifecycles.

Caveats and Tips for the IT Department in their Role in the AI System Development Process

Developing and implementing AI systems can be complex, and the IT department plays a crucial role in ensuring success. Here are some critical caveats and tips for the IT department in its role in AI systems development and implementation:

Critical Caveats

1. **Ethical Considerations**

   Caveat: Ethical issues, including bias, fairness, and interpretability, can arise in AI systems. Biased training data may lead to biased models, and unethical AI practices can have significant consequences.

   Tip: IT should work closely with data scientists to implement ethical AI practices, conduct thorough bias assessments, and prioritize fairness and transparency in AI models.

2. **Data Privacy and Security**

   Caveat: Inadequate data protection measures can lead to privacy breaches and security vulnerabilities, especially when dealing with sensitive information.

   Tip: Implement robust security protocols, encryption, and access controls. Regularly audit and monitor systems for potential vulnerabilities, and ensure compliance with data protection regulations.

3. **Scalability Challenges**

   Caveat: Scalability issues may arise if the IT infrastructure is not designed to handle increased workloads or if resources are not optimized efficiently.

   Tip: Plan for scalability from the beginning, use scalable infrastructure, and continuously monitor and optimize resource allocation based on system demands.

4. **Interdisciplinary Collaboration**

   Caveat: Lack of collaboration between IT, data scientists, and domain experts can hinder successful AI system development.

   Tip: Foster a collaborative culture, encourage regular communication, and ensure that IT professionals understand the domain-specific requirements to align technical solutions with business goals.

Additional Tips for IT Departments

1. **Continuous Learning**

   Tip: Stay abreast of the latest advancements in AI technologies, frameworks, and best practices. Encourage continuous learning among IT professionals to adapt to evolving industry trends.

2. **Agile Development Practices**

   Tip: Adopt agile development methodologies to facilitate flexibility and responsiveness to changing requirements. This allows for iterative development, quick adaptations, and faster delivery of AI solutions.

3. **Transparent Documentation**

   Tip: Maintain transparent and detailed documentation throughout the AI system development lifecycle. This includes documenting processes, configurations, decisions, and any challenges faced, facilitating easier troubleshooting and future updates.

4. **Regulatory Compliance**

   Tip: Stay informed about relevant data protection and AI regulations. Develop a thorough understanding of compliance requirements and work proactively to ensure that AI systems adhere to legal and ethical standards.

5. **Robust Monitoring and Logging**

   Tip: Implement comprehensive monitoring and logging systems to track system performance, identify issues, and provide valuable insights. This helps in proactive issue resolution, performance optimization, and troubleshooting.

6. **Collaboration with Stakeholders**

   Tip: Foster strong collaboration with stakeholders, including business leaders, data scientists, and end users. Understand their needs, gather feedback, and ensure that IT solutions align with the broader organizational objectives.

7. **Knowledge Transfer**

   Tip: Facilitate knowledge transfer within the IT department and between IT and other teams. This ensures that expertise is shared, reducing dependencies on individual team members and enhancing overall system resilience.

8. **Focus on Explainability**

   Tip: Prioritize the interpretability and explainability of AI models. This helps build trust in the system, allows users to understand model decisions, and facilitates easier debugging in case of unexpected behavior.

9. **DevOps Practices**

   Tip: Embrace DevOps practices to streamline collaboration between development and operations teams. This includes continuous integration, continuous deployment, and automation, which can enhance efficiency and reduce the likelihood of errors.

10. **User Training and Support**

    Tip: Provide training and support for end users interacting with AI systems. Ensure that users understand how to use and interpret the outputs of AI models and offer assistance when needed.

By considering these caveats and tips, the IT department can navigate the complexities of AI system development more effectively, contributing to the successful implementation and responsible governance of AI technologies within the organization.

Key Points

- The IT department must keenly assess the computational demands of AI algorithms and models, ensuring the infrastructure is not just available but is also scalable.
- The IT department ensures the establishment and upkeep of systems for data storage, processing, and retrieval, tailored to support AI functionalities, emphasizing data quality.
- Effective data management is a cornerstone of AI systems, as the quality and organization of data directly impact the performance, accuracy, and efficiency of these systems.
- IT facilitates system integration, ensuring AI systems seamlessly connect with existing infrastructure, databases, and applications.
- The IT implements comprehensive security measures to safeguard AI systems and data, aligning with relevant regulations and standards.
- Monitoring systems are put in place to detect any operational issues, performance degradation, or security breaches.
- The IT department monitors system performance, identifies bottlenecks, and implements optimizations to improve efficiency and responsiveness.
- Regular updates, security patches, and maintenance are essential for the longevity and security of AI systems.
- The IT department develops training materials, conducts workshops, and provides technical assistance, enabling users to leverage AI applications.
- The synergy between IT and data science teams is vital for the seamless deployment and operation of AI systems.
- The IT department ensures that AI systems and data are backed up and that contingency plans are in place to recover functionality in the event of failures.

- The IT department plays a crucial role in ensuring AI practices adhere to principles of transparency, fairness, and accountability, collaborating with governance and legal teams to uphold responsible AI deployment.
- While AI systems have shown great promise, there have been instances of failures and challenges in development and deployment, often involving the IT department.
- In the Problem Definition phase, IT collaborates with domain experts and stakeholders, they harness their technical acumen to assess the feasibility of proposed AI solutions.
- In the Data Collection phase, IT is important to establish robust data collection mechanisms that prioritize the relevance, reliability, and ethical provenance of data sources.
- In the Data Preparation phase, IT elevates data quality through rigorous data cleaning, preprocessing, and transformation practices.
- In the Model Selection and Training phase, IT professionals lend their support to data scientists to choose the most suitable machine learning models.
- In the Model Evaluation phase, IT helps in assessing model performance, with a keen eye on addressing potential biases, ensuring fairness, and enhancing model interpretability.
- In the Model Deployment phase, IT ensures the secure integration of AI models with existing systems and establishes monitoring mechanisms to oversee model performance.
- In the Monitoring and Maintenance phase, IT implements continuous monitoring and maintenance, tracking real-world performance.
- In the Retirement phase, IT coordinates with stakeholders to assist in decommissioning obsolete models to ensure data is handled and disposed of in compliance with regulatory standards.

Key Glossary Terms

Bias: In the context of AI systems, "bias" refers to systematic errors or unfair prejudices in the data, algorithms, or decision-making processes that lead to partial, skewed, or unfair outcomes.

Data management: The processes, practices, and technologies involved in acquiring, validating, storing, protecting, and processing required data to ensure its accessibility, reliability, and timeliness for the creation and operation of AI models.

Decommissioning: Safely and systematically retiring an AI model from active use. This can involve several steps, including removing the model from production environments, securely archiving its data and learning parameters, and ensuring that all associated resources are appropriately reallocated or disposed of.

Facial recognition systems: A category of biometric software that can identify or verify a person's identity using their face. These systems capture, analyze, and compare patterns based on the individual's facial details.

Infrastructure: The comprehensive suite of hardware, software, network resources, and services required for the development, deployment, operation, and support of AI systems and applications.

Risk analysis: In the context of AI systems, refers to the systematic process of identifying, assessing, and managing potential risks associated with the development, deployment, and use of AI technologies.

Scalability: Refers to the ability of the system to handle growing amounts of work or its capacity to accommodate growth in complexity, size, or scope effectively. This concept is pivotal as AI applications increasingly become integrated into various aspects of business operations, public services, and consumer products, where demands can rapidly change or escalate.

Notes

1 Lu Phillips & Yang, "The Impact of Cloud Computing and AI on Industry Dynamics and Concentration," National Bureau of Economic Research, Working Paper 32811, Accessed May 14, 2025, https://www.nber.org/papers/w32811.

2 Sekar, "The Critical Role of Data Engineering in Generative AI," International Journal of Computer Engineering and Technology, July-August 2024, Article ID: IJCET_15_04_073, www.iaeme.com.

10 AI Governance Considerations for Business Units

It is fairly common to find organizations that perceive little business value in the Information Governance (IG) protocols that they have implemented. Often, these initiatives are viewed as a necessary evil. They are considered overhead, an administrative burden, and a cost of doing business. But business units must provide the business justification and use case(s), with IG considerations folded in.

Unfortunately, this viewpoint often becomes a self-fulfilling prophecy, as an IG initiative viewed negatively stands little chance of getting adequate time, attention, and funding for it to contribute to the organization's operations—and profitability—rather than detract from them, and perhaps even finding ways to increase innovation, improve collaboration, and even help to increase revenue by monetizing or adding value to information.

Organizations that embrace the view that information is a valuable, if not the most valuable, asset, and invest in IG accordingly are those most likely to achieve the greatest gains from their information resources.

With AI, this "you get what you focus on" effect is strongly amplified. AI is proving to be the strongest, most transformational technology lever ever applied to business outcomes. And, given that social organizations (businesses or otherwise) are the most productive output of our collective human intellect, the ability of AI to bring dramatic changes to how our organizations operate and produce value cannot be overstated.

The degree to which AI stands to change how organizations operate is far greater than the impact of the personal computer, the Internet, social media, cloud computing, or any number of other information technologies deployed over the last half-century. Hence, approaching the implementation of AI Information Governance must be viewed as an enabling step, rather than a cost of doing business, in order to ensure success.

AI Governance involves the development and implementation of policies, processes, and controls to ensure ethical, legal, and responsible use of AI technologies. It aims to mitigate risks, address biases, and ensure that AI applications align with organizational goals and values.

Governance of AI programs is crucial to ensure responsible and effective use of AI within business units. Following is an outline of the role and specific steps that business units can take to properly govern AI programs:

1. **Establish a Governance Framework**
   - *Define clear goals and objectives for AI implementation aligned with overall business strategy*

Defining clear goals and objectives for AI implementation aligned with overall business strategy is a critical step in effective AI Governance. This process ensures that AI initiatives contribute meaningfully to the organization's mission and business objectives.

Firstly, the business unit leaders must thoroughly understand the overall business strategy, its key objectives, priorities, and challenges. Engaging stakeholders, including executives and department heads, is essential to gather insights into business priorities and areas where AI can provide value.

Next, business units should *actively seek out opportunities within the business strategy where AI can drive innovation and efficiency*, exploring avenues for automation, optimization, and data-driven decision-making.

Setting specific and measurable AI program objectives aligned with broader business objectives is crucial. And it helps get executive buy-in. Quantifiable objectives with established metrics that "bubble up" or represent key milestones toward making progress in accomplishing AI program objectives facilitate the assessment of success along the way, and prioritizing these objectives based on strategic importance and potential impact ensures a focused approach.

Alignment with core values and ethical principles is paramount, considering both internal and external implications. *Creating a roadmap with defined phases, milestones, and timelines facilitates effective AI implementation.*

Establishing measurable **key performance indicators** (KPIs) directly linked to AI objectives and assessing progress against benchmarks ensures ongoing success.

Addressing potential risks (see the risk management chapter for more detail) associated with AI implementation and developing mitigation strategies demonstrates proactive AI Governance. Evaluating data readiness, including the quality and availability of necessary data, and fostering a data-driven culture through education and promotion are critical steps.

Collaboration across departments is essential for cross-functional alignment, particularly between data science and IT, Privacy, Security, Risk Management, Records and Information Management (RIM), Legal, and, where appropriate, other business units.

Adequately allocating resources, including budget, technology, and personnel, is crucial to match the scale and scope of defined objectives.

Defining success criteria for each AI objective and communicating the strategy and expected outcomes to all stakeholders fosters a shared commitment to the implementation plan.

Implementing a robust monitoring and evaluation system allows for regular reviews of progress against objectives, making adjustments as needed.

Staying informed about industry trends and seeking external input from experts and industry networks ensures that the organization remains adaptable to emerging technologies and best practices.

Regularly reviewing and iterating the AI strategy based on lessons learned and changes in the business environment ensures continuous improvement.

In summary, business units are integral to the holistic governance of AI, ensuring that AI initiatives not only align with business strategy but also contribute meaningfully to the organization's mission and objectives.

Summary:

Defining clear goals and objectives for AI implementation is a dynamic and collaborative process that involves understanding the business context, engaging stakeholders, and aligning AI initiatives with strategic priorities. By following these detailed steps, organizations can ensure that their AI Governance strategy is well-aligned with broader business objectives, setting the stage for successful AI implementation and impactful business outcomes.

- *Identify key stakeholders and establish their roles and responsibilities in the AI Governance framework.*

Identifying key stakeholders and establishing their roles and responsibilities is a crucial step in developing an effective AI Governance framework. This ensures that relevant perspectives are considered, responsibilities are clearly defined, and there is accountability throughout the AI lifecycle.

Some key steps for identifying key stakeholders and establishing their roles and responsibilities in the AI Governance framework are delineated below:

To begin, it is crucial to define the scope of AI Governance, outlining the specific areas and processes that will be covered while determining the boundaries of responsibility for AI initiatives. Identifying primary business owners, typically represented by specific business units or departments, ensures clarity in accountability.

Engaging executive leadership is essential, involving them in the communication of the importance of AI Governance and securing their commitment and support for the framework.

A comprehensive stakeholder mapping exercise is then conducted, encompassing internal contributors such as data scientists, IT professionals, Legal, Compliance, Privacy, Security, Records and Information Management, and Risk Management teams. External stakeholders, including customers, vendors, regulators, and industry associations, are also identified, with a focus on understanding and involving them in the governance process. Stakeholder analysis is performed to grasp their interests, influence, and potential contributions, while also identifying expectations and concerns related to AI Governance.

With this understanding, roles and responsibilities are clearly defined for each stakeholder within the AI Governance framework.

Governance committees or working groups are established, ensuring representation from various stakeholders, with well-defined purposes, compositions, and responsibilities. Decision-making authority is clearly articulated for different aspects of AI Governance, specifying individuals or groups with the final say in critical decisions.

Effective communication is key in this process, where expectations regarding roles, responsibilities, and the importance of contributions are clearly communicated to stakeholders. Cross-functional collaboration is promoted to foster a culture of open communication and shared responsibility. Training programs should be offered to stakeholders on AI Governance principles and best practices, complemented by resources, guidelines, and documentation to support their roles.

To maintain transparency and accountability, reporting mechanisms are established, allowing stakeholders to communicate progress, issues, and concerns regularly.

Stakeholder performance is monitored, and feedback mechanisms are implemented for continuous improvement. A feedback loop should be established, enabling stakeholders to provide input on the effectiveness of the AI Governance framework, which is then used to refine and enhance governance practices.

Recognizing the dynamic nature of organizational structures, roles, and responsibilities, the framework is designed to stay adaptable. Regular reassessment ensures alignment with changing organizational needs. Collaboration with legal and compliance teams ensures that stakeholder roles align with legal and ethical standards, addressing any compliance-related concerns promptly. Finally, all defined roles and responsibilities are documented in a clear and accessible manner, often compiled in a governance handbook or documentation repository for easy reference.

In conclusion, these steps help organizations build a robust foundation for AI Governance by engaging key stakeholders, clarifying their roles, and fostering a collaborative and accountable environment for responsible AI practices.

- *Develop policies and guidelines for ethical AI use, data privacy, and compliance with relevant regulations.*

Business units play a crucial role in shaping and implementing effective AI Governance, particularly in the development of policies and guidelines for ethical AI use, data privacy, and compliance with relevant regulations.

To begin, it is essential for business units to thoroughly understand applicable regulations and standards governing AI use in their industry and region. This includes identifying key AI-related regulations, privacy and data protection frameworks such as GDPR, HIPAA, CCPA, CPRA, other applicable state (or provincial) privacy laws, key standards from ISO and IEEE, and any industry-specific standards that may apply. Conducting a **regulatory impact assessment** allows organizations to *evaluate how each regulation or standard influences AI activities, pinpointing specific requirements related to data processing, consent, transparency, and accountability.*

A comprehensive **data privacy policy** is crucial, outlining how personal and sensitive data will be handled in AI processes. This includes specifying data collection, storage, processing, and sharing practices.

Privacy by Design is emphasized, integrating privacy considerations into the entire AI development lifecycle from the outset of projects.

Data governance practices, encompassing policies for data quality, integrity, and security, are developed consistently across business units, with defined roles and responsibilities to ensure accountability for data management.

A **compliance framework** should be established to align AI activities with legal and regulatory requirements, specifying procedures for monitoring and ensuring compliance. Roles and responsibilities for compliance are clearly defined, assigning accountability for regulatory adherence and reporting. Policies are developed to ensure AI systems are *explainable and transparent* in their decision-making processes, considering the need for interpretability in sensitive applications.

The implementation of **bias detection and mitigation policies** is critical, with regular audits and updates to address emerging challenges. Continuous monitoring processes are implemented to ensure ongoing adherence to policies, with regular reviews and updates based on evolving risks and regulations. Policies for obtaining user consent in AI applications and communication practices to inform users about AI use and its implications are defined.

Business units, perhaps working with the Human Resources department, should also be responsible for developing training programs to educate employees on ethical AI use, data privacy policies, and compliance requirements, fostering a culture of awareness and responsibility.

An **incident response plan** is developed to address potential breaches, violations, or ethical concerns, with clear procedures for reporting and responding to incidents. Collaboration with external stakeholders, including customers, partners, and regulators, is encouraged to gather input and ensure alignment with external expectations while staying informed about industry best practices.

Establishing a periodic review schedule for policies and guidelines, updating them based on changes in regulations, technology, or organizational needs, ensures ongoing relevance and effectiveness.

Seeking legal counsel is advisable to ensure policies align with legal requirements and to obtain legal advice on the interpretation and application of regulations.

Lastly, business units must ensure that AI policies are accessible and well-communicated within the organization and publicize relevant policies to external stakeholders to demonstrate transparency.

2. **Risk Assessment and Management**
   - *Conduct a comprehensive risk assessment to identify potential risks associated with AI implementations.*

In the establishment of AI Governance guidelines, business units play a critical role by conducting a comprehensive **risk assessment**, in consultation with in-house or external risk professionals, to identify and mitigate potential risks associated with AI implementations.

Firstly, take the defined scope of the AI implementation and specify the objectives of the risk assessment. This ensures a clear understanding of the goals and parameters of the assessment.

Identifying stakeholders from various departments, including IT, Legal, Compliance, Risk Management, Privacy, Security, Records and Information Management, data science, and business units, ensures a holistic perspective and diverse expertise in the risk assessment process.

Ethical considerations are integrated into the risk assessment, with a focus on societal impact, privacy, and potential discrimination issues.

Understanding the AI system is vital, involving a deep dive into its purpose, functionality, data sources, and integration points. A **data governance assessment** is conducted to evaluate the quality, integrity, and security of the data used by the AI system. This includes assessing data governance practices, such as data collection, storage, processing, and sharing.

Algorithmic risks are evaluated, focusing on potential biases, fairness issues, and unintended consequences of the algorithms. The interpretability and explainability of model outputs are also considered in this evaluation.

Compliance with relevant regulations, such as the EU Artificial Intelligence Act[1], the Algorithmic Accountability Act of 2023 in the United States, and also privacy regulations like GDPR, CCPA, CPRA, and other state laws, or industry-specific standards like HIPAA, is ensured to identify and address potential legal and regulatory risks associated with AI implementation.

A **security assessment** is conducted to identify vulnerabilities and potential cybersecurity risks, including an evaluation of the robustness of the AI system against adversarial attacks.

Vendor and third-party risks are assessed, including those associated with pre-trained models, APIs, and external data sources. The security and compliance practices of AI vendors are verified.

Operational risks, such as system downtime, data breaches, and performance issues, are identified and evaluated in terms of their potential impact on business operations. User acceptance and adoption risks are assessed, considering potential resistance or challenges and identifying communication and training needs to mitigate these risks.

Documentation related to AI development, including model documentation, codebase, and implementation guidelines, is thoroughly reviewed to ensure transparency and accessibility of relevant information.

Identified risks are then prioritized based on their potential impact and likelihood, with a focus on high-priority risks that have significant consequences. Risk mitigation strategies are developed for each identified risk, considering both preventive and corrective measures, and responsibilities for implementing these strategies are clearly defined.

A **continuous monitoring plan** is established to monitor the AI system's performance and associated risks in real-time, implementing tools and processes for proactive risk detection.

A **communication plan** is developed to keep stakeholders informed about identified risks, mitigation strategies, and ongoing monitoring efforts, fostering a culture of transparency and accountability. The entire risk assessment process, including findings, prioritized risks, and mitigation strategies, is documented, and regular reports are generated for stakeholders and management.

Procedures for **regulatory reporting** in case of incidents or breaches are established to ensure compliance with reporting requirements stipulated by relevant authorities. Scenario planning exercises are conducted to simulate potential risk scenarios, testing the effectiveness of mitigation strategies under different circumstances.

Periodic **audits** are conducted to review the effectiveness of risk mitigation measures, and the risk assessment is continuously updated based on changes in the AI system or the external environment. This iterative approach ensures that the AI Governance framework remains adaptive and robust over time.

By following these steps, organizations can conduct a comprehensive risk assessment that helps identify and mitigate potential risks associated with AI implementations, ensuring responsible and secure deployment.

- *Develop strategies and controls to mitigate identified risks, including legal, ethical, and operational considerations.*

Business units are integral in developing a robust AI Governance framework, particularly in the formulation and implementation of strategies and controls to mitigate identified risks, encompassing legal, ethical, and operational considerations. The approach should be methodical and systematic.

Below are key steps, bearing in mind legal, ethical, and operational considerations.

The first step involves *prioritizing identified risks* based on their potential impact and likelihood, categorizing them into legal, ethical, and operational dimensions for targeted mitigation strategies.

On the legal front, business units should review and update policies to ensure compliance with relevant laws and regulations, while implementing mechanisms for regular monitoring and adaptation to changes in legal requirements.

Ethical considerations are addressed through the development or updating of ethical guidelines that align with the organization's values.

Algorithmic fairness and bias mitigation are critical risk aspects to assess, requiring the implementation of algorithms and tools to detect and mitigate biases in AI models. Regular audits and updates to models ensure ongoing efforts to address fairness concerns and ensure equitable outcomes.

To enhance **transparency** and **explainability,** business units should work toward making AI decision-making processes more transparent and providing clear explanations for AI-generated outcomes to users and stakeholders.

Data privacy safeguards are strengthened through measures such as encryption, anonymization, and access controls, with regular audits to ensure compliance with privacy regulations. Robust **cybersecurity** measures are implemented to protect AI systems from unauthorized access and attacks, with regular updates to security protocols to address emerging threats.

Assessing third-party risk: Clear contractual obligations for vendors and partners regarding security and compliance are established to mitigate potential risks.

User consent mechanisms are implemented, ensuring clear and user-friendly methods for obtaining informed consent and empowering users to control the use of their data in AI processes.

Operational resilience planning is essential to address downtime, system failures, and other operational risks. Comprehensive plans are developed and tested through simulations and drills to refine strategies.

Continuous monitoring systems for AI operations are implemented, utilizing real-time monitoring tools to detect anomalies and potential risks promptly. User feedback mechanisms are established to allow users to provide input on AI system performance, enabling the identification of potential issues and areas for improvement. Regular audits are conducted to assess compliance with legal and ethical standards, using audit findings to refine and update governance policies.

Scenario-based **risk mitigation strategies** are developed to address specific legal, ethical, and operational challenges. These strategies are tested through simulated scenarios to ensure their effectiveness in real-world situations.

Documentation of all risk mitigation strategies, controls, and their implementations is essential. Regular reports are provided to leadership and stakeholders on the status of risk mitigation efforts, promoting transparency and accountability. A communication plan is developed for addressing legal and ethical concerns transparently, and efforts are made to proactively communicate risk mitigation to stakeholders, customers, and the public. This comprehensive approach ensures that business units actively contribute to the development and maintenance of a robust AI Governance framework.

By following these steps, organizations can create a robust framework for mitigating and reducing identified risks associated with AI implementations, addressing legal, ethical, and operational considerations in a comprehensive manner.

- *Regularly review and update risk assessments as technology and organizational landscapes evolve.*

Regularly reviewing and updating risk assessments is crucial to ensure that AI Governance remains effective and aligned with evolving technology and organizational landscapes. Below, key steps are listed for this ongoing process.

Firstly, organizations should establish a regular schedule for these reviews, taking into consideration factors such as the pace of technological change and the organization's risk appetite. Engaging cross-functional teams, including IT, Legal, Records and Information Management (RIM), Privacy, Security, Risk, Audit, compliance, data science, and business units, in the review process ensures diverse perspectives are considered, capturing a comprehensive understanding of risks.

Organizational changes, including shifts in structure, processes, or strategies, should be assessed for their influence on AI risks and governance requirements.

Regular reviews of risks associated with third-party components, including vendor and partner relationships, should align with the organization's risk tolerance.

Monitoring user acceptance and adoption of AI technologies helps identify challenges or resistance that may pose risks to successful deployment.

Regular audits of AI algorithms for bias and fairness, as well as assessing the effectiveness of cybersecurity measures in place, are crucial.

The effectiveness of training programs on ethical AI use, data privacy, and compliance should be evaluated, and content should be updated to address new challenges and reinforce key principles. Revision of documentation related to AI Governance policies, guidelines, and risk assessments is necessary to ensure all information is up-to-date and accessible.

Engaging with external stakeholders, including customers, partners, and regulators, allows organizations to incorporate external feedback and insights into the risk assessment process. Regular communication of updates to the risk assessment process internally ensures transparency regarding changes and their implications. Seeking legal guidance is advised to ensure that risk assessments align with the latest legal landscape and to obtain advice on interpreting and applying new regulations.

Staying informed about emerging best practices in AI Governance and incorporating these practices into the organization's risk assessment methodology ensures continuous improvement. Documenting the entire review process, including findings, updates, and decisions made, maintains a clear record of the evolution of risk assessments over time, facilitating accountability and transparency within the organization. *The RIM department should be involved in creating retention and disposition schedules and guidelines for all documentation.*

By consistently following these steps, organizations can adapt their AI Governance strategies to changes in technology and organizational landscapes, ensuring that risk assessments remain relevant and effective in the dynamic field of AI.

3. **Data Governance**
   - *Implementing robust data governance practices in business units helps to ensure the quality, integrity, and security of data used for AI training and decision-making.*

Implementing robust **data governance** practices is essential for ensuring the quality, integrity, and security of data used for AI training and decision-making (please see Chapter 3 on Lifecycle management for more details on developing data governance processes).

In consultation with the RIM function, establishing data retention and deletion policies to manage the lifecycle of data used in AI ensures compliance with legal and regulatory requirements regarding data storage. Implementing version control for datasets used in AI training, tracking changes, and maintaining a version history for reproducibility are important steps.

Ethical considerations should be integrated into data governance practices, addressing issues such as bias, fairness, and responsible AI use, with measures implemented to identify and mitigate biases in training data.

Ensuring that data governance practices align with **data privacy** regulations and implementing mechanisms for obtaining and managing user consent for data use are crucial for maintaining trust.

Performing **data impact assessments** to evaluate the potential consequences of data breaches or unauthorized access and developing mitigation strategies based on the assessment findings are important for proactive risk management. Implementing monitoring and auditing tools to track data usage patterns and regularly auditing data access logs helps identify and address unauthorized or suspicious activities.

Providing **data governance training programs** in the business units to educate employees on data governance policies and best practices fosters a culture of awareness and responsibility regarding data management. Establishing a schedule for the regular review and update of data governance policies ensures that these policies remain aligned with organizational goals and evolving industry standards.

Finally, fostering a culture of continuous improvement in data governance, soliciting feedback from stakeholders, and using lessons learned to refine and enhance data governance practices contribute to the ongoing effectiveness of the data governance framework.

By following these steps, organizations can establish and maintain robust data governance practices, ensuring the quality, integrity, and security of data used for AI training and decision-making. This approach contributes to the responsible and effective deployment of AI systems within an organization.

- *Establish data access controls and permissions to protect sensitive information.*

Establishing robust **data access controls** and permissions is crucial for protecting sensitive information in the context of AI Governance. Below are detailed steps to achieve this.

The initial steps involve identifying and **classifying** data, particularly sensitive data such as personally identifiable information (PII) and confidential information, and classifying it based on sensitivity and criticality. Following this, organizations need to define clear and comprehensive data access policies, outlining who can access specific types of data and specifying the conditions under which access is granted or restricted.

A **data access needs assessment** should be conducted to understand the specific data access requirements of different roles within the organization, identifying teams or individuals that require access to specific datasets for AI purposes. Implementing **Role-Based Access Control** (RBAC) is crucial, where permissions are assigned based on job roles and responsibilities, following the **Principle of Least Privilege** (i.e., providing information only on a "need to know" basis).

Data stewards should be appointed in the business units to oversee and manage data access controls, ensuring they understand the importance of enforcing access policies.

Fine-grained access controls, which specify access permissions at the attribute or field level within datasets, provide granular control over who can access specific pieces of information. Leveraging **Access Control Lists** (ACLs) helps define specific permissions for individual users or groups, with regular reviews and updates based on changing requirements.

Attribute-Based Access Control (ABAC) should be implemented, utilizing attributes such as user attributes, data classification, and environmental conditions to determine access, enhancing flexibility in controlling access based on dynamic factors.

Enhancing security measures includes the implementation of **Multi-Factor Authentication** (MFA) for users accessing sensitive data, adding an additional layer of protection beyond traditional username and password.

Encrypting sensitive data, both in transit and at rest, ensures that only authorized individuals with the appropriate decryption keys can access the information. Monitoring and auditing access activities, coupled with regular reviews of access controls to align with organizational changes, are essential for maintaining the security posture.

Data masking and anonymization techniques should be applied **to protect sensitive information**, ensuring that only authorized users see the complete, unmasked data. Regular training programs should educate employees on data access policies and the importance of secure data handling, reinforcing awareness of security practices.

Emergency access procedures need to be well-defined, documented, time-limited, and subject to post-event review.

Automating access provisioning and deprovisioning ensures that access is promptly revoked for employees who leave the organization or change roles. Collaboration with IT and security teams is vital to align data access controls with broader security measures, addressing vulnerabilities and implementing unified security practices. Regular access reviews validate that individuals still require their assigned access permissions, adjusting controls based on changes in job roles or responsibilities.

Ensuring compliance with regulations, such as the EU Artificial Intelligence Act[2], the Algorithmic Accountability Act of 2023 in the United States, and also privacy regulations like GDPR, CCPA, CPRA, and other state laws, or industry-specific standards like HIPAA, involves aligning data access controls with relevant compliance standards and regularly reviewing and updating controls to meet evolving regulatory requirements.

Finally, **periodic security audits** are essential to evaluate the effectiveness of data access controls, using audit findings to continuously improve and enhance security measures.

By following these steps, organizations can establish a robust framework for data access controls and permissions, ensuring that sensitive information is protected from unauthorized access and aligned with AI Governance principles.

- *Address bias and fairness issues in the training data to avoid unintended consequences in AI models.*

Addressing bias and fairness issues in training data is crucial for ensuring responsible and equitable AI models. Below are key considerations to mitigate bias and promote fairness:

To begin, teams must be educated on the concept of bias in AI, emphasizing that biases can be unintentionally introduced during the development process. Your team should be keenly aware of the sources of training data, the potential inherent biases that may occur in the data, and the methods to root out or counterbalance biases.

Clear fairness objectives, aligned with organizational values and ethical considerations, should be defined, along with specific fairness metrics relevant to the AI application. Diversifying the AI development team is crucial to bring in varied perspectives and reduce the risk of biased decision-making.

An **audit of the training data** is essential to identify potential biases, analyzing data across different demographic groups to uncover disparities. Ensuring the representativeness of the training data of the population the AI model is intended to serve is crucial, and addressing underrepresented groups is important. Employing **bias detection tools** helps identify and measure bias in both the training data and model outcomes, with regular updates as new methods emerge. Model fairness must be assessed across various subgroups using fairness metrics to quantify disparities and assess performance.

Scrutinizing features in the training data that may contribute to bias is essential, and adjustments or elimination of features disproportionately impacting certain groups may be necessary.

Pre-processing techniques applied to the model training data, such as re-sampling, re-weighting, or generating synthetic data, can mitigate bias.

Enhancing model interpretability through techniques like **LIME** (Local Interpretable Model-agnostic Explanations) or **SHAP** (Shapley values) aids in understanding how the model makes decisions. Inclusive design practices should be integrated from the outset of AI development, considering diverse user needs and scenarios during the design phase.

Continuous **updates to training data** to reflect changes in the real-world environment are crucial, incorporating **feedback loops** to address biases identified post-deployment.

Collaboration with domain experts in the business units who understand the context and nuances of the data is invaluable. Thorough testing is required to identify unintended consequences of bias mitigation strategies, ensuring vigilance for unintended negative impacts on other groups. Exploration and implementation of fairness-aware algorithms during the training process can proactively reduce biases.

Introducing a **fairness review process** as part of the model development lifecycle and conducting regular reviews to assess fairness and identify areas for improvement is essential. Documenting decision-making processes related to model development maintains transparency regarding choices made to address bias and fairness.

Engagement with external stakeholders, including impacted communities and advocacy groups, is crucial for understanding potential biases and fairness concerns from diverse perspectives. Stakeholders, including end users, should be educated on potential biases in AI models, providing clear explanations of model limitations and fairness considerations.

Finally, the establishment of **continuous monitoring systems** to detect and address bias in real-time is necessary, with regular reviews and updates to mitigation strategies based on ongoing assessments. By following these steps, organizations can actively address bias and fairness issues in training data, promoting responsible AI development and mitigating unintended consequences. It's essential to approach bias mitigation as an ongoing and collaborative effort involving diverse expertise and perspectives.

4. **Model Development and Validation**
    - *Implement a transparent and reproducible model development process.*

Implementing a transparent and reproducible model development process is a cornerstone of effective AI Governance. To achieve this, it is crucial to follow a comprehensive set of steps throughout the development lifecycle. The process begins with:

1. Clearly documenting the project objectives, encompassing the problem statement, desired outcomes, and success criteria.
2. A **version control system**, such as **Git**, should be established to track changes consistently across code, data, and model artifacts.
3. Detailed documentation of data pre-processing steps, including cleaning, normalization, and feature engineering, ensures that the data pipeline is reproducible.
4. Feature selection rationale and the chosen process should be well-documented, employing techniques that shed light on feature importance.
5. The model architecture, encompassing model type, layers, activation functions, and hyperparameter settings, should be documented comprehensively.
6. The parameters used during training, such as learning rate and batch size, must be recorded and kept consistent across experiments.
7. Implementing **cross-validation techniques** is essential for robustly assessing model performance, and this process should be documented, specifying the number of folds and chosen evaluation metrics.
8. Model evaluation metrics, including accuracy, precision, recall, and F1 score, should be recorded for thorough documentation. The validation process, including adjustments made based on validation results, needs clear documentation.

9. To enhance interpretability, model interpretability **F1 score** techniques should be applied, and their impact on understanding the model's decisions should be documented.
10. Sensitivity analysis, which explores how changes in input features affect predictions, should be conducted and documented. Model outputs on test datasets or real-world data should be recorded for traceability and auditing. A standardized model documentation template should be developed, covering data, architecture, training, and evaluation details. Code should be shared in a way that ensures reproducibility, including detailed comments, dependencies, and instructions for running the code.

Creating a **model card**—a concise summary of the model, its intended use, performance metrics, and potential limitations—ensures accessibility to stakeholders and end users. Collaborative and regular code and documentation reviews maintain consistency and quality.

Continuous integration systems should be set up to automate testing and validation, incorporating checks for reproducibility. Containerization using tools like **Docker** ensures consistent environments across development stages. Procedures for sharing and deploying trained models, along with regular updates to model documentation, complete the process, fostering transparency and reproducibility in AI model development.

- *Regularly validate AI models to ensure they perform as intended and remain unbiased over time.*

From an AI Governance perspective, regular validation of AI models is crucial to ensure ongoing performance and prevent unintended biases over time.

The first step involves defining validation metrics that align with the specific use case, incorporating performance indicators such as accuracy, precision, recall, and fairness metrics. A comprehensive **validation plan** is then established, outlining the frequency, methods, and criteria for model validation. This plan includes a defined schedule with regular intervals and triggers for ad hoc validation.

To maintain the relevance of the validation process, regular data updates are essential. Collecting new data helps ensure that the validation dataset reflects the current distribution of real-world scenarios. As data evolves, the representativeness of the validation dataset should be reassessed to confirm coverage of diverse scenarios and an accurate reflection of the target population.

Bias and fairness audits on the validation dataset are critical steps to identify and measure biases across different subgroups.

Employing **cross-validation** techniques enhances the robustness of model performance assessment, considering different validation folds and ensuring consistency in results. Continuous monitoring systems are implemented to assess the model's sensitivity to **concept drift** and detect deviations from expected behavior in real-time.

Model interpretability is revisited to guarantee that the model's decisions remain understandable and aligned with expectations.

Sensitivity to drift is evaluated to address changes in the relationships between features and outcomes over time. A/B testing is employed to compare the current model's performance with potential new versions or alternative models, facilitating controlled experiments to validate changes in model behavior.

Continuous monitoring systems, including real-time alerts, are implemented to detect deviations promptly. User feedback is solicited and analyzed, incorporating valuable insights to identify issues and improve the model. Fairness metrics are regularly updated, and adjustments are made to model parameters or retraining is conducted if bias is detected.

Maintaining a **model registry** becomes integral for traceability and auditing purposes, tracking versions of the model, training data, and validation results over time. Engaging external auditors or third-party experts for periodic reviews brings external perspectives and valuable insights to the validation process.

Documentation of validation results, including identified issues and corrective actions, is essential for maintaining a historical record, which the RIM department can advise on.

Regular updates to validation protocols are conducted based on lessons learned and changes in the AI landscape, ensuring alignment with best practices and industry standards. Stakeholder education emphasizes the importance of ongoing model validation and fosters awareness of potential biases. Finally, a regular review of AI Governance policies and guidelines related to model validation ensures compliance with evolving best practices and regulatory requirements.

- *Document the decision-making process during model development and maintain an audit trail for accountability.*

Documenting the decision-making process during AI model development and maintaining an audit trail are critical components of AI Governance for accountability and transparency. Key decision points throughout the AI model development lifecycle, such as data selection, feature engineering, model architecture, hyperparameter tuning, and deployment decisions, must be clearly defined. To systematically capture these decisions, a **decision log** is established, encompassing fields like decision description, rationale, decision-maker, date, and supporting references.

The individuals or teams responsible for decision-making at each point in the process are identified, and roles and responsibilities are specified, ensuring accountability.

Criteria for data selection and preprocessing, including considerations for data quality, representativeness, and potential biases, are documented. Feature engineering choices and their impact on model performance are recorded, and decisions related to model architecture and algorithms are justified based on factors like interpretability, complexity, and performance.

The **hyperparameter tuning process**, including chosen hyperparameters and their values, is documented, along with the criteria for selecting optimal hyperparameters.

Evaluation metrics used to assess model performance, as well as the criteria for determining whether the model meets acceptance thresholds, are recorded. Results of model validation, including observed biases, fairness issues, or unexpected behavior, are documented, along with details on how validation results influenced subsequent decisions.

The methods used to enhance model interpretability are documented, emphasizing their contribution to transparency and understanding. Decisions related to model deployment, deployment environments, and considerations for scalability are recorded, including any ethical or legal considerations addressed during the deployment decision.

Ethical considerations made during the development process, addressing potential biases and fairness issues, are documented.

Decisions related to model updates and retraining, including triggers for retraining and the impact of new data or environmental changes on model performance, are detailed. Stakeholder input from users, domain experts, and external reviewers is documented, specifying how stakeholder input influenced decision-making. An **audit trail** is established to capture the entire decision-making process, ensuring accessibility, security, and regular updates.

Version control systems are leveraged to track changes in code, data, and model artifacts, associating decision logs with specific versions to maintain a chronological record.

External expert opinions are considered, especially in areas such as ethics, bias mitigation, and legal compliance, with the input received and its incorporation into decisions carefully documented.

Regular reviews of decision logs and audit trail documentation are scheduled to update documentation to reflect changes, new insights, and lessons learned. AI development teams are provided training on the importance of documenting decisions and maintaining an audit trail, fostering a culture of accountability and transparency within the organization. Documentation practices are aligned with overarching AI Governance policies, with regular reviews and updates to reflect evolving best practices and standards.

By systematically documenting decision-making processes and maintaining a robust audit trail, organizations can enhance accountability, transparency, and the overall governance of AI models. This documentation serves as a valuable resource for internal review, external audits, and ongoing improvement of AI systems.

5. Explainability and Transparency

Explainability in AI refers to the capacity of an AI system to provide understandable and comprehensible explanations for its decision-making processes. It involves making the internal workings of complex machine learning models accessible and interpretable to humans. Explainability is crucial for building trust, accountability, and transparency in AI systems, particularly when they are deployed in applications that impact individuals, society, or sensitive domains.

Explainability is not a one-size-fits-all concept; its implementation varies based on the complexity of the model, the application domain, and the requirements of stakeholders. *In contexts where AI decisions have significant consequences, such as healthcare or finance, the need for explainability becomes even more critical* to ensure responsible and trustworthy AI deployment. Key steps in establishing explainability include:

1. **Interpretable Models:** Explainability begins with the choice of models. Some models, like decision trees or linear models, inherently offer interpretable outputs due to their transparent structures. Decision trees, for instance, allow for a clear understanding of how input features contribute to predictions. On the other hand, advanced machine learning models like deep neural networks are often considered black-box models, as their intricate internal mechanisms make it challenging to interpret their decision-making processes. Achieving explainability in these cases necessitates the application of additional techniques and methodologies to shed light on the model's operations.
2. **Model-Agnostic Techniques:** Model-agnostic techniques play a crucial role in achieving explainability, especially for complex black-box models. **LIME** (Local Interpretable Model-agnostic Explanations) and **SHAP** (SHapley Additive exPlanations) are two prominent approaches. *(LIME perturbs input data, observes changes in model predictions, and fits a local interpretable model to approximate the black-box model's behavior for a specific instance. SHAP values, rooted in cooperative game theory, provide a fair distribution of "credit" for the model's output to individual input features. These techniques offer a way to unravel the complexity of advanced models.)*

3. **Feature Importance:** Central to explainability is the communication of the importance of individual features in the decision-making process. This involves conveying to end users which aspects of the input data had the most significant influence on the model's output. By highlighting feature importance, users gain insights into the factors that contribute most to the AI system's decisions, fostering a clearer understanding of the model's behavior.
4. **Contextual Explanations:** Accurate explanations are not only about providing correct information but also about presenting it in a way that is comprehensible to end users. Contextual explanations go beyond raw data by providing relevant information and context. This contextualization makes the reasoning behind the model's decisions more accessible and relatable to users, enhancing the overall interpretability of the AI system.
5. **Visualizations:** Visual representations are powerful tools in enhancing model interpretability. Graphs, charts, and heatmaps offer intuitive visualizations of model outputs, decision boundaries, and feature importance. These visual aids simplify complex information, making it more accessible to a wider audience, including stakeholders who may not have a deep understanding of the underlying technical aspects of the AI system.
6. **Human-in-the-Loop:** In human-in-the-loop systems, human involvement becomes integral to the decision-making process. Users have the ability to query the model for explanations, and human experts can provide input and validation on model decisions. This approach ensures that human judgment and expertise contribute to decision-making, combining the strengths of AI systems with human insights.
7. **Ethical Considerations:** Ethical considerations are paramount in the pursuit of explainability. Ensuring that explanations do not inadvertently reinforce biases, discrimination, or unfair practices is critical. Rigorous evaluation of explanations is necessary to identify and address any potential biases, thereby aligning AI systems with ethical standards and promoting fair and just decision-making.
8. **Regulatory Compliance:** Compliance with regulations such as the General Data Protection Regulation (GDPR) emphasizes the right to explanation. AI systems must provide meaningful and understandable explanations for automated decisions to adhere to regulatory requirements. Ensuring regulatory compliance not only protects individuals' rights but also contributes to the overall transparency and accountability of AI systems.
9. **User Feedback:** Actively encouraging users to provide feedback on model explanations is a valuable practice in refining AI systems. User feedback can reveal gaps in understanding, highlight areas for improvement, and contribute to the continuous enhancement of AI models. This iterative feedback loop ensures that AI systems align with user expectations and are continually optimized for user comprehension.
10. **Continuous Improvement:** Achieving and maintaining explainability is an iterative and ongoing process. Regularly reviewing and updating explainability practices becomes essential as AI models evolve, new data becomes available, and user needs change. This commitment to continuous improvement ensures that AI systems remain transparent, trustworthy, and aligned with the evolving landscape of technology and user expectations.

Transparency in AI is closely related to explainability and refers to the openness and accessibility of the processes, decisions, and underlying mechanisms of AI systems. It involves making the actions and behaviors of AI models clear, understandable, and accountable to stakeholders, users, and the wider community. Transparency is a fundamental aspect of responsible AI development, and it complements the goal of achieving explainability.

Transparency in AI Governance is a foundational principle that underscores the openness and accessibility of the processes, decisions, and underlying mechanisms of AI systems. It serves as a key component of responsible AI development, working in tandem with the goal of achieving explainability. At its core, transparency involves making the actions and behaviors of AI models clear, comprehensible, and accountable to a broad range of stakeholders, including users, decision-makers, and the wider community.

In the context of AI, transparency is about demystifying the often complex and intricate operations of machine learning models. It ensures that the decision-making processes and outcomes are not concealed behind an impenetrable veil, especially in cases where AI impacts individuals, society, or sensitive domains. Transparent AI systems empower users and stakeholders to understand how and why certain decisions are made, fostering trust and confidence in the technology.

Transparency extends beyond merely revealing the final outputs of AI models; it encompasses the entire lifecycle of AI development. This includes openness about the data used to train models, the selection and engineering of features, the choice of algorithms, and the tuning of hyperparameters. By providing insight into these aspects, transparency enables stakeholders to assess the fairness, ethical considerations, and potential biases inherent in AI systems.

Crucially, transparent AI practices contribute to accountability. When the decision-making processes are laid bare, it becomes easier to attribute responsibility for the outcomes. This accountability is not only essential for maintaining trust but is also increasingly demanded by regulatory frameworks. Transparency aligns AI development with ethical standards and legal requirements, ensuring that organizations adhere to guidelines that emphasize openness and responsible use of AI technologies.

In practice, achieving transparency often involves the documentation and communication of AI processes in a clear and accessible manner. This includes creating comprehensive documentation that details the development steps, decision points, and validation processes. Moreover, transparent AI systems may employ tools and methodologies that facilitate external scrutiny, allowing third-party audits and assessments.

Transparency is a collaborative effort that involves developers, data scientists, ethicists, and stakeholders working together to establish a culture of openness and disclosure. By prioritizing transparency in AI Governance, organizations not only foster accountability and trust but also contribute to the responsible advancement of artificial intelligence, acknowledging the societal impact of these technologies and the importance of ensuring their ethical and fair use.

Transparency in AI Governance encompasses a multifaceted approach to openness and accessibility in the development and deployment of AI systems.

The first aspect involves a comprehensive understanding of model behavior, where transparency requires providing stakeholders with a clear insight into how an AI model processes input data and arrives at specific decisions or predictions. This transparency is foundational for building trust and validating the reliability of the AI system.

Accessible information is another pivotal dimension of transparency. Transparent AI systems make relevant details such as model architecture, training data sources, feature importance, and decision-making criteria readily accessible to users, developers, and other stakeholders. This accessibility ensures that those interacting with the system can scrutinize and comprehend the fundamental components driving its functionalities.

The disclosure of **model architecture** and **parameters** is a critical facet of transparency. This includes openly sharing details about the type of model employed, the structure of layers in the case of neural networks, and the specific hyperparameter values utilized during the training process. By providing this information, organizations enhance the interpretability and scrutiny of their AI models.

- *Transparency extends to the origins of the training data, known as **data provenance**.*

Organizations committed to transparency spell out how data was collected, pre-processed, annotated, and any transformations applied. Clear explanations of data provenance contribute to a more complete understanding of potential biases and the ethical considerations associated with the data.

Documentation of decisions throughout the AI model lifecycle is a practice intrinsic to transparent AI development. This documentation spans decisions related to data selection, feature engineering, model architecture, and deployment. It creates a traceable record that aids in accountability, analysis, and the improvement of decision-making practices.

Open-source practices and collaboration are key contributors to transparency. Open-sourcing the code of an AI model allows the wider community to inspect, review, and contribute, fostering collaboration and external validation. Such practices align with the principle that transparency benefits from diverse perspectives.

Maintaining detailed **audit trails** is another critical aspect of transparency, ensuring a historical record of changes in code, data, and model versions. This record serves as a comprehensive account that supports accountability and allows for a retrospective analysis of the development process.

Addressing ethical considerations openly is part of transparent AI Governance. This involves acknowledging potential biases, privacy concerns, and societal impacts. It also includes robust efforts to mitigate biases and uphold ethical standards in AI decision-making, aligning with broader societal values.

User-friendly explanations tailored to diverse audiences are essential for transparency. Transparent AI systems provide explanations that are accessible and contextual, enhancing user understanding and fostering trust.

Transparency is crucial for adhering to **data protection** and **privacy** regulations that emphasize the need for individuals to understand and challenge decisions made by AI systems.

Risk disclosure is inherent in transparent AI, as organizations openly communicate potential risks and limitations associated with their models. This includes recognizing situations where the model may struggle or make inaccurate predictions, ensuring that users are informed about the system's boundaries.

User feedback mechanisms are integral to transparency, as they provide avenues for users to offer feedback on the model's behavior. This practice uncovers issues, improves understanding, and drives continuous improvement, creating a feedback loop that enhances the transparency and effectiveness of the AI system.

Finally, transparency is an ongoing commitment that requires continuous improvement. Organizations must strive to refine communication, enhance documentation practices, and address emerging challenges as AI models evolve over time. This iterative approach ensures that transparency remains a dynamic and integral part of AI Governance.

- *Communicate AI decisions and predictions in a clear and understandable manner to stakeholders.*

In the realm of AI Governance, effectively communicating AI decisions and predictions to stakeholders is a fundamental aspect that demands careful consideration. To achieve this, understanding the audience is paramount.

Identifying a diverse range of stakeholders, which may include decision-makers, end users, and both technical and non-technical audiences, enables tailoring the communication approach to meet the specific needs and expertise levels of each group. Recognizing that different stakeholders may have varying levels of familiarity with AI concepts allows for a more nuanced and targeted communication strategy.

Defining communication goals is the next crucial step. Clearly outlining the objectives, such as building trust, informing decisions, or addressing concerns, establishes a roadmap for effective communication. It is essential to articulate what stakeholders should take away from the communication, aligning the messaging with the desired outcomes.

Providing context and background information about the AI system, its purpose, and the specific problem it aims to solve is an essential foundation. Offering this information sets the stage for stakeholders to better grasp the significance of AI decisions within a broader context, fostering a more informed understanding.

The use of clear and simple language is a guiding principle for effective communication. Avoiding technical jargon and translating complex AI concepts into easily understood terms ensures that the information is accessible to a wider audience. This approach is crucial for conveying intricate ideas to nonexperts.

Visualizing model outputs through charts, graphs, or heatmaps is a powerful tool for enhancing interpretability. Visual aids make complex information more accessible, helping stakeholders interpret AI decisions and facilitating a deeper understanding.

In communicating AI decisions, explaining **feature importance** is vital. Clearly conveying the significance of individual features in influencing decisions provides stakeholders with insights into the factors most impactful in the model's predictions.

The provision of **probabilistic information** is a key aspect of transparent communication. Rather than presenting predictions as absolutes, it is crucial to communicate them as probabilities. *Clearly explaining that AI models provide likelihoods, not definite outcomes, helps manage stakeholder expectations.*

Highlighting **model confidence levels** adds another layer of transparency. Sharing information about the confidence levels associated with predictions indicates when the model is more or less certain about its outputs, contributing to a nuanced interpretation.

Addressing uncertainty and limitations head-on is an essential practice. Transparently communicating the uncertainties and limitations associated with the AI model, and being forthright about situations where the model may struggle or predictions may be less reliable, builds trust by managing expectations.

Providing insight into the mechanisms used to make the AI model interpretable is a crucial component. This involves explaining any model-agnostic techniques, visualizations, or tools that have been employed to facilitate understanding.

Crafting user-friendly explanations tailored to the stakeholders' domain knowledge is a best practice. Using analogies or real-world examples to illustrate complex concepts ensures that the information resonates with the audience, fostering comprehension.

Incorporating **feedback loops** establishes a mechanism for stakeholders to provide feedback on AI decisions. This encourages a continuous improvement cycle, enhancing communication and addressing any concerns or misunderstandings that may arise.

Utilizing interactive interfaces or dashboards that allow stakeholders to explore and interact with AI predictions adds an extra layer of engagement. Enabling users to query the system and understand how different inputs influence outcomes promotes a deeper understanding.

Documenting communication protocols is a foundational step. Developing clear documentation that outlines communication protocols for AI decisions specifies how and when communication will occur, especially in critical situations or when significant changes are made to the model.

Educating stakeholders is a proactive approach. Providing educational materials or workshops helps stakeholders understand AI concepts, terminology, and processes, fostering an environment where they are informed and empowered to engage with AI decisions.

Establishing a comprehensive **communication plan** is pivotal. Developing a plan that outlines how and when AI decisions will be communicated to stakeholders ensures consistency and alignment with organizational policies.

Engaging in two-way communication channels is encouraged. Allowing stakeholders to ask questions and seek clarification fosters an environment of openness. Actively listening to stakeholder feedback and addressing concerns promptly contributes to a collaborative and transparent communication process.

Ensuring compliance with relevant regulations is a non-negotiable aspect of AI communication. Aligning communication practices with regulations related to data protection, privacy, and automated decision-making is essential for legal and ethical adherence.

Providing clear contact points for stakeholders to reach out with queries or concerns establishes a support system. This transparency in communication channels ensures that stakeholders feel heard and supported in their interactions with the AI system.

Conducting training sessions for teams involved in AI communication is a strategic investment. Enhancing their ability to convey complex information clearly and effectively, especially in sensitive communication scenarios, ensures that communication aligns with organizational objectives and values.

By following these steps, organizations can establish effective communication practices that enhance stakeholder understanding, trust, and confidence in AI decisions. Clear and transparent communication is a key component of responsible AI Governance.

6. Ethical Considerations

- *Develop ethical guidelines for AI use, considering the potential societal impact and consequences.*

Developing ethical guidelines for AI use within business units is a cornerstone of AI Governance, ensuring that the deployment of AI is conducted responsibly and with accountability. The establishment of a diverse **ethics committee** is foundational, bringing together experts from AI, ethics, law, social sciences, and diverse stakeholder groups to provide a comprehensive and varied perspective on ethical considerations. This diversity ensures that a broad range of ethical considerations is addressed, promoting robust and inclusive guidelines.

Clear objectives are crucial in guiding the development of ethical guidelines. Articulating the values and principles that these guidelines aim to uphold, with a focus on factors such as fairness, transparency, accountability, and societal well-being, provides a clear direction for ethical AI development.

Conducting stakeholder engagement further enhances this process, involving end users, affected communities, advocacy groups, and industry experts to gather input on concerns, values, and expectations related to AI use.

A thorough review of existing **ethical frameworks** both within and outside the organization informs the development of new guidelines. Incorporating relevant principles and best practices from established frameworks ensures that the guidelines align with industry standards and ethical norms.

Identifying potential ethical risks and harms through a comprehensive risk assessment is a vital step, considering issues like bias, discrimination, privacy infringement, and unintended consequences in the development and deployment of AI.

Establishing core ethical principles is fundamental to guiding AI development and deployment. Common principles such as fairness, transparency, accountability, privacy, inclusivity, and harm avoidance provide a solid foundation for ethical AI practices. Specific attention to addressing bias and promoting fairness, ensuring transparency and explainability, and prioritizing accountability throughout the AI lifecycle are critical aspects of these guidelines.

Protecting user **data privacy** is a key ethical consideration, and guidelines should detail how personal data will be handled, ensuring compliance with data protection regulations. Encouraging inclusivity and accessibility helps avoid disparities and ensures equal access and benefits from AI systems. Considering the environmental impact, especially energy consumption, is essential, with guidelines encouraging the development of energy-efficient AI models and infrastructure.

Guidelines should explicitly address the potential dual-use or misuse of AI technologies, considering ethical implications in both intended and unintended applications. Defining ethical decision-making processes and establishing procedures for ethical reviews, especially in situations involving ambiguous ethical considerations, ensures that ethical considerations are embedded in AI development.

A culture of **continuous learning** and improvement in AI ethics is fostered through mechanisms for ongoing training and education on emerging ethical challenges and advancements.

Alignment with legal and regulatory standards is paramount, ensuring that ethical guidelines comply with existing and evolving legal frameworks. **Ethical impact assessments** should be integrated into the development process to systematically evaluate the ethical implications of AI projects.

Establishing channels for **whistleblowing and reporting ethical concerns**, along with ensuring protection for individuals who report violations, promotes accountability within organizations. Public awareness campaigns and educational resources contribute to informing users and the broader community about the ethical considerations of AI. Regularly reviewing and updating guidelines through a periodic review process ensures that they remain relevant and effective in the face of new insights, technological advancements, and societal changes.

By following these detailed steps, organizations can develop ethical guidelines for AI use that prioritize societal impact and consequences. Ethical AI Governance ensures responsible and sustainable deployment, fostering trust and positive contributions to society.

- *Encourage a culture of responsible AI use among employees and stakeholders.*

Developing a culture of responsible AI use within an organization is a fundamental aspect of ensuring ethical and effective deployment of AI technologies. The following twenty key points provide detailed insights into fostering such a culture:

1. **Develop Clear Ethical Guidelines:** Establishing clear and comprehensive ethical guidelines is crucial for shaping responsible AI practices within the organization. These guidelines should articulate the values, principles, and expectations related to AI use.
2. **Communicate Organizational Values:** Clear communication of the organization's commitment to responsible AI use is essential. This communication should align AI initiatives with the broader mission, vision, and values of the organization.
3. **Provide Training and Awareness Programs:** Offering training programs that educate employees and stakeholders on responsible AI use is essential. These programs should cover key concepts such as bias mitigation, fairness, transparency, and the ethical implications of AI decisions.
4. **Tailor Training to Different Roles:** Customizing training programs to the specific roles and responsibilities of different employees and stakeholders ensures targeted guidance based on their level of technical expertise and involvement with AI technologies.
5. **Encourage Continuous Learning:** Fostering a culture of continuous learning involves providing ongoing educational resources and updates on AI ethics. This approach ensures that employees are informed about emerging ethical considerations and best practices in AI.
6. **Establish an AI Ethics Committee:** Creating an AI Ethics Committee with representatives from various departments empowers the organization to guide and monitor responsible AI practices. This committee plays a crucial role in overseeing ethical considerations.
7. **Include Ethical Considerations in Decision-Making:** Integrating ethical considerations into decision-making processes related to AI initiatives is a critical step. Teams should be encouraged to weigh the ethical implications of their choices throughout the AI development lifecycle.
8. **Promote Transparency and Open Communication:** Cultivating an open communication culture where employees feel comfortable discussing ethical concerns related to AI is paramount. Promoting transparency in AI decision-making and outcomes builds trust within the organization.
9. **Establish Clear Reporting Mechanisms:** Implementing clear mechanisms for reporting ethical concerns or violations related to AI ensures that employees can report issues without fear of retaliation. This encourages a culture of accountability.
10. **Incorporate Ethical Reviews into Workflows:** Integrating ethical reviews into the regular workflows of AI projects ensures that ethical considerations are assessed at key milestones, including data collection, model development, and deployment.
11. **Recognize and Reward Ethical Behavior:** Recognizing and rewarding employees who demonstrate responsible AI practices reinforces the importance of ethical behavior. Acknowledging ethical considerations in performance evaluations and organizational recognition programs is crucial.
12. **Provide Ethical Decision-Making Support:** Offering tools and resources that assist employees in making ethical decisions related to AI is beneficial. Providing decision-making frameworks and guidelines helps navigate complex ethical considerations.

13. **Encourage Collaboration Across Teams:** Promoting collaboration between technical and non-technical teams to address ethical considerations fosters an interdisciplinary approach. Diverse perspectives contribute to well-rounded ethical decision-making.
14. **Offer Channels for Ethical Discussions:** Creating forums or channels for employees to engage in discussions about AI ethics provides a platform for sharing insights and exploring ethical challenges. Regular meetings or workshops can facilitate these discussions.
15. **Engage Stakeholders in Ethical Dialogue:** Including external stakeholders, such as customers and partners, in ethical discussions around AI ensures that diverse perspectives are considered. Seeking input and feedback from a broader audience enhances ethical decision-making.
16. **Implement Responsible AI Champions:** Appointing Responsible AI Champions within different teams or departments who serve as advocates for ethical practices helps disseminate knowledge throughout the organization.
17. **Embed Ethical Considerations in Governance Policies:** Integrating ethical considerations into overarching governance policies related to AI ensures that ethical guidelines become an integral part of the organizational DNA.
18. **Conduct Ethical Impact Assessments:** Implementing Ethical Impact Assessments (EIAs) as a proactive approach to assess the ethical implications of AI projects helps guide decision-making and identify potential ethical challenges.
19. **Encourage a Culture of Accountability:** Promoting individual and collective accountability for ethical AI practices emphasizes that responsible AI use is a shared responsibility across the organization.
20. **Regularly Evaluate and Update Initiatives:** Regularly evaluating the effectiveness of initiatives aimed at promoting responsible AI use and iterating on programs based on feedback, evolving ethical standards, and organizational needs ensures continuous improvement in fostering a culture of responsible AI.

By following these detailed steps, organizations can cultivate a culture of responsible AI use among employees and stakeholders. This culture helps ensure that AI technologies are deployed ethically, aligning with organizational values and contributing positively to society.

7. **Monitoring and Auditing**
    - *Implement monitoring mechanisms to track the performance of deployed AI models in real-world scenarios.*

Implementing monitoring mechanisms to track the performance of deployed AI models in real-world scenarios is crucial for ensuring ongoing effectiveness, identifying issues, and maintaining ethical and responsible AI practices.

From an AI Governance perspective, the process involves several detailed steps:

First, it's important to define **Key Performance Indicators** (KPIs) that align with the objectives and success criteria of the AI model, encompassing metrics such as accuracy, precision, recall, and fairness.

Following this, establishing baseline **performance metrics** upon deployment serves as a reference point for monitoring changes over time.

Real-time **monitoring mechanisms** are then implemented to track performance continuously, with alerts set up to identify and address deviations promptly. Tracking and analyzing inputs and outputs in real-world scenarios allow for the detection of shifts or anomalies that may affect model performance. Regular assessments of accuracy, precision, and robustness ensure that the model consistently provides reliable results under different conditions, including adversarial testing to enhance resilience. Monitoring for bias and fairness across diverse demographic groups is crucial, with necessary adjustments made to mitigate bias. Additionally, tracking model confidence levels and implementing feedback loops from end users and stakeholders help identify issues and improve performance.

Regular **audits** ensure compliance with ethical guidelines and regulatory requirements, with a focus on generalization performance and adaptability to evolving data patterns. Ethical and societal impacts are also considered, with documentation of monitoring processes maintained for transparency and accountability. External auditors may be engaged for independent assessments, and version control is implemented to track model evolution. Accountability mechanisms are defined to address performance issues and ethical concerns, while regular updates incorporate improvements and adapt to changing conditions.

Integration with **incident response** mechanisms ensures prompt addressing of performance issues, and compliance with regulations and standards governing AI deployment is maintained through ongoing awareness of emerging guidelines for responsible AI practices.

By following these detailed steps, organizations can establish effective monitoring mechanisms to track the performance of deployed AI models in real-world scenarios. This proactive approach helps maintain ethical standards, address issues promptly, and ensures that AI technologies continue to align with organizational goals and societal expectations.

8. Employee Training and Awareness

- *Provide training programs to employees to enhance their understanding of AI technologies and the importance of responsible AI use.*

Here are key steps for providing training programs to employees from an AI Governance perspective:

Initiating with an assessment of employees' existing AI knowledge and awareness levels regarding AI technologies and governance, organizations can identify specific areas requiring additional training.

Clear **training objectives** should be defined, aligning with AI Governance goals and organizational values.

Customized training content, tailored to different employee roles, should cover AI fundamentals, ethical principles, legal considerations, and governance policies. The inclusion of real-world examples and case studies can illustrate the practical implications of AI technologies, emphasizing responsible AI use and the consequences of ethical lapses.

Ethical frameworks and principles should be integrated into the training content, emphasizing fairness, transparency, accountability, and inclusivity in AI decision-making.

Providing insights into relevant **legal and regulatory frameworks** governing AI use ensures employees understand the legal implications of AI activities. Utilizing interactive learning methods, such as workshops and simulations, fosters engagement by encouraging discussions, questions, and practical applications. Offering flexibility in training formats, including in-person sessions, virtual classes, and self-paced resources, accommodates different learning preferences.

Engaging **subject matter experts** (SMEs), including AI specialists, ethicists, and legal professionals, as trainers or guest speakers, allows employees to interact with experts and gain deeper insights. Practical exercises that enable employees to apply theoretical concepts should be incorporated to reinforce responsible AI practices and decision-making. Establishing a training schedule ensures all employees have the opportunity to participate, with ongoing sessions addressing emerging trends and updates in the AI field.

Engaging **outside experts** may be beneficial. Once experts are selected, initial discussions are initiated to clarify expectations, discuss methodologies, and address any concerns. Signing **non-disclosure agreements** (NDAs) is a critical step to safeguard the confidentiality of sensitive information shared during the assessment. Providing external experts with access to relevant information, including documentation, datasets, and policies, is essential for a comprehensive evaluation.

Coordination of on-site visits or virtual meetings enables external experts to interact with key stakeholders, observe AI systems in action, and gain a deeper understanding of governance practices.

Facilitating **cross-functional collaboration** during training emphasizes the **interdisciplinary nature of responsible AI Governance**. Providing resources for self-learning, such as articles and research papers, creates a repository for continuous learning. Implementing pre- and post-assessments gauges baseline knowledge and measures knowledge retention, contributing to the overall assessment of the training program's effectiveness.

Fostering a culture of questioning and implementing a feedback mechanism gathers input from employees, refining and improving future training sessions. Incorporating relevant case studies showcases positive and challenging AI implementations, extracting valuable lessons learned and best practices. Emphasizing the importance of continuous learning in the rapidly evolving field of AI encourages employees to stay informed about industry developments and ethical considerations. Lastly, recognizing and celebrating instances of responsible AI use within the organization serves to showcase examples of employees applying their training to make ethical and informed decisions.

By following these detailed steps, organizations can develop and implement comprehensive training programs that enhance employees' understanding of AI technologies and emphasize the importance of responsible AI use within the framework of AI Governance.

- *Participate in industry collaborations and standards development to stay informed about best practices and emerging trends in AI Governance.*

Participating in industry collaborations and standards development is helpful for staying informed about best practices and emerging trends in AI Governance. Here are detailed steps from an AI Governance perspective:

To begin, organizations need to identify relevant industry collaborations, consortiums, alliances, or working groups dedicated to AI Governance and standards. Researching existing standards organizations, such as **IEEE, ISO,** and industry-specific bodies, helps to understand the landscape of established norms and practices.

After evaluating the relevance of these collaborations to the specific sector and AI applications, organizations should assess membership requirements, considering costs, commitments, and benefits associated with joining. Actively participating in these groups (such as the Certified Information Governance Officers Association, CIGOA) as members allows organizations to gain access to valuable resources, networks, and collaborative initiatives.

Engaging in working groups within industry collaborations or standards organizations that focus on AI Governance is a proactive step. Organizations can contribute their expertise, share experiences, and collaborate with peers from different backgrounds. Staying informed about developments in

AI Governance, standards, and best practices involves actively participating in meetings, webinars, and conferences organized by these groups, as well as regularly reviewing publications and updates.

Building relationships with experts in AI Governance within these collaborations and standards organizations is essential. Engaging in discussions, seeking mentorship, and leveraging the collective knowledge of the community contribute to the organization's growth. Hosting or attending workshops, seminars, and training sessions organized by these groups provides insights into emerging trends, challenges, and solutions in AI Governance.

Active participation in policy and advocacy initiatives led by industry collaborations or standards organizations allows organizations to shape industry guidelines and influence regulatory frameworks related to AI. Facilitating cross-industry collaboration and encouraging dialogue between organizations with diverse experiences fosters a collaborative environment that addresses shared challenges in AI Governance.

Implementing learnings and best practices gained from these collaborations within the organization ensures alignment with emerging standards and guidelines. Seeking **certification programs** (such as the **Certified Information Governance Officer/AI** from CIGOA.org) offered by industry collaborations or standards organizations demonstrates a commitment to responsible AI practices. Regularly monitoring changes in industry standards and best practices allows organizations to adapt internal governance processes and policies in response to evolving norms.

Contributing actively to the evolution of standards by providing feedback, participating in revision processes, and staying engaged in ongoing discussions is desired. Participating in industry events, conferences, and forums organized by these collaborations helps network with professionals, share experiences, and stay updated on the latest developments. Sharing success stories and challenges within these collaborations contributes to a culture of transparency and shared learning.

Demonstrating leadership in AI Governance within the industry involves actively participating in discussions, leading initiatives, and contributing thought leadership. This showcases the organization's commitment to responsible and ethical AI practices, establishing it as a leader in the evolving landscape of AI Governance.

9. **Continuous Improvement**
    - *Establish a process for continuous improvement of AI Governance practices based on feedback, evolving technologies, and changing regulatory landscapes.*

Establishing a robust process for the continuous improvement of AI Governance practices is indispensable for organizations seeking to adapt to evolving technologies, address feedback, and remain compliant with changing regulatory landscapes.

The initial step involves defining clear governance objectives, including ethical considerations, regulatory compliance, and alignment with organizational goals. Measurable metrics are essential to assess the effectiveness of governance practices, emphasizing transparency and accountability.

Identifying **key performance indicators** (KPIs) that align with AI Governance objectives is crucial for monitoring progress and addressing specific areas of concern.

Feedback mechanisms should be implemented to capture input from stakeholders, fostering a culture where reporting concerns and suggestions for improvement are actively promoted. Regular audits and assessments of AI Governance practices are essential, ensuring ongoing compliance with internal policies, industry standards, and regulatory requirements.

Keeping informed about regulatory changes related to AI and data privacy is important. Organizations need to stay vigilant, monitor evolving regulations, and adapt policies accordingly. Regularly reviewing and updating AI Governance policies and procedures to reflect changes in regulations, technologies, and industry best practices is an ongoing responsibility, and accessibility of these policies to relevant stakeholders is key.

Establishing a **risk management framework** is critical to identify, assess, and mitigate risks associated with AI implementations. This involves conducting regular risk assessments to proactively address potential challenges.

Cross-functional collaboration between departments, including IT, Legal, RIM, Risk Management, Privacy, Security, Compliance, Audit, and business units, is necessary to address the diverse aspects of AI Governance comprehensively.

Providing **continuous training and education** to keep employees updated on AI Governance practices, ethical considerations, and regulatory changes is essential. Tailoring training content to address evolving challenges and advancements ensures relevance. Conducting incident response drills is crucial to assess the organization's readiness to handle AI-related incidents and identify areas for improvement.

Utilizing external assessments by engaging external experts or third-party assessors for periodic evaluations enhances the organization's perspective, identifying blind spots and areas for improvement. Fostering an environment of open communication where employees feel comfortable sharing concerns and insights related to AI Governance is crucial. Establishing channels for anonymous reporting, if needed, contributes to an open and honest feedback culture.

Regularly evaluating user feedback and experiences with AI systems is key. Considering user satisfaction, perception of fairness, and concerns raised by end users informs improvements. Implementing monitoring mechanisms to continuously track the performance of AI models in real-world scenarios, assessing accuracy, bias, and overall effectiveness over time, is crucial.

Regularly reviewing data governance practices ensures the quality, integrity, and security of data used for AI training and decision-making. Enhancing data governance processes based on lessons learned and emerging requirements is part of the continuous improvement process. Adopting and promoting ethical AI principles within the organization and integrating ethical considerations into the development and deployment of AI systems are essential.

Documenting lessons learned from incidents, audits, and feedback is a valuable practice. Insights gained can inform future decision-making and governance improvements. Prioritizing high-impact improvements based on their potential impact on AI Governance objectives is necessary, addressing critical issues promptly and allocating resources strategically.

Forming a dedicated team responsible for overseeing continuous improvement initiatives in AI Governance is beneficial. Including members from relevant departments ensures diverse perspectives. Transparently communicating improvements made in AI Governance practices to internal and external stakeholders builds trust by demonstrating a commitment to learning and adapting over time.

By following these detailed steps, organizations can establish a robust process for continuous improvement of AI Governance practices. This iterative approach ensures that governance frameworks remain adaptive, effective, and aligned with the evolving landscape of AI technologies, regulatory requirements, and ethical considerations.

Key Points

- Business units play a pivotal role by aligning AI initiatives with the broader business strategy.
- Defining clear goals and objectives for AI implementation aligned with overall business strategy is a critical step in effective AI Governance, and it ensures that AI initiatives contribute to the organization's business objectives.
- Establishing key performance indicators (KPIs) directly linked to AI objectives and assessing progress against benchmarks ensures ongoing success.
- Addressing potential risks associated with AI implementation and developing mitigation strategies demonstrate proactive AI Governance.
- Collaboration across departments is essential for cross-functional alignment.
- Implementing a robust monitoring and evaluation system allows for regular reviews of progress against objectives, making adjustments as needed.
- Regularly reviewing and iterating the AI strategy based on lessons learned and changes in the business environment ensures continuous improvement.
- Identifying key stakeholders and establishing their roles and responsibilities is a crucial step in developing an effective AI Governance framework.
- Business units play a crucial role in shaping and implementing effective AI Governance in the development of policies for ethical AI use, data privacy, and compliance.
- Engaging executive leadership is essential, involving them in communicating the importance of AI Governance and obtaining their support for the framework.
- Conducting a regulatory impact assessment allows organizations to evaluate how each regulation or standard influences AI activities, pinpointing specific requirements related to data processing, consent, transparency, and accountability.
- Conducting a regulatory impact assessment allows organizations to evaluate how each regulation influences AI activities related to data processing, consent, transparency, and accountability.
- A data privacy policy is crucial, outlining the handling of sensitive data in AI processes, including specifying data collection, storage, processing, and sharing practices.
- Privacy by Design is emphasized, integrating privacy considerations into the entire AI development lifecycle from the outset of projects.
- The implementation of bias detection and mitigation policies is critical, with regular audits and updates to address emerging challenges.
- An incident response plan is developed to address potential breaches, violations, or ethical concerns, with clear procedures for reporting and responding to incidents.
- Seeking legal counsel is advisable to ensure policies align with legal requirements.
- Business units play a critical role by conducting a comprehensive risk assessment, in consultation with risk professionals, to identify and mitigate potential risks.
- Ethical considerations are integrated into the risk assessment, with a focus on societal impact, privacy, and potential discrimination issues.
- Identified risks are then prioritized based on their potential impact and likelihood, with a focus on high-priority risks.
- Algorithmic risks are evaluated, focusing on potential biases, fairness issues, and unintended consequences of the algorithms.

- Risk mitigation strategies are developed for each identified risk, considering both preventive and corrective measures, and assigning responsibilities for these strategies.
- A data governance assessment is conducted to evaluate the quality, integrity, and security of the data used by the AI system.
- Documentation related to AI development, including model documentation, codebase, and implementation guidelines, is thoroughly reviewed to ensure transparency.
- A communication plan is developed to keep stakeholders informed about identified risks, mitigation strategies, and ongoing monitoring efforts.
- Procedures for regulatory reporting in case of incidents or breaches are established to ensure compliance.
- Periodic audits are conducted to review the effectiveness of risk mitigation measures, and the risk assessment is continuously updated.
- Data privacy safeguards are strengthened through measures such as encryption, anonymization, and access controls, with regular audits to ensure compliance.
- Continuous monitoring systems for AI operations are implemented, utilizing real-time monitoring tools to detect anomalies and potential risks promptly.
- User feedback mechanisms are established to allow users to provide input on AI system performance, enabling the identification of potential issues and areas for improvement.
- Regularly reviewing and updating risk assessments is crucial to ensure that AI Governance remains effective and aligned.
- Regular reviews of risks associated with third-party components, including vendor relationships, should align with the organization's risk tolerance.
- Implementing robust data governance practices is essential for ensuring the quality, integrity, and security of data used for AI training and decision-making.
- Creating an inventory of all data assets used in AI processes and classifying data based on sensitivity, criticality, and relevance are crucial steps.
- Data quality standards need to be established, defining acceptable levels of accuracy, completeness, consistency, and timeliness.
- Ensuring data traceability by implementing mechanisms to trace the origin and lineage of data used in AI models is essential.
- Clear data ownership should be defined for each dataset, and data stewards appointed to oversee the quality and integrity of specific datasets.
- Creating a centralized data catalog that provides metadata and documentation for all datasets is important for transparency.
- Access controls should be defined and enforced to restrict data access based on roles and responsibilities, and encryption and anonymization techniques should be implemented to protect sensitive data.
- In consultation with the RIM function, establishing data retention and deletion policies to manage the lifecycle of data used in AI ensures compliance.
- It is important to perform data impact assessments to evaluate the potential consequences of data breaches or unauthorized access and developing mitigation strategies to offset them.
- Providing data governance training programs to educate employees on data governance policies fosters a culture of awareness and responsibility regarding data management.

- Establishing robust data access controls and permissions is crucial for protecting sensitive information in the context of AI Governance.
- Role-Based Access Control (RBAC) is crucial, where permissions are assigned based on job roles and responsibilities, following the Principle of Least Privilege.
- Attribute-Based Access Control (ABAC) should be implemented, utilizing attributes such as user attributes, data classification, and environmental conditions to determine access.
- Data masking and anonymization techniques should be applied to protect sensitive information.
- Emergency access procedures need to be well-defined, documented, time-limited, and subject to post-event review.
- Automating access provisioning and deprovisioning ensures that access is promptly revoked for employees who leave the organization or change roles.
- An audit of the training data is essential to identify potential biases, analyzing data across different demographic groups to uncover disparities.
- Employing bias detection tools helps identify and measure bias in both the training data and model outcomes, with regular updates as new methods emerge.
- Pre-processing techniques, such as re-sampling, re-weighting, or generating synthetic data, can mitigate bias.
- LIME is a valuable tool in the broader field of explainable AI (XAI), helping bridge the gap between complex models and the need for transparency and interpretability.
- Continuous updates to training data to reflect changes in the real-world environment are crucial, incorporating feedback loops.
- Implementing a transparent and reproducible model development process is a cornerstone of effective AI Governance.
- A version control system, such as Git, should be established to track changes consistently across code, data, and model artifacts.
- To enhance interpretability, *model interpretability* F1 score *techniques* should be applied, and their impact on understanding the model's decisions should be documented.
- The F1 score is the harmonic mean of precision and recall. It provides a balance between precision and recall and is especially useful when there is an uneven class distribution.
- Sensitivity analysis, which explores how changes in input features affect predictions, should be conducted and documented.
- From an AI Governance perspective, regular validation of AI models is crucial to ensure ongoing performance and prevent unintended biases over time.
- Continuous monitoring systems are implemented to assess the model's sensitivity to concept drift and detect deviations from expected behavior in real-time.
- Model interpretability is revisited to guarantee that the model's decisions remain understandable and aligned with expectations.
- Maintaining a model registry becomes integral for traceability and auditing purposes, tracking versions of the model, training data, and validation results over time.
- Hyperparameters are set in advance and influence the learning process of a machine learning model.
- Version control systems are leveraged to track changes in code, data, and model artifacts, associating decision logs with specific versions to maintain a chronological record.

- Explainability is a fundamental aspect of AI Governance that revolves around making the *decision-making processes of AI systems understandable and transparent to humans.*
- *In contexts where AI decisions have significant consequences, such as healthcare or finance, the need for explainability becomes even more critical.*
- Transparency extends beyond merely revealing the final outputs of AI models; it encompasses the entire lifecycle of AI development.
- Transparency extends to the origins of the training data, known as data provenance.
- In the realm of AI Governance, effectively communicating AI decisions and predictions to stakeholders is a fundamental aspect that demands careful consideration.
- Protecting user data privacy is a key ethical consideration, and guidelines should detail how personal data will be handled, ensuring compliance with data protection regulations.
- Risk disclosure is inherent in transparent AI, as organizations openly communicate potential risks and limitations associated with their models.
- Establishing channels for whistleblowing and reporting ethical concerns, along with ensuring protection for individuals who report violations, promotes accountability.
- Implementing monitoring mechanisms to track the performance of deployed AI models in real-world scenarios is crucial for ensuring ongoing effectiveness, identifying issues, and maintaining ethical and responsible AI practices.
- Providing training programs to employees is key to their understanding of AI technologies and the importance of responsible AI use.
- Initiating with an assessment of employees' existing AI knowledge can identify specific areas requiring additional training.
- Engaging with external experts, consultants, or organizations for independent assessments of AI systems and governance practices is a valuable step in ensuring objectivity, thorough evaluation, and adherence to best practices.
- Participating in industry collaborations and standards development is crucial for staying informed about best practices and emerging trends in AI Governance.
- Establishing a robust process for the continuous improvement of AI Governance practices is indispensable for organizations seeking to adapt to evolving technologies, address feedback, and remain compliant with changing regulatory landscapes.

Key Glossary Terms

Data provenance: The history of data throughout its lifecycle. It encompasses information about the origin, ownership, processing steps, transformations, and any changes that occur to the data from its initial collection to its utilization.

F1 score: A metric commonly used in ML that combines both precision and recall into a single value. Precision is the number of true positive predictions divided by the total number of positive predictions made by the model. It measures the accuracy of the positive predictions. Recall the number of true positive predictions divided by the total number of actual positives in the dataset. It measures the model's ability to capture all the positive instances.

- Precision is the number of true positive predictions divided by the total number of positive predictions made by the model. It measures the accuracy of the positive predictions.
- Recall the number of true positive predictions divided by the total number of actual positives in the dataset. It measures the model's ability to capture all the positive instances.

Feature Importance: Central to explainability is the communication of the importance of individual features in the decision-making process. This involves conveying which aspects of the input data had the most significant influence on the model's output.

Human-in-the-Loop: Systems that include human involvement in the decision-making process.

Hyperparameters: External configuration settings that are not learned from the training data but are set before the training process begins. These influence the learning process of a machine learning model and are set in advance.

LIME (Local Interpretable Model-agnostic Explanations): A technique designed to enhance the interpretability of complex machine learning models.

Model card: A concise summary of the model, its intended use, performance metrics, and potential limitations that ensures accessibility to stakeholders and end users.

Probabilistic: Information presents predictions as probabilities, rather than absolutes.

SHAP: A model-agnostic technique to provide explainability of complex models. SHAP is rooted in cooperative game theory, providing a fair distribution of "credit" for the model's output to individual input features.

Notes

1 "What is the EU AI Act?" EU Artificial Intelligence Act, accessed July 16, 2024. https://artificialintelligenceact.eu/.

2 Ibid

11 The Role of Auditing in AI Governance

The auditing function in AI Governance plays a crucial role in ensuring that AI programs are properly governed, compliant with regulations, and meet ethical standards. An AI Governance program may look great on paper, but until it is audited to prove that the actions documented were, in fact, in place, there is no complete assurance that AI systems are being properly governed. *Auditing provides an independent and objective assessment of AI systems, helping organizations identify and mitigate risks.*[1]

Defining the **scope** and objectives of an AI audit is the initial step in ensuring that the audit process is effective and aligns with the goals of an AI Governance. A clear definition of the audit scope is vital by specifying the systems, processes, and components that will be included. This may involve determining whether the audit will cover the entire AI lifecycle or focus on specific phases.

To establish **audit objectives**, first, it is essential to gain a thorough understanding of the organization's business goals, strategies, and the role of AI within its processes. This understanding provides context for setting audit objectives.

Next, reviewing the existing **AI Governance Framework**, policies, and procedures helps in understanding how AI is currently managed, deployed, and governed within the organization. This will include, at a minimum, an **AI Governance Program Charter**, a listing of roles and responsibilities for key team members, cited core standards and regulations that must be followed as guardrails, key business objectives, and metrics that allow for progress toward business objectives to be tracked.

Identifying relevant regulatory and ethical requirements is crucial to align audit objectives with these considerations and assess compliance.

Collaboration with key stakeholders, including AI development teams, data scientists, privacy and security professionals, risk management staff, compliance officers, legal advisors, RIM professionals, and business unit leaders, *ensures a comprehensive understanding of AI processes.*

Considering **data governance** within the audit scope is essential to assess how data is collected, processed, stored, and used in AI systems, *ensuring alignment with data protection and privacy regulations.*

The evaluation of practices and methodologies employed in **AI model development**, as well as the assessment of model deployment and integration into existing systems, *helps in understanding the entire AI lifecycle.* The audit should also review **explainability** and **interpretability** of AI models, examining bias, fairness, and algorithmic accountability throughout the development and deployment phases.

Assuring security measures, including

1. data security,
2. access controls, and
3. protection against adversarial attacks

are critical aspects of the audit.

Ethical considerations, such as the *impact on societal values, privacy, and human rights*, should be included in the examination. If AI systems involve **automation and autonomy**, the audit should assess *controls and governance mechanisms in place to manage and oversee autonomous decision-making processes.*

Defining **performance metrics** for the audit, aligning with organizational **risk priorities,** and documenting the defined scope and objectives are crucial steps. Finally, seeking *approval from relevant stakeholders, including executive leadership, ensures consensus* on the focus areas and key aspects of the AI audit, contributing to the overall effectiveness of the auditing function in AI Governance.

By following these steps, organizations can establish clear and meaningful audit objectives that address the key aspects of AI Governance, compliance, and ethical considerations. This ensures that the audit process is targeted, effective, and aligned with organizational priorities.

Identify specific areas of focus, such as data privacy, model fairness, and security.

Identifying specific areas of focus for AI audit objectives is crucial to ensure a comprehensive assessment of AI programs. Below are the steps involved in establishing audit objectives with a focus on data privacy, model fairness, and security.

The process begins with conducting a thorough **risk assessment** of the AI systems, where potential risks associated with **data privacy, model fairness**, and **security** are identified. This involves considering the impact and likelihood of these risks on the organization.

Next, it is important to review relevant regulatory requirements, including data privacy regulations such as GDPR and HIPAA, CPRA and CCPA, and various state privacy regulations as guidelines on model fairness and cybersecurity standards. *This step ensures that audit objectives align with specific legal and regulatory expectations.*

Collaboration with key stakeholders, including legal, compliance, data science, IT, privacy, security, risk, RIM, and business teams, is essential. Understanding their concerns and priorities regarding data privacy, model fairness, and security helps in tailoring the audit objectives to meet organizational needs. The establishment of **audit objectives** related to **data privacy** involves *considerations such as how personally identifiable information (PII) is handled, compliance with data protection laws, and processes for obtaining and managing consent.*

Furthermore, the assessment of **data handling practices** within AI systems *evaluates how data is collected, processed, stored, and shared.* This includes an examination of whether adequate measures are in place to protect sensitive information and if data handling practices align with privacy regulations. The audit also includes an assessment of **consent mechanisms**, ensuring that user consent for data processing is obtained in an informed and explicit manner, in accordance with regulatory requirements.

Regarding **model fairness**, audit objectives are established by:

1. Considering methods used to assess and mitigate bias.
2. Monitoring mechanisms for fairness during model deployment.
3. Evaluation of the impact of model decisions on different demographic groups.

This involves reviewing bias mitigation strategies and defining and evaluating specific fairness metrics relevant to the organization and the application of AI.

For **security objectives**, the audit focuses on *the protection against unauthorized access, measures in place to prevent data breaches, and resilience against adversarial attacks*. Security audits evaluate the effectiveness of security measures in AI systems, including encryption practices, access controls, and monitoring for suspicious activities. Additionally, the review of **incident response plans** ensures that the organization has documented procedures for responding to security incidents and breaches related to AI systems.

Considering overarching governance objectives related to data privacy, model fairness, and security is crucial for a holistic assessment. These overarching objectives may encompass the effectiveness of governance structures and policies.

The final steps involve *clearly documenting the identified areas of focus and corresponding audit objectives, ensuring alignment with organizational priorities, regulatory requirements, and stakeholder expectations*. Stakeholder approval, including executive leadership, legal, and compliance teams, is sought for the defined audit objectives, and the objectives are communicated clearly to the audit teams involved in the assessment. This meticulous process ensures that the AI audit is comprehensive, targeted, and aligned with organizational goals.

By following these steps, organizations can tailor their audit objectives to specific areas of focus, such as data privacy, model fairness, and security, ensuring a targeted and effective audit process.

Collaborate with key stakeholders to understand business objectives and AI system functionalities.

Collaborating with key stakeholders is essential to establishing effective audit objectives that align with business objectives and AI system functionalities. Here are the steps involved in this process:

1. **Identify Key Stakeholders**
   Identify and compile a list of key stakeholders involved in AI development, deployment, and usage. This may include executives, data scientists, IT professionals, legal and compliance experts, and representatives from business units
2. **Conduct Stakeholder Meetings**
   Schedule and conduct meetings with key stakeholders to discuss the overall business objectives and strategies. Understand their perspectives on the role of AI in achieving these objectives and how AI systems contribute to business functions.
3. **Understand Business Objectives**
   Engage in discussions to gain a clear understanding of the organization's broader business objectives. Explore how AI initiatives support or enhance these objectives. Identify key performance indicators (KPIs) relevant to AI's impact on business success.
4. **Align AI Goals with Business Goals**
   Work with stakeholders to align the goals of AI initiatives with broader business goals. Identify specific AI-related objectives that contribute to achieving business outcomes. Ensure that AI projects are strategically aligned with the organization's mission and vision.

5. **Identify Critical AI Functionalities**

   Collaborate with technical stakeholders, including data scientists and IT professionals, to understand the critical functionalities of AI systems. This includes aspects such as data processing, model development, deployment, and integration with existing systems

6. **Assess AI System Architecture**

   Review the architecture of AI systems with technical stakeholders. Understand the technical components, data flows, and integration points. Identify potential areas of risk, such as data privacy concerns, model biases, or security vulnerabilities

7. **Discuss Ethical Considerations**

   Engage in discussions about ethical considerations related to AI. Collaborate with stakeholders to understand their perspectives on fairness, transparency, and accountability in AI decision-making processes. Address any ethical concerns raised by stakeholders.

8. **Explore Regulatory Requirements**

   Collaborate with legal and compliance experts to explore regulatory requirements relevant to AI. Understand the legal landscape and any industry-specific regulations that may impact AI Governance. Identify compliance goals and expectations.

9. **Document Stakeholder Inputs**

   Document the insights gathered from stakeholder meetings. Capture key business objectives, AI functionalities, architectural considerations, and ethical considerations, and regulatory requirements. Use this documentation as a foundation for defining audit objectives.

10. **Facilitate Cross-Functional Collaboration**

    Encourage cross-functional collaboration between business, technical, legal, and compliance teams. Create a collaborative environment where stakeholders from different domains can contribute their expertise to shape AI Governance and audit objectives.

11. **Validate Assumptions and Expectations**

    Validate assumptions and expectations with stakeholders to ensure a shared understanding. Address any discrepancies or conflicting viewpoints. Seek clarification on specific areas that may impact the establishment of audit objectives.

12. **Iterative Discussions and Refinement**

    Conduct iterative discussions with stakeholders to refine and fine-tune audit objectives. Ensure that the objectives accurately reflect the organization's priorities, mitigate risks, and align with the expectations of various stakeholders.

13. **Seek Executive Approval**

    Seek approval from executive leadership for the finalized audit objectives. Ensure that the objectives are endorsed at the highest levels of the organization to demonstrate commitment to AI Governance and compliance

14. **Communicate Objectives to Audit Teams**

    Clearly communicate the established audit objectives to the audit teams responsible for the assessment. Provide context on how the objectives align with business goals, functionalities, and stakeholder expectations.

By following these steps, organizations can collaboratively define audit objectives that are well-aligned with business objectives, AI system functionalities, and the expectations of key stakeholders. This collaborative approach ensures a holistic and informed perspective in the establishment of audit objectives.

- **Align audit objectives with regulatory requirements and industry standards.**

Aligning audit objectives with regulatory requirements and industry standards is a pivotal aspect of ensuring that AI programs adhere to legal and ethical guidelines.

The first step involves conducting a comprehensive analysis to *identify applicable regulations and industry standards* that impact AI systems.[2] This encompasses data protection laws, privacy regulations, industry-specific compliance standards, and ethical guidelines. Collaborating with **legal and compliance** experts within the organization is crucial during this process, as their insights are instrumental in gaining a deep understanding of the regulatory landscape and legal requirements relevant to AI Governance.

In addition to legal requirements, *ethical considerations are paramount.* Auditors should review ethical guidelines and frameworks specific to AI, which may be provided by industry organizations, governmental bodies, or international associations. These guidelines typically cover principles related to fairness, transparency, accountability, and non-discrimination. The audit objectives should reflect these ethical considerations to ensure that AI systems adhere to responsible practices.

Data protection and **privacy** requirements, especially those outlined in laws like GDPR and HIPAA, should be a focal point in defining audit objectives. The audit should assess how these regulations impact the collection, processing, and storage of personal and sensitive data within AI systems. Bias and fairness guidelines should also be considered, and audit objectives should be developed to assess the fairness of model outcomes and mitigate biases.

Security standards and best practices must be incorporated into audit objectives to ensure the robustness of AI systems against:

1. unauthorized access,
2. data breaches, and
3. other cybersecurity threats.

If applicable, regulations or standards emphasizing the **explainability** and **interpretability** of AI models should be taken into account. Audit objectives should assess whether AI systems provide clear explanations of decisions, particularly in sensitive or high-stakes applications.

Guidelines related to accountability and governance in AI should be reviewed to *establish audit objectives that assess the effectiveness of governance structures, decision-making processes, and mechanisms for addressing accountability.*

Transparency requirements from regulations or industry standards *should also be integrated into audit objectives* to ensure that AI systems provide understandable and transparent information to end users and stakeholders about their functionality and decision-making processes.

Documenting specific regulatory compliance goals derived from identified regulations and standards is crucial, and audit objectives should align with these documented goals.

Collaboration with regulatory authorities or industry bodies, when applicable, is recommended to gain insights into their expectations regarding AI Governance. This collaboration can provide clarification on specific audit areas that align with regulatory priorities.

Validation of compliance expectations with legal and compliance experts is necessary to ensure that audit objectives accurately reflect the organization's commitment to meeting regulatory requirements and industry standards. Integrating **continuous monitoring** mechanisms into audit objectives supports ongoing compliance with evolving regulations and standards. This includes developing audit criteria that facilitate continuous assessment and adaptation to changes in the regulatory landscape.

Lastly, *providing training to audit teams on specific regulatory requirements and industry standards relevant to AI Governance is essential.* This ensures that auditors are well-versed in the legal and ethical considerations associated with AI programs, enabling them to effectively assess and ensure compliance during the audit process.

By following these steps, organizations can align audit objectives with regulatory requirements and industry standards, thereby enhancing the effectiveness of AI Governance and ensuring compliance with legal and ethical guidelines.

Risk Assessment

- **Conduct a comprehensive risk assessment of AI programs.**

Conducting a comprehensive risk assessment of AI programs is essential for identifying and mitigating potential risks associated with their development, deployment, and use. Here are the steps involved in conducting a thorough risk assessment for AI programs (for more detail see the chapter on Risk Management).

In conducting a comprehensive AI system risk assessment for audits, a meticulous and structured approach is essential. First, the **scope of the risk assessment** must be clearly defined, delineating the boundaries across the AI program's lifecycle, encompassing development, deployment, maintenance, and usage phases. Subsequently, explicit **risk assessment objectives** should be set, aligning them with organizational goals and priorities. Objectives may center around operational, ethical, legal, or technical risks, or a combination thereof.

Identifying **key stakeholders** *and experts forms the next crucial step, including data scientists, developers, legal experts, compliance officers, and* end users. Engaging subject matter experts ensures a nuanced understanding of specific risks associated with AI technologies. Thoroughly compiling information on AI program components, including algorithms, data sources, training processes, deployment environments, and use cases, serves as the foundational step for understanding potential risks.

Data quality and **bias evaluation** should be conducted, scrutinizing the training data's quality and potential biases that may lead to unfair outcomes, particularly with regard to different demographic groups. Analyzing **model complexity and explainability** becomes key, acknowledging that complex models may pose challenges in interpreting and explaining decisions, impacting transparency and trust.

Legal and **regulatory compliance** *assessment is essential*, requiring a review of applicable laws governing AI technologies, with a specific focus on data protection, privacy, anti-discrimination, and other legal requirements. The ethical and societal impacts of AI technologies must also be scrutinized, evaluating issues related to fairness, accountability, transparency, and the broader societal implications of AI-driven decisions.

Analyze **security risks**, *including vulnerabilities in software, exposure to cyber threats, and risks related to unauthorized access.* Deployment and operational risks, such as system integration challenges and scalability issues, are then assessed, recognizing the potential impact of changing operational environments.

Vendor and **third-party risks** *are scrutinized if external components or services are integrated into the AI program.* This involves an evaluation of data privacy, security, and the reliability of external services. Quantifying and qualifying risks follows, assigning risk levels based on likelihood and potential impact, utilizing a mix of quantitative and qualitative methods, and prioritizing risks according to organizational significance.

Proposing effective risk mitigation strategies is the subsequent step, involving adjustments to the AI model, enhancements in data quality, fortified security measures, or operational procedure modifications. Documenting and communicating findings is crucial, detailing identified risks, potential consequences, and recommended mitigation strategies to relevant stakeholders, including executives, developers, and compliance officers.

Finally, recognizing the dynamic nature of the risk landscape, organizations are urged to iterate and update their risk assessments periodically. Establishing a proactive process ensures ongoing vigilance and adaptability to address emerging risks effectively.

By following these steps, organizations can conduct a comprehensive risk assessment of AI programs, enabling them to make informed decisions, implement effective risk mitigation strategies, and enhance the overall governance of AI technologies.

Compliance Check

- **Verify that AI programs comply with relevant laws and regulations**. (Note: See more detail in the Legal chapter.)

Conducting a **compliance check** to verify that AI programs adhere to relevant laws and regulations is imperative for ensuring ethical and lawful AI deployment.

To begin, organizations need to *create a comprehensive list of laws, regulations, and standards applicable to AI in their industry and geographic location.*[3] This includes considering data protection laws, industry-specific regulations, ethical guidelines, and international standards. Following this, a compliance framework should be established, outlining specific requirements and obligations set forth by identified laws and regulations. Criteria defining AI program compliance should be clearly defined, referring to specific legal requirements such as GDPR, HIPAA, US state privacy laws, or industry-specific regulations.

Documenting the design and functionality of the AI system is crucial, encompassing data sources, processing methods, decision-making algorithms, and any external components. This documentation forms the basis for assessing compliance. *The evaluation process should include an assessment of data handling practices,* ensuring alignment with data protection regulations and verifying the presence of consent mechanisms, anonymization techniques, and data retention policies.

Moreover, it is *essential to check model training and validation procedures, focusing on the representativeness, unbiased nature, and diversity of* **training data**. Measures to mitigate algorithmic bias and discrimination in decision-making processes should be examined. The **explainability** and **transparency** of the AI model should be assessed, particularly in critical applications like finance, healthcare, or employment.

Verification of **accountability mechanisms** is equally important, confirming the existence of oversight, monitoring, and processes for handling accountability in cases of adverse events or unintended consequences.

Privacy measures and **consent mechanisms** need to be reviewed to ensure compliance with privacy regulations, including how user consent is obtained, stored, and managed throughout the AI lifecycle.

The assessment should extend to fairness and non-discrimination in AI decision-making, evaluating steps taken to identify and mitigate bias in algorithms. Additionally, cybersecurity measures must be evaluated to protect AI systems from unauthorized access, data breaches, and other security threats, ensuring compliance with relevant regulations and industry standards.

An **ethical impact assessment** should be conducted to evaluate broader societal implications, considering social, economic, and cultural impacts in alignment with ethical guidelines and principles.

Collaboration with legal and compliance teams is crucial to staying updated on regulatory changes and ensuring accurate interpretation and application of laws and regulations.

Documentation of compliance findings is essential for internal **records** and potential external **audits**.

If compliance gaps are identified, corrective action plans should be developed, outlining timelines for implementation and assigning responsibilities for each action item. Regularly updating and repeating compliance checks is critical, especially with changes in regulations, laws, or the AI program itself, to ensure ongoing compliance.

Considering external auditors or third-party experts for an independent assessment of compliance is advisable, providing an additional layer of assurance and objectivity. Finally, communicating the compliance status to relevant stakeholders, including leadership, legal teams, and regulatory authorities, is key for building trust and transparency about compliance efforts and outcomes.

By systematically following these steps, organizations can conduct a thorough compliance check to ensure that their AI programs align with relevant laws and regulations, fostering ethical and responsible AI deployment. This process contributes to the overall governance framework and risk management strategy within the organization.

- **Ensure adherence to internal policies and industry standards.**

Ensuring adherence to internal policies and industry standards is a critical aspect of the compliance check in AI Governance.

To begin, organizations must thoroughly *review their internal policies related to AI development, deployment, and usage.* This examination ensures that internal policies align with ethical guidelines, legal requirements, and industry best practices. Simultaneously, *identifying relevant industry standards is crucial,* as organizations need to compile a comprehensive list of industry-specific standards and guidelines applicable to AI systems in their sector. This includes **ISO standards, IEEE standards, industry consortium guidelines,** and other relevant benchmarks.

Understanding **ethical guidelines** and principles governing AI usage, such as fairness, transparency, accountability, and non-discrimination, is fundamental.

Organizations should develop a **compliance framework** *that encompasses internal policies, industry standards, and ethical guidelines.* This framework should clearly outline the specific requirements and expectations for AI systems within the organization.

Documenting internal policies and industry standards applicable to AI Governance is essential, ensuring accessibility to relevant stakeholders and regular updates as policies and standards evolve.

Aligning the design and development of AI programs with the principles outlined in internal policies and industry standards is crucial. This alignment covers various aspects, including data handling practices, model training methodologies, and decision-making processes.

Verification of **model interpretability** is necessary, especially for compliance with standards that emphasize transparency and interpretability. Evaluating **security measures** to ensure compliance with internal cybersecurity policies and industry-specific security standards is equally important. This assessment verifies protection against unauthorized access, data breaches, and other security threats.

In terms of **data privacy compliance**, organizations need to ensure that AI systems comply with internal data privacy policies and industry regulations, such as GDPR, HIPAA, US state privacy laws, or other regional data protection laws. This involves assessing mechanisms for obtaining and managing user consent, anonymization practices, and data access controls.

Checking for bias mitigation measures is important, ensuring alignment with internal policies and industry standards addressing fairness and non-discrimination. Verification of **accountability mechanisms**, such as responsibilities for oversight, monitoring, and addressing issues during AI system operation, is also important.

Continuous monitoring practices must be in place to align with internal policies and industry standards. This involves regularly assessing AI systems for performance, security, and compliance, and implementing corrective actions as needed. *Documentation of specific measures implemented to ensure compliance serves as evidence* during internal reviews or external audits.

Periodically conducting internal audits is recommended to assess the effectiveness of compliance measures, identify areas for improvement, and ensuring ongoing alignment with policies and standards.

Providing training sessions for employees involved in AI development and deployment, ensuring awareness and understanding of internal policies and industry standards, fosters a culture of compliance within the organization.

Considering **external certification** or **engaging third-party auditors** to validate compliance with industry standards adds an additional layer of assurance and credibility. Finally, staying abreast of changes in internal policies and industry standards and regularly reviewing and updating documentation to reflect the latest requirements is crucial for maintaining compliance.

By systematically following these steps, organizations can conduct a comprehensive compliance check to ensure adherence to internal policies and industry standards, contributing to the ethical and responsible deployment of AI systems.

Data Governance Assessment

- **Evaluate the processes and controls related to data governance in AI.**

Conducting a Data Governance Assessment is crucial to ensure that AI programs adhere to established data governance processes and controls. Here are the steps involved in evaluating data governance for AI:

1. **Define Assessment Objectives**

   Clearly outline the objectives of the data governance assessment. Identify key aspects such as data quality, data integrity, data security, data privacy, and compliance with relevant regulations.

2. **Identify Stakeholders**

   Identify and involve key stakeholders, including data scientists, data engineers, IT personnel, legal and compliance teams, and business representatives. Ensure representation from various departments that contribute to or are impacted by AI data.

3. **Review Data Governance Framework**

   Examine the existing data governance framework within the organization. This includes policies, procedures, and guidelines related to data management, data quality, and data security.

4. **Understand Data Lifecycle**

   Map out the entire data lifecycle, from data acquisition and storage to processing, analysis, and disposal. Understand how data moves through the organization and its use in AI applications.

5. **Identify Data Sources**

   List and categorize the sources of data used in AI systems. Identify internal and external data sources, ensuring that data origins are well-documented and comply with data governance standards.

6. **Evaluate Data Quality**

   Assess the quality of data used in AI models. Consider factors such as accuracy, completeness, consistency, and timeliness. Implement data profiling techniques to identify potential issues in data quality.

7. **Assess Data Security Measures**

   Review the security measures in place to protect data used in AI systems. Evaluate access controls, encryption practices, and measures to prevent unauthorized access or data breaches.

8. **Examine Data Privacy Controls**

   Assess how well data privacy controls are implemented in the context of AI applications. Ensure compliance with relevant data protection laws (e.g., GDPR, HIPAA) and assess mechanisms for obtaining and managing consent.

9. **Check Data Ownership and Responsibility**

   Clarify data ownership and responsibilities. Identify individuals or teams responsible for different stages of the data lifecycle, including data collection, processing, and storage.

10. **Verify Data Cataloging and Metadata Management**

    Evaluate the effectiveness of data cataloging and metadata management practices. Ensure that there is a comprehensive catalog of available data, along with metadata that describes the characteristics and context of each dataset.

11. **Review Data Access and Usage Policies**

    Assess the policies governing data access and usage. Ensure that there are clear guidelines on who can access specific datasets, how data can be used, and any restrictions in place.

12. **Evaluate Data Governance Tools**

    Assess the tools and technologies in use for data governance. Consider whether there are adequate tools for data profiling, metadata management, data lineage tracking, and other aspects of effective data governance.

13. **Assess Data Governance Training and Awareness**

    Evaluate the training programs and awareness initiatives related to data governance. Ensure that employees involved in AI activities are knowledgeable about data governance principles and best practices.

14. **Check for Compliance with Regulations**

    Ensure that data governance practices align with relevant data protection and privacy regulations. Conduct regular compliance checks to verify adherence to laws such as GDPR, HIPAA, or industry-specific standards.

15. **Conduct Data Risk Assessment**

    Identify and assess potential risks associated with data usage in AI applications. This includes risks related to data quality, security, privacy, and compliance.

16. **Document Findings and Recommendations**

    Document the findings from the data governance assessment. Clearly outline areas of strength and weakness, and provide recommendations for improvement.

17. **Develop a Data Governance Roadmap**

    Based on the assessment, create a roadmap for enhancing data governance practices. Prioritize actions that address critical issues and contribute to a more robust data governance framework.

18. **Implement Continuous Monitoring**

    Establish mechanisms for continuous monitoring of data governance practices. Regularly review and update processes based on changes in data sources, regulations, or organizational requirements.

Establish mechanisms for continuous monitoring of data governance practices. Regularly review and update processes based on changes in data sources, regulations, or organizational requirements.

By systematically following these steps, organizations can conduct a comprehensive data governance assessment to ensure that AI programs are built on a foundation of reliable, secure, and ethically managed data.

- **Assess data quality, integrity, and privacy practices** (see Privacy module for more details).

Conducting a Data Governance Assessment to evaluate data quality, integrity, and privacy practices involves a series of steps. Below is a detailed description of the key steps in assessing these aspects.

In conducting a comprehensive Data Governance Assessment within the AI Governance audit process, a systematic approach is imperative to evaluate data quality, integrity, and privacy practices.

The first step involves clearly outlining the assessment objectives, emphasizing a focus on key criteria and indicators for each aspect—data quality, integrity, and privacy. To ensure a holistic perspective, the involvement of key stakeholders from relevant departments is important, including data stewards in business units, data scientists, data engineers, IT personnel, compliance officers, and individuals responsible for data privacy and cybersecurity.

A critical examination of the existing **data governance framework** *within the organization is the subsequent step,* delving into policies, procedures, and guidelines pertaining to data quality, integrity, and privacy. Mapping out the entire data lifecycle is necessary, emphasizing critical touchpoints vulnerable or critical to these aspects. Employing data profiling and analysis techniques, the assessment proceeds to evaluate data quality, considering factors such as accuracy, completeness, consistency, timeliness, and relevance, utilizing statistical methods and data profiling tools.

The integrity of data is then assessed, ensuring accuracy and unaltered status throughout the lifecycle, with scrutiny for mechanisms preventing corruption, loss, or unauthorized modifications. Evaluating data privacy controls is a key next step, ensuring compliance with relevant data protection laws and assessing mechanisms for obtaining and managing consent, along with reviewing anonymization and pseudonymization practices.

Reviewing **security measures**, including access controls, encryption practices, and measures to prevent unauthorized access or data breaches, is essential. The *effectiveness of* **data cataloging** *and* **metadata management** *practices is then evaluated to ens*ure a comprehensive catalog and detailed metadata for each dataset.

Continuous monitoring of data quality is assessed, verifying the presence of mechanisms for identifying and addressing deviations from established standards. Evaluation of tools and technologies used for data governance, particularly those related to data quality and integrity, is conducted. Training programs and awareness initiatives related to data privacy are assessed, ensuring employee knowledge of data privacy principles and awareness of their responsibilities.

Practices related to data retention and deletion are scrutinized, emphasizing secure deletion when data is no longer needed. The review extends to policies addressing data quality, integrity, and privacy, checking for clarity, completeness, and alignment with regulatory requirements. Privacy Impact Assessments (PIAs) for systems handling sensitive data are examined for effectiveness in identifying and mitigating privacy risks.

Verification of compliance with relevant data protection and privacy regulations, such as GDPR, HIPAA, or industry-specific standards, is essential. Documenting findings related to data quality, integrity, and privacy practices follows, outlining areas of strength and weakness, alongside recommendations for improvement. Based on the assessment, a roadmap is developed to enhance data governance practices, prioritizing actions addressing critical issues and contributing to a more robust framework. Establishing mechanisms for continuous monitoring is the final step, ensuring regular review and updates based on changes in data sources, regulations, or organizational requirements.

By following these steps, organizations can systematically assess and enhance their data governance practices, ensuring that data quality, integrity, and privacy are effectively managed across the AI lifecycle.

- **Review data management policies and procedures.**

In enforcing AI Governance, reviewing data management policies and procedures as part of a **Data Governance Assessment** involves a series of critical steps to *ensure that the organization's approach to handling data is comprehensive, effective, and aligned with its objectives.*

Firstly, it is essential to define the assessment objectives clearly. This includes specifying areas of focus, such as data collection, storage, processing, sharing, and disposal.

Identifying **key stakeholders** *from relevant departments is crucial*, ensuring diverse representation from end users or data stewards, data scientists, data engineers, IT personnel, compliance officers, legal, privacy, security, risk, RIM, and individuals responsible for data governance.

The assessment should begin with a review of the overall data governance framework within the organization. This involves examining the presence and effectiveness of policies and procedures governing data management practices. A compilation of all policies and procedures related to data management is then created, covering aspects such as data **classification**, **retention,** ownership, sharing, and more.

To ensure the effectiveness of these policies, it is important to assess their clarity and completeness. This involves *evaluating whether policies are clearly articulated*, easy to understand, and cover all necessary aspects of data management. Checking alignment with regulatory requirements is also crucial, verifying that data management policies align with relevant data protection laws, industry regulations, and organizational standards.

Specifically, ***the review should include policies that define data ownership and responsibility, data classification, data sharing and access, data retention and disposal, data quality management, data security, data privacy, and incident response and breach notification.*** The effectiveness of training programs related to data governance policies should be assessed to ensure that employees are adequately trained in data management practices and are aware of their responsibilities.

The evaluation should extend to the tools and technologies used to enforce data management policies. This ensures that there are mechanisms for monitoring and enforcing compliance with policies effectively. Documenting the findings from the review is critical, outlining areas of strength and weakness, and providing recommendations for improvement. Subsequently, a **data governance roadmap** should be developed based on the assessment, prioritizing actions that address critical issues and contribute to a more robust data governance framework.

Lastly, to maintain the effectiveness of data management policies and procedures, it is important to implement **continuous monitoring** mechanisms. Regularly reviewing and updating policies based on changes in regulations, technology, or organizational requirements ensures that the data governance framework remains adaptive and resilient.

Model Validation and Performance Assessment

- **Verify the accuracy and reliability of AI models.**

In the audit process of AI Governance enforcement, Model Validation and Performance Assessment involves a series of key steps to verify the accuracy and reliability of AI models.

To begin, it is essential to define the **assessment objectives**, clearly outlining criteria for accuracy, reliability, and other relevant performance metrics. This process requires the involvement of key stakeholders, including data scientists, machine learning engineers, domain experts, and business representatives, collaborating to understand business requirements and expectations.

Reviewing **model documentation** is a foundational step, examining details such as model architecture, algorithms used, and hyperparameters. This ensures clear documentation on the model's purpose, limitations, and expected performance.

Understanding the data used for training is crucial, requiring a comprehensive assessment of the quality, diversity, and representativeness of the training dataset[4]. Verification of data preprocessing steps, including normalization and handling of missing values, ensures that preprocessing techniques are appropriate and consistent.

The model training process is thoroughly reviewed, including:

1. optimization algorithms,
2. convergence criteria, and
3. validation techniques.

The accuracy of the AI model is then assessed on a separate validation dataset, utilizing appropriate evaluation metrics tailored to the problem at hand. Evaluating the model for bias and fairness involves examining predictions across different demographic groups, utilizing fairness metrics and techniques to identify and mitigate biases.

Assessing model robustness includes testing the model against adversarial attacks or variations in input data to evaluate generalization to unseen or perturbed data.

Alignment with business requirements is crucial to ensure that the model meets specified objectives and contributes to intended business outcomes. Evaluating model **explainability** involves assessing the **interpretability** and explainability of predictions using techniques such as **feature importance analysis** (which involves assessing and understanding the significance of individual features (input variables) in influencing the model's predictions) or **model-agnostic interpretability** (techniques that can be applied to understand and interpret the decisions or predictions made by machine learning models) methods (see detailed definitions in Glossary).

The stability of the model's performance over time and across different environments is checked, ensuring reliability and accuracy in real-world scenarios. Reviewing the model deployment process, including versioning, monitoring, and rollback procedures, ensures a robust deployment pipeline.

Sensitivity analysis *is conducted to understand how changes in input features impact predictions, identifying critical features, and potential sources of model uncertainty.*

Validating the model's performance in the production environment involves real-time or batch monitoring to detect deviations from expected behavior.

Collecting *user feedback from end users and stakeholders provides valuable insights* that are incorporated into the assessment.

Documenting findings and recommendations is important, highlighting areas of strength, potential improvements, and any deviations from expected performance.

Based on the assessment, a **Model Improvement Plan** is created, prioritizing actions that address identified issues, enhance model performance, and align with business objectives.

Finally, **continuous monitoring** mechanisms are established to regularly review and update the model based on changes in data patterns, user feedback, and evolving business requirements, ensuring the ongoing accuracy and reliability of AI models.

By following these steps, organizations can systematically assess the accuracy, reliability, and overall performance of AI models, ensuring that they meet business objectives and adhere to ethical and regulatory standards. Continuous monitoring and improvement are essential components of maintaining the reliability of AI models over time.

- **Assess the performance against predefined metrics and objectives.**

In the process of conducting a Model Validation and Performance Assessment against metrics and objectives, several key steps are followed to comprehensively evaluate the performance of AI models.

The first crucial step involves defining performance metrics, which could encompass accuracy, precision, recall, F1 score, area under the ROC curve, or other domain-specific metrics.

Aligning these metrics with the broader business objectives is essential to ensure that the evaluation is meaningful and relevant. Moreover, regulatory and ethical considerations are taken into account to address fairness, bias, and compliance with legal standards.

To establish a baseline for comparison, historical or benchmark datasets are used, allowing for a thorough assessment of improvements or deviations. The selection of appropriate evaluation datasets, distinct from the training data, is crucial to represent the diversity of real-world scenarios. Consistency in data preprocessing steps, such as normalization and feature engineering, is maintained to reflect actual deployment conditions. The model is then evaluated using standard procedures like cross-validation or holdout validation to obtain reliable and unbiased performance estimates.

Upon obtaining metric results, a detailed analysis is conducted to understand the model's strengths and weaknesses. Regulatory limits are considered, and fairness and bias are assessed, especially if the AI system impacts different demographic groups. Misclassifications are scrutinized to identify root causes, and **sensitivity analysis** is performed to understand the influence of input features on predictions. The model is also validated against use-case specific metrics aligned with business objectives.

User feedback becomes a necessary element in the assessment, providing valuable insights into practical effectiveness and user satisfaction. Findings are documented, including performance metrics, areas of improvement, and any identified issues. The assessment process is iterative, involving adjustments to hyperparameters, retraining with additional data, or enhancements to specific components based on evaluation results.

Clear communication of assessment results to key stakeholders, such as business leaders, data scientists, and regulatory compliance teams, is prioritized for transparency. **Continuous monitoring mechanisms** are established to track the ongoing performance of the model in production, allowing for regular reviews and updates to adapt to changing conditions. Finally, model documentation is updated to reflect the latest evaluation results, changes made to improve performance, and any lessons learned during the assessment process. This comprehensive approach ensures a robust evaluation of AI model performance throughout its lifecycle.

By following these steps, organizations can systematically assess AI model performance against predefined metrics and objectives, ensuring that the models meet business goals and adhere to regulatory and ethical standards. Regular evaluation and improvement are integral to maintaining the effectiveness and reliability of AI models over time.

- **Review the model development lifecycle, including data preparation, feature engineering, and training.**

When conducting a Model Validation and Performance Assessment to scrutinize the model development lifecycle, meticulous steps are undertaken to ensure the robustness, fairness, and effectiveness of the artificial intelligence (AI) model, including data preparation, feature engineering, and training. Follow the steps delineated below (see the module on Lifecycle for more detail):

The initial phase involves a comprehensive review of **Data Collection and Preparation**. This encompasses an assessment *of methods for data cleaning, handling missing values, and addressing outliers, with a critical focus on ensuring the training data's representation of real-world scenarios.*

Data Bias and Fairness should be evaluated in the next phase, assessing the dataset for potential bias issues and determining whether the training data reflects the diversity of the target population.

Feature Engineering is then examined, delving into the process of selecting and creating features to ascertain their alignment with the problem statement and meaningful contribution to predictive performance.

The subsequent steps involve a detailed review of **Feature Scaling** and **Transformation** methods to ensure appropriate handling of numeric and categorical features. **Data Splitting** for Training and Validation is evaluated to verify the randomness and consistency of the split, guarding against data leakage and ensuring the model's generalization to unseen data.

The **Model Selection phase** assesses the rationale behind the choice of the machine learning algorithm or model architecture, emphasizing suitability for the given problem and alignment with the AI application goals. **Hyperparameter Tuning** is then reviewed, evaluating the optimization process and the systematic approach used to explore the hyperparameter space.

Cross-Validation is verified to assess the model's robustness across different subsets of the training data, considering the number of folds used and the consistency of performance metrics.

The **Model Training process** is reviewed, including parameter initialization, optimization algorithms, convergence evaluation, and the appropriate application of regularization techniques to prevent overfitting.

Model Evaluation Metrics are examined to ensure alignment with problem objectives and a comprehensive understanding of model effectiveness. The **Validation Set Performance** is evaluated, scrutinizing the model's performance on the validation set and identifying any discrepancies between training and validation results.

Error Analysis *is conducted to understand the types of errors the model makes, identifying common misclassification patterns and assessing their impact.* Model Explainability is assessed by evaluating interpretability techniques such as feature importance analysis or model-agnostic interpretability methods.

Robustness Testing follows, assessing how the model handles perturbations in input data and its resilience to small variations or adversarial attacks.

Model Versioning is reviewed to verify the existence of a version control system tracking changes in the model over time, ensuring documentation of model versions and traceability of changes.

The **Model Deployment Plan** is then reviewed, with an eye to considerations such as scalability, monitoring, and integration with existing systems. Documentation completeness and clarity related to the model development lifecycle are assessed, covering data sources, preprocessing steps, model architecture, hyperparameters, and training procedures.

Collaboration and Communication practices among team members involved in the model development process are evaluated to ensure knowledge sharing and documentation promote a transparent and collaborative environment. Finally, plans for continuous model improvement are reviewed, assessing the establishment of feedback loops to incorporate insights from performance evaluations and user feedback into future iterations.

By systematically reviewing each stage of the model development lifecycle, organizations can ensure the reliability, transparency, and effectiveness of their AI models. This comprehensive assessment contributes to the overall governance of AI systems, supporting compliance with regulations and ethical standards.

- **Assess model outputs for biases and fairness, using appropriate evaluation metrics.**

When conducting a Model Validation and Performance Assessment to evaluate model outputs for biases and fairness, a series of key steps are followed along with appropriate evaluation metrics.

The first step involves defining **evaluation metrics** *specifically tailored to assess biases and fairness in model predictions.* Common metrics such as disparate impact, equalized odds, and statistical parity are identified and defined to quantify the fairness of the model across different subgroups.

Sensitive attributes, such as gender, race, or age, are selected based on their relevance to the application and potential association with biases.

Legal and ethical considerations play a crucial role in the selection of these attributes. Demographic disparities in model predictions are calculated by comparing the distribution of predicted outcomes across subgroups, and a disparate impact analysis is conducted using metrics like the adverse impact ratio.

Equalized odds analysis is then performed *to ensure that the model provides equal false positive and false negative rates across different demographic groups*. The odds ratio for various groups is evaluated to identify any disparities. Statistical parity analysis is employed to assess whether the distribution of predicted outcomes is statistically different across demographic groups by comparing the predicted probabilities.

Intersectional analysis, *considering biases at the intersection of multiple sensitive attributes*, is conducted to unveil biases that may not be apparent when analyzing each attribute independently. **Fairness-aware evaluation metrics**, such as fairness-aware accuracy or F1 score, are utilized to account for both overall performance and disparities across subgroups.

Exploration of **threshold optimization techniques** allows for *adjusting decision thresholds based on different subgroups, aiming for a more balanced trade-off between false positives and false negatives. Leveraging bias detection tools and libraries th*at automate the assessment of biases becomes instrumental, utilizing statistical methods, visualizations, and fairness metrics to gain insights.

Model **explainability** and interpretability techniques are employed to understand the factors contributing to biases in model predictions. Explainable AI methods help identify features or decision points that contribute to disparities. Collecting user feedback and stakeholder input provides qualitative information that complements quantitative metrics, offering a comprehensive view of fairness considerations.

Continuous monitoring of model outputs is implemented to detect and address biases over time. Automated monitoring systems are set up to alert when significant changes in biases are observed. The results of bias and fairness assessments, including the metrics used, demographic disparities identified, and any corrective actions taken, are meticulously documented. Reports are prepared for both internal and external stakeholders.

Establishing an iterative improvement process is vital, incorporating ongoing assessments and feedback to enhance model fairness. Improvements can be implemented in model architecture, data collection, or preprocessing to address identified biases.

Throughout the entire process, legal and ethical considerations remain a focal point, ensuring that the model's treatment of sensitive attributes aligns with legal requirements and ethical standards. This comprehensive approach ensures a thorough examination of biases and fairness in AI model outputs.

By systematically evaluating model outputs for biases and fairness using these steps, organizations can enhance the transparency, accountability, and ethical considerations of their AI systems. This approach contributes to robust AI Governance and aligns with principles of fairness and responsible AI development.

Ethical Considerations and Bias Assessment

(Note: More Detail in the Risk Chapter)

- **Examine AI systems for ethical considerations and potential biases.**

In the pursuit of an AI Governance initiative, **Ethical Considerations** and **Bias Assessment** play a pivotal role in ensuring responsible development and deployment of AI systems. When considering ethical considerations and conducting a bias assessment for AI systems, follow the steps described below:

The initial step involves the explicit definition of **Ethical Principles** that should guide the entire process, encompassing fairness, transparency, accountability, privacy, and inclusivity. A nuanced understanding of the Context in which the AI system will operate is then pursued, considering societal, cultural, and domain-specific factors that may influence ethical considerations.

Identifying Stakeholders becomes imperative, engaging end users, affected communities, domain experts, and ethical specialists to capture diverse perspectives and ensure a comprehensive understanding of potential ethical issues. The assessment then delves into the examination of **Data Collection Practices**, scrutinizing potential biases in the training data and evaluating its representativeness and impartiality.

The **Model Training phase** is subject to evaluation, with a *focus on identifying biases introduced during this process*. This includes a meticulous analysis of feature selection, data preprocessing, and algorithmic choices to uncover potential biases. *A comprehensive assessment of Model Outputs follows, aiming to identify biases in predictions and evaluate whether the model's decisions disproportionately impact specific groups.*

Examination of **Feature Importance** is then conducted, ensuring that sensitive attributes do not unduly influence predictions, particularly in relation to protected characteristics like gender or race.

Fairness Metrics and Disparate Impact Analysis are employed to quantitatively assess fairness in model predictions, identifying disparities in outcomes among different demographic groups.

Assessing **Human-AI Collaboration** becomes crucial, ensuring that the AI system supports human decision-makers and promotes collaborative decision-making, particularly in sensitive domains. Prioritizing **Explainability and Interpretability** in AI models is emphasized to enhance the understandability of decisions, especially in cases with significant ethical implications.

User Feedback and Impact Assessments are conducted, involving stakeholders to collect feedback on the AI system's impact on different groups and performing impact assessments to understand the consequences on individuals and communities. **Mitigation Strategies** are developed and implemented for identified biases, ranging from algorithm adjustments to refining training data or incorporating fairness-aware techniques.

Continuous Monitoring is instituted to detect and address ethical issues over time, establishing mechanisms for ongoing assessment and adjustment as the system interacts with new data. **Documentation and Transparency** are integral, with comprehensive documentation of steps taken to address ethical considerations and share information about the ethical principles guiding the AI system.

Considering the establishment of an **Ethics Review Board** or incorporating ethical reviews into existing governance structures is suggested to provide oversight and guidance on ethical considerations throughout the AI lifecycle. Compliance with Ethical Standards is emphasized, aligning the AI system's behavior with broader ethical norms and principles.

Communication and education efforts are directed towards relevant stakeholders, ensuring transparency about ethical considerations and steps taken to address biases. This involves educating users, developers, and decision-makers about the ethical principles guiding the AI system. An iterative improvement process is advocated, fostering ongoing enhancements in ethical practices based on continuous assessments, feedback, and advancements in ethical AI practices.

By following these steps, organizations can systematically examine AI systems for ethical considerations and potential biases, fostering the development of responsible and ethically sound AI applications. This approach contributes to building trust, transparency, and accountability in AI Governance.

- **Evaluate the fairness and transparency of decision-making processes.**

When evaluating the fairness and transparency of decision-making processes in AI Governance, a comprehensive approach involves multiple key steps.

First and foremost, defining **fairness criteria** is essential, considering metrics like demographic parity and equalized odds based on the specific context of the AI application. Understanding the intricacies of decision-making processes, including the role of input features, algorithms, and influencing factors, forms the basis for the assessment.

Identifying sensitive features within the dataset and decision-making process, such as race or gender, is crucial to pinpoint potential sources of bias.

An examination of the training data ensures its diversity and representation of different groups, while an evaluation of the model training process identifies biases introduced during this phase. **Fairness metrics**, including disparate impact and equal opportunity, quantify and measure fairness, aligning with the predefined criteria.

Leveraging **bias detection tools** automates the identification of biases, providing valuable insights. Prioritizing algorithmic transparency and explainability ensures that decisions are interpretable, with techniques like LIME aiding in this process.

User-friendly explanations of decisions enable affected individuals to comprehend influencing factors, and feedback loops facilitate continuous improvement through user challenges. Fairness-aware techniques, such as **reweighing training instances** (a technique used in machine learning to address bias in training datasets), and **bias mitigation strategies**, such as adjusting algorithms, address and reduce biases. Continuous monitoring of decision-making processes ensures timely detection and correction of fairness issues.

Compliance with ethical guidelines and industry standards is paramount, aligning decision-making behavior with broader ethical norms. Integrating **human-in-the-loop** approaches, with human oversight in critical decisions, prevents and corrects biases that may elude the AI system.

The auditability of decision-making processes is maintained through detailed logs and **records**, facilitating accountability.

Consideration of an **ethics review board** or ethical reviews within existing governance structures provides oversight and guidance.

Documentation of the evaluation steps, transparency about criteria and strategies, ensures a clear and transparent process in promoting fairness and transparency in AI decision-making.

By following these steps, organizations can systematically evaluate the fairness and transparency of decision-making processes in AI systems, promoting ethical AI practices and mitigating biases that could lead to unfair outcomes. This approach contributes to building trust, transparency, and accountability in AI Governance.

- **Collaborate with ethics committees and data science teams to understand the ethical framework.**

In establishing a robust ethical framework and conducting a thorough bias assessment in AI Governance, a series of key steps should be followed. First and foremost, clear communication channels need to be set up between ethics committees and data science teams, fostering an open and collaborative environment for discussions on ethical considerations. Subsequently, collaboration with ethics committees is essential to define the ethical framework that will guide the assessment, articulating relevant principles and values. Identifying and prioritizing ethical principles, such as fairness, transparency, accountability, privacy, and human dignity, should be a joint effort.

To align the ethical framework with practical implementation, it is best to gain a comprehensive understanding of data science objectives and goals. This involves examining the intended use of AI models, their impact on end users, and potential ethical challenges tied to data and algorithms. Identifying potential sources of bias in data, algorithms, or decision-making processes is a collaborative process that should align with the defined ethical framework. Engaging in discussions about **fairness metrics** and **evaluation criteria** is also vital, selecting metrics that align with the outlined ethical principles.

Addressing potential ethical dilemmas that may arise during development and deployment is another essential step, considering scenarios where ethical principles may conflict and establishing guidelines for resolution.

Collaboratively assessing data collection practices ensures alignment with ethical considerations, covering issues of privacy, consent, and unintentional biases. Additionally, *evaluating model training processes, including algorithmic choices, is critical for understanding their impact on the ethical dimensions of the AI system.*

To enhance **transparency** and **explainability** in AI models, collaboration on strategies for making decision-making processes more understandable to end users is essential. Privacy preservation measures should also be discussed, aligning with the ethical principles of data protection. Exploring the incorporation of **human-in-the-loop** approaches, (where human judgment is involved in critical decision points), contributes to ethical decision making.

Furthermore, providing ethics training for data scientists is paramount to ensure awareness of the ethical framework, understanding its implications, and equipping teams to make ethical decisions. Establishing documentation and reporting practices collaboratively is essential, defining how ethical considerations, including bias assessments, will be documented and reported for transparency and accountability.

Continuous feedback and improvement mechanisms should be established, encouraging an ongoing dialogue between ethics committees and data science teams to address emerging ethical issues and continuously refine the ethical framework. Creating **ethical impact statements** for AI systems, offering a clear overview of anticipated ethical impacts in line with the defined framework, enhances accountability.

Collaboration on the development of a review and approval process is important, specifying how ethical considerations will be reviewed and approved by ethics committees throughout the AI system's lifecycle.

Facilitating **multidisciplinary workshops** involving members from ethics committees and data science teams provides a platform for in-depth discussions and collaborative problem-solving.

Scenario analysis, in collaboration with both parties, is imperative to evaluate how the AI system behaves under different conditions, anticipating potential ethical challenges and establishing guidelines for addressing them. Finally, conducting an **ethical risk assessment** with ethics committees and data science teams is vital, identifying and prioritizing potential ethical risks associated with the AI system and developing strategies to mitigate them.

By following these steps, organizations can foster effective collaboration between ethics committees and data science teams, ensuring a shared understanding of the ethical framework and facilitating the incorporation of ethical considerations throughout the AI Governance process. This collaborative approach contributes to the development of responsible and ethically aligned AI systems.

- **Implement fairness and bias assessment tools and methodologies.**

Implementing fairness and bias assessment tools and methodologies is pivotal to addressing ethical considerations in AI systems. First, it is crucial to clearly define the assessment criteria, pinpointing sensitive attributes like race, gender, and age, along with factors that may introduce bias into the system. Following this, selecting appropriate **fairness metrics**, such as disparate impact, equalized odds, and demographic parity, aligned with the defined criteria *is essential*. Understanding the distribution of data used for training and testing the AI model is a fundamental step, analyzing the representation of different groups within the dataset and identifying potential imbalances.

To automatically identify patterns of bias, integrating **bias detection tools** like **Fairness Indicators, AI Fairness 360**, and **Themis** (see Glossary for definitions) into the AI development pipeline is necessary.

Exploratory data analysis (EDA) further *uncovers potential biases in the dataset, examining summary statistics and distributions to identify disparities among different groups.* Evaluating the importance of features in the model's decision-making process helps identify whether sensitive attributes disproportionately influence predictions.

Assessing the model's outputs across different demographic groups and utilizing **confusion matrices** (a table used in machine learning to evaluate the performance of a classification model) to understand prediction outcomes is a critical step.

Post-processing techniques like **re-ranking, re-weighting**, and **adversarial debiasing** (see Glossary) can be applied to mitigate bias in model predictions. Additionally, evaluating the model for intersectional bias, where biases interact across multiple dimensions, ensures a comprehensive assessment.

Fairness assessments must be conducted across different versions of the model to identify and address biases introduced during updates.[5] *Collaboration with domain experts, ethicists, and representatives from affected communities enriches the assessment process* with external perspectives. Documenting the results of fairness and bias assessments in a detailed report, including methodologies used and steps taken to address biases, enhances transparency.

Establishing an iterative process for **fairness assessment**, using feedback to continuously refine fairness metrics and methodologies, is crucial for ongoing improvement. Educating stakeholders about the importance of fairness and bias assessments promotes a culture of awareness and responsibility among developers, data scientists, and decision-makers.

Integrating ethical considerations into the development lifecycle, "ethics by design" essentially ensures that fairness assessments align with broader ethical principles, fostering transparency, accountability, and the responsible use of AI. Staying informed about advancements in fairness assessment methods and regularly updating assessment methodologies based on emerging best practices ensures ongoing effectiveness in addressing biases in AI systems.

By following these steps, organizations can implement a comprehensive fairness and bias assessment framework, promoting the development of AI systems that are more ethical, accountable, and aligned with principles of fairness. Regular assessments and continuous improvement contribute to building responsible and unbiased AI solutions.

Security Audit

- **Conduct a thorough security audit of AI systems.**

Conducting a thorough security audit of AI systems is essential to identify and mitigate potential vulnerabilities. Here are the steps involved in the process (see the Cybersecurity chapter for more detail):

1. **Define Audit Objectives**

   Clearly define the objectives of the security audit for the AI system. Specify the scope, goals, and critical security areas to be assessed.

2. **Identify Assets and Components**

   Identify and document all assets and components related to the AI system, including hardware, software, data, models, and interfaces. Understand the dependencies and interactions between these components.

3. **Establish Security Standards**

   Define security standards and best practices applicable to the AI system. This may include adherence to industry-specific standards, regulatory requirements, and internal security policies.

4. **Conduct Risk Assessment**

   Perform a comprehensive risk assessment to identify potential security threats and vulnerabilities. Evaluate the impact and likelihood of each risk, and prioritize them based on their severity.

5. **Access Controls Audit**

   Audit access controls and authentication mechanisms to ensure that only authorized individuals and systems have access to the AI system. Verify the effectiveness of user authentication, authorization, and role-based access controls.

6. **Data Security Audit**

   Assess the security of data handling processes, including data storage, transmission, and processing. Verify the implementation of encryption protocols and mechanisms to protect sensitive data.

7. **Model Security Review**

   Review the security of machine learning models deployed in the system. Assess model robustness, evaluate against adversarial attacks, and ensure that models are resistant to manipulation.

8. **Infrastructure Security Audit**

   Audit the security of the underlying infrastructure supporting the AI system. This includes servers, databases, network configurations, and cloud services. Identify and address vulnerabilities in the infrastructure.

9. **Network Security Audit**

   Evaluate the security of network configurations and protocols used by the AI system. Assess firewall rules, network segmentation, and data flows to identify and mitigate potential threats.

10. **Incident Response Audit**

    Review the incident response plan for the AI system. Ensure that there is a well-defined process for detecting, responding to, and recovering from security incidents. Test the effectiveness of incident response procedures.

11. **Security Patching and Updates**

    Audit the process for applying security patches and updates to all components of the AI system. Ensure that software dependencies, libraries, and frameworks are regularly updated to address known vulnerabilities.

12. **External Integrations Audit**

    Assess the security of external integrations and APIs connected to the AI system. Verify that third-party services and applications adhere to security best practices and do not introduce vulnerabilities.

13. **Evaluate Logging and Monitoring**

    Review the logging and monitoring mechanisms in place. Ensure that logs capture relevant security events, and monitoring tools provide real-time alerts for suspicious activities.

14. **Personnel Security Audit**

    Audit personnel access and permissions related to the AI system. Ensure that only authorized individuals have access to sensitive information and that user accounts are properly managed.

15. **Physical Security Review**

    If applicable, review the physical security measures in place for any hardware components of the AI system. This may include data centers, servers, and other physical infrastructure.

16. **Compliance Assessment**

    Ensure that the AI system complies with relevant security regulations and standards. This may include GDPR, HIPAA, ISO 27001, or industry-specific requirements.

17. **Document Findings and Recommendations**

    Document the findings of the security audit, including identified vulnerabilities, risks, and areas of noncompliance. Provide clear recommendations for mitigating risks and improving security measures.

18. **Implement Remediation Measures**

    Work with relevant teams to implement remediation measures based on the audit findings. Prioritize and address identified vulnerabilities and weaknesses in a timely manner.

19. **Regularly Update Security Policies**

    Update security policies and procedures based on lessons learned from the security audit. Ensure that security measures evolve to address emerging threats and changes in the AI system.

20. **Continuous Monitoring**

    Implement continuous monitoring practices to detect and respond to security threats in real time. Regularly review and update security measures to adapt to the evolving threat landscape.

    Implement continuous monitoring practices to detect and respond to security threats in real time. Regularly review and update security measures to adapt to the evolving threat landscape.

By following these steps, organizations can conduct a comprehensive security audit of their AI systems, enhancing the overall security posture and ensuring compliance with relevant standards and regulations. Regular security audits contribute to the ongoing improvement of security practices and help organizations stay resilient against evolving cybersecurity threats.

- **Assess vulnerabilities and potential risks related to data breaches or unauthorized access.**

Conducting a security audit for AI systems involves a systematic and comprehensive process to *assess vulnerabilities and potential risks associated with data breaches or unauthorized access.*

The initial step is to clearly define the scope of the security audit, outlining the specific AI systems, data, and infrastructure to be assessed, while simultaneously establishing objectives such as:

1. Identifying vulnerabilities
2. Assessing compliance
3. Evaluating the effectiveness of security controls.

Understanding the AI system architecture is key, requiring a thorough examination of data flows, storage mechanisms, processing components, and external interfaces.

Asset identification and cataloging, encompassing hardware, software, data, and personnel, should be conducted alongside mapping the flow of data throughout the system—from collection to storage, processing, and output.

The assessment then delves into evaluating how sensitive data is handled, processed, and stored within the AI system, scrutinizing encryption methods, access controls, and data retention policies. The effectiveness of **access controls** and **authentication mechanisms** is also reviewed, ensuring that only authorized personnel have access to sensitive data and critical components of the AI system.

Network security is a crucial aspect, involving the examination of network configurations and security protocols to identify and address vulnerabilities that could be exploited for unauthorized access. A thorough review of software components, including AI algorithms, libraries, and third-party dependencies, is essential. This includes scanning for known vulnerabilities and ensuring that software patches are up to date.

The audit extends to external interfaces, reviewing connections with external systems, APIs, and third-party services. The security of data exchanges and the overall integrity of communication channels are validated. Controlled **penetration testing** is then performed to simulate attacks and identify potential weaknesses, testing for common attack vectors like SQL injection, cross-site scripting, and unauthorized access attempts.

Evaluating security policies and ensuring compliance with relevant regulations and standards, such as GDPR, HIPAA, and various US state privacy laws, or industry-specific guidelines, is a critical checkpoint.

Incident response planning is also reviewed, ensuring that established procedures for detecting, responding to, and mitigating security incidents are in place.

Documentation and reporting of findings, vulnerabilities, and recommendations follow the assessment phase. This includes generating a comprehensive report with:

1. an executive summary,
2. detailed findings,
3. risk assessments, and
4. recommendations for remediation.

The final steps involve *collaborating with responsible teams to address identified vulnerabilities, implementing corrective measures*, and establishing a follow-up process to monitor the ongoing effectiveness of remediation efforts, ensuring a continuous commitment to security.

By following these steps, organizations can conduct a thorough security audit to identify and address vulnerabilities in AI systems, reducing the risk of data breaches and unauthorized access.

- **Collaborate with IT security teams to review access controls, encryption practices, and network security.**

Collaborating with IT security teams is essential when conducting a security audit for AI programs to ensure a comprehensive review of access controls, encryption practices, and network security. *Please see the Cybersecurity Role in AI Governance chapter for more detail.*

Effective collaboration between AI Governance and IT security teams is crucial for a successful security audit, promoting a holistic approach to addressing vulnerabilities and ensuring compliance with regulations and ethical standards.

- **Conduct penetration testing and vulnerability assessments.**

Penetration testing and vulnerability assessments are critical components of a security audit for AI programs. They help identify weaknesses and potential entry points for attackers. *Please see the Cybersecurity Role in AI Governance chapter for more detail.*

Model Explainability and Documentation

- **Verify that AI models are explainable and well documented.**

Ensuring model **explainability** and creating comprehensive documentation are pivotal elements of effective AI Governance. The first step involves defining documentation standards and guidelines that align with industry best practices and regulatory requirements. This includes documenting the model architecture in detail, providing information about the type of model, layers, nodes, and any specific algorithms or techniques employed.

Feature engineering, a critical aspect of model development, is explained in the documentation, highlighting the selected features and their relevance to the model. Additionally, any transformations or preprocessing steps applied to the input data are detailed. Capturing information about the training data, including sources, size, and distribution, along with documenting any data cleaning or augmentation during the training process, contributes to transparency.

Model training parameters, such as learning rates, batch sizes, and regularization methods, are documented, along with an explanation of the rationale behind choosing specific **hyperparameter** values. **Model evaluation metrics**, aligned with the goals and objectives of the AI application, are recorded to provide insights into the model's performance.

Bias and fairness considerations are addressed in the documentation, covering steps taken to mitigate biases in the training data. *Techniques employed for model interpretability, such as* **feature importance analysis** *or* **LIME** or **SHAP values**, *are documented*, emphasizing their role in understanding the model's decision-making process.

Validation against established **explainability standards** is essential, ensuring adherence to guidelines provided by regulatory bodies or industry organizations.

Creating user-friendly documentation is emphasized, employing clear language and visualizations to make the information accessible to both technical and nontechnical stakeholders.

The documentation includes information about the model's limitations and assumptions, clearly articulating scenarios where the model may not perform optimally. Ethical considerations, such as privacy concerns, potential biases, and societal impacts, are also documented, along with measures taken to mitigate ethical risks.

Model audits specifically focused on explainability are conducted, involving internal and external stakeholders, domain experts, and end users. Subject matter experts (SMEs) are actively engaged in reviewing and contributing to the documentation to ensure accuracy and completeness, addressing any domain-specific nuances impacting model interpretation.

Establishing a process for regularly updating the documentation is crucial to reflect changes in the model, data, or deployment environment. The documentation is made easily accessible to relevant stakeholders, including developers, data scientists, regulatory bodies, and end users, facilitating ongoing transparency and accountability in the AI system.

By following these steps, organizations can verify that AI models are explainable and well-documented, fostering transparency, accountability, and compliance with ethical standards and regulations.

- Ensure transparency in model decision-making processes.

In the pursuit of AI Governance, ensuring transparency in the decision-making processes of AI models is paramount for building trust, meeting ethical standards, and complying with regulations. The initial step involves clearly defining Transparency Goals, specifying the objectives of achieving transparency and identifying key stakeholders who stand to benefit, such as end users, regulators, and internal teams.

Selecting appropriate Explainability Techniques is the subsequent focus, where methods like feature importance analysis, SHAP values, LIME, or other model-agnostic and model-specific techniques are chosen based on the type and complexity of the model.

Documenting **Feature Importance** becomes integral, with clear documentation of individual features' influence on predictions, providing insights into the decision-making logic.

Visualizing Decision Processes is advocated to aid stakeholder understanding, employing diagrams, charts, and interactive tools to illustrate how input features impact the model's output. **Contextual Explanations** are encouraged, relating model predictions to real-world scenarios and explaining the relevance of specific features in alignment with domain knowledge.

The assessment addresses **Bias and Fairness**, with a thorough evaluation and documentation of the model's performance in these aspects. Explanations for observed biases are provided, accompanied by descriptions of efforts taken to address or mitigate them. Clear articulation of **Model Assumptions** is emphasized, elucidating how these assumptions might impact decisions and predictions.

Model Limitations are documented comprehensively, specifying scenarios where the model may not perform well or where its predictions may be less reliable. Uncertainties and potential risks associated with the model are communicated transparently. Providing **decision examples** becomes crucial, including detailed explanations for specific instances, encompassing both positive and negative examples to illustrate the range of decisions the model can make.

Collaboration with Domain Experts is encouraged to validate and enhance the transparency of the model's decision-making processes. Incorporating feedback from experts ensures accuracy and relevance. **Natural Language Explanations** are proposed to translate technical details into understandable language for non-technical stakeholders, enhancing accessibility and facilitating broader comprehension.

Incorporating **User Feedback** involves collecting input from end users and stakeholders regarding the clarity and comprehensibility of model explanations. This feedback is then utilized to refine and improve transparency features. Documenting the **Decision Threshold** is essential, clearly articulating the confidence level at which the model's predictions are considered reliable and explaining how different thresholds may affect performance.

Creating **comprehensive documentation** consolidates all aspects of model transparency, including architecture, algorithms, parameter choices, methodology, features, limitations, and decision examples. This documentation should be organized in a structured and easily accessible format.

Regular **audits** are established as a continuous process, ensuring that documentation remains accurate and reflective of any changes in the model or data.

Educating stakeholders is emphasized through the provision of educational materials, explaining the importance of transparency and guiding stakeholders on how to interpret the information presented in the documentation. Training sessions or workshops are facilitated to enhance understanding and foster a collaborative and informed AI Governance environment.

By following these steps, organizations can enhance the transparency of AI models, enabling stakeholders to better understand and trust the decision-making processes. Transparent models contribute to ethical AI practices and regulatory compliance.

Incident Response Simulation

- **Simulate AI-related incidents to test the organization's incident response capabilities.**

Simulating AI-related incidents through **incident response simulations** is a proactive measure to test an organization's ability to handle unforeseen challenges.

The process begins by defining simulation objectives, specifying the scenarios to be tested, and the goals to be achieved. Identifying AI-specific threat scenarios follows, encompassing potential issues such as model bias, adversarial attacks, data poisoning, or unauthorized model access. Detailed scenarios are then developed for each threat, outlining the incident's progression and potential impacts, defining the starting point, key events, and expected outcomes.

Cross-functional teams, including business units, IT, privacy, security, legal, risk, RIM, communications, and relevant AI specialists, are actively involved in the simulation to ensure a realistic response. Participants are notified in advance, emphasizing the simulation's importance as a real incident test. The simulation is initiated by presenting the identified **incident scenario**, and teams respond in real time, activating the organization's incident response plan.

Simulated communication channels, both internal and external, are assessed, including coordination among teams, communication with stakeholders, and potential public relations responses.

The technical response to the incident is evaluated, focusing on issue identification, containment measures, threat eradication, and recovery efforts. Legal and regulatory compliance during the incident response is scrutinized, assessing **data privacy management**, disclosure obligations, and other legal considerations.

Observations and feedback are collected during and after the simulation, identifying strengths, weaknesses, and areas for improvement in the incident response process. A debriefing session is conducted immediately after the simulation, discussing observations and lessons learned, and reviewing the effectiveness of incident response actions.

Findings, including strengths, weaknesses, and recommendations for improvement, are documented. The insights gained from the simulation are then used to iterate and improve incident response plans, procedures, and capabilities. Corrective actions are implemented to address any identified weaknesses.

Regularly scheduled incident response simulations ensure ongoing preparedness and test improvements based on previous simulations. *Scenarios are adapted to reflect emerging threats and changes in the AI landscape.* **Incident response training** is provided based on lessons learned during simulations, ensuring that team members are well-equipped to handle AI-related incidents in real-world scenarios. This iterative and proactive approach strengthens an organization's overall readiness to respond effectively to unforeseen challenges in the AI domain.

By conducting incident response simulations specific to AI-related incidents, organizations can identify and address vulnerabilities, enhance coordination among teams, and continuously improve their incident response capabilities in the context of AI Governance.

- **Conduct tabletop exercises to simulate various AI-related scenarios.**

Tabletop exercises are valuable for simulating various AI-related incidents in a controlled environment and testing an organization's incident response capabilities. Here are the steps involved in conducting tabletop exercises for AI-related scenarios:

1. **Define Exercise Objectives**

   Clearly define the objectives of the tabletop exercise, specifying the AI-related scenarios to be simulated and the goals to be achieved.

2. **Identify Key Participants**

   Identify and invite key participants, including representatives from IT, security, legal, communications, AI specialists, and other relevant stakeholders.

   Ensure a diverse group that covers all areas involved in incident response.

3. **Create AI-Specific Scenarios**

   Develop realistic AI-related scenarios that could impact the organization. Consider scenarios such as adversarial attacks, data poisoning, or bias-related issues.

   Clearly define the starting point, key events, and the expected outcomes of each scenario.

4. **Prepare Scenario Materials**

   Prepare materials, including scenario descriptions, timelines, and any necessary documentation for participants.

   Ensure that the materials provide sufficient context for participants to understand the simulated incidents.

5. **Conduct Briefing Session**

   Conduct a pre-exercise briefing session to provide an overview of the tabletop exercise, explain the objectives, and distribute scenario materials.

   Answer any initial questions and ensure that participants understand their roles.

6. **Initiate the Tabletop Exercise**

   Start the tabletop exercise by presenting the first scenario to the participants.

   Facilitate discussions as participants navigate through the incident response process.

7. **Simulate Decision-Making**

   Simulate decision-making processes by presenting new information and challenges to participants at predefined intervals.

   Encourage participants to discuss and decide on appropriate responses.

8. **Coordinate Communication**

   Emphasize the importance of effective communication between participants and teams.

   Simulate internal and external communication channels, including coordination among different departments.

9. **Introduce Injects**

   Introduce injects or additional elements to the scenario to escalate or complicate the incidents.

   These injects should challenge participants and test their ability to adapt to evolving situations.

10. **Facilitate Discussions**

    Facilitate discussions among participants to encourage collaboration, information sharing, and coordination.

    Prompt participants to discuss their decision rationale and how they are addressing the simulated incidents.

11. **Assess Legal and Regulatory Compliance**

    Assess how well participants address legal and regulatory compliance requirements during the incident response.

    Discuss how data privacy, disclosure obligations, and other legal considerations are being managed.

12. **Gather Observations and Feedback**

    Collect observations and feedback from participants during and after the tabletop exercise.

    Identify strengths, weaknesses, and areas for improvement in the incident response process.

13. **Debrief and Review**

    Conduct a debriefing session immediately after the tabletop exercise to discuss observations and lessons learned.

Review the incident response actions taken and evaluate their effectiveness.

14. **Document Findings and Recommendations**

    Document findings, including strengths and weaknesses identified during the tabletop exercise.

    Provide recommendations for improving incident response plans, processes, and capabilities.

15. **Iterate and Improve**

    Use the insights gained from the tabletop exercise to iterate and improve incident response plans, procedures, and capabilities.

    Identify areas for improvement in incident response processes.

    Implement corrective actions to address any identified weaknesses or gaps.

16. **Repeat Tabletop Exercises Periodically**

    Schedule regular tabletop exercises to ensure ongoing preparedness and to test improvements made based on previous exercises.

    Adapt scenarios to reflect emerging threats and changes in the AI landscape.

17. **Incident Response Training**

    Provide training based on the lessons learned during the tabletop exercise.

    Ensure that team members are well-equipped to handle AI-related incidents in real-world scenarios.

By conducting tabletop exercises for AI-related scenarios, organizations can effectively assess their incident response capabilities, identify areas for improvement, and enhance their preparedness to address incidents in the context of AI Governance, compliance, and ethical standards.

Audit Trail and Documentation

- **Verify the existence and completeness of audit trails.**

Establishing and maintaining an audit trail is a critical component of transparency, accountability, and compliance in AI Governance.

To begin this process, defining **Audit Trail Requirements** is essential, encompassing regulatory standards, organizational policies, and ethical considerations. Specific events, actions, and changes that necessitate logging are identified, forming the foundation for an effective audit trail.

Mapping the **Data Flow** and **System Components** of the AI system follows, allowing for a clear understanding of where critical events and activities occur and which components are integral to the audit trail.

Identifying Critical Events is then examined, outlining events such as model training, deployment, data access, and system configuration changes that warrant inclusion in the audit trail.

Selecting appropriate **Audit Trail Tools and Technologies** aligns with the AI system's requirements, ensuring the capture of critical events. The subsequent step involves implementing **Logging Mechanisms** within the AI system to capture relevant events in real time, with logs including essential details such as timestamps, user IDs, and event descriptions.

To safeguard the integrity and security of audit trail data, measures such as encryption, access controls, and other security protocols are implemented. **Defining retention policies, in collaboration with the Records and Information Management department,** is imperative, specifying the duration logs should be retained in alignment with regulatory requirements and organizational needs.

Regularly **monitoring and reviewing logs** is a continuous process, with assigned personnel responsible for identifying anomalies or suspicious activities. Automating log analysis further assists in detecting patterns or deviations from expected behavior, enabling a proactive response to critical events.

Conducting **periodic audits** ensures the existence and completeness of the audit trail, comparing recorded events with predefined critical events to confirm the comprehensive logging of relevant activities. Sampling and testing of audit trail data are conducted to verify its accuracy and consistency with documented processes and activities.

Documenting Audit Trail Procedures, including guidelines for responding to identified issues or discrepancies, is crucial for organizational clarity and consistency. Integrating Audit Trail Information into System Documentation further enhances transparency, providing details about logged events, storage locations, and access methods.

Ensuring compliance with **standards** involves verifying that the audit trail implementation aligns with industry standards and regulatory requirements, meeting the expectations of external auditors and regulatory bodies. Training personnel on audit trail processes is integral to ensure individuals are well equipped to maintain the integrity and completeness of the audit trail.

Regularly **updating audit trail documentation** reflects changes in processes, tools, or system configurations, keeping the documentation aligned with the evolving nature of the AI system. Documenting corrective actions is emphasized, detailing measures taken to address discrepancies and implementing improvements to prevent similar issues in the future.

By following these steps, organizations can establish a robust audit trail, verify its existence and completeness, and ensure that the logging mechanisms effectively capture critical events in the AI system. This contributes to transparency, accountability, and compliance in AI Governance.

Reporting and Communication

- Prepare comprehensive audit reports with findings and recommendations.

Preparing comprehensive audit reports with findings and recommendations is a critical aspect of effective AI Governance. To begin, *it is crucial to define reporting objectives clearly, specifying the scope, purpose, and intended audience of the audit report*. These objectives should align with the broader goals of AI Governance, compliance requirements, and ethical standards. Identifying key stakeholders, such as executives, AI development teams, compliance officers, privacy, and legal teams, ensures that the report addresses the needs of relevant parties.

The report should commence with a detailed overview of the audit scope and methodology, explaining the criteria used, including relevant regulations, organizational policies, and ethical guidelines. A concise summary of the audit process follows, highlighting key activities, methodologies, and approaches used during the audit, including details on data sources, interviews conducted, and tools utilized.

Presenting high-level findings at the outset provides a quick overview of the audit results, summarizing major observations, positive aspects, and areas of concern. The subsequent section details audit findings, categorizing them based on relevance and severity, with a clear articulation of specific issues, deficiencies, or noncompliance areas. *Supporting evidence, such as documentation, logs, screenshots, or other artifacts obtained during the audit, is included in an organized manner to substantiate the findings.*

While acknowledging positive practices and areas of strength observed during the audit, the report provides actionable recommendations to address identified issues and improve **AI Governance**. Recommendations are prioritized based on significance and potential impact, distinguishing those requiring immediate attention from those that can be addressed over a longer timeframe.

Quantifying and qualifying risks associated with findings and non-compliance aids stakeholders in prioritizing remediation efforts. Providing context and detailed explanations for each finding and recommendation helps clarify implications and rationale. *Customizing communication for different audiences ensures that technical details are accessible to specialists while executive summaries are clear for non-technical stakeholders.*

The report includes an assessment of compliance with relevant regulations, standards, and ethical guidelines, clearly articulating the organization's standing in terms of adherence to legal and ethical requirements. Encouraging feedback and collaboration fosters effective resolution of identified issues through stakeholder collaboration.

An **action plan** outlining steps to address findings and recommendations, along with a specified timeline for implementation, is a key component of the report. Considerations for the future, including ongoing improvement, emerging risks, and potential changes in regulations or ethical standards, are highlighted. An executive summary at the beginning of the report provides a quick overview for busy stakeholders.

Establishing a review and approval process before finalizing and disseminating the report ensures that key stakeholders, including audit team leads and executive management, have the opportunity to review and approve it. The communication of audit findings and recommendations should be done effectively through appropriate channels, such as formal presentations, meetings, or written communication, using clear and concise language to facilitate understanding.

Lastly, establishing a follow-up mechanism to track the implementation of recommendations and conducting periodic reviews to assess progress and update stakeholders on the status of remediation efforts ensures the ongoing effectiveness of AI Governance.

By following these steps, organizations can prepare comprehensive audit reports that effectively communicate findings, recommendations, and action plans, contributing to enhanced AI Governance, compliance, and adherence to ethical standards.

- Communicate audit results to relevant stakeholders, including executives and AI development teams.

Effectively communicating audit results to relevant stakeholders, including executives and AI development teams, is essential for driving understanding, accountability, and action. Here are the steps involved in communicating AI audit results:

1. **Understand Stakeholder Profiles**

   Identify and understand the profiles of relevant stakeholders, including executives, AI development teams, legal teams, compliance officers, and any other key individuals.

Tailor the communication approach to meet the needs and perspectives of each stakeholder group.

2. **Define Communication Objectives**

   Clearly define the objectives of the communication, specifying what key messages need to be conveyed to each stakeholder group. Align communication objectives with the overall goals of AI Governance, compliance, and ethical standards.

3. **Prepare an Executive Summary**

   Create a concise executive summary that provides a high-level overview of the audit results.

   Summarize key findings, recommendations, and the overall impact on AI Governance and compliance.

4. **Use Clear and Non-Technical Language**

   Use clear and non-technical language to ensure that the information is easily understandable by all stakeholders, including those who may not have a technical background.

5. **Provide Context and Background**

   Begin the communication by providing context and background on the audit, including the scope, methodology, and key considerations.

   Help stakeholders understand the importance and relevance of the audit results.

6. **Highlight Positive Aspects**

   Acknowledge positive aspects and achievements observed during the audit.

   Balance the communication by recognizing areas of compliance, effective governance practices, and ethical considerations.

7. **Present Findings in a Structured Manner**

   Present audit findings in a structured manner, categorizing them based on relevance and significance.

   Clearly articulate each finding, providing details on the observed issues and their implications.

8. **Offer Practical Recommendations**

   Clearly communicate recommendations in a practical and actionable format.

   Ensure that recommendations are presented with a focus on how they can be implemented to address identified issues.

9. **Discuss Risks and Impacts**

   Discuss the risks associated with identified findings and noncompliance.

   Clearly articulate the potential impacts of the findings on AI programs, compliance, and overall business operations.

10. **Facilitate Q&A Sessions**

    Schedule Q&A sessions or open forums to allow stakeholders to ask questions and seek clarifications.

    Create an environment that encourages dialogue and ensures that stakeholders feel comfortable seeking additional information.

11. **Customize Communication Channels**

    Utilize various communication channels to reach different stakeholder groups effectively.

Consider using presentations, reports, meetings, and email communications based on the preferences of each group.

12. **Engage Executives in a Briefing Session**

    Conduct a dedicated briefing session for executives to present the audit results.

    Present findings in a clear and understandable manner.

    Provide an opportunity for executives to ask questions, share insights, and discuss the strategic implications of the findings.

    Collaborate with management to address and remediate identified issues.

13. **Collaborate with AI Development Teams**

    Engage in collaborative sessions with AI development teams to discuss technical aspects of the audit findings.

    Encourage open communication and a shared understanding of the implications for ongoing development efforts.

14. **Emphasize the Importance of Compliance**

    Emphasize the importance of compliance with regulations, organizational policies, and ethical standards.

    Reinforce the organization's commitment to ethical AI practices and responsible use of AI technologies.

15. **Provide Resources for Remediation**

    Offer resources and support for implementing remediation efforts.

    Provide documentation, training materials, or access to subject matter experts to facilitate the resolution of identified issues.

16. **Encourage Action and Accountability**

    Clearly communicate the need for action and accountability in addressing audit findings.

    Establish timelines for implementing recommendations and monitor progress.

17. **Follow Up on Action Items**

    Follow up with stakeholders to ensure that action items are being addressed and implemented.

    Provide regular updates on the status of remediation efforts.

18. **Document and Archive Communications**

    Document all communication related to audit results and archive records for future reference.

    Maintain a clear record of discussions, decisions, and actions taken in response to the audit.

19. **Facilitate Continuous Dialogue**

    Establish a framework for continuous dialogue with stakeholders on AI Governance, compliance, and ethical considerations.

    Foster an environment of transparency and collaboration to address emerging challenges.

20. **Seek Feedback**

    Actively seek feedback from stakeholders on the communication process and the clarity of presented information.

    Use feedback to improve future communication efforts.

By following these steps, organizations can ensure that audit results are communicated effectively to relevant stakeholders, fostering a shared understanding of findings, promoting accountability, and driving actions to enhance AI Governance and compliance.

Continuous Improvement

- **Provide feedback for continuous improvement of AI Governance processes.**

Continuous improvement is essential for enhancing AI Governance processes and ensuring that AI programs evolve to meet changing standards and expectations. Here are the steps involved in providing feedback for continuous improvement of AI Governance processes:

1. **Establish a Feedback Mechanism**

   Set up a structured feedback mechanism to gather insights and opinions on AI Governance processes.

   Encourage stakeholders to provide feedback through surveys, interviews, suggestion boxes, or other channels.

2. **Define Clear Objectives for Feedback**

   Clearly define the objectives of seeking feedback for continuous improvement.

   Identify specific areas of AI Governance, compliance, or ethical considerations that require input and insights.

3. **Engage Stakeholders**

   Engage a diverse set of stakeholders, including AI development teams, compliance officers, legal teams, data scientists, and end users.

   Ensure representation from different departments and levels within the organization.

4. **Encourage Open and Honest Communication**

   Foster an environment of open and honest communication to encourage stakeholders to share their perspectives without fear of retribution.

   Emphasize the importance of constructive feedback for driving improvements.

5. **Define Feedback Criteria**

   Clearly define criteria for evaluating feedback.

   Establish parameters such as relevance, specificity, and actionable insights to ensure that feedback is valuable for improvement.

6. **Collect Data on AI Performance**

   Collect quantitative and qualitative data on AI performance, including metrics related to accuracy, reliability, and compliance.

   Use data analytics to identify trends and patterns that may highlight areas for improvement.

7. **Conduct Regular Audits and Assessments**

   Conduct regular audits and assessments of AI Governance processes.

   Use internal or external audit teams to evaluate adherence to policies, regulatory requirements, and ethical standards.

8. **Review Incident Reports and Responses**

   Review incident reports and responses related to AI programs.

Analyze how incidents were handled, identify root causes, and assess the effectiveness of incident response mechanisms.

9. **Analyze Stakeholder Satisfaction**

   Analyze stakeholder satisfaction by seeking feedback on their experiences with AI applications.

   Understand end users' perceptions, concerns, and expectations related to AI technologies.

10. **Identify Opportunities for Automation**

    Identify opportunities to automate aspects of AI Governance processes to enhance efficiency and reduce manual interventions.

    Evaluate the use of advanced technologies such as AI-driven analytics for continuous monitoring.

11. **Assess Training and Awareness Programs**

    Assess the effectiveness of training and awareness programs on AI Governance.

    Ensure that stakeholders are well informed about policies, procedures, and ethical considerations through regular training sessions.

12. **Benchmark Against Best Practices**

    Benchmark AI Governance processes against industry best practices.

    Stay informed about emerging standards and guidelines to align governance practices with the latest advancements in the field.

13. **Conduct Root Cause Analysis**

    Conduct root cause analysis for any identified issues or shortcomings in AI Governance.

    Determine the underlying causes of problems to implement targeted and effective solutions.

14. **Prioritize Improvement Initiatives**

    Prioritize improvement initiatives based on the severity and impact of identified issues.

    Allocate resources and efforts to address high-priority areas first.

15. **Develop Action Plans**

    Develop action plans outlining the steps to be taken for continuous improvement.

    Assign responsibilities, set timelines, and establish milestones for implementing improvements.

16. **Implement Changes Incrementally**

    Implement changes incrementally to avoid disruptions to ongoing AI projects.

    Roll out improvements in phases, monitoring the impact at each stage.

17. **Monitor and Evaluate Progress**

    Establish mechanisms to monitor and evaluate the progress of improvement initiatives.

    Use key performance indicators (KPIs) to measure the effectiveness of implemented changes.

18. **Iterate Based on Feedback**

    Iterate based on ongoing feedback and performance evaluations.

    Continuously refine AI Governance processes in response to changing requirements, feedback, and industry developments.

19. **Document Changes and Lessons Learned**

    Document all changes made to AI Governance processes.

    Capture lessons learned from improvement initiatives to inform future decision-making and strategies.

20. **Promote a Culture of Continuous Improvement**

    Promote a culture of continuous improvement across the organization.

    Encourage all stakeholders to actively participate in providing feedback and contributing to the enhancement of AI Governance processes.

By following these steps, organizations can create a robust feedback loop for continuous improvement, ensuring that AI Governance processes remain effective, compliant, and aligned with ethical standards in a dynamic and evolving landscape.

Conclusion

The auditing function in AI Governance ensures accountability, transparency, and compliance with established standards. By systematically evaluating AI systems, the auditing function contributes to the overall risk management and governance framework. Regular audits help organizations adapt to evolving threats, maintain ethical standards, and continuously improve their AI Governance processes. Collaboration between auditors, IT professionals, data scientists, and other stakeholders is essential for a robust and effective AI Governance framework.

Key Points

- Auditing provides an independent and objective assessment of AI systems, helping organizations identify and mitigate risks.
- Collaboration with key stakeholders ensures a comprehensive understanding of AI processes.
- Considering data governance within the audit scope is essential to assess how data is collected, processed, stored, and used in AI systems.
- The evaluation of practices and methodologies employed in AI model development helps in understanding the entire AI lifecycle.
- Ethical considerations, such as the impact on societal values, privacy, and human rights, should be included in the audit examination.
- The establishment of audit objectives related to data privacy involves considerations such as how personally identifiable information (PII) is handled, compliance with data protection laws, and processes for obtaining and managing consent.
- Collaborating with key stakeholders is essential to establishing effective audit objectives that align with business objectives and AI system functionalities.
- Guidelines related to accountability and governance in AI should be reviewed to establish audit objectives that assess the effectiveness of governance structures, decision-making processes, and mechanisms for addressing accountability.
- Providing training to audit teams on specific regulatory requirements and industry standards relevant to AI Governance is essential.

- Conducting a comprehensive risk assessment of AI programs is essential for identifying and mitigating potential risks associated with their development, deployment, and use.
- Vendor and third-party risks are scrutinized if external components or services are integrated into the AI program.
- Organizations need to create a comprehensive list of laws, regulations, and standards applicable to AI in their industry and geographic location.
- It is essential to check model training and validation procedures, focusing on the representativeness, unbiased nature, and diversity of training data.
- The assessment should extend to fairness and non-discrimination in AI decision-making.
- Aligning the design and development of AI programs with the principles outlined in internal policies and industry standards is crucial.
- Identifying relevant industry standards is crucial.
- Periodically conducting internal audits is recommended to assess the effectiveness of compliance measures.
- Practices related to data retention and deletion are scrutinized, emphasizing secure deletion when data is no longer needed.
- A data management review should include policies that define data ownership and responsibility, data classification, data sharing and access, data retention and disposal, data quality management, data security, data privacy, and incident response and breach notification.
- Understanding the data used for training is crucial, requiring a comprehensive assessment of the quality, diversity, and representativeness of the training dataset.
- The stability of the model's performance over time and across different environments is checked, ensuring reliability and accuracy in real-world scenarios.
- Error Analysis is conducted to understand the types of errors the model makes, identifying common misclassification patterns and assessing their impact.
- Equalized odds analysis is performed to ensure that the model provides equal false positive and false negative rates across different demographic groups.
- Intersectional analysis, considering biases at the intersection of multiple sensitive attributes, is conducted to unveil biases that may not be apparent when analyzing each attribute independently.
- Exploration of threshold optimization techniques allows for adjusting decision thresholds based on different subgroups, aiming for a more balanced trade-off between false positives and false negatives.
- A comprehensive assessment of model outputs aims to identify biases in predictions and evaluate whether the model's decisions disproportionately impact specific groups.
- Scenario analysis is imperative to evaluate how the AI system behaves under different conditions.
- Exploratory data analysis (EDA) uncovers potential biases in the dataset, examining summary statistics and distributions to identify disparities among different groups.
- Network security is a crucial aspect, involving the examination of network configurations and security protocols to identify and address vulnerabilities that could be exploited for unauthorized access.
- Ensuring transparency in the decision-making processes of AI models is paramount for building trust, meeting ethical standards, and complying with regulations.

- Simulating AI-related incidents through **incident response simulations** is a proactive measure to test an organization's ability to handle unforeseen challenges.
- Supporting evidence, such as documentation, logs, screenshots, or other artifacts obtained during the audit, is included in an organized manner to substantiate the findings.

Key Glossary Terms

Equalized odds analysis in AI systems refers to a *fairness assessment technique that evaluates whether a model provides equal false positive and false negative rates across different demographic groups or subpopulations.* This analysis is particularly important in scenarios where the impact of errors may have disparate consequences for different groups, such as in lending, hiring, or criminal justice applications.

To understand equalized odds, let's break down the components:

1. **False Positive Rate (FPR):** The proportion of actual negatives that are incorrectly predicted as positives by the model.
2. **False Negative Rate (FNR):** The proportion of actual positives that are incorrectly predicted as negatives by the model.

Equalized odds analysis involves comparing these rates across various demographic groups to ensure that the model's error rates are similar for all groups. The goal is to avoid situations where certain groups are disproportionately affected by false positives or false negatives.

Equalized odds is one of several fairness metrics used to assess and mitigate biases in AI models. It aims to promote fairness by ensuring that the model's predictive errors are distributed fairly among different demographic groups, avoiding scenarios where certain groups are disproportionately affected by specific types of errors.

Reweighing training instances is a technique used in machine learning to address bias in training datasets, especially when certain groups are underrepresented or overrepresented. The goal is to mitigate bias in the model by adjusting the weights assigned to different instances during the training process.

In the context of bias mitigation, "reweighing" involves assigning different weights to instances based on their sensitive attributes. These sensitive attributes could include characteristics like race, gender, or any other attribute that is identified as potentially leading to bias.

The process typically involves the following steps:

1. **Identification of Sensitive Attributes:** Identify the sensitive attributes in the dataset that are associated with potential biases.
2. **Weight Adjustment:** Assign different weights to instances based on their sensitive attributes. Instances from underrepresented groups may be assigned higher weights, while instances from overrepresented groups may be assigned lower weights.
3. **Training the Model:** Train the machine learning model using the reweighted dataset. The model will now give more importance to instances from underrepresented groups, helping to balance the impact of these instances during training.
4. **Evaluation:** Evaluate the model's performance using fairness metrics to ensure that bias has been reduced. Common fairness metrics include disparate impact, equalized odds, and statistical parity.

The reweighing technique is part of a broader set of strategies aimed at promoting fairness and mitigating bias in machine learning models. It recognizes the importance of addressing imbalances in training data to ensure that models make predictions that are fair and unbiased across different demographic groups.

Some common **bias mitigation strategies** in AI system deployment include:

1. **Diverse and Representative Training Data:** Ensure that the training dataset used to train the AI model is diverse and representative of the population it is meant to serve. This helps in capturing a comprehensive range of scenarios and reduces the risk of biased model behavior.
2. **Bias Detection and Measurement:** Implement tools and techniques to detect and measure bias in the AI system. This involves using specific metrics and evaluation methods to identify areas where bias may be present.
3. **Fairness-aware Algorithms:** Choose or develop algorithms that are designed to be inherently fair. Fairness-aware algorithms are designed to minimize biases and ensure equitable treatment across different groups.
4. **Re-weighing Training Instances:** Adjust the weights of different instances in the training dataset to address imbalances and biases. This technique involves assigning different weights to instances based on their importance in mitigating bias.
5. **Adversarial Training:** Incorporate adversarial training, where the model is trained to resist adversarial attempts to introduce bias. This involves training the model against scenarios specifically designed to induce bias.
6. **Bias-aware Regularization:** Apply regularization techniques that penalize the model for making decisions that are strongly correlated with sensitive attributes. This encourages the model to disregard features that may lead to biased outcomes.
7. **Inclusive Feature Engineering:** Be mindful of the features used in model training and avoid features that may lead to biased outcomes. Additionally, include features that promote fairness and inclusivity.
8. **Algorithmic Transparency and Explainability:** Prioritize transparency and explainability in your algorithms. Models that provide clear explanations for their decisions are easier to audit, and biases can be more readily identified and addressed.
9. **User Feedback Loops:** Implement mechanisms for users to provide feedback on model outputs. This feedback can be invaluable in identifying instances where the model may exhibit bias or make unfair decisions.
10. **Threshold Optimization:** Explore optimization of decision thresholds based on different subgroups to achieve a more balanced trade-off between false positives and false negatives for each group.
11. **Continuous Monitoring:** Set up continuous monitoring systems to track the model's performance over time. Regularly review and update the model based on changes in data patterns, user feedback, and business requirements.
12. **Ethical and Multidisciplinary Oversight:** Establish ethical oversight boards or involve multidisciplinary teams, including ethicists, domain experts, and stakeholders, in the decision-making process. This can provide diverse perspectives on potential biases.

These strategies can be applied individually or in combination, depending on the specific characteristics and requirements of the AI system and its use cases. It's important to continuously assess and improve these strategies throughout the deployment lifecycle.

1. **Fairness Indicators:** Fairness Indicators is a tool developed by Google that aids in assessing and visualizing fairness in machine learning models. It provides metrics to evaluate model performance across different subgroups defined by sensitive attributes, helping to identify and address potential biases. Fairness Indicators is designed to integrate seamlessly into **TensorFlow**, a popular open-source machine learning framework.
2. **AI Fairness 360 (AIF360):** AI Fairness 360 is an open-source toolkit developed by IBM to help detect and mitigate biases in machine learning models. It provides a comprehensive set of algorithms and metrics for fairness assessment, allowing users to measure and address biases related to various attributes such as race, gender, or age. AIF360 supports integration with popular machine learning frameworks and can be applied throughout the model development pipeline.
3. **Themis:** Themis is a **Python** library designed to address bias in machine learning models, focusing on disparate impact and disparate mistreatment. It provides a set of tools for bias detection and fairness-aware machine learning, allowing users to assess and mitigate biases in their models. Themis supports integration with popular machine learning frameworks and is aimed at providing a flexible and customizable solution for fairness in AI systems.

A **confusion matrix**, also known as an **error matrix**, is a table used in machine learning to evaluate the performance of a classification model. It provides a comprehensive summary of the model's predictions by comparing them to the actual outcomes in a dataset. The matrix is particularly useful when assessing the model's outputs across different demographic groups or classes.

In a binary classification scenario, a confusion matrix typically consists of four components:

1. **True Positive (TP):** Instances where the model correctly predicted the positive class.
2. **True Negative (TN):** Instances where the model correctly predicted the negative class.
3. **False Positive (FP):** Instances where the model incorrectly predicted the positive class when the actual class was negative (Type I error).
4. **False Negative (FN):** Instances where the model incorrectly predicted the negative class when the actual class was positive (Type II error).

The confusion matrix is organized as a 2x2 table, where the rows represent the actual classes and the columns represent the predicted classes. Each cell in the matrix corresponds to the count of instances falling into a particular category. The diagonal elements (top-left to bottom right) represent correct predictions, while the off-diagonal elements represent errors.

Confusion matrices are crucial for evaluating model performance, especially in the context of assessing disparities in predictions across different demographic groups. By examining the values in the matrix, one can calculate various performance metrics such as accuracy, precision, recall, and F1 score, which provide insights into the model's ability to make correct predictions and its performance across different subgroups or classes.

1. **Re-ranking:** Re-ranking is a post-processing technique used to mitigate bias in AI model predictions. After the initial predictions are made, re-ranking involves adjusting the order or ranking of the predictions based on certain fairness criteria. This technique aims to ensure that the final outcomes are more equitable and less influenced by biases. By re-evaluating and reordering the predictions, re-ranking seeks to address disparities that may have arisen during the initial model inference.
2. **Re-weighting:** Re-weighting is a post-processing technique that involves assigning different weights to instances in the dataset based on their sensitive attributes or other

relevant factors. The goal is to give more or less importance to certain instances during the model's training or prediction phases. By adjusting the weights, re-weighting aims to counteract biases present in the data, ensuring that the model pays equal attention to all relevant groups. This technique is often applied to balance the impact of different demographic groups on the model's performance.

3. **Adversarial Debiasing:** Adversarial debiasing is a post-processing technique designed to reduce bias in AI models by incorporating an adversarial training approach. In this method, a debiasing adversary is introduced during the training process to penalize the model for making predictions that correlate with sensitive attributes. The model is simultaneously trained to minimize prediction errors and to withstand the adversarial attempts to introduce bias. Adversarial debiasing aims to create a model that is more robust to biases and less likely to produce unfair or discriminatory outcomes.

Threshold optimization techniques allow for *adjusting decision thresholds based on different subgroups, aiming for a more balanced trade-off between false positives and false negatives.*

Notes

1 Mökander, Curl & Kshirsagar, "A Blueprint for Auditing Generative AI," SSRN, July 12, 2024, accessed May 14, 2025, https://papers.ssrn.com/sol3/papers.cfm?abstract_id=4887768.

2 Huttenlocher, Ozdaglar & Goldston, "A Framework for U.S. AI Governance," Massachusetts Institute of Technology, November 28, 2023, accessed May 12, 2025, https://computing.mit.edu/wp-content/uploads/2023/11/AIPolicyBrief.pdf.

3 Oluoch, "Crossing Boundaries: The Ethics of AI and Geographic Information Technologies," University of Twente, March 9, 2024, accessed May 15, 2025, https://www.mdpi.com/2220-9964/13/3/87.

4 Whang, Roh, Song & Lee, "Data Collection and Quality Challenges in Deep Learning: A Data-Centric AI Perspective," ARXIV.org, December 26, 2022, accessed May 18, 2025, https://arxiv.org/pdf/2112.06409.

5 Lalor, Abbasi, et al., "Should Fairness Be a Metric or a Model? A Model-Based Framework for Assessing Bias in Machine Learning Pipelines," Association for Computing Machinery, March 22, 2024, accessed May 20, 2025. https://dl.acm.org/doi/abs/10.1145/3641276.

Appendix
Additional Legal Citations

1.1 Liability and Accountability

Establishing liability when AI systems cause harm or make incorrect decisions is a challenge that involves a complex interplay of various legal frameworks. Here are some key areas of law that may be relevant when addressing liability for AI-related harm:

1.1.1.1 Product Liability Laws

Product liability laws hold manufacturers, distributors, and sellers responsible for defective products that cause harm to consumers. If an AI system is considered a "product," product liability laws may come into play when the AI system causes harm. These laws vary by jurisdiction but generally require proving that the product was defective or unreasonably dangerous.

1.1.1.2 Negligence Law

Negligence laws may apply when the harm caused by an AI system results from the failure of individuals or entities to exercise reasonable care. This can include negligence in the design, development, testing, or deployment of AI systems.

1.1.1.3 Contract Law

Liability for AI-related harm may be governed by contractual agreements between parties involved in the development, deployment, or use of AI systems. Contracts may define responsibilities, warranties, and indemnification provisions in the event of harm.

1.1.1.4 Strict Liability

Some jurisdictions have adopted strict liability principles, which hold parties liable for harm caused by a product or activity regardless of fault. Strict liability may be applicable if an AI system is considered an abnormally dangerous or ultra-hazardous activity.

1.1.1.5 Agency Law

Agency principles may be relevant when determining liability for AI decisions, especially in situations where the AI acts on behalf of a human or a legal entity. Questions of agency and whether the AI's actions can be attributed to a specific party may arise.

1.1.1.6 *Data Protection and Privacy Laws*

If harm results from a violation of data protection or privacy laws, entities involved in the processing of personal data through AI systems may be held liable. For example, the General Data Protection Regulation (GDPR) in the United States imposes strict obligations on entities processing personal data.

1.1.1.7 *Ethical Guidelines and Industry Standards*

Adherence to ethical guidelines and industry standards may influence liability considerations. Failing to comply with established ethical norms or industry standards could be a factor in determining legal responsibility.

1.1.1.8 *Regulatory Compliance*

Compliance with specific regulations governing AI use, such as safety and security standards, may impact liability. Regulatory frameworks are evolving, and adherence to relevant laws and guidelines is crucial.

1.1.1.9 *Tort Law*

Tort law, including concepts such as intentional torts or tortious interference, may be relevant in cases where harm results from intentional actions or interference with contractual relations.

1.1.1.10 *AI-Specific Legislation*

Some jurisdictions are considering or have implemented specific legislation addressing liability for AI systems. These laws may outline the responsibilities of developers, users, and other stakeholders in mitigating risks and ensuring accountability.

It's important to note that the legal landscape concerning AI liability is dynamic. Legal advice tailored to the specific circumstances and jurisdiction is essential to navigate the complexities of establishing liability for harm caused by AI systems.

1.2 Intellectual Property (IP)

There are several legal frameworks that may be relevant in addressing the ownership and protection of intellectual property (IP) used in or generated by AI systems. The complexity arises because AI often involves a combination of human and machine contributions. Here are some key legal aspects and laws to consider:

1.2.1.1 *Patent Laws*

Depending on jurisdiction, existing patent laws may require clarification on whether AI-generated inventions are eligible for patent protection.

1.2.1.2 Copyright Law

Copyright protects original works of authorship fixed in a tangible medium of expression. In the context of AI-generated content, the question of authorship becomes crucial. Some jurisdictions, like the United States, typically grant copyright to human authors, raising questions about the eligibility of AI-generated works for copyright protection. Some countries, however, have recognized AI as a creator for copyright purposes.

1.2.1.3 Trade Secret Law

Trade secret laws protect confidential and proprietary information. If an AI system is used to develop a trade secret, the protection of that secret can be crucial. Companies should take measures to ensure the confidentiality of their AI algorithms and training data.

1.2.1.4 Contract Law

Ownership and licensing of AI-generated IP can be defined through contracts. Clear contractual agreements between parties involved in AI development, including employees, contractors, and collaborators, can help establish ownership rights over the generated IP.

1.2.1.5 Data Protection and Privacy Laws

Data protection laws, such as the General Data Protection Regulation (GDPR) in the European Union, may impact the use of personal data in AI systems. Complying with these laws is essential to avoid legal issues related to the collection and processing of data.

1.2.1.6 Antitrust Law

In cases where AI-generated IP results from collaboration or agreements between multiple entities, antitrust laws may come into play to ensure fair competition and prevent anticompetitive behavior.

1.2.1.7 Ethical Guidelines and Industry Standards

Industry-specific ethical guidelines and standards can provide guidance on responsible AI development and use. Adhering to these guidelines can help organizations navigate ethical considerations and potential legal challenges.

1.2.1.8 Regulatory Frameworks for AI

Emerging regulatory frameworks for AI, such as those being developed in various jurisdictions, may address issues related to AI-generated IP. These frameworks often include considerations for transparency, accountability, and the ethical use of AI.

1.2.1.9 Common Law Principles

In some cases, common law principles related to agency and ownership may be applied to determine ownership of AI-generated IP. Courts may consider factors such as the degree of human involvement in the AI's creation.

It's important to note that the legal landscape surrounding AI-generated IP is evolving, and there may be variations in how different jurisdictions approach these issues. Legal advice specific to the jurisdiction and industry context is crucial for organizations dealing with AI-generated intellectual property to navigate the complexities and ensure compliance with relevant laws and regulations.

1.3 Additional Legal Considerations

1.3.1 Healthcare Regulations

The use of AI in healthcare introduces regulatory considerations related to patient safety and data security. Furthermore, many jurisdictions have substantial regulation over health data privacy, as such data is viewed as having particular sensitivity to personal sovereignty.

1.3.2 Employment and Labor Laws

Guarding the impact of AI on employment, workforce dynamics, and potential legal implications. The intersection of AI systems and employment and labor laws involves considerations related to workforce management, privacy, discrimination, and intellectual property. While specific laws may vary by jurisdiction, here are some general areas of employment and labor laws that pertain to AI systems and development from a governance perspective.

1.3.2.1 Health and Safety Regulations

Workplace safety regulations may be applicable when deploying AI systems in work environments. Employers must ensure that AI technologies do not compromise the health and safety of workers.

1.3.2.2 Employee Monitoring Laws

Laws related to the monitoring of employees, such as electronic communications and surveillance, may impact the deployment of AI systems that involve monitoring or data collection. Compliance with these laws is crucial for protecting employee privacy.

1.3.2.3 Intellectual Property Laws

Organizations should consider intellectual property laws when developing AI systems. Employment contracts and intellectual property laws may dictate ownership of AI-generated innovations and developments.

1.3.2.4 Wage and Hour Laws

Compliance with wage and hour laws, including regulations on minimum wage, overtime pay, and working hours, remains essential when implementing AI systems that impact employee work schedules and compensation.

1.3.2.5 Employee Training and Education

Employers should consider providing training and education to employees regarding AI systems and technologies to ensure a smooth integration into the workplace and mitigate potential concerns.

1.3.2.6 Ethical Guidelines and Best Practices

While not legal requirements, ethical guidelines and best practices can play a crucial role in AI Governance. Organizations may adopt ethical principles to guide the responsible and fair use of AI in employment contexts.

AI Governance in the employment context requires a comprehensive approach that considers legal, ethical, and practical considerations. Organizations should work closely with legal and HR professionals to navigate the complex landscape of employment and labor laws in the context of AI system development and deployment.

1.3.3 National Security and Cybersecurity

AI systems may be vulnerable to cybersecurity threats, raising concerns about national security. Further, as AI systems are particularly susceptible to vulnerabilities introduced into training data or introduced into an iterative-learning AI via user interactions, security efforts must be comprehensive, ongoing, and constantly evolving to the evolving threat environment.

The deployment of AI in sensitive sectors, particularly those related to national security, is subject to various laws and regulations aimed at addressing cybersecurity threats and safeguarding national interests. The legal landscape varies across countries, but there are common themes in the regulation of AI in sensitive sectors.

1.3.4 Antitrust and Competition Laws

The concentration of AI capabilities in a few large entities may raise antitrust concerns. This is particularly true of generative AI platforms such as Large Language Models (LLMs), which are extremely demanding of computing and storage capacity. The costs to implement the latest iterations of LLMs are scaling into the billions of dollars per generation, deeply concentrating the expertise and control of this technology domain.

2 Examples of Regulations Governing AI

2.1 Examples of Privacy Regulations

The following is a representative sample of privacy regulations from around the world. The list is ever-growing, further complicating governance and compliance.

2.2 Personal Privacy

2.2.1.1 North America

2.2.1.2 United States, General Data Protection Regulation (GDPR)

The GDPR is a comprehensive regulation that applies to the processing of personal data of EU residents. It has extraterritorial reach, impacting organizations outside the EU if they process the personal data of EU residents.

2.2.1.3 California, California Consumer Privacy Act (CCPA)

The CCPA grants California residents certain rights regarding their personal information. It imposes obligations on businesses to be transparent about data collection practices, allow consumers to opt out of certain data sharing, and provide access and deletion rights.

2.2.1.4 California Privacy Rights Act (CPRA)

CPRA builds on the CCPA and introduces additional privacy rights and obligations. It establishes the California Privacy Protection Agency to enforce and implement privacy laws.

2.2.1.5 Virginia: Virginia Consumer Data Protection Act (CDPA)

The CDPA is similar to the CCPA and provides consumers with certain rights over their personal data. It applies to businesses that process the personal data of Virginia residents and has specific requirements for data controllers and processors.

2.2.1.6 Colorado: Colorado Privacy Act (CPA)

The CPA grants Colorado residents certain rights over their personal data and imposes obligations on businesses. It requires businesses to conduct data protection assessments for certain processing activities and provides consumers with the right to opt out of certain data processing.

2.2.1.7 New York: Stop Hacks and Improve Electronic Data Security (SHIELD) Act

The SHIELD Act imposes data breach notification requirements on businesses that collect private information of New York residents. It also requires businesses to implement reasonable data security measures.

2.2.1.8 Other States

Several other states have introduced or are in the process of considering data protection laws. For example, Washington, Texas, and Massachusetts have proposed or discussed comprehensive privacy legislation.

2.2.1.9 Biometric Information

Some states, like Illinois (Biometric Information Privacy Act - BIPA), have specific laws regulating the collection and use of biometric information. AI systems that use biometric data should comply with these regulations.

2.2.1.10 Canada: Personal Information Protection and Electronic Documents Act (PIPEDA)

PIPEDA governs the collection, use, and disclosure of personal information by private-sector organizations. It applies to organizations engaged in commercial activities across the United States.

2.2.1.11 Europe

2.2.1.12 European Union: General Data Protection Regulation (GDPR)

The GDPR is a comprehensive regulation that applies to the processing of personal data of EU residents. It has extraterritorial reach, impacting organizations outside the EU if they process the personal data of EU residents.

2.2.1.13 ePrivacy Directive

This directive concerns the processing of personal data and the protection of privacy in the electronic communications sector. It works in conjunction with the GDPR and is currently being updated to become the ePrivacy Regulation.

2.2.1.14 Asia

2.2.1.15 Singapore

Singapore's primary data privacy law is the Personal Data Protection Act (PDPA), which came into effect on January 2, 2013, with various amendments since then. The PDPA governs the collection, use, and disclosure of personal data by organizations in Singapore, with the aim of protecting individuals' personal information while facilitating the legitimate use of data for business and other purposes.

2.2.1.16 People's Republic of China (PRC)

China's primary data privacy law is the Personal Information Protection Law (PIPL), which came into effect on November 1, 2021. The PIPL is considered one of the most comprehensive data protection laws in China and establishes rules for the collection, processing, and transfer of personal information by both government agencies and private entities.

2.2.1.17 Japan

Japan's primary data privacy law is the Act on the Protection of Personal Information (APPI), which was first enacted in 2003 and has undergone several amendments since then. The APPI governs the handling of personal information by businesses, government agencies, and other organizations in Japan, aiming to protect individuals' privacy rights while promoting the responsible use of personal data.

2.2.1.18 South Korea

South Korea's primary data privacy law is the Act on the Protection of Personal Information (APPI), also known as the Personal Information Protection Act (PIPA). This law governs the collection, use, and handling of personal information by businesses, government agencies, and other organizations in South Korea, with the aim of protecting individuals' privacy rights and ensuring the secure and responsible handling of personal data.

2.2.1.19 Middle East

2.2.1.20 Saudi Arabia

Saudi Arabia implemented its Regulations of the Personal Data Protection Law on September 7, 2023. The KSA's first comprehensive national data protection legislation is broadly modeled on the European GDPR. The legal framework applies across all industry sectors and prescribes strict obligations on almost anyone dealing with personal data, such as reporting data breaches within seventy-two hours, appointing a Data Protection Officer in certain circumstances, carrying out legitimate interest assessments and data protection impact assessments, and maintaining a record of processing activities.

2.2.1.21 South America

2.2.1.22 Colombia

The main legislation related to data protection in Colombia is Law 1581 of 2012, which Issues General Provisions for the protection of personal data. The Personal Data Protection Law was enacted to guarantee the constitutional right of individuals to know, update, and rectify the information that has been collected about them in databases and to ensure that their personal data is processed in accordance with their privacy rights.

2.2.1.23 Brazil

Brazil's General Data Protection Law (LGPD), amended in 2019, provides for the processing of personal data, including by digital means, by a natural person or a legal entity of either public or private law, with the purpose of protecting the fundamental rights of freedom and privacy and the free development of the personality of the natural person.

AI practitioners should regularly monitor updates to these laws and guidelines, as regulatory frameworks in the field of AI are evolving rapidly. Additionally, seeking legal advice to ensure compliance with specific regional laws is crucial.

2.3 *Bias and Fairness Regulations*

In the United States, addressing biases in training data and mitigating potential discrimination in AI systems involves compliance with various regulations beyond Title VII of the Civil Rights Act. Here are some key regulations and guidelines that apply:

2.3.1.1 Fair Credit Reporting Act (FCRA)

The FCRA regulates the collection, dissemination, and use of consumer information, including credit reports. It aims to ensure fairness, accuracy, and privacy of consumer information used by credit reporting agencies and businesses. AI systems used in credit scoring or lending must comply with FCRA requirements to prevent discriminatory practices.

2.3.1.2 Equal Employment Opportunity Commission (EEOC) Guidelines

The EEOC provides guidelines and regulations to enforce federal laws that prohibit employment discrimination. These guidelines help employers navigate issues related to fairness, objectivity, and non-discrimination in the context of AI tools used in hiring and employment decisions.

2.3.1.3 Age Discrimination in Employment Act (ADEA)

The ADEA prohibits employment discrimination against individuals aged forty or older. AI systems used in hiring and workforce management should be designed to avoid age-based discrimination, and compliance with the ADEA is crucial.

2.3.1.4 Americans with Disabilities Act (ADA)

The ADA prohibits discrimination against individuals with disabilities in various aspects, including employment. AI tools used in recruitment, hiring, and workplace decision-making should be accessible and not discriminate against individuals with disabilities.

2.3.1.5 Fair Housing Act (FHA)

The FHA prohibits discrimination in housing and related services based on race, color, religion, sex, disability, familial status, or national origin. AI systems involved in real estate, property management, or housing-related decisions should adhere to FHA regulations.

2.3.1.6 Uniform Guidelines on Employee Selection Procedures (UGESP)

These guidelines, issued by federal agencies, provide standards for assessing the impact of employment selection procedures on different demographic groups. Organizations using AI in employment decisions should align their practices with UGESP to ensure fairness.

2.3.1.7 Office of Federal Contract Compliance Programs (OFCCP) Requirements

Federal contractors and subcontractors are subject to specific requirements by the OFCCP, which monitors and enforces affirmative action and equal employment opportunity regulations. AI tools used by federal contractors must comply with these requirements.

2.3.1.8 Consumer Financial Protection Bureau (CFPB) Guidance

The CFPB provides guidance on fair lending practices and discrimination prevention in the financial sector. AI systems used in credit scoring and lending must comply with these guidelines to prevent discriminatory outcomes.

2.3.1.9 State-Specific Laws

Some states have enacted additional laws addressing discrimination and bias in the context of AI. For example, the Illinois Artificial Intelligence Video Interview Act regulates the use of AI in video interviews for employment purposes.

2.3.1.10 Algorithmic Accountability Act of 2022

The Algorithmic Accountability Act aims to address bias and discrimination concerns in AI systems by requiring companies to assess and mitigate risks.

2.4 Example Transparency Regulations

2.4.1.1 Algorithmic Accountability Act of 2022

This US bill aims to address concerns related to the transparency and accountability of automated decision systems.

2.4.1.2 Equal Employment Opportunity Commission (EEOC) Guidelines

The EEOC provides guidelines and regulations to enforce federal laws that prohibit employment discrimination. These guidelines help employers navigate issues related to fairness, objectivity, and non-discrimination in the context of AI tools used in hiring and employment decisions.

2.4.1.3 Age Discrimination in Employment Act (ADEA)

The ADEA prohibits employment discrimination against individuals aged 40 or older. AI systems used in hiring and workforce management should be designed to avoid age-based discrimination, and compliance with the ADEA is crucial.

2.4.1.4 Americans with Disabilities Act (ADA)

The ADA prohibits discrimination against individuals with disabilities in various aspects, including employment. AI tools used in recruitment, hiring, and workplace decision-making should be accessible and not discriminate against individuals with disabilities.

2.4.1.5 Fair Housing Act (FHA)

The FHA prohibits discrimination in housing and related services based on race, color, religion, sex, disability, familial status, or national origin. AI systems involved in real estate, property management, or housing-related decisions should adhere to FHA regulations.

2.4.1.6 Uniform Guidelines on Employee Selection Procedures (UGESP)

These guidelines, issued by federal agencies, provide standards for assessing the impact of employment selection procedures on different demographic groups. Organizations using AI in employment decisions should align their practices with UGESP to ensure fairness.

2.4.1.7 Office of Federal Contract Compliance Programs (OFCCP) Requirements

Federal contractors and subcontractors are subject to specific requirements by the OFCCP, which monitors and enforces affirmative action and equal employment opportunity regulations. AI tools used by federal contractors must comply with these requirements.

2.4.1.8 Consumer Financial Protection Bureau (CFPB) Guidance

The CFPB provides guidance on fair lending practices and discrimination prevention in the financial sector. AI systems used in credit scoring and lending must comply with these guidelines to prevent discriminatory outcomes.

2.4.1.9 State-Specific Laws

Some states have enacted additional laws addressing discrimination and bias in the context of AI. For example, the Illinois Artificial Intelligence Video Interview Act regulates the use of AI in video interviews for employment purposes.

2.5 Relevant Privacy Regulations

Several data protection and privacy laws around the world govern the transfer of data across borders, reflecting concerns about the protection of individuals' privacy rights. Here are some key global laws and regulations addressing privacy and data protection issues:

Europe

2.5.1.1 General Data Protection Regulation (GDPR)

The GDPR is a comprehensive data protection regulation applicable to the European Union (EU) and the European Economic Area (EEA). It imposes strict requirements on the transfer of personal data outside the EU/EEA. Adequate safeguards, such as Standard Contractual Clauses (SCCs) or Binding Corporate Rules (BCRs), must be in place for lawful cross-border data transfers.

United States

2.5.1.2 Privacy Shield (No Longer Valid)

The EU-US Privacy Shield was a framework designed to facilitate data transfers between the EU and the US. However, it was invalidated by the Court of Justice of the European Union (CJEU) in the "Schrems II" decision in 2020. Companies now need to rely on alternative mechanisms, such as SCCs or BCRs.

2.5.1.3 Standard Contractual Clauses (SCCs)

SCCs are contractual clauses approved by data protection authorities that provide a legal basis for transferring personal data outside the EU/EEA. Organizations can use SCCs as a tool to ensure the protection of data subjects' rights during cross-border transfers.

Asia-Pacific

2.5.1.4 Personal Data Protection Act (PDPA) - Singapore

The PDPA in Singapore regulates the collection, use, and disclosure of personal data. It includes provisions for cross-border data transfers and requires organizations to ensure that the recipient country has a comparable standard of data protection.

2.5.1.5 Personal Information Protection Law (PIPL) - China

The PIPL in China, effective as of November 2021, includes provisions related to the cross-border transfer of personal information. It requires data controllers to conduct assessments before transferring data outside of China.

Canada

2.5.1.6 Personal Information Protection and Electronic Documents Act (PIPEDA)

PIPEDA governs the collection, use, and disclosure of personal information in the private sector. Organizations subject to PIPEDA must ensure that cross-border data transfers comply with the law.

Latin America

2.5.1.7 General Data Protection Law (LGPD) — Brazil

The LGPD in Brazil governs the processing of personal data and includes provisions related to cross-border data transfers. Organizations must follow specific requirements when transferring data outside of Brazil.

International Initiatives

2.5.1.8 Convention 108+ of the Council of Europe

Convention 108+, an international treaty for the protection of individuals with regard to the processing of personal data, provides a framework for data protection cooperation. It emphasizes the need for safeguards when transferring data to countries outside the convention.

2.5.1.9 APEC Cross-Border Privacy Rules (CBPR) System

The Asia-Pacific Economic Cooperation (APEC) CBPR System establishes a framework for the cross-border transfer of personal information among participating APEC economies.

2.5.1.10 Convention for the Protection of Individuals with Regard to Automatic Processing of Personal Data (Convention 108)

Convention 108, under the Council of Europe, serves as the first legally binding international treaty related to data protection.

It's crucial for organizations engaged in cross-border data transfers to understand and comply with the data protection laws applicable in the regions where they operate. Given the evolving nature of these laws, staying informed about updates and seeking legal advice is essential for ensuring compliance.

2.6 Example Employment and Labor Regulations

2.6.1.1 Fair Labor Standards Act (FLSA)

In the US, concerns may arise about compliance with wage and hour laws as AI systems automate certain tasks.

2.6.1.2 Non-Discrimination Laws

2.6.1.3 Title VII of the Civil Rights Act (United States)

Title VII prohibits discrimination based on race, color, religion, sex, or national origin in employment decisions. AI systems used in hiring and personnel management should comply with these non-discrimination provisions.

2.6.1.4 Equality Act (United States)

The Equality Act addresses discrimination based on various protected characteristics, including age, disability, gender, and race. Organizations using AI in employment decisions should ensure compliance with these anti-discrimination provisions.

2.6.1.5 Fair Employment Practices

Various jurisdictions have laws governing fair employment practices. For example, the Fair Employment Practices Act (FEPA) in the US prohibits discriminatory practices in employment based on factors such as race, color, religion, or national origin.

2.6.1.6 Labor Union and Collective Bargaining Laws

Organizations using AI systems in the workplace should be mindful of labor union laws and collective bargaining agreements that may govern issues such as working conditions, wages, and employee rights.

2.6.1.7 Health and Safety Regulations

Workplace safety regulations may be applicable when deploying AI systems in work environments. Employers must ensure that AI technologies do not compromise the health and safety of workers.

2.6.1.8 Employee Monitoring Laws

Laws related to the monitoring of employees, such as electronic communications and surveillance, may impact the deployment of AI systems that involve monitoring or data collection. Compliance with these laws is crucial for protecting employee privacy.

2.6.1.9 Intellectual Property Laws

Organizations should consider intellectual property laws when developing AI systems. Employment contracts and intellectual property laws may dictate ownership of AI-generated innovations and developments.

2.6.1.10 Wage and Hour Laws

Compliance with wage and hour laws, including regulations on minimum wage, overtime pay, and working hours, remains essential when implementing AI systems that impact employee work schedules and compensation.

2.6.1.11 Employee Training and Education

Employers should consider providing training and education to employees regarding AI systems and technologies to ensure a smooth integration into the workplace and mitigate potential concerns.

2.6.1.12 Ethical Guidelines and Best Practices

While not legal requirements, ethical guidelines and best practices can play a crucial role in AI Governance. Organizations may adopt ethical principles to guide the responsible and fair use of AI in employment contexts.

AI Governance in the employment context requires a comprehensive approach that considers legal, ethical, and practical considerations. Organizations should work closely with legal and HR professionals to navigate the complex landscape of employment and labor laws in the context of AI system development and deployment.

2.7 Sample Healthcare Regulations

2.7.1.1 European Union

2.7.1.2 General Data Protection Regulation (GDPR)

The GDPR, applicable across the European Union (EU), regulates the processing of personal data. Healthcare providers and AI developers in the healthcare sector must comply with GDPR requirements, ensuring patient data privacy and security.

2.7.1.3 Medical Device Regulation (MDR)

The MDR sets standards for the safety and performance of medical devices, including certain AI applications used in healthcare. AI-based medical devices may need to undergo a conformity assessment and obtain CE marking to be marketed in the EU.

2.7.1.4 United States

2.7.1.5 Health Insurance Portability and Accountability Act (HIPAA)

HIPAA is a US federal law that sets standards for the privacy and security of protected health information (PHI). Covered entities, including healthcare providers and insurers, must comply with HIPAA when using AI systems that involve patient data.

2.7.1.6 Federal Food, Drug, and Cosmetic Act (FD&C Act)

The US Food and Drug Administration (FDA) oversees the regulation of medical devices, including certain AI applications. Developers of AI-based medical devices may need to obtain FDA clearance or approval before marketing them.

2.7.1.7 21st Century Cures Act

The 21st Century Cures Act includes provisions related to the development and use of health information technology, aiming to improve interoperability and patient access to health information.

2.7.1.8 Canada

2.7.1.9 Personal Information Protection and Electronic Documents Act (PIPEDA)

PIPEDA regulates the collection, use, and disclosure of personal information, including health information. Healthcare providers and AI developers must adhere to PIPEDA when handling patient data.

2.7.1.10 United Kingdom

2.7.1.11 Data Protection Act 2018 (DPA 2018)

The DPA 2018 supplements the GDPR in the UK and includes provisions specific to the processing of health data. Healthcare organizations and AI developers must comply with both the GDPR and DPA 2018.

2.7.1.12 Australia

2.7.1.13 Privacy Act 1988

The Privacy Act in Australia governs the handling of personal information, including health information. Healthcare providers and AI developers must comply with privacy principles outlined in the Act.

2.7.1.14 International Initiatives

2.7.1.15 World Health Organization (WHO) Global Strategy on Digital Health

The WHO provides guidance on the use of digital health technologies, including AI, to promote patient safety, data security, and ethical considerations.

2.7.1.16 International Medical Device Regulators Forum (IMDRF)

The IMDRF provides a forum for international collaboration on the regulation of medical devices, including AI-based medical devices.

2.7.1.17 International Organization for Standardization (ISO)

ISO standards, such as ISO 13485 (Quality Management for Medical Devices) and ISO/IEC 27001 (Information Security Management), provide frameworks for ensuring the quality and security of medical devices and health information.

Organizations deploying AI in healthcare must stay informed about the specific regulations applicable in their jurisdictions, ensuring compliance with data protection laws, medical device regulations, and other relevant standards. It's essential to conduct thorough risk assessments, prioritize patient safety, and implement robust data security measures in alignment with applicable laws and guidelines.

2.7.2 Example National Security and Cybersecurity Regulations

Here are some key laws and regulations globally that address cybersecurity and national security concerns, impacting the deployment of AI in sensitive sectors

2.7.2.1 United States

2.7.2.2 National Defense Authorization Act (NDAA)

The NDAA includes provisions related to cybersecurity and the use of emerging technologies, including AI, within the US Department of Defense (DoD). It outlines requirements and funding for AI research, development, and deployment.

2.7.2.3 Cybersecurity and Infrastructure Security Agency (CISA)

CISA, part of the US Department of Homeland Security, plays a critical role in enhancing the cybersecurity posture of the nation. It collaborates with government and private sector entities to address cybersecurity threats.

2.7.2.4 Executive Order on Improving the Nation's Cybersecurity

Executive orders issued by the President, such as the one focused on improving the nation's cybersecurity, outline measures to enhance the resilience of federal networks and critical infrastructure against cyber threats, including those involving AI.

2.7.2.5 European Union

2.7.2.6 Network and Information Systems (NIS) Directive

The NIS Directive aims to ensure a high common level of cybersecurity across the EU. It applies to operators of essential services, including those in the energy, transportation, and healthcare sectors. AI systems deployed in critical infrastructure may be subject to these regulations.

2.7.2.7 United Kingdom

2.7.2.8 National Cyber Security Strategy

The UK's National Cyber Security Strategy outlines the government's approach to improving the nation's cybersecurity. It includes initiatives to address cyber threats in critical sectors, and the deployment of AI is considered within the context of enhancing national security.

2.7.2.9 Australia

2.7.2.10 Security of Critical Infrastructure Act

The Security of Critical Infrastructure Act in Australia focuses on strengthening the security and resilience of critical infrastructure. Sectors identified as critical may include those where the deployment of AI has implications for national security.

2.7.2.11 International Initiatives

2.7.2.12 The Wassenaar Arrangement

The Wassenaar Arrangement is an international agreement that controls the export of conventional arms and dual-use technologies, including certain cybersecurity technologies. It aims to prevent the proliferation of technologies that could be used for malicious purposes.

2.7.2.13 International Telecommunication Union (ITU) Guidelines

The ITU provides guidelines and recommendations related to the security of information and communication technologies, which can impact the deployment of AI systems in telecommunications and critical infrastructure.

In addition to these laws, national security considerations may also be addressed through classified measures and government directives that are not publicly disclosed. Organizations involved in deploying AI in sensitive sectors should work closely with relevant regulatory authorities, comply with applicable laws, and adhere to best practices for securing AI systems in the context of national security.

2.7.3 Example Antitrust and Competition Laws

Here are some key laws and regulations globally that address antitrust concerns in the context of AI and technology markets

United States

2.7.3.1 Sherman Antitrust Act

Enacted in 1890, the Sherman Antitrust Act is a fundamental US antitrust law. It prohibits anticompetitive practices, including conspiracies to restrain trade and monopolization.

2.7.3.2 Clayton Act

The Clayton Act addresses various antitrust issues, including mergers and acquisitions that may substantially lessen competition. It also prohibits certain anti-competitive practices, such as price discrimination and exclusive dealing.

2.7.3.3 Federal Trade Commission Act (FTC Act)

The FTC Act empowers the Federal Trade Commission to prevent unfair methods of competition and unfair or deceptive acts or practices. The FTC has the authority to investigate and take action against anti-competitive behavior.

2.7.3.4 European Union

2.7.3.5 Antitrust Laws of the European Union

The EU has a comprehensive framework of antitrust laws that includes Articles 101 and 102 of the Treaty on the Functioning of the European Union (TFEU). These articles prohibit anti-competitive agreements and the abuse of a dominant market position.

2.7.3.6 Merger Regulation

The EU Merger Regulation regulates mergers and acquisitions that may affect competition within the European Single Market. It requires notification to and approval by the European Commission for transactions meeting certain thresholds.

2.7.3.7 Japan

2.7.3.8 Antitrust Act

Japan's Antitrust Act prohibits various forms of anti-competitive behavior, including cartels, abuse of dominance, and unfair trade practices. The Japan Fair Trade Commission (JFTC) enforces these provisions.

2.7.3.9 United Kingdom

2.7.3.10 Competition Act

The UK Competition Act prohibits anti-competitive agreements and abuse of a dominant market position. The Competition and Markets Authority (CMA) is responsible for enforcing competition law in the UK.

2.7.3.11 International Initiatives

2.7.3.12 Organization for Economic Cooperation and Development (OECD) Guidelines

The OECD provides guidelines on competition policy that member countries follow. These guidelines include principles to address anti-competitive practices and promote fair competition.

2.7.3.13 International Competition Network (ICN)

The ICN is an international organization focused on promoting competition enforcement and cooperation among competition authorities. It facilitates dialogue and coordination on global antitrust issues.

2.7.3.14 Proposed Legislation

2.7.3.15 Competition and Antitrust Laws Worldwide

Various countries are considering or have proposed legislation to update and strengthen their antitrust laws, reflecting the challenges posed by the digital economy and concentration of power in technology markets.

Acknowledgments

Thank you to our contributors, Michael Esola, Dr. Patricia Franks, and Dr. Pieter Van der Walt, for adding their insights and expertise to this important book. Their work elevated the content in the especially important AI Governance areas of data privacy, cybersecurity, and records and information management.

We would also like to thank the editing team at Bloomsbury and our literary agent, Jeff Herman, who worked tirelessly and patiently to find a home for this book.

Index

About the Authors

Robert F. Smallwood, MBA, CIGO, CIGO/AI, is the world's leading author, researcher, and trainer in Information Governance (IG), with nine published books on IG topics. He is an AI & Information Governance SME, consultant, keynote speaker, and the noted author of the seminal textbook *Information Governance: Concepts, Strategies, and Best Practices* (2014, 2020). Robert's IG book is being used to guide corporations in their IG programs as well as teaching graduate students IG at major universities like Oxford, the University of Michigan, San Jose State, and others. Robert is also the author *of Managing Electronic Records: Methods, Best Practices, and Technologies* (2013); *Safeguarding Critical E-Documents: Implementing a Program for Securing Confidential Information Assets* (2012); *Information Governance for Healthcare Professionals* (2021); *Introduction to Information Governance* (2016), and several others. He has also developed several annual research studies on IG and written White Papers covering emerging IG topics. His first published article on AI and IG was published in 2018.

Chris Surdak is an award-winning author and an expert in Data Analytics, Social Media, Regulatory Compliance, and Digital Transformation. He is the founder and CEO of ReLeaf Financial, a crypto payments platform working to lift billions of the world's poorest people out of poverty.

www.ingramcontent.com/pod-product-compliance
Ingram Content Group UK Ltd.
Pitfield, Milton Keynes, MK11 3LW, UK
UKHW050641160826
474436UK00005B/51

9 798881 800833